Farm Servants and Labour in Lowland Scotland
1770–1914

Edited by
T. M. DEVINE
Reader in History
University of Strathclyde

JOHN DONALD PUBLISHERS LTD
EDINBURGH

ISBN 0 85976 105 3

Exclusive distribution in the United States of America and Canada by Humanities Press Inc., Atlantic Highlands, NJ 07716, USA.

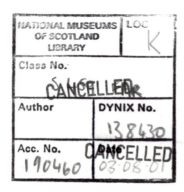

Printed in Great Britain by Bell and Bain Ltd., Glasgow.

Preface

The aim of this collection of essays is to present a history of farm service and labour in lowland Scotland between the Agricultural Revolution of the later eighteenth century and the First World War. In the earlier period most Scots lived on the land and the majority worked wholly or partly in agriculture. A hundred years later, farm work only attracted a dwindling minority in an expanding industrialised society as migration thinned the rural population and mechanisation permitted more production with less labour. Yet, even on the eve of the Great War, there was much that would have been familiar to the farm servants and day labourers of earlier generations. The horse remained the main source of power and traction and horsemen maintained their principal position in the hierarchy of the farm. Terms and conditions of engagement, hours of work and accommodation arrangements changed little over the years. Such traditional institutions as the hiring-fairs (or feeing-markets) survived into the twentieth century. This volume, therefore, covers a coherent phase in the development of a key section of the Scottish labour force in the nineteenth century, an era which spanned the years between radical agrarian reform from c. 1770 and the coming of the tractor later in the twentieth century.

The authors approach the subject from a range of perspectives. The introductory study sets the scene, describes the economic context of farm service and relates it to the evolving society of nineteenth-century Scotland.

An important principle is here established that the experience of farm workers can only be meaningfully examined against the broad background of national demographic and economic changes. The peculiar structure of agricultural labour in Scotland was a direct consequence not only of Scottish agrarian capitalism but also of developments in other sectors of the economic system. Variety in climate, soil and topography within the lowlands produced contrasting farm systems which also profoundly influenced the composition and characteristics of the work force. The contributors in Part II seek to clarify these distinctions by focusing their analyses on the locality and the region. Finally, the essays in Parts III and IV concentrate on key groups among the rural population and on themes of particular interest and significance to an understanding of the labour force as a whole.

The volume does not claim to be either comprehensive or definitive. There is, for example, no extended discussion of standards of life or of the national history of rural trade unionism. It is to be hoped, however, that a

v

structure has been assembled which later research can refine and extend. Each author worked independently on his subject, occasionally with some resulting differences in interpretation and emphasis. Careful readers should reach their own general conclusions on the basis of the evidence presented.

I am grateful to my fellow contributors for their forbearance and for making the task of editor both pleasant and stimulating. John Tuckwell of John Donald Ltd. provided support and guidance in equal measure. Mrs. Irene Scouller of the Department of History at Strathclyde University coped with my obscure handwriting with characteristic speed and efficiency. The jacket illustration is reproduced by kind permission of the Dick Institute, Kilmarnock.

T. M. Devine

Contents

Contributors

David Buchan
Professor of Folklore, Memorial University of Newfoundland, Canada.

R. H. Campbell
Professor Emeritus of Economic History, University of Stirling.

Ian Carter
Professor of Sociology, University of Auckland, New Zealand.

T. M. Devine
Reader in History, University of Strathclyde.

Alexander Fenton
Director, National Museum of Antiquities of Scotland.

Malcolm Gray
Formerly Reader in Economic History, University of Aberdeen.

William Howatson
Research Student, University of Edinburgh and Journalist.

Ian Levitt
Lecturer in Social Administration, Plymouth Polytechnic.

Alastair Orr
Formerly Lecturer in Economics, Madras Christian College, India.

Michael Robson
Director, Border Country Life Museum, Berwickshire

Christopher Smout
Professor of Scottish History, University of St. Andrews.

Gavin Sprott
Curator, Scottish Agricultural Museum, Ingliston, Edinburgh.

1

Introduction: Scottish Farm Service in the Agricultural Revolution

T. M. Devine

The agrarian revolution of the later eighteenth and early nineteenth century was a major watershed in Scottish historical development. A radical increase in the production of foods and raw materials was achieved by a series of related innovations in farm organisation, crop rotations, technical improvement and the deployment of labour.[1] The new efficiency of the agricultural sector then became one of the prime foundations for self-sustaining growth in manufacturing and urban expansion. By the early nineteenth century, the Scottish agricultural system was attracting international attention for its excellence. Farming in the Scottish lowlands was advanced and highly efficient and was widely copied elsewhere. Yet, underpinning this modern agrarian regime, was a structure of labour recruitment and payment which seemed to have more in common with the previous era of unimproved agriculture and in some ways was apparently hardly touched by the wide-ranging changes in modes of production characteristic of the period after c. 1780. Most permanent farm workers in Scotland were farm *servants* (rather than labourers), who were hired over a period of one year, if married, and for six months if single. Married servants, who predominated in the Lothians, the most improved of all the lowland regions, were paid almost entirely in kind, receiving such allowances as oats, barley, pease, the keep of a cow and ground for planting potatoes. The rental of the cottage was paid for by the labour of the wife or daughter during harvest and fuel was carted from town at the farmer's expense.[2] Unmarried male and female servants, who were especially common in the north-eastern and western lowlands, did obtain a cash wage but were also boarded within the farm steading and received both food and accommodation as part of their contracts.

The main outlines of this system were already present in Scottish agriculture in the sixteenth and seventeenth centuries — the habit of rewarding married men mainly in kind and a small area of land; the custom of boarding unmarried servants in the steading; the principle of the long hire.[3] Farm service was indeed common throughout Britain up to the later eighteenth century but only in Scotland and parts of the north of

1

England did it survive into the era of agrarian revolution.[4] Elsewhere service had become obsolete by the early nineteenth century. The most fundamental changes occurred in that other centre of advanced agriculture, southern England.[5] Long hires were in rapid decay there and were generally being replaced by short contracts of a month, a week or even less. Labour in that region was predominently paid in cash with only vestigial remains of traditional allowances in kind. The custom of boarding unmarried servants in the farmhouse or steading was fast disappearing. Instead most labourers by the 1800s were recruited from local villages whenever required.

This basic shift in the structure of labour recruitment in the south developed logically from the economics of the new farming. In most counties south of the line from the Trent to the Severn, the enormous expansion in demand for food grains resulted in a great increase in the production of wheat, a crop for which the region was especially suited both in terms of soil and climate. This new level of specialisation accentuated the cycle of seasonal demand for labour. On the one hand, more workers than ever before were required at harvest; on the other the rapid adoption of the threshing machine, from the early nineteenth century, began to reduce the need for an enhanced labour supply in the early winter months. Demand for labour therefore tended to fluctuate even more markedly throughout the year and farmers in southern England had a clear incentive to eliminate the long hire and, instead, take on workers as and when required. At the same time, the steep rise in wheat prices during the Napoleonic Wars compelled an erosion in the traditional system of paying labour in kind. In a period of inflation there was obvious advantage in changing to payment in cash; continuation of 'in kind' rewards in the 1790s would have increased the wage in real terms. The old custom of boarding servants in the farmhouse was also doomed. As farmers moved to short hires there was less need to have a regular labour supply around the farm. In addition, the rising living standards of the employing classes made them less willing for social reasons to board workers in improved farmhouses.

By the early nineteenth century, then, two contrasting structures of labour recruitment had emerged in British agriculture. In comparison with the system which had evolved in southern England, that of the Scottish lowlands (and parts of northern England) seemed archaic and old-fashioned. Indeed, in his classic study of the English agricultural labourer, W. Hasbach dismissed regions where farm service and payment in kind survived as 'conservative' and lagging behind the more advanced areas of the south.[6] It is difficult, however, to accept this argument as entirely convincing. Scottish farmers were among the most progressive in Europe and they were unlikely to be any less skilled in the deployment of labour than in other aspects of farm management. Moreover, while farm service was retained, other elements associated with the old society, such as the numerous class of sub-tenants and cottars who had supplied most of the labour needs of traditional agriculture, were swept aside as irrelevant to the requirements of the new farming.[7] This might suggest that farm service survived because it was found both appropriate and necessary in the modern agricultural system.

In fact, farm service had a basic rationale in lowland Scotland. The perpetuation of the long hire reflected the new routine of farming and the general economic circumstances of Scotland in the later eighteenth century. The fundamental distinction between southern England and lowland Scotland lay in labour supply. If the period 1780 to 1830 is considered as a whole, then it is clear that there was a glut of agricultural labour in the south produced by population growth, and the contraction of industrial employment and its concentration in northern England, together with limited migration from the region.[8] Farmers therefore did not need to tie labour to long contracts to ensure a regular supply: it was hardly ever scarce and, after 1815, usually available at low cost. Indeed, the problem became one of supporting through the Poor Law an increasing population of agricultural labourers many of whom were surplus to requirements even at the busy season.

Scottish farmers faced a quite different labour market. Natural population increase was probably less rapid in the lowlands in the eighteenth century, there was a greater willingness and opportunity for the rural population to move to urban employment and, above all, to 1815 farmers had to contend with strong and persistent competition for labour from industry.[9] Industrial and agrarian change proceeded both simultaneously and in close geographical proximity in the central and eastern lowlands. Instead of a contracting industrial sector, as in southern England, there developed in lowland Scotland a new manufacturing structure which by the second half of the nineteenth century dominated the economy. In the later eighteenth century, however, industry and agriculture were intimately linked because textile work in the spinning and weaving of linens, cottons and woollens was widespread and expanding in the countryside.[10] Competition for labour before 1815 was therefore intense and accentuated by the manpower demands of the Napoleonic Wars. In addition, Scottish farmers were now keener to employ full-time, skilled workers over whom they could exert greater powers of discipline and control. The long hire therefore survived, not as a hangover from a previous age, but because it was well suited to ensuring a regular supply of labour in the new circumstances.

It had two other advantages.[11] First, the cycle of labour activity on Scottish farms differed radically from the pattern in southern England. The hiring of labour there on a short-term basis was a logical response to the seasonal discontinuities of arable farming. In the north, however, both climate and soil dictated a regime of mixed agriculture in which stock-rearing, fattening and cropping were systematically combined. Increasing production within mixed husbandry required an extension of acreage under root crops and sown grasses, a development which in turn encouraged a lengthening of the working year and an evening out rather than an accentuation of seasonal labour needs. This was an inevitable result of the varied tasks of weeding, dunging, singling and intensive ploughing associated with the classic Scottish five-course rotation.[12] In essence, then, the social effects of agrarian change in a mixed farming region were almost the reverse of those in a specialist cereal zone. Work was spread through the farming year and labour had to be hired over lengthy periods.

Secondly, the long-hiring of ploughmen and the custom of boarding them in the steading reflected the crucial position of horsepower and horse management in the productivity of the new farming system.[13] The whole routine in Scottish agriculture from the later eighteenth century began to centre round maximising the efficiency of the horses used in ploughing and carting. Hours of labour and the numbers of workers employed were closely related to the number of horse-teams and their rate of work. Each ploughman took sole responsibility for a pair of horses, and his entire routine from early morning to evening concerned the preparation, working and final grooming of his animals. Such a system required that ploughmen be permanent servants, boarded within the farm steading, close to their horses. It also followed that they would have to be paid at least partly in kind because many farms were far from villages or other markets where the necessities of life could be obtained in return for cash. The accommodation of workers in the steading and the custom of payment on kind were therefore interrelated. Not until the second half of the nineteenth century, when transport and marketing networks in the countryside improved, was there a rapid decline of 'in kind' allowances.[14]

The survival of farm service in lowland Scotland had important consequences for both the economy and society of the rural lowlands in the nineteenth century. Scottish agriculture became internationally famous for its high levels of labour productivity.[15] This partly reflected the tight labour market already described, where industry and agriculture were in close competition for workers — farmers therefore had a vested interest in fully exploiting relatively scarce labour resources.[16] But it was probably also linked to the structure of farm service. Since farmers had fixed, certain and clear obligations to their work force over periods of six months or a year, they were encouraged to tailor their labour requirements exactly to the number required for the proper running of the farm and to ensure that the organisation of the work-team was such that it was fully exploited when at work. The conventional day became one of ten hours divided by a midday rest of two hours. To rest and feed the horses at this time would not be practicable unless the ploughmen lived close to their work and the stables. In East Anglia, however, work began at 7.00 a.m. when the stableman handed over his team to the ploughmen from the village to be worked continuously until 3.00 p.m. It was estimated in the 1860s that, as a result, Scottish farmers obtained two more hours' work than those in southern England.[17] Within the superficially traditional and archaic structure of farm service great economy of labour was practised. Significantly, when Scottish farmers moved to East Anglia in the depression of the 1880s, their first action was to reduce the number of men and horses.[18]

The survival of farm service also helps to explain the contrasting social experience of southern England and lowland Scotland. In the south agrarian capitalism and demographic pressures produced considerable unrest and discontent. There were risings by farm labourers in East Anglia in 1816, again in the same area in 1822, and all over the south and east of England in the famous 'Captain Swing' riots of 1830. These disturbances had no counterpart in the Scottish lowlands, and society there was remarkably stable throughout the late eighteenth and early nineteenth centuries.[19] Since Scottish farm servants were either wholly or partly paid in kind, they were insulated from the market price of food when in employment. This was especially important in the period 1792–1815 when grain prices rocketed and food rioting spread to many parts of Britain. Significantly, however, Scottish farm servants were not associated with the 'meal mobs' of this period.[20] Married ploughmen were accustomed to sell a proportion of their 'in kind' payments in local markets or to day-labourers wholly paid in cash. As vendors rather than purchasers of food they were not only afforded an impregnable security when prices rose but stood to gain from the increase in the real value of their 'in kind' earnings.[21]

Moreover, the transition from a sub-tenancy structure (prevalent in the early eighteenth century) in which land was given in return for labour to a system where landless employees were engaged in return for payment was facilitated by the survival of the farm servant system. There were indeed differences between the sub-tenants of the old order and the farm servant class of the new. Sub-tenants and cottagers seemed to have a greater degree of independence and security because of their access to land, whereas the 'landless' servant was more dependent upon the employer class and hence more vulnerable to unemployment. Yet, the difference between the two was at most one of degree rather than kind, and it is by no means certain that service was less secure than sub-tenancy. Sub-tenants held the merest fragments of land and had no option but to seek work in adjacent larger farms to obtain a full subsistence. Grinding poverty was the lot of many sub-tenant families, and there is abundant contemporary comment about the miserable conditions in which they often lived.[22] The major weakness in their position was the extensive seasonal underemployment which characterised agriculture before the adoption of the new rotation systems and the associated extension of the busy season. On the other hand, married servants were allowed ground for planting lint, potatoes and the keep of a cow and were given security of employment for a year. Cash income derived partly from the sale of butter and cheese from the cow and from the cash wages of their sons and daughters. Thus, in the 1780s and 1790s, when the destruction of sub-tenancy was underway, the structure of farm service provided a bridge between the old world and the new.

However, the vital role of farm service in maintaining social stability in the rural areas only really became apparent from 1815. In southern England, after the end of the Napoleonic Wars, the development of a massive surplus of agriculture labour fuelled social discontent. Scotland was advantaged in this respect because industry provided an alternative source of employment to agriculture. But it is important to keep the significance of industrial development in perspective. The plight of the urban handloom weavers between 1810 and 1840 and the problem of casual labour in the Scottish cities are reminders that the industrial economy was not sufficiently developed to provide employment on a regular basis for the majority of migrants from rural areas.[23] Rather, the evidence suggests that many were being forced out of the countryside after 1815 into towns already suffering from a surplus of labour. Scotland had a problem of surplus labour before 1840. It was, however, mainly confined to the towns and cities. The countryside was rendered free of the consequences of structural unemployment by a ruthlessly efficient system for channelling labour which was surplus to requirements off the land.[24]

Within the long-hire system accommodation and employment were linked. To be unemployed, therefore, meant not simply to be without work but without a home. In the later eighteenth century it had become a major principle of Scottish 'improving' policy that only that population essential for proper cultivation ought to be retained permanently on the land. Accommodation in and around the farm was therefore strictly limited to the specific labour needs of the farmer. Cottages surplus to such requirements were pulled down and the building of new accommodation rigorously controlled. The unemployed farm worker had often therefore no alternative but to move to seek work.[25] There was no encouragement to his continued residence in the neighbourhood. Moreover, the hiring-fairs or feeing-markets were very effective media for relating the number of available places to the number of potential servants required for periods of between six months and one year.[26] Those not engaged were faced with the choice of unemployment until the next fair, taking the chance of finding a job as a day-labourer or moving elsewhere. They could not, like the rural unemployed of southern England, depend as easily on the Poor Law, partly because of the social stigma attached to poor relief and also because the able-bodied unemployed in Scotland had no legal right to a dole. Finally, for single male servants, migration was likely at the age of marriage. In some areas, such as the east-central and north-east lowlands, only unmarried servants were hired in any numbers, and at marriage many had to move out of the district because of the scarcity of family cottages.[27] The entire system, therefore, was geared to the establishment of an equilibrium between demand and supply of labour. Only in the second half of the nineteenth century, with the second phase of industrial expansion based on coal, iron, steel and shipbuilding, did agricultural labour become scarce again. Until then the balance was maintained in most years.

When examined from this perspective, then, farm service hardly seems an eccentric survival from an older world. Rather, it can be viewed as a dynamic system which became an integral component of agrarian capitalism in nineteenth-century Scotland and one which proved remarkably adaptable to the needs of the new and more efficient system of food production. The essays which follow clarify its nature and characteristics, the economic structure within which it functioned and the experience of the ploughmen, women workers and seasonal labourers who spent the greater part of their lives engaged in it.

NOTES

1. The features of the new system are explored in detail in M. Gray, 'Scottish Emigration: the social impact of agrarian change in the rural lowlands, 1775–1875', *Perspectives in American History*, VII (1973).

2. See Chapter 11, pp. 156–187 for an appraisal of regional and local variation in wages in the early 1840s.

3. Margaret H. B. Sanderson, *Scottish Rural Society in the 16th Century* (Edinburgh, 1982) pp. 44–5; Ian Whyte, *Agriculture and Society in Seventeenth Century Scotland* (Edinburgh, 1979), pp. 39–40. See also below, pp. 10–12, 30, 75–76.

4. Ann Kussmaul, *Servants in Husbandry in Early Modern England* (Cambridge, 1981).

5. E. J. Hobsbawm and G. Rudé, *Captain Swing* (London, 1973 edition), pp. 3–70; E. L. Jones, 'The Agricultural Labour Market in England 1793–1872', *Economic History Review*, 2nd ser., xvii (1965–6), pp. 329ff; N. Gash, 'Rural Unemployment, 1815–34', *Economic History Review*, vi (1935–6), pp. 90–3.

6. W. Hasbach, *A History of the English Agricultural Labourer* (London, 1908), p. 4.

7. Gray, 'Scottish Emigration', pp. 139–140. See also, below, pp. 7, 16, 100.

8. Gash, 'Rural Unemployment', pp. 90–3.

9. T. M. Devine and D. Dickson, 'In Pursuit of Comparative Aspects of Irish and Scottish Development', in T. M. Devine and David Dickson, eds., *Ireland and Scotland 1600–1850* (Edinburgh, 1983), pp. 261–272; M. Gray, 'Migration in the Rural Lowlands of Scotland 1750–1850' in T. M. Devine and D. Dickson, eds. *Ireland and Scotland, 1600–1850* (Edinburgh, 1983), pp. 110–112.

10. N. Murray, *The Scottish Hand Loom Weavers, 1790–1850* (Edinburgh, 1978), pp. 22–26; A. J. Durie, *The Scottish Linen Industry in the Eighteenth Century* (Edinburgh, 1979), pp. 95–114.

11. For a fuller discussion see T. M. Devine, 'Social Stability and Agrarian Change in the Eastern Lowlands of Scotland, 1810–1840', *Social History*, 3, no. 3, October 1978, pp. 331–346.

12. Anon., 'On the Hiring Markets in the Counties of Northumberland, Berwick and Roxburgh', *Quarterly Journal of Agriculture* V (1834–5), pp. 379–80.

13. See below, pp. 13, 15, 17–18, 38, 99–100.

14. J. T. Duncan, 'Scottish Farm Labour', *Scottish Journal of Agriculture*, II (1919), pp. 499–504. See also below, pp. 17, 245–7.

15. W. Burness, 'Our Agricultural Labourers — English, Irish and Scotch', *Trans, of the Highland and Agricultural Society*, new ser. 1849–51, pp. 450–1; Leonce de Lavergne, *Essai sur l'Economie Rurale de l'Angleterre, de l'Ecosse et de l'Irelande* (Paris, 1854).

16. E. H. Hunt, *Regional Wage Variations in Britain, 1850–1914* (Oxford, 1973), pp. 204–207.

17. *Royal Commission on the Employment of Children, Young Persons and Women in Agriculture. Fourth Report. Appendix. Part I. Parliamentary Papers* 1870, xiii, p. 47.

18. P. McConnell, 'Experiences of a Scotsman on the Essex Clays', *Journal of the Royal Agricultural Society*, 3rd ser., II (1891), p. 317.

19. Devine, 'Social Stability', pp. 331–346; Andrew Charlesworth, ed., *An Atlas of Rural Protest in Britain 1548–1900* (London, 1983), pp. 131–163

20. Kenneth J. Logue, *Popular Disturbances in Scotland 1780–1815* (Edinburgh, 1979), p. 197.

21. R. Somerville, *General View of the Agriculture of East Lothian* (London, 1805) p. 210.

22. Patrick Graham, *Agricultural Survey of Clackmannanshire* (Edinburgh, 1814), p. 332; *Old Statistical Account*, VIII, p. 610; I. Carter, *Farm Life in Northeast Scotland, 1840–1914* (Edinburgh, 1979), pp. 16–17.

23. Murray, *Handloom Weavers, pp. 122–9*; J. H. Treble, *Urban Poverty in Britain* (London, 1979), pp. 51–90.

24. For the evidence that unemployment in the rural lowlands between 1815 and 1840 was limited in both space and time, see G. Houston, 'Farm Wages in Central Scotland from 1814 to 1870', *Journal of the Royal Statistical Society*, Series A (General), 118 (1955), pp. 224–7; T. M. Devine, 'The Demand for Agricultural Labour in East Lothian after the Napoleonic Wars', *Trans. East Lothian Antiquarian and Natural History Society*, 16 (1979), pp. 49–61; see also below, pp. 21, 37.

25. T. M. Devine, 'Social Stability in the Eastern Lowlands of Scotland during the Agricultural Revolution, 1780–1840', in T. M. Devine, ed., *Lairds and Improvement in the Scotland of the Enlightenment* (Dundee, 1979), pp. 65–66.

26. Ibid.

27. Gray, 'Scottish Emigration', pp. 142–3.

Part I. Regional Perspectives

2

Farm Workers in North-East Scotland

Malcolm Gray

The area of this study, comprising the lowlands and foothills of the counties of Angus, Kincardine, Aberdeen, Banff and Moray together with Perthshire north of the Tay, contains wide local variations in climate, soil and elevation, from the south-facing, sheltered and rich clay lands of the Carse of Gowrie to the thin, cold upland soils of Aberdeenshire and Banffshire. Equally, farming practice must always have varied from place to place; and different farming practices may well imply differences in the type of labour required to help the tenants in working the land — workers might be married or unmarried, hired by the day or over longer term, full-time or merely seasonal — and consequently in the forms of society built around farm labour. Yet before the 1770s when innovations were few and slow to evolve, the similarities from place to place overshadowed the differences, and in spite of discernible variations of detail there did exist a broadly uniform system of farming and a rough similarity of practice in hiring labour.[1]

In the earlier eighteenth century individual holdings of land were generally small with most of them requiring only a single plough, but the tenants who rented them formed on the whole a group of special privilege in a social position that could only be upheld by the hiring of labour from a lower and larger stratum of cottagers and servants. Even in the quieter seasons of the year the smallest of independent farmers found it difficult to manage on their own. Threshing, the making of *muck feal* — a compost of dung and turf which was the main and very necessary fertiliser — the spreading of the mixture, the carriage of grain to market, (or to the laird's girnal), the droving of beasts, rough weeding, herding — however later writers might jeer at the idleness of farmers in this traditional scheme, the work was unremitting. In addition, the tenant as a privileged man demanded help in the non-farming activities on which his household depended. Most important was the cutting, drying and transporting of peats which in most parts formed the chief fuel and which engaged all available labour for several weeks in the summer. There were other tasks, too, such as making and maintaining farm equipment or building and thatching to take up the time of the farm staff. The other side of the medal for the tenant was the often onerous duties to be performed for the laird.

10

To help in the steady year-round work any tenant who aimed to live independently on his land would engage at least one male servant.[2] The hiring was for at least six months at a time and would normally be renewed, or the hired man replaced, to cover the needs of all seasons. The general custom, particularly in Aberdeenshire and Banffshire, was for servants to be unmarried, to occupy rough sleeping places around the farm buildings, to feed in the farm kitchen and to receive a small fee in addition. Frequently, too, there would be at least one female servant hired under similar terms but for an even smaller monetary payment; such servants worked both 'in and out', at kitchen and dairying tasks and outdoors at general farm work. Male servants were generally in the majority, but clearly the work of the farm depended crucially on hired female labour. In the southern parts of Kincardineshire, in Angus and in Perthshire there were rather more married servants, who would occupy cottages on the farm and would receive an allowance of meal and milk as subsistence;[3] like those who lived in, they would be in constant attendance at the farm and would be remunerated by a small fee, paid six-monthly.

On top of the miscellaneous tasks that kept the long-hire labour busy through the year there came the concentrated demands of the seasonal peaks of spring and autumn. Ploughing at this time was heavily concentrated in the spring period; only for the bere crop would an extra ploughing be given in the autumn, together with a rib-furrow for the second or third year of oats.[4] Harvesting when there was little hay to be cut was both confined in time and very laborious, being performed by sickle. A considerable body of additional labour, then, was required in spring and autumn. There was little reserve of day-labourers to be called upon for such occasional work.[5] In fact, day labour could only provide a livelihood when combined with either work as an independent tradesman or the holding of some land, and small-holdings to be rented directly of the proprietors of land were few. The arrangement that most neatly fitted the needs both of the potential employer and of the small-holder seeking the opportunity for day labour was the subset of small portions of the primary tenant's land. Thus were accommodated numerous cottagers. Much of the seasonal labour, male and female, came out of these cottages, and a substantial proportion of the rural population was contained in their families. The cottager would receive a stance for his cottage, ground for a kailyard, a rig or two in the cropped land, and rights of grazing a cow or cows. The employing farmer would often undertake the ploughing of his sub-tenant's land. In return, the latter would be obliged to give a few days' labour, normally at seed-time and harvest, although help in working the peat might also be demanded. But his usefulness to the farmer did not end there. Additional days might be worked at day labour rates, and sometimes he could be called upon compulsorily, although for payment; also, very importantly, his wife and family would be ready to give additional help at daily rates of pay.[6] Altogether such cottages seem to have been the main source of seasonal aid; and they were certainly crucial to the farming economy, not least because they could provide the young lads to be hired as servants, a position they would occupy till they were ready to marry and take subtenancies on their own.

On the whole, then, unmarried servants employed for the year-round work and cottagers providing only occasional services formed the greater part of the labour force. Together they made a close-knit social group in which individuals moved in the different phases of their lives from one position to the other — from birth and childhood in the cottage to full-time service on a larger farm and, on marriage, back to a cottage from which the new family was involved in a diversity of farm tasks. Even where more substantial numbers of married servants were perpetuated from within their own ranks, the farmers also used the part-time services of subtenants. Whatever may have been the numerical proportions in the farmer's roll of labourers as between married and unmarried servants and between servants and subtenant cottagers, it was the cottages of the last-named which ultimately formed the basis and source of the bulk of farm labour.[7] And it was on the cottages that most of the people centred their lives. The livelihood of the cottager can scarcely be stated in precise terms as can, for example, the material sustenance of the married servant. Clearly family incomes came from various sources, some of them non-agricultural. His land and grazing rights were important for the cottager — particularly to ensure a supply of milk — but some meal would have to be bought and other items pressed upon him. There were, we have seen, some earnings to be made from day labour in the fields, but an important support to the whole system was the work to be had in the two great domestic occupations of the area, linen-spinning in the southern part and stocking knitting in Aberdeenshire and Banffshire.[8]

By 1790, farming had been much altered by a number of interconnected innovations. They came at different rates in different districts and they tended towards quite sharply differing systems of farming. Inevitably, they also brought new demands on the labour force and slowly shaped new terms of employment. Many of the old features in terms of engagement and ways of living persisted, and these continued to vary somewhat from place to place. But also new technology everywhere brought a sharper definition and a greater specialisation in farm tasks while the employing farmer demanded the full-time service of more and more of his labourers. The social consequences were considerable, for the basis of the cottage economy was eroded. The cottagers who survived had to submit to new terms of service or to increase their earnings from outside farming even while some sectors of domestic industry were also shrinking.

The district in which the rate of change was greatest and in which the new demands to be made on farm labour were most evident was the Carse of Gowrie, the fertile and flat stretch lying to the north of the lower reaches of the Tay. A heavy but fertile soil, a southern exposure and a coastal position making export easy combined to encourage intensive wheat growing. The new and profitable pattern of cropping, developed in the 1770s, was a six-year rotation. One year in the six was a summer fallow in which the land would be cleaned by several ploughings; the following five years saw grain alternating with beans or pease, and grass. At first one year of wheat would be taken but the tendency was to increase the wheat acreage either by 'robbing' from the other grain crops or by stretching the rotation.[9] A predominating characteristic, then, was the frequent ploughing both in the fallow period and in the yearly preparations for sowing, particularly for the wheat crop. With a heavy clay soil one plough and its team would be required for every thirty or forty acres in rotation.[10] The need for so much ploughing was met in part by the introduction of new designs of plough which by gradual improvement reduced the required team to two horses manageable by one man.[11]

On the Carse, then, with the new intensive cropping system, the farmer needed above all a sufficiency of labour for ploughing. The draught animals were now heavily built horses which were expensive to maintain, and strict farm economy meant that they had to be used continuously to the full extent of their power. In fact, the emergent system of husbandry gave 200 days of ploughing in the year to each team. Since there was horsework to occupy fully the other available work-days, the horses' power could indeed be used to the utmost.[12] But it was clearly also essential that the ploughman be a full-time and specialised employee. He was therefore hired on the yearly or six-monthly terms that had long prevailed for servants and in service acquired a specialised skill that gave dignity and importance, his position being further fortified by the practice of giving each man the sole and continuing charge of a particular pair of horses.[13] It was, of course, traditional for some of the farm labour force to be engaged at long term, but it was new for so many of the workers and for all of the ploughmen to be of this type; and it had not been customary for ploughing to be so much a specialised task. Indeed, the usefulness of the subtenant who could give occasional help on the farm and who might well do some of the seasonal ploughing was fading; and as they ceased to be useful to the farmer, so were subtenants having no guaranteed tenure turned off the land.[14] Subtenants and cottagers were progressively removed to be replaced by an increasing number of men and women in full-time service. Some of these servants would be married, living in cottages attached to the farm and receiving stated amounts of meal and milk together with other perquisites, as well as a small money wage. But increasingly the majority was unmarried.[15] One of the advantages to the employing farmer of having numerous cottager subtenants had been the availability of family labour for the rush seasons of the year. This advantage he was now prepared to forego partly because there was little summer labour other than ploughing required with the rotations characteristic of the Carse, partly because the growth of population in the weaving villages as well as in the greater towns provided a source of part-time day labour.[16]

The relationship of the unmarried male servant to his employer was itself changing as farms were reorganised. A possibly romanticised picture has been drawn of the old conditions with the servant almost a member of his employer's family; he undoubtedly slept rough but he had his meals in the farm kitchen, and when farmhouses were no more than but-and-ben cottages, this meant at the farmer's table. Now master and servant were drawing apart. Farmhouses would have a parlour as well as a kitchen and the tenant would not take his food in the kitchen. Some servants continued to receive their meals in the kitchen, but for others there was further banishment from the intimacy of the farmhouse. Some farmers took to housing their unmarried men in dormitory buildings where they could look to their own needs, each man receiving an allowance of meal and milk which he cooked as he might.[17] These were the bothies, remaining common through the nineteenth century in certain areas, of which the Carse was an outstanding example.[18] In places the bothy life became the lot of a large proportion of the servants. The arrangement was criticised much and often as causing the young men to live almost wholly isolated from society, without restraint or discipline. Some of the men themselves, however, saw it differently: the bothies gave, they felt, valued freedom from the disciplines imposed by the masters, who clearly took it upon themselves to exert moral as well as working controls.[19] It is probably true that in isolation the young male group lost something in civilisation. Their allowances of meal and milk were plentiful enough but they could only be ill-cooked, and little attention was paid to the cleaning of the buildings. As with all farm servants, personal possessions would have to be kept in a kist, but this was partly the consequence of their prized mobility. At least the bothy would have a fireplace, unlike the lofts and other individual sleeping-places around the steadings.

This composite process of change, affecting farm labour as well as farming methods, was well advanced in the Carse of Gowrie by the mid-nineties. The flat land was nearly all under the new form of rotation, with intensive cropping replacing many areas of waste or intermittent outfield cultivation, although the nearby hilly, 'black land' areas had more of the old system left with stretches of outfield and sometimes unremitting sequences of oats and bere.[20] The reorganisation of the labour force was probably some way behind the reform of farming methods. Many of the smaller farms had been consolidated into larger units with considerable farm staffs, and most of the work was certainly done by servants on long hire, many of them being unmarried men living in bothies; but still some subtenants were to be found giving their occasional services and daily aid to the main tenants.[21]

The Carse of Gowrie, a tiny sub-section of the whole north-eastern area, was a forerunner in development, showing clearly many aspects of the new systems of farm work that would eventually prevail everywhere north of the Tay. But in some ways it was, and remained, exceptional. Further north, except in a few favoured coastal areas, the growing season was shorter, the soil tended to be much lighter and many parts were remote and difficult of access. Peat continued to be the fuel of the remote areas well into the nineteenth century. In the eighteenth century nearly all parishes except those of the mountainous fringes were self-sufficient in grain and many had a surplus for export; but the rearing and sale of livestock, particularly cattle, was also universally important. The first important innovation in these more pastoral areas was the cultivation of sown grasses, and by the 'nineties a considerable proportion of the arable land was being put down to a three- or four-year ley. Yet the framework of infield and outfield remained and the grass would be followed by the traditional successions of oats, bere and possibly pease.[22] As elsewhere, new ploughs were being introduced from the 1770s on, but even by the mid-nineties this was little more than experiment, at least in the more northerly areas, and very few of the two-horse types were to be found.[23] Thus at that time innovation was still so limited as to put few new demands on labour, except for an increase in winter herding, a task that was normally carried out by youngsters. Much of the farm work would still be done by the tenant calling upon his subtenants.

By 1795 turnips were being grown all over the area, but always in small quantities and often without being set in drills.[24] But in the next ten or fifteen years the growing of turnips was to advance to become the very hinge of the farm-work of the north-east. Brought into the standard rotations which were taking over the old land both of infield and outfield, the root covered up to one-fifth of the cultivated acres.[25] But its importance is not to be measured in the extent of land occupied. Within a rotation the turnip year was the occasion of thorough preparation by early ploughing and continued cleaning through the period of growth. The crop set up an altogether new requirement for labour as the work in the fields intensified through the summer months. The ploughing would begin in the autumn, while there was further ploughing and spreading of dung — the good supply of which was itself the result of indoor feeding of cattle with the root — until the time of sowing. After sowing there was the singling of the plants and the hoeing of the drills through the period of growth, while the carting of the crop eventually meant more horse-work.[26] As in the areas of heavy soils and intensive grain production, the need for trained horsemen increased. For the change to the horse as the chief draught animal — and particularly to the two-horse team — was proceeding with the advance of turnip husbandry, may indeed have been a condition of that advance; certainly the horse was required for the light plough with which the drills were prepared. In fact, just as had happened in the more southerly areas, the ploughman with his pair takes his place as the essential skilled man of farm operation;[27] employed the year round, with a working day determined by the capacity of the horses, his routine tended to set the pattern for other farm hands. By about 1820, the changeover to the horse, and particular to the Clydesdale,[28] seems to have been general even in the laggard areas, at least on farms big enough to give full employment to such a plough-team.[29] But the dependence on full-time ploughmen, each with his pair of horses, was not so complete. In Aberdeenshire, an arrangement is found in which ploughmen with small crofts might be engaged for nine months, leaving them free to work their own land and to see to their peat supply during the summer.[30] In Moray and Nairn it was reported in 1813 that there were still few pairs of horses worked by the tenants.[31] And in Angus about the same time there were still cot-towns populated by small-holders who were obliged to give some days' service to the tenants.[32]

By the 1830s, however, the forms of employment on the farms of the north-east had settled into a new pattern which was scarcely to be altered, at least in outline, for the next hundred years. Certain principles prevailed throughout the region. The crushing of the subtenants had proceeded everywhere, and most of the farm work had now come to be done by men and women on long hire.[33] The unmarried men and women were engaged for six months at a time, the married for a year. Notoriously, many at least of the unmarried men did not stay with the one employer for longer than the minimum term. The hiring was done at fixed times of the year, the term days of May and November, Whitsun and Martinmas, and most of the bargains were struck at the feeing markets which were held in many of the small towns and which had come into existence for the most part in the first quarter of the century.[34] The markets were occasions of holiday and reputedly wild behaviour, but the serious bargaining was hard and realistic as employees waited for an offer that would please and employers judged the individuals offering themselves in service, bethought themselves of the farming prospects for the coming months and made their offers.[35] The prevailing rates were highly sensitive to the conditions of the day, with yearly fluctuations, but each bargain was an individual affair, settled according to the reputation and appearance of the servant on the one hand and the known, and sometimes notorious, conditions of work and food of the particular farms on the other.

A second almost invariable principle was that all fee'd servants must reside on the farm. Servants might be married, living with their families in farm cottages, or cottar houses. In Aberdeenshire and Banffshire probably less than one-fifth of the men were so accommodated,[36] but in Angus, in Kincardineshire and in the southern part of Strathmore the proportion might be around one-half.[37] In the northern tier the unmarried majority — and also some of the married men — were maintained, except in the case of the comparatively few bothies that were to be found, under a kitchen system, sleeping in individual places, or 'chaumers'.[38] Further south the bothy was the usual accommodation provided for the unmarried men.[39] In any case the bulk of the servants and their families knew no social life beyond that of the farm community itself. Such were the hours of work that they had little chance to move away from farm-house, steading or cottage. Any accommodation was held strictly for the period of engagement, and none even of the married men had cottages that they could occupy with certainty over more than a few months. In fact the men scarcely allowed an attachment to a particular farm or employer to lengthen into anything that could be the basis for long-term home-making. The cottages were of comparatively recent construction, dating from no earlier than the phase of farm reconstruction which had scarcely ended by 1830. On the whole they had been improved from the original standard of one room towards a minimum of two rooms, sometimes with wooden flooring, plastered walls and ceiling, but they remained stark and strictly functional. There were no ovens for home-baking, no furniture beyond what could be carried from place to place and little attempt at decorative gardening. Even more grim were the chaumers. A common place for the men to sleep was in a loft above the stable or byre. No artificial heating was provided, and frequently the 'room' was neither wind- nor water-proof.[40] Bothies were perhaps more likely to be weather-proof and might have a fireplace, but its ineffectiveness is indicated by the fact that men often preferred to sleep two to a bed for warmth.[41]

The remuneration of all was still largely in kind — rough accommodation and food in the kitchen or an allowance of meal, milk and potatoes and possibly coal. Money payments were tending to increase, and by the late 'sixties they were worth somewhat more than the allowances in kind.[42] The money component could be further increased by the common practice, at least of the bothymen, of selling as much as half their allowance of meal. Thus were bread, tea and syrup added to the diet.[43]

A firm specialisation of function and a hierarchy of status now prevailed among the fee'd men. The largest group was made up by the ploughmen or horsemen.[44] They stood clearly apart, since each man would have the sole charge of a pair of horses, achieved only after several years of farm service, at the age perhaps of sixteen or seventeen. Their work was all to do with horses, and only they could undertake the ploughing. Even among the ploughmen there was a strict order of precedence which prescribed deference down the line from the first as far perhaps as the sixth ploughman, an order reflected in social behaviour and in rates of pay.[45] But whatever their rank, all were bound to a scheme of work basically defined by the capacity of the horses, although at certain times of year abbreviated by shortening hours of daylight. The heart of the working day was the ten hours of ploughing which was standard over the greater part of the area; where soils were particularly heavy, however, this was shortened to nine hours.[46] The ploughing itself usually started at six or seven a.m. and continued without interruption for five hours; then followed a meal break of two hours in which the ploughman and his team would return to the steading, and finally a further four or five hours in the fields. The working day, however, was much longer. Before threshing machines were commonly in use, that is on smaller farms till at least the middle of the century, the ploughman might well have to thresh his horses' feed for the day, starting at 4.00 a.m. or even earlier;[47]; then, as well as the tasks of yoking and unyoking and the trek to and from the fields, there was evening work in the stables in grooming and 'suppering' the horses. In the winter-time the ploughing day was inevitably shorter but other tasks would make up the working day. There was no ploughing or work in the fields of a Sunday but the horses still needed attention; such Sunday work was usually shared so that a ploughman might have a day partly free say on alternate weeks.[48] At harvest time the conventional limits on the working schedule vanished and it was toil for all from dawn to dusk.

The increased specialisation of farm work and the comparatively narrow definition of the ploughman's tasks meant that every farm of any size had its complement of other types of servant. Herding of the cattle remained an important function until the coming of cheap wire made general enclosure possible after 1870. Traditionally, herding was the work of the youngsters. Boys would be engaged on a seasonal basis from the age of nine.[49] Full-time farm service would follow at the age of thirteen or fourteen, and for the next three or four years the youths, now within the full grip of farm discipline and routine, would be classed as halflins, performing miscellaneous tasks. Most of them would then become ploughmen. But some remained as general farm servants or orramen, with lower pay and status than the ploughmen. Cattlemen formed a distinct group, but it appears that young men before their acceptance as ploughmen might be assigned both the title and duties of cattleman;[50] at the other end of the age-range cattlemen might be ploughmen who with advancing years no longer had the strength for the more taxing duties of their younger days.[51] Female servants, with the same form of engagement as the men although with much lower pay, took part in the heavy farm work such as the spreading of dung as well as in the gentler indoor duties.[52] The larger farms would have at least two who might well alternate the outdoor and indoor stints between them. All the servants whatever the category or age followed a working day of a length determined by the routine of the horsemen.

At certain seasons of the year the farmer had to take on extra labour. Notably there were the summer tasks of weeding and singling in the turnip fields and the overwhelming demands of the harvest period. This problem of finding seasonal aid was made the more difficult by the virtual disappearance of subtenants from whose cottages so much of the tenants' more variable need for labour had once been met. They were only partially replaced by married full-time servants whose families could be called upon for help, and in general the tendency to use unmarried servants had stripped agriculture of one of its most important sources of part-time labour.[53] Men whose sole livelihood lay in finding agricultural work by the day were comparatively few, probably less than one-fifth of the whole force of full-time workers.[54] Nor were there many to combine agricultural with industrial work such as quarrying or lime-burning. The solution was to use female labour from two main outside sources. In Aberdeenshire and Banffshire, where the dependence on unmarried servants was at its most extreme, a continuing expansion of the land under crop was secured largely by the creation of small holdings or crofts which were too small and often on too poor soil to give a full livelihood to the holders.[55] In general there came to be at least as many crofts as there were farms of sufficient size. Unlike so many of the cottagers of old, the crofters held their land directly of the landowners and owed no service to the tenant farmers. But necessity drove them to seek work where they could find it, and their wives and daughters, with the faltering of cottage industry, increasingly went to the fields of the greater farmers. They might be hired and paid by the day or they might take seasonal engagements for the summer months.[56] Increasing dependence on coal as a fuel made these summer engagements more feasible. The second recourse was to the villages where the main male employment would be non-agricultural. The northerly belt was strong in fishing villages — which did, indeed, supply some labour — but in spite of the founding of many planned villages, rural industry remained limited. But in Angus and in Perthshire linen weaving kept the villages growing till about 1850 and, added to the greater number of married servant households, they produced a good supply of female day labour. Towns of greater size — say, upwards of 5,000 inhabitants — were quite numerous in this area and, together with the major centres of Dundee and Perth, produced a considerable and in the end more enduring quota of workers.[57] In total these various sources were not quite sufficient, particularly with the decline of handloom weaving after 1850, and the help of the highland areas, both nearby and more distant, was used. Some farms would engage highland girls for the summer, housing them in bothies.[58] In parts of Angus, too, small holdings, or pendicles, were numerous enough to supply labour, as did the crofts further north.[59]

Among the many small differences in the forms of farm employment from place to place there was one outstanding factor which tended to produce substantial distinctions in ways of living. A sufficiency of farm cottages — to be used by married servants — formed the basis for a course of life for the typical worker which was substantially different from that forced on the workers where cottages were scarce. One consequence of a sufficient supply of cottages such as was to be found through large parts of the more southern counties was an adequate flow of recruits to the farm work-force from the families of existing full-time employees.[60] The lads would enter service, train as ploughmen, work for a period unmarried but with the full skills of their trade, and then, after marriage, take a farm cottage where they would complete a life-time in service and raise the families which would produce the next generation of servants. This made for a society of fixed positions, with lifelong wage-earners standing outside the community of holders of land. Further north, in Aberdeenshire, in

Banffshire and in Moray, the predominating condition was scarcity of cottages and insufficient numbers, therefore, of married servants to provide the lads to fill the places on the farms. The solution lay in the numerous crofts. Many of the farm workers began life on a croft to be fee'd part-time as early perhaps as the age of nine; then would come the full-time fee at the age of thirteen or fourteen and service as halflin and then ploughman, usually living in, until his mid-twenties. But the impulse to marriage would bring severe problems: how would he then follow his trade, being unable to find a cottar house? Ideally he might obtain a croft of his own, and undoubtedly a place of his own was the ambition of many a fee'd man.[61] But the crofts were too few to provide this ultimate fulfilment for many. Some appear to have left for the towns; some, too, would become day labourers, living in rooms rented in the villages.[62] The agony of the choice is most clearly shown, however, by the considerable numbers who opted to live among the unmarried men and to keep their families in village or town; usually the family's accommodation was no more than a single rented room. A survey of eleven scattered Aberdeenshire parishes shows that, in a work-force of 1271 full-time employees, 92 out of 212 married men were living thus.[63] They might well be able to see their families only once in two weeks.[64] Ultimately, however, the day labourers and the men maintaining their families off the farm might, well into middle age, succeed to a croft.[65]

Thus in one type of rural economy, found most notably in the extreme north-eastern corner, the land was worked largely by young unmarried men; these were mostly related to the families settled on the numerous small holdings which gave less than full livelihood but which were worked independently of the control of any larger farmer. The young men faced their employers in hard bargaining postures, acting as wage-earners without land and with no other recourse than selling their labour. But they would often have been born to crofting families and in the end might well come to the possession of small pieces of land on which they could have a form of independence.[66] The apparently separate groups of servants, day labourer and crofter were, in fact, all held within a network of family relationships, and one man would move in the succeeding phases of his life from one group to the other. On the other hand, where, as in many of the southerly districts, there were comparatively few holdings accessible to the labourers, it was bound to be otherwise. Here farm cottages were more numerous and the strands were knit together within the servants' families. Probably most young men would spend part of their lives as bothymen, temporarily beyond the reach of their families; but soon they would return to occupy farm cottages, in the dependent position of full-time wage-earners. The only land they could use in any sense as their own would be the potato ground or cows' grazing that they held, if at all, under the strict control of an employing farmer.[67]

Thus towns and villages as well as crofts and cottages meshed in providing the varied types of labour required on the land, and incomes derived from farm labour percolated broadly through communities of varying description. Through the middle decades of the century cultivation was tending to expand and intensify but the north-east was yet able to meet most of its needs for farm labour by tapping the various sources within its own boundaries. Even the expanded needs of summer and autumn could be met by relatively small migrations from the highlands, especially to the more southerly areas. Only in the Carse of Gowrie were there substantial signs of a hampering shortage before 1870, one factor there being the decline of handloom weaving which hastened migration from the villages and diminished the supply of female day labourers.[68] But the supply never became excessive. Few were forced to live solely on occasional employment in agriculture; there is little evidence of any large body of men lacking employment and staying in the countryside, although it may be that the jobless simply moved to towns or emigrated;[69] and, while conditions of work and housing remained harsh, wages, with more and more proportionately paid in money, increased faster than did urban earnings although they never reached the same level.[70]

The threat of labour scarcity, first evident in Perthshire, became obvious in all parts of the north-east after 1870. Rural population in the area after decades of growth began to show general decreases in 1861 and the fall continued, continuously through the decades although at varying pace, until the end of our period. In all, the population of the rural parishes fell by rather more than one-quarter between 1851 and 1911.[71] One reason was a falling rate of natural increase, but also important was migration from the country areas. There was much comment on this migration and in particular on its selective force as tending to erode the supply of good, country-bred servants.[72] In addition fewer women out of a given population would offer themselves for farm work. Not only were they attracted to other jobs but also there was a positive and growing revulsion from the harshness of outdoor agricultural work.[73]

The methods of farming were also changing, partly in response to this very drying up of some of the sources of labour, but in part quite independently of conditions on the labour market. The fall in agricultural prices and consequent depression did not strike the stock-rearing sections of the north-east — that is, the greater part of the area — until the 1880s, and then not so severely as in the south. Indeed, at no time was there any marked decline in the area under crop.[74] But prices moved in such a way as to shift the balance of farming effort further from grain to livestock production, and in the north-east farmers tended to lengthen rotations by adding a year of grass, thus diminishing the ploughing to be done.[75] A decline in the labour required for harvesting showed itself after 1850 as the horse-drawn reaper took over from the scythe, itself an instrument of economy, but more decisive was the invention of the reaper-binder; by the end of the century the numbers employed in harvesting had been drastically cut.[76] At the same time the completion of enclosure by use of wire fencing dispensed with herding.[77] Further, even the smallest farmers were increasingly able to use threshing machines which had been given mobility by use of steam tractors.[78] There was some movement to take crofts into larger farms — which would react upon labour supply — but on the whole the smaller units weathered the depression well and most of the crofting sector was left intact.[79]

The new condition of farming and of the labour market altered the patterns of employment. There was much complaint in particular about the shortage of female labour and indeed of anyone to perform the 'orra' work.[80] Day labourers became even scarcer and farmers were forced to depend more upon the hired servants and particularly upon ploughmen who in turn were put to jobs other than the traditional horse-work.[81] In fact the labour force was narrowing in composition, and it was men and boys permanently on the farm who did most of the work.[82] Only where crofts were numerous and also in the neighbourhood of towns and villages did the old mix of day labourers with the always predominant servants continue.[83] Casual labourers continued to be hired on an individual basis. The towns were also increasingly important to the farmers, as from them came many of the youths to engage as servants; such was the rate and nature of migration from the land that the springs of supply from the rural areas were drying up.[84] The change was not welcomed by employers because they saw in it a deterioration in the quality of labour; fee'd servants were no longer bred from their earliest days to a knowledge of country ways.[85] Still, the numbers coming forwards were sufficient to tackle the increasing variety of tasks facing the ploughmen. The land was not labour-starved in that an undiminished acreage was sustained in rotation crops, tended with full efficiency although with a larger proportion of grass.[86]

In fact, the changes served to emphasise what had been from early in the century the heart of the system of labour provision and discipline. Lads still came into farm service at thirteen or fourteen and graduated after three or four years to the full charge of a pair. And we have seen more and more of the farm work devolving upon these halflins and unmarried ploughmen. On marriage many were faced with the same awkward choices as their forerunners had been. The shortage of cottages had been slightly alleviated in parts of Aberdeenshire and Banffshire but the prevailing condition was still scarcity; indeed there was increased complaint about a shortage in parts of Angus.[87] Some married men, then, still chose to live among their unmarried co-workers and keep their families in villages and towns that might be ten miles distant.[88] Fewer evidently took to day labouring, and crofting was probably a less attractive aim than once it had been.[89] More than ever, then, marriage brought a decision to leave the land, for a nearby town perhaps but also, in spasmodically increasing numbers, to emigrate overseas.[90]

Living conditions and work routines remained very much the same. The districts characterised by numerous bothies, or by a predominant kitchen system, or by a fairly numerous complement of married servants remained, in spite of some experiment with alternative systems, much as they had been defined in the earlier years of the century.[91] There was, however, some slight softening of the rigours of the farm worker's life. In places sleeping accommodation had been improved. Apartments might be constructed separated from the functional sections of the steading, with better protection against the weather and a fireplace. But many bad places remained.[92] Bothies had sometimes been divided to give each man a separate cubicle for sleeping, and it was more common for the cooking and cleaning to be done for the men by a female servant.[93] Cottages were now almost all up to the two-room standard, although the division might have to be made by a box-bed.[94] Some estates were providing two-storey units with two or three bedrooms but they might not be liked by the occupants because they were cold and expensive to furnish.[95] Real wages continued to rise through the last quarter of the nineteenth century and there was a slight shortening of the working day, as the early morning threshing demanded before the start in the fields was now almost gone and there was a tendency for evening work in the stables to be shortened.[96] A great improvement in the quality of the farm servant's life come with the widespread sale of bicycles, which, indeed, became as common a personal possession as the kist had always been.[97] But fundamentally the ploughman, and with him the other servants, continued to be held to the long working day of nine or ten hours in the fields, together with other duties in the stable and steading.[98] The domination by the horse of the hours of labour, the system of engagement, the form of housing, and indeed the very texture of social life, was not to be substantially eroded till the fourth decade of the twentieth century.

NOTES

1. For an account of the annual round in a traditional system of agriculture see Thomas P. Soper, 'Monymusk, 1770–1850' (unpublished Ph.D. thesis, University of Aberdeen, 1954), pp. 76–81. On more specific points with regard to peat see James Anderson, *General View of the Agriculture of the County of Aberdeen* (Edinburgh, 1794), p. 107; George Skene Keith, *General View of the Agriculture of the County of Aberdeen* (Aberdeen, 1811), p. 531.

2. John Stuart, ed., *List of Pollable Persons within the Shire of Aberdeen, 1696* (Aberdeen, 1844) shows how numerous throughout the county were the unmarried servants attached to the households of even small farmers. See also Sir John Sinclair, ed., *The Statistical Account of Scotland*, New Edition, 20 vols. (Wakefield, 1973–) (*O.S.A.*), XV, p. 127; XVI, p. 660; William Leslie, *General View of the Agriculture of the Counties of Moray and Nairn* (London, 1813), pp. 350–1.

C

3. James Headrick, *General View of the Agriculture of the County of Angus or Forfarshire* (Edinburgh, 1813), p. 493; George Robertson, *Rural Recollections* (Irvine, 1829), p. 421; Sir John Sinclair, *General Report of the Agricultural State and Political Circumstances of Scotland*, 3 vols. (Edinburgh, 1814), III, p. 232; Keith, *Aberdeenshire*, p. 514.

4. The many retrospective statements about the feeble and limited ploughing given to the land are vague and generally exaggerated. The best indication of the practice of ploughing is itself retrospective, being that given in *O.S.A.*, XVI, p. 657.

5. Keith, *Aberdeenshire*, p. 520; *General Report*, III, pp. 237–8.

6. Henry Hamilton, ed., *Selections from the Monymusk papers, 1713–1755* (Scottish History Society, Edinburgh, 1945), pp. xxv–vi, lxxvi–vii; William Littlejohn, *Stories of the Buchan Cottars from the Year 'One'* (Aberdeen, 1929), pp. 16–17; Robert A. Dodgshon, *Land and Society in Early Scotland* (Oxford, 1981), pp. 213–4; Sir Archibald Grant, *Dissertation on the Chief Obstacles to the Improvement of land* (Aberdeen, 1760), p. 47; *O.S.A.*, XI, pp. 17, 346, 553, 556; XIII, pp. 231, 374, 470, 604–5; XV, pp. 245, 503, 516–7, 555.

7. Sir John Sinclair, *Analysis of the Statistical Account of Scotland*, 2 vols, (Edinburgh, 1827), I, p. 262; Grant, *Dissertation*, pp. 59–60, 70; *O.S.A.*, XIII, p. 231; Andrew Wight, *Present State of Husbandry in Scotland*, 4 vols. (Edinburgh, 1778–84), III Pt. 2, p. 614.

8. Keith, *Aberdeenshire*, p. 149; *O.S.A.*, XIII, pp. 76, 345, 509, 643; XIV, pp. xxv–vi; XV, pp. xxviii–xxix.

9. James E. Handley, *The Agricultural Revolution in Scotland* (Glasgow, 1963), p. 135; *O.S.A.*, XI, pp. 167–8, 269, 373, 380.

10. *Royal Commission on the Employment of Children, Young Persons and Women in Agriculture. Fourth Report. Appendix, Part I. Parliamentary Papers 1870, XIII* (hereafter *Fourth Report on Women in Agriculture, 1870*), p. 50; *O.S.A.*, XI, pp. 170–1.

11. The evidence from all the Carse parishes in *O.S.A.* is that the two-horse plough was, by then, almost universal. See also Handley, *Agricultural Revolution*, pp. 124, 136, 139, 147; James Robertson, *General View of the Agriculture of the County of Perth* (Perth, 1813), p. 125.

12. Sir John Sinclair, *An Account of the Systems of Husbandry adopted in the more Improved Districts of Scotland*, 2 vols. (Edinburgh, 1814), I, pp. 139, 142.

13. *Fourth Report on Women in Agriculture, 1870* App., I, pp. 46–7, 50.

14. *O.S.A.*, XI, pp. 251, 271, 346, 556.

15. *O.S.A.*, XI, pp. 20, 271; Sinclair, *Analysis*, I, p. 262; *Fourth Report on Women in Agriculture, 1870*, App., I, p 50.

16. Levitt and Smout argue that farmers were forced to employ unmarried men because of the movement of families to find employment in the towns. Nevertheless there is ample evidence that much of the required day labour came from villages and towns and that labourers were easier to find close to the towns and bigger villages. Farmers' needs seem to have been adequately met at least until 1850, after which the decline of handloom weaving tended to make farm labour scarcer. Ian Levitt and Christopher Smout, *The State of the Scottish Working-Class in 1843* (Edinburgh, 1979), p. 71; Headrick, *Angus*, p. 495; Sinclair, *General Report*, III, p. 237; *Fourth Report on Women in Agriculture, 1870*, App., I, p. 50.

17. *O.S.A.*, XI, p. 345; *Fourth Report on Women in Agriculture, 1870*, App., I, p. 50.

18. *O.S.A.*, XI, pp. 171, 345; *Fourth Report on Women in Agriculture, 1870*, App., I, p. 50.

19. For example, farmers might insist on taking their young servants through the catechism.

20. *O.S.A.*, XI, p. 21.

21. *O.S.A.*, XI, pp. 252, 550.

22. The survival of the infield/outfield distinction is amply illustrated in the *O.S.A.* reports for Aberdeenshire and Banffshire and, to a lesser extent, Angus.

23. Anderson, *Aberdeenshire*, pp. 74–6. Again *O.S.A.* shows the widespread survival of ploughing with oxen and with teams of four or more animals.

24. Anderson suggests that by 1794 the growing of turnips was widespread through Aberdeenshire, but it is clear from *O.S.A.* parish reports that this only meant that each farmer would have a tiny acreage devoted to turnips. Anderson, *Aberdeenshire*, p. 64.

25. George Robertson, *Rural Recollections*, pp. 459–60; Keith, *Aberdeenshire*, p. 513. The *New Statistical Account (N.S.A.)* shows turnips occupying an important place in the rotations pursued in most districts north of the Carse of Gowrie. *New Statistical Account of Scotland*, 15 vols. (Edinburgh, 1835–45).

26. Sinclair, *General Report*, III, pp. 184–6; Anderson, *Aberdeenshire*, p. 67; Keith, *Aberdeenshire*, p. 513.

27. Headrick, *Angus*, p. 492; *O.S.A.*, XVI, p. 165.

28. The adoption of the heavy work-horses in the north was a slow adaptation, starting with the importation of stallions to breed with the local mares. Anderson, *Aberdeenshire*, p. 83; Handley, *Agricultural Revolution*, pp. 124, 136, 139, 147.

29. In areas of lighter soil one ploughman could deal with between fifty and eighty acres of land under rotation. *Fourth Report on Women in Agriculture, 1870*, App., I, p. 32; Leslie, *Moray and Nairn*, p. 327.

30. Sinclair, *General Report*, III, p. 233; Keith, *Aberdeenshire*, p. 575.

31. Leslie, *Moray and Nairn*, p. 350.

32. Headrick, *Angus*, pp. 492, 494.

33. *O.S.A.*, XI, pp. 346, 553, 556; XIII, pp. 63, 144, 231, 374; XIV, pp. 5, 62, 224; XV, p. 195; XVI, pp. 165, 211–3.

34. *Fourth Report on Women in Agriculture, 1870*, App., I, pp. 34, 36.

35. Ian Carter, *Farm Life in Northeast Scotland, 1840–1914* (Edinburgh, 1979), pp. 144–8; *Fourth Report on Women in Agriculture, 1870*, App., I, p. 36. For an account based on personal experience of feeing markets in the twentieth century see David Toulmin, *A Chiel Among Them* (Aberdeen, 1982), pp. 85–8.

36. See below, p. 191. Also Sinclair, *General Report*, III, p. 233; Keith, *Aberdeenshire*, p. 514; *Fourth Report on Women in Agriculture, 1870*, App., I, p. 38; Levitt and Smout, *Scottish Working Class*, pp. 70–76, 83.

37. Robertson, *Rural Recollections*, p. 421; *Fourth Report on Women in Agriculture, 1870*, App., I, p. 39; Levitt and Smout, *Scottish Working Class*, pp. 70–76, 83; James Macdonald, 'The agriculture of the counties of Forfar and Kincardine', *Transactions of the Highland and Agricultural Society*, (*T.H.A.S.*), XIII (1882), p. 170.

38. *Fourth Report on Women in Agriculture, 1870*, App., I, p. 41; Carter, *Farm Life*, pp. 120–32.

39. *Fourth Report on Women in Agriculture, 1870*, App., I, pp. 40, 50–51; Macdonald, 'Forfar and Kincardine', p. 170.

40. *Eleven Years at Farm Work, being a True Tale of Farm Servant Life from 1863 onwards* (Aberdeen, 1879), pp. 16–21.

41. *Royal Commission on Labour:* The Agricultural Labourer Vol. III, Scotland, Part II, Parliamentary Papers 1893–94, XXXVI (hereafter *R.C. on Labour, 1893*), pp. 148, 155.

42. *Fourth Report on Women in Agriculture, 1870*, App., I, p. 35; Levitt and Smout, *Scottish Working Class*, pp. 72–75.

43. *Fourth Report on Women in Agriculture, 1870*, App., I, p. 36; *R.C. on Labour, 1893*, p. 110.

44. Carter, *Farm Life*, p. 109. In eleven Aberdeenshire parishes that have been surveyed in detail there were, in 1861, 703 ploughmen, 234 cattlemen and 314 general servants (male). Census 1861, Enumerators' Books [for the parishes of Aberdour, Aboyne, Alford, Auchendoir, Auchterless, Keith Hall, Kinnellar, Lonmay, Lumphanan, Methlick, Old Deer].

45. John R. Allan, *Farmer's Boy* (London, 1935), p. 113; Carter, *Farm Life*, pp. 117, 139–42.

46. The hours of ploughing as reported in the second decade of the nineteenth century were the same as those of the 1890s and indeed of the 1920s. They seem in all cases to have been shorter than those required for ploughing by oxen. Wight, *State of Husbandry*, III, Pt. 2, p. 693; Sinclair, *Improved Districts*, II, pp. 244–5; Sinclair, *General Report*, III, pp. 184–6; *Fourth Report on Women in Agriculture, 1870*, App., I, pp. 46–47; *R.C. on Labour, 1893*, pp. III, 132, 150; Toulmin, *Chiel Among Them*, pp. 127–8.

47. Anderson, *Aberdeenshire*, p. 80; Keith, *Aberdeenshire*, p. 522; *R.C. on Labour*, pp. 113, 141.

48. *Fourth Report on Women in Agriculture, 1870*, App., I, p. 38; *R.C. on Labour 1893*, p. 111.

49. Keith, *Aberdeenshire*, p. 575; *Fourth Report on Women in Agriculture, 1870*, App., II, p. 9.

50. Ian Carter, 'Class and culture among farm servants in the north-east', in A. Allan Maclaren, ed., *Social Class in Scotland: Past and Present*, (Edinburgh, 1976), p. 107; Carter, *Farm Life*, p. 109.

51. This again is indicated by the age-distribution among the different categories of servant. Carter, 'Class and Culture', p. 107; Carter, *Farm Life*, p. 109; *R.C. on Labour 1893*, p. 118.

52. *Fourth Report on Women in Agriculture, 1870*, App., II, p. 25.

53. *O.S.A.*, XI, p. 20; XIII, p. 329; Headrick, *Angus*, p. 136; Sinclair, *Analysis*, I, p. 262; *Fourth Report on Women in Agriculture, 1870*, App. I, pp. 51–2.

54. National figures for the proportion of day labourers in the farm labour force are given in Malcolm Gray, 'Migration in the Rural Lowlands of Scotland, 1750–1850', in T. M. Devine and David Dickson, eds., *Ireland and Scotland, 1600–1850* (Edinburgh, 1983), p. 109. In the north-eastern counties (not including Perthshire) day labourers amounted to 17 per cent of the farm work-force (including farmers) and to 23 per cent of the labour force (excluding farmers). *Census of Scotland 1861, Parliamentary Papers 1864, LI, Occupations of the People*, pp. 167–92.

55. See Gray, 'North-east Agriculture', pp. 93–4; Carter, *Farm Life*, pp. 28–31.

56. *Fourth Report on Women in Agriculture, 1870*, App., I, p. 34.

57. Sinclair, *Central Report*, III, p. 239; Macdonald, 'Forfar and Kincardine', p. 83. *Fourth Report on Women in Agriculture, 1870*, App. I, pp. 51–52; *N.S.A.*, XI, *Angus*, pp. 242, 6.

58. *Fourth Report on Women in Agriculture, 1870*, App., I, pp. 41, 52.

59. Macdonald, 'Forfar and Kincardine', p. 83; *N.S.A.*, XI, Angus, pp. 405, 501; *Fourth Report on Women in Agriculture, 1870*, App., I, pp. 21, 23–25.

60. Sinclair, *Improved Districts*, I, p. 269; *Fourth Report on Women in Agriculture, 1870*, App., I, p. 38.

61. The harshness but also the strange appeal of the life of the crofter is vividly recalled in David Kerr Cameron, *Willie Gavin, Crofter Man* (London, 1980). See also Gray, 'North-east Agriculture', p. 100.

62. The type of village accommodation in which the families lived is shown in *Fourth Report on Women in Agriculture, 1870*, App., I, p. 38; App. II, p. 13. See also Gray, 'North-east Agriculture', pp. 99–100.

63. Census, 1861, Enumerators' Books.

64. *Fourth Report on Women in Agriculture, 1870*, App., I, p. 38.

65. Gray, 'North-east Agriculture', pp. 100, 102.

66. The independence of the crofter was qualified but prized. Cameron, *Willie Gavin*, pp. 60–74; Carter, *Farm Life*, pp. 92–97; Gray, 'North-east Agriculture', p. 95–96, 100.

67. *Fourth Report on Women in Agriculture, 1870*, App., I, p. 35; App., II, Answers to questions 58–63; *Royal Commission on the Poor Laws in Scotland. Appendix, Part V. Parliamentary Papers 1844*, XXII (hereafter *R.C. on Scottish Poor Laws, 1844*). Answers to question 9.

68. *Fourth Report on Women in Agriculture, 1870*, App., I, p. 51.

69. *R.C. on Scottish Poor Laws, 1844*, Answers to question 22.

70. See below, pp. 251– .

71. Gray, 'Migration in the Rural Lowlands', p. 114; *Census of Scotland, 1851, Parliamentary Papers, 1853*, LXXXVI, *Numbers of the Inhabitants*; *Census of Scotland, 1911, Parliamentary Papers, 1912*, LXXX, Table VII, *Population of Civil Parishes*.

72. *R.C. on Labour, 1893*, pp. 109, 112, 130.

73. *R.C. on Labour, 1893*, pp. 109, 114, 117, 135, 141–2, 155; T. M. Devine, 'Temporary Migration and the Scottish Highlands in the Nineteenth Century', *Economic History Review*, 2nd Series, XXXII, 3, 1979, p. 350. See also below, pp. 119–20 for a fuller discussion of this point.

74. Carter, *Farm Life*, pp. 79–85.

75. *Report of the Royal Commission on Agriculture*, Parliamentary Papers, 1894, XVI Pt. 1. Report by Mr. James Hope, pp. 4–7, 15; *R.C. on Labour, 1893*, pp. 129–30.

76. *R.C. on Labour, 1893*, pp. 109, 115.

77. *Fourth Report on Women in Agriculture, 1870*, App., I, p. 34; James D. Young, 'On Wire Fences', *T.H.A.S.*, IV, 1849–51, pp. 242–62.

78. James Black, 'On the Agriculture of Aberdeen and Banff Shires', *T.H.A.S.*, III, 1870–1, p. 32; Cameron, *Willie Gavin*, p. 72.

79. Carter, *Farm Life*, pp. 92–96.

80. *R.C. on Labour, 1893*, pp. 117, 130, 139–40, 142, 148, 156.

81. *Ibid.*, pp. 130, 138, 142.

82. *Ibid.*, p. 148.

83. *Ibid.*, pp. 109, 112, 117, 130, 148.

84. *Ibid.*, pp. 109, 112, 121, 130.

85. *Ibid.*, pp. 109, 117, 140.

86. *Ibid.*, pp. 109, 130.

87. *Ibid.*, pp. 112, 148.

88. *Ibid.*, pp. 110, 118, 124, 126, 134, 139.

89. Carter, *Farm Life*, pp. 94–97; Cameron, *Willie Gavin*, pp. 60–88; *R.C. on Labour, 1893*, pp. 112, 148.

90. R. Molland and G. Evans, 'Scottish Farm Wages from 1870 to 1900' *Journal of the Royal Statistical Society*, Series A (General), CXIII Pt. 2, 1950, p. 225; *R.C. on Labour, 1893*, p. 109.

91. *Report of the Royal Commission on the Housing of the Industrial Population of Scotland, Rural and Urban. Parliamentary Papers*, 1917–18, XXXI (hereafter *R.C. on Housing, 1918*), pp. 162, 174; *R.C. on Labour, 1893*, pp. 111, 114–23, 131–2, 135–48; Carter, *Farm Life*, pp. 126–7.

92. *R.C. on Housing, 1918*, p. 171; *R.C. on Labour, 1893*, pp. 132, 137–8, 142. An example of an improved sleeping place is fully described in Allan, *Farmer's Boy*, pp. 111–2.

93. *R.C. on Housing, 1918*, p. 172; *R.C. on Labour, 1893*, pp. 118, 120–3, 131–2, 137, 141.

94. *R.C. on Housing, 1918*, pp. 163–4.

95. *R.C. on Housing, 1918*, p. 164; *R.C. on Labour, 1893*, pp. 112, 116, 118.

96. *R.C. on Labour, 1893*, pp. 113, 159.

97. David Toulmin, *Hard Shining Corn* (Aberdeen, 1972), p. 81; *R.C. on Labour, 1893*, p. 150; Allan, *Farmer's Boy*, p. 112.

98. Toulmin, *Chiel Among Them*, pp. 127–8.

3

Farm Servants and Farm Labour in the Forth Valley and South-East Lowlands

Alastair Orr

The south-east lowlands were the source of Scotland's international reputation for agricultural improvement. By the 1830s, Lothian husbandry held up a mirror to the future: large farms, the latest technology, massive capital investment, and a compliant labour force. The region is thus ideally suited for testing current generalisations about the form of the transition to capitalist agriculture in Britain. What follows, therefore, is not a general survey of agricultural labour in five counties (East, West, and Midlothian, Stirlingshire and Clackmannanshire), but a study of the impact of this transition on farm labour.[1]

The impact of British capitalist agriculture on the labour force has been summed up by historians in the world 'proletarianisation'. At least three processes were involved.[2] First, the separation of employers from employed by the abolition of farm service. Second, the substitution of money wages for payment in kind. Third, the replacement of annual labour contracts by short-term weekly or daily engagements. As we shall discover, none of the above, derived from Hobsbawm and Rudé's study of southern England, accurately describes the transition to capitalist agriculture in the south-east lowlands of Scotland. Here, in the region where the forces of production developed faster than in most other areas of Britain, relations of production remained stubbornly traditional.

I shall divide my analysis of this paradox into four parts. The first section examines labour relations; the second, the labour market; the third, labour productivity; the final section looks at labour's response to technological change.

1. Labour Relations

The agricultural revolution between 1780 and 1840 which revolutionised modes of production was accompanied by an agrarian revolution which transformed labour relations. One aspect of this change which has recently attracted attention was the abolition of farm service.[3] Traditionally, much of the labour force in Britain consisted of young, unmarried servants living in the farmhouse with the farmer and his family. With the commercialisation of agriculture, however, farm servants were no longer welcome in the farmer's family. Instead, they were housed separately in cottages or bothies, a physical separation which symbolised the new social division between farmer and labourer.

Service lay at the heart of traditional labour relations in the south-east. The typical employer in the Lothians was the 'gudeman', a rich peasant using family labour but also hiring servants. Farm servants as a group consisted broadly of three subdivisions: married ploughmen (called 'hinds' in the Lothians) living in a cottage attached to the farm; unmarried ploughmen boarded in the farmer's house, and domestic servants who were usually women. It is possible that farm servants were recruited from the families of cottars, poor peasants who farmed the small crofts scattered around the compact holdings of the gudemen.[4] In 1780 'the greater number' of farm servants in the Lothians were said to be unmarried servants boarding in the farmer's house.[5] A typical gudeman with 100 acres might employ, besides two hinds, as many as five farm servants (two ploughmen and three maid servants) who shared his table and slept in the ben.[6] Such servants must have been numerous because gudemen were common. A census in East Lothian in 1769 revealed 506 farms over sixty acres.[7]

By 1840, the agrarian revolution in Britain had reduced many farm servants to the status of labourers. Yet the abolition of farm service was far from universal in all regions. The 1831 Census shows that farm servants still formed a significant proportion of the labour force in the south-east, especially in Stirlingshire (see Fig. 1 and Appendix pp. 48–9). Moreover, many servants continued to live in the farmhouse. Unfortunately, data on indoor farm servants only become available in 1861. However, they show indoor farm servants were still numerous.

As late as 1861, a large proportion of the agricultural labour force still consisted of farm servants (40 per cent). Moreover, nearly half of these, 20 per cent of the labour force, lived in the farmhouse. Indeed, indoor farm servants were actually more common than outdoor servants in two counties, Stirling and West Lothian. Their numbers were insignificant only in East Lothian, the source of so many generalisations about capitalist agriculture.

The remarkable survival of farm service in the south-east can be attributed to two factors. Firstly, instead of accommodating their servants in cottages or bothies, many farmers simply redesigned their houses to provide separate quarters and kitchens for servants. One observer estimated that over half the farmhouses in the Lothians were rebuilt between 1778 and 1810.[8] Plans of such houses show separate quarters for servants.[9] Thus, although the meaning of service had changed, the form

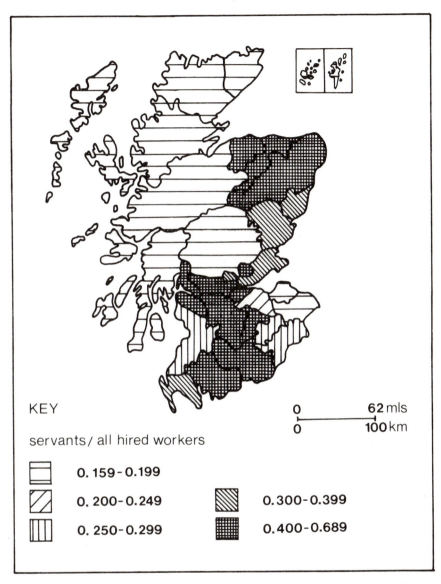

Fig. 1. Composition of the hired agricultural labour force (servants/all hired workers), the Scottish Lowlands, 1831.

remained the same. This enabled the farmer to secure his labour supply without compromising his social superiority. Secondly, outside East Lothian many farms in the south-east remained small, and the social gulf between farmer and servant was a narrow one. As one observer wrote, 'the kitchen system can exist only where a farmer is willing to associate with his

Table 1   *Indoor farm servants as a proportion of hired workers, 1861*

County	Indoor Servants	Outdoor Servants	Labourers	Total
West Lothian	585	537	1384	2506
	(23.34)	(21.42)	(55.22)	(100.00)
Midlothian	1068	1577	3809	6454
	(16.54)	(24.43)	(59.01)	(100.00)
East Lothian	165	1738	4067	5970
	(2.76)	(29.11)	(68.12)	(100.00)
Stirling	2044	617	1651	4312
	(47.40)	(14.30)	(38.28)	(100.00)
Clackmannan	98	211	329	648
	(15.12)	(32.56)	(52.31)	(100.00)
Total	3960	4680	11250	19890
Average	(19.90)	(23.52)	(56.56)	(100.00)

Source: *Census of Scotland, 1861.*
Note: Figures within parentheses are percentages.

work people, and dine at the same table. But when farms increase in size, and the tenant rises in the social scale, he objects to mingle with his servants...'[10] In Stirlingshire, where the average farm size in 1851 was only fifty acres, indoor servants predominated and were still numerous in the late nineteenth century.[11]

Where the kitchen system broke down, an alternative was to house unmarried ploughmen in bothies. Such was the practice in Clackmannan, where it was estimated that 90 per cent of the single men lived in bothies by the 1890s.[12] Yet bothies for ploughmen were uncommon in the Lothians. As one East Lothian farmer wrote, 'There are no bothies for men, in the common sense of the term, and I doubt if a single Scotch workman inhabits a bothy in the county'.[13] Instead, unmarried farm servants were recruited from the families of the hinds. This prevented the growth of bothies.[14] When the practice of obtaining labour from the hind's families died out in the later nineteenth century, bothies became more common.[15] These local differences in labour relations are best explained by variations in the size of farms. Where farms were small, as in Stirlingshire, unmarried servants continued to be boarded in the farmhouse. Where farms were large, as in the Lothians, they were housed either in the farmhouse or in cottages. Only in Clackmannan, where farms were not so small as in Stirlingshire nor yet so large as in the Lothians, do we find few indoor servants and male bothies.

Other aspects of labour relations in the south-east are equally at odds with the historical model. Capitalist labour relations are supposedly characterised by the absence of social and extra-economic ties between labourers and farmer. Yet a striking feature of labour relations in the south-east was the survival of traditional forms of dependence, in the custom of family contracts and the system of 'bondage'.

Family contracts were common among hinds. Besides his own labour, the married ploughman also pledged to provide a worker at harvest time (normally his wife or daughter) for anything from eighteen days to one month, in return for his cottage. In Borthwick parish in the 1840s, for example, the hind's rent was fixed at twenty days' work at harvest, plus labour to carry the corn from the stackyard to the barn for threshing in winter.[16] Labour-tying was thus a convenient way of obtaining casual labour at peak periods: 'In the family of the cottar there is a fund of labour from which great benefit is derived in busy seasons, and in which lies a great inducement to arable farmers to study and promote their general well-being'.[17]

Hinds also contracted to supply the farmer with labour for longer periods. This was known as the 'bondage' system:

> By the bondage system I mean the practice of compelling each hind, or rather cottage holder, to provide an outworker, generally understood to mean a woman. Usually the outworker is the daughter or sister of the hind or cottager; but in case the head of the house is not blessed with a daughter or sister prepared to 'work the bondage', under this system he is obliged to hire a woman, whom he boards and lodges, receiving from the farmer a certain allowance in money for every day she is employed on the farm.[18]

This form of labour-tying was to the farmer's advantage since it meant labour was always available but was paid only when it worked. On average, a bondager might work for 180 days in the year.[19] While idle, she had to be supported by the hind. Not surprisingly, bondage was deeply unpopular with farm servants, and the Farm Servants Protection Society (established in 1865) campaigned for its abolition.[20] The custom was rare in this region by the 1890s.[21] Yet as late as 1914, the distinctive bondager dress of wide-brimmed straw hat, blouse, and drugget skirt, together with boots buttoning up the side of the leg, could still be seen in the Lothians.[22] Similarly, the system of family contracts remained widespread in the south-east even after the First World War.[23]

The custom of recruiting family labour explains two important structural features of agriculture in the south-east. Firstly, it explains the high proportion of women in the agricultural labour force. After the abolition of sub-tenancies, farmers turned increasingly to the wives and daughters of farm servants for their labour supply. 'Women are now employed for every farming activity except ploughing and threshing,' wrote Patrick Graham of Stirlingshire in 1812.[24] Their large numbers may also be explained by the widespread cultivation of green crops and the predominance of heavy industry in central Scotland, which required male labour.[25] The importance of women in the composition of the labour force between 1851–1911 is shown in Table 2.

Table 2 *Composition of the farm labour force in the South-East and Forth Valley, 1851–1911*

| | | | (000's) | | |
| | | | Hired workers | | |
Date	Farmers	Relatives	(male)	(female)	Others
1851	2.8	1.2	15.3	5.1	3.3
1861	2.6	0.8	14.3	5.6	2.6
1871	2.2	2.4	11.0	5.1	2.6
1881	2.1	0.7	10.3	5.3	1.5
1891	2.1	0.8	9.2	4.0	3.7
1901	2.1	0.7	7.5	3.7	3.5
1911	2.1	1.0	4.8	2.2	2.4

Source: *Census of Scotland, 1851–1911.*
Note: Classification follows F. W. D. Taylor, 'United Kingdom: numbers in agriculture', *Farm Economist*, vol. 8, No. 4 (1955), pp. 36–40.

With the demise of the bondage system, female outworkers were obtained by importing labour from the Highlands and Ireland.[26] Instead of being boarded with hinds or cottagers, the immigrants were housed separately in bothies. These were common on large farms. A survey of twenty-seven arable farms in the Lothians in the 1870s revealed that women (mostly young girls under eighteen) made up 46 per cent of the work force.[27] The ready supply of cheap female labour from the Highlands explains why the proportion of female workers in the south-east rose by over 30 per cent between 1851 and 1911, whereas in England the proportion fell.[28] Absolute numbers remained constant until the 1890s, when the supply at last began to dry up.

Secondly, the use of family labour explains the absence of a numerous class of day labourers. Before 1780, large numbers of day labourers had been unnecessary because farms were small; there were only ten farms over 300 acres in the Lothians by that date.[29] The need for casual labour at peak seasons had been met through the custom of labour services ('bonnage', literally bondage), supplied by poor peasants farming small crofts or sub-tenancies.[30] With the enlargement of farms, small crofts disappeared, and this source of labour dried up. Instead, the increased demand for casual labour was met by adapting the traditional system of labour supply from small crofts into what became known as the 'cottage system', namely the practice of recruiting labour from the family of the hind through joint contracts and the bondage system. Thus, the evolution of small crofters hiring out labour into cottagers supplying family labour, checked 'the overgrowth of an agricultural population, and that accumulation of catch-labourers, depending greatly on the Poor Law for support, which is such a distressing feature in many southern English villages'.[31] Most of those classified as labourers by the 1831 Census were in fact bondagers or male labourers housed on the farm. Such men were called 'orramen', or 'spade-hinds'.[32] Orramen were jacks-of-all-trades who did the hedge-cutting, draining, and heavy fieldwork considered unsuitable for women. Both in their wages and annual or six-monthly contracts they enjoyed a similar status to the hind.[33] Indeed, spade-hinds were themselves the sons of hinds, boarded in their father's cottage or that of a close relative.[34] No farm was complete without its orraman, and large farms employed several.[35]

2. The Labour Market

The second feature of the historical model of the transition to capitalist agriculture is of changes in the labour market. These took the form of the substitution of cash wages for payment in kind, and the introduction of short-term weekly or daily labour contracts.

Once again, the south-east does not fit this paradigm. The usual mode of payment for farm servants remained payment in kind. This was known as the 'boll wage', the boll being a Scottish measure. The precise composition of the boll wage varied from county to county, but it generally consisted of oats, barley, peas or beans, as well as the keep of a cow, food at harvest time, and a plot of land for growing potatoes or flax (in addition to a garden), and sometimes the keep of hens or pigs as well. Conversely, hinds rarely paid cash for the rent of their cottages; instead, they supplied a worker at harvest and a bondager at other times of the year. A good example of the kind of items included in the boll wage is shown below by the hinds' earnings in East Lothian in 1852.[36] Opposite each payment in kind is shown the cash equivalent:

	£.	s.	d.
8 quarters oats at 28s	12	12	0
2¼ quarters barley at 36s	4	1	0
1 quarter beans at 42s	2	2	0
Lint and hens	1	1	0
Keep of a cow and pig	6	0	0
Harvest meat	1	0	0
1,200 yards of potatoes	3	0	0
Free house, garden and manure	2	10	0
Coals carted	1	0	0
Total	33	6	0

The boll wage frequently included a cash component, but this was not large. As late as 1867 in the Lothians, for example, out of a total wage of £42 only £14 was paid in cash.[37] Not until the 1880s did Lothian farm servants begin to receive most of their wages in money.[38] In East Lothian, a quarter of the hind's wage was still paid in kind in the 1890s, and the practice survived into the twentieth century.[39]

As with wages, so with contracts. Long-term engagements continued to be the most common form of labour contract in the south-east. Married ploughmen were hired by the year, unmarried ploughmen and female farm servants by the half year. Nor were such contracts given only to farm servants. Orramen were also hired for long periods.[40] Annual contracts not only afforded farm servants security of employment but also entitled them to sick pay. 'By law we are obliged to give him his food and wages for six successive weeks, if ill health does not keep him away longer than that from working'.[41] However, this provision did not apply to female servants.[42] Hiring was therefore a twice-yearly occasion, at Whitsunday and Martinmas. Until the 1860s, however, the market for skilled agricultural labour was segmented. Only single farm servants frequented hiring fairs — hinds were hired on the farm.[43] This informal hiring system was advantageous for both employer and employed. The hind retained some control over his choice of employer, while farmers could obtain character references which ensured good workmen. Hiring fairs for married servants only became common after the 1860s, when they were deplored as 'loosening ... the tie which binds master and servant together'.[44] The custom of annual and six-monthly contracts persisted, since it was in the farmers' interest. As one wrote, 'the efficiency and steadfastness of the Scotch labourers have been promoted by regular service and long engagements'.[45]

Changes in the supply and demand of labour are best analysed through movements in wages. Unfortunately, the construction of a wage series for Scottish agriculture poses special problems since farm servants received part of their wages in kind. The data in Tables 3 and 4 refer only to money wages, and do not represent changes in earnings. Given the problems of valuing income in kind, an index based on cash wages alone is probably the best possible guide to changes in income.[46] Wage series are given for four different categories of agricultural labour. For the sake of consistency, the three wage series for farm servants are all drawn from the same county, Stirlingshire, while the wage series for day labourers refers to the Lothians.

Money wages during the period of the agricultural revolution (Table 3) show a steady rise until 1814. This is to be expected given a period of rapid agricultural change fuelled by the war-time demand for food, which brought about an extension in the arable area, coinciding with industrial expansion. There are even suggestions of labour shortage, from the increasing use of women for farm work to the popularity of labour-saving

Table 3 *Agricultural money wages. South-East and Forth Valley, 1780–1840*

Date	(1) Married Ploughmen (£)	(2) Unmarried ploughmen (£)	(3) Female farm servants (£)	(4) Day labourers
1780–89	7.0	5.0	2.5	10½d.
1790–99	10.0	8.6	4.0	1/4d.
1800–09	—	—	—	1/6d.
1810–19	—	13.3	10.0	1/10d.
1820–29	17.0	13.5	6.7	1/8d.
1830–39	20.0	11.0	6.0	1/7d.

Sources: (1) 1780–89: M. Goldie, 'The Standard of Living of Scottish Farm Labourers', (unpublished M.Sc. thesis, University of Edinburgh, 1970), Appendix, Table 6; 1820–29: *Stirling Journal* (1823, 28, 29); 1830–39: Goldie, 'Standard of Living', Table 5C, Appendix, Table 1.5; (2) 1780–89: Goldie, 'Standard of Living', Appendix, Table 6; 1810–19: A. L. Bowley, 'The Statistics of Wages in the United Kingdom during the last Hundred Years (Part 1. Agricultural Wages — Con'td. Scotland', *Journal of the Royal Statistical Society*, vol. LXII (1899), p. 148, Table 3; 1820–39: *Stirling Journal* (1823, 28, 29, 31); Goldie, 'Standard of Living', Appendix, Table 1.5; (3) 1780–99: Goldie, 'Standard of Living', Appendix, Tables 6, 1E; 1810–39: *Stirling Journal* (1823, 28, 29, 31); Goldie, 'Standard of Living', Appendix, Table 5C; (4) 1780–99: Robertson, *Rural Recollections*, p. 400; 1800–19: Robertson, *Rural Recollections*, p. 400; 1820–29: *First Report from Select Committee on Agricultural Distress. Parliamentary Papers Part II–VII*, 1836, Evidence of John Brodie; 1830–39: *Report from Select Committee on Present State of Agriculture. Parliamentary Papers*, V, 1833, Q. 2647; Goldie, 'Standard of Living', p. 116.

innovations. Conversely, farmers were not averse to innovations which reduced productivity in order to obtain labour. The introduction of harvest piece work ('threaving') during the Napoleonic Wars is a good example. Harvesters cutting and binding individually were less efficient than five reapers in a 'bandwin'. Nevertheless, piece work effectively mopped up residual pools of labour among the elderly and semi-employed. Its popularity among farmers indicates that, in the labour market of the 1790s, innovations which increased productivity were less important than those which attracted labour.[47]

After 1814 wages plummeted as grain prices fell, but the depression was not so prolonged as in England. Ploughmen's wages began to recover in 1819, and by the 1830s money wages for married ploughmen were higher than ever before. Hardest hit were female farm servants and day labourers. Their wages fell sharply, and by 1840 were still lower than they had been twenty years before.[48]

Table 4   *Agricultural money wages, South-East and Forth Valley, 1840–1914*

Date	(1) Married ploughmen (£)	(2) Unmarried ploughmen (£)	(3) Female farm servants (£)	(4) Day labourers
1840–49	—	16.5	6.9	1/7d.
1850–59	19.0	15.0	7.0	1/10d.
1860–69	22.0	17.5	8.2	2/3½d.
1870–79	28.0	24.0	13.8	3/-
1880–89	27.5	21.5	12.6	2/9d.
1890–99	33.0	27.0	15.0	3/1d.
1900–09	38.0	30.0	19.2	3/3d.
1910–14	41.0	35.0	18.5	—

Sources: (1) 1850–1914: *Stirling Journal* (1857–1914); *Second Report by Mr. Wilson Fox on the Wages, Earnings and Conditions of Employment of Agricultural Labourers in the United Kingdom, Parliamentary Papers*, vol. XCVII, 1905 (hereafter *Wilson Fox's Report on Agricultural Labourers, 1905*), p. 217; (2) 1840–49: Houston, 'Farm Wages', p. 225, Table 1; 1850–1914: *Stirling Journal* (1857–1914); *Wilson Fox's Report on Agricultural Labourers, 1905*, p. 217; (3) 1840–59: Farmer, 'Present position of Agriculture', *Journal of Agriculture*, New Series, vol. XXI (July 1857–March 1859), p. 545; 1860–1914: *Stirling Journal* (1860–1914); (4) 1840–99: Bowley, 'Wages', p. 141, Table 1; 1845–49: *Fourth Report on Women in Agriculture, 1870*, p. 65; 1855–59: Anon., 'Physical Condition of the People', *Journal of Agriculture*, New Series, vol. XXI (July 1857–March 1859), p. 450; 1875–79: Thomas Farell, 'On the Agriculture of the Counties of Edinburgh and Linlithgow', *T.H.A.S.*, 4th Series, vol. IX (1877), No. 1, p. 46; 1895–99, 1905–09: Hunt, *Regional Variations*, pp. 62–3, Table 1.3.

This divergence in money wages between skilled and unskilled labour was partly a reflection of the new division of labour produced by the agricultural revolution. The increased horsepower demanded by the new technology meant that ploughmen were fully occupied throughout the year: on the Marquis of Tweeddale's estates in East Lothian in 1870, ploughmen worked 280 days in the year.[49] Hinds became specialised workmen, entrusted with care of the farmer's valuable horses, who could no longer be spared even for work in peak seasons, like cutting and threshing corn.[50] Their new professionalism elevated hinds almost to the status of a separate caste, entry to which required a two-year apprenticeship.[51] High wages permitted a lifestyle which further distinguished them from other farm servants. Their social aspirations were reflected in the prizes at their ritual ploughing matches (£5 and the use of a silver tea service for a year at Buchlyvie in 1905),[52] the sober black suits they wore on Sundays,[53] and the fact that few allowed their wives to work in the fields after marriage.[54]

The period 1840–1914 saw a steady rise in money wages except in the decade 1880–89 when all groups experienced a fall (Table 4). Overall, money wages for all groups rose by at least 100 per cent. The major contrast with the earlier period, besides the sustained increase, is that wages for unskilled labour kept pace with those of ploughmen. Indeed, during this period wages for agricultural labourers rose faster than in most other areas in Britain.[55] This was probably due chiefly to competition for labour from industry. But there were other reasons for the buoyant demand for farm labour.

Everywhere in the south-east, turnips and potatoes were replacing summer fallow and playing a more important role in the rotation.[56] The spread of green crops to the wet clays was made possible by subsoil drainage and cheap manure. Peruvian guano quadrupled the area under turnips in East Lothian before 1853.[57] The importance of green crops in the south-east is shown by the statistics of crop acreages collected after 1866 (Table 5). They occupied 64,000 acres by the 1860s, and they remained a constant proportion of the arable acreage until 1914. Cultivation on such a scale required an enormous labour force. On the farm of East Barns, near Haddington, where 335 acres of potatoes were grown every year, there was a resident farm population of 150, and over 100 extra workers were needed to lift the crop.[58]

In the Lothians, this demand was met in the later nineteenth century by importing Highland and Irish labour. Single girls served as outworkers and were housed together in cottages or in bothies on the farm. About half the female labour force in the Lothians in the 1860s were immigrants.[59] The demand for female labour explains the disproportionate rise in money wages for women farm servants after 1870 (Table 4). By the 1890s, young girls were reported to earn as much as orramen.[60] With the Highlanders came the Irish, who constituted a reservoir of casual labour in villages and

Table 5 *Cropping pattern in the South-East and Forth Valley, 1860–1914*

| | | (000 acres) | | | | |
Date	Crops & grass	Arable	Corn	Green crops	Hay	Grass
1860–69	400	298	142	64	83	99
1870–79	424	305	137	63	96	117
1880–89	442	306	128	59	110	134
1890–99	440	295	116	57	114	143
1900–09	429	283	111	58	106	143
1910–14	421	266	109	57	93	152

Sources: Crop structures derived from Scottish agricultural statistics published in Parliamentary Papers for the relevant years. See n. 14, p. 68.

D

towns. Before long they supplied most of the unskilled male labour in the south-east.[61] In East Lothian 'nearly the whole of the drainage operations are now executed, not by the native population, but by the immigrant Irish — the local population being really all absorbed by the demand for hired servants as ploughmen, cattle keepers and barn men'.[62] In time they also replaced female labour. When the practice of importing Highland outworkers died out in the 1890s, their place was taken by Irish immigrants.[63]

The role of immigrant workers is important in the south-east for two reasons. The supply of cheap female labour from the Highlands helps explain the high proportion of women in the labour force. Without such a supply of females from the north and the cottages of married servants, the extensive cultivation of green crops (and the high farming for which the Lothians became famous) would have been impossible.[64] Lothian husbandry was a triumph not just of mechanical ingenuity but of human muscle. Secondly, immigrants formed a rural proletariat alien in language and culture to the local population. The division between skilled and unskilled agricultural labour in the south-east was not merely economic, but also social and cultural. This served to reinforce the élitism of the hinds.

Money wages for unskilled labour remained high after the 1890s, despite the fall in prices and the consequent decline in the arable area. This was because in the south-east the contraction in the arable area took the form of a fall in the acreage under corn, rather than under green crops (Table 5). Instead, on some mixed husbandry farms there was even an increase in the demand for casual labour. However, the decline in corn meant there was less demand for ploughmen.[65] High wages for unskilled labour also reflected the cumulative impact of the drift from the land. By the 1890s, the days of cheap female labour were virtually over. For the daughters of the hind, domestic service promised better pay and working conditions than the farmer was prepared to offer.[66]

3. Labour Productivity

Did the agricultural revolution raise labour productivity? According to one view, 'The English agricultural revolution raised land, not labour productivity'.[67] Timmer's conclusion was based on a comparison of the labour requirements before and after the introduction of turnips, which enabled farmers to keep more cattle and increase the supply of manure, thereby increasing yields. He demonstrated that, on a 500-acre farm under the Norfolk rotation, turnips increased labour requirements by 45 per cent. Hence, in this view, the agricultural revolution actually lowered labour productivity.

But the agricultural revolution was not confined to the use of fodder crops. Besides turnips, there were other innovations which *reduced* labour requirements. Such innovations were particularly important in the Scottish context, since much of the new labour-saving technology was invented there. The period 1780–1840 saw four major changes in farming technology. The sickle replaced the serrated hook, to be succeeded in turn by the scythe. Threshing machines replaced flails. Machine fanners came into use. Finally, Small's two-horse plough ousted the traditional, four-horse model. The last three innovations were Scottish in origin.[68] Together with improved farm layouts and a more efficient organisation of labour, they produced a significant increase in labour productivity.

Increases in labour output can be measured in terms of the total labour force, of each worker, or per unit of labour time. Here we adopt the third method.[69] The increase in labour productivity during the agricultural revolution is shown by comparing the labour requirements for each crop, measured in mandays per acre of ten hours' duration, the standard working day in the south-east (Table 6).

A comparison of labour inputs in the 1760s, before the agricultural revolution, with those in the 1790s and 1840s, shows that labour-saving technology in this area raised labour productivity per acre for cereal crops. Most of this increase can be attributed to improved organisation of labour and to three Scottish innovations (Small's plough, machine threshing, and

Table 6   *Labour inputs to Scottish agriculture, 1760–1914*

	(mandays per acre)							
Date	Wheat	Barley	Oats	Peas/ beans	Potatoes	Turnips	Hay	Summer fallow
c. 1760	36.09	33.63	17.98	21.83	—	—	—	—
c. 1790	25.54	22.99	13.16	15.36	36.7	27.48	14.8	10.04
c. 1840	23.97	22.02	12.59	14.79	36.7	27.48	14.8	10.04
c. 1860	17.86	16.88	11.40	13.58				
c. 1880	17.01	16.03	10.55	10.81				
c. 1914	12.64	11.96	8.36	5.08				
1958	2.8	2.8	3.6	3.2	16.0	9.6	1.6	0.4

Sources: 1760–1840: Alastair Orr, 'Productivity and Innovation in Traditional Agriculture' (unpublished Ph.D. thesis, University of Edinburgh, 1982), ch. 2; 1860–1914: author's estimates, based on primary printed sources; 1958: J. T. Coppock, 'Regional Differences in Labour Requirements in England and Wales', *Farm Economist*, vol. 10. No. 9 (1964), p. 386, Table 1.

Note: Innovations comprise (1790) two-horse plough, smooth hook, two horsepower threshing machine, machine fanning; (1840) scythe; (1860) steam threshing, steam ploughing, machine reaping, machine mowing, and horse rake; (1880) improved steam threshing, rick lifter and horse fork, tine cultivator, manure spreader.

machine fanning) introduced by 1790. By contrast, the scythe, introduced after 1790, had a relatively small impact on labour inputs. Overall, in the south-east by 1840 it took 50 per cent less labour to grow one acre of wheat, barley, or oats than in 1760.

Simultaneously with this fall in labour requirements came the introduction of fodder crops. Turnips were highly labour-intensive, potatoes even more so: thirty-six mandays per acre, three times the labour input for oats. To measure the effect on productivity, Timmer's method has been adopted and labour requirements on a typical farm compared before and after the agricultural revolution, this time taking labour-saving technology into account. The farm in 1760 follows an infield-outfield rotation, and in 1840 a six-course rotation, of types which were common in the south-east.[70] The results are shown in Table 7.

Total labour requirements on a typical Stirlingshire carse farm in 1840 were about 690 mandays per annum after the introduction of turnips, and about 750 mandays per annum after the introduction of potatoes. In neither case did labour requirements exceed those under infield–outfield. Instead, the figures show a drop in labour inputs of between 15–25 per cent. However, these figures require careful handling. It would be unwise to generalise on the basis of evidence from a single farm, however representative. The figures take no account of variations in labour requirements within the time period. Yet, it is possible that labour requirements may have risen during the Napoleonic Wars, then fallen. Above all, although most arable farms in the south-east followed a six-course rotation similar to that in the Stirlingshire carse, the rotation was flexible enough to permit considerable variation in cropping patterns within the region, and therefore in labour requirements. Until more local studies are forthcoming, the impact of the agricultural revolution on labour productivity even in this region must remain an open question. In at least

Table 7   *Labour inputs on a Stirlingshire carse farm, 1760–1840*

	(mandays)			
	Acres		Labour inputs	
Crop	1760	1840	1760	1840
Oats	12	6	215.76	75.54
Barley	12	6	403.56	134.52
Pea and beans	12	6	257.76	88.74
Wheat		6		143.82
Hay		6		88.80
Turnips		6		164.88
Total	36	36	877.08	696.30

Source: Orr, 'Productivity and Innovation', ch. 3.

one area of the south-east, however, the agricultural revolution appears to have raised both land *and* labour productivity.

Whether productivity increases create unemployment depends on the social and economic context in which they occur. So far as the economic context is concerned, it seems unlikely that mechanical innovation before 1840 was a response to labour shortage. Threshing machines and machine fanners were introduced primarily to speed the delivery of grain to market in order to take advantage of higher prices. Savings in unit costs were significant only for farms above 300 acres.[71] Similarly, while the introduction of the two-horse plough may suggest a shortage of skilled labour, quicker ploughing was essential to maintain the strict timetable required by the new rotations. Finally, although the scythe economised on labour time, it also required male labour, whereas the sickle could be used equally well by women. The only innovation before 1840 directly attributable to labour shortage was the introduction of 'threaving' or harvest piece-work. Paradoxically, this practice actually increased labour requirements.

One important aspect of the social context of innovation is that the new fodder crops increased the demand for female, not male, labour. Hoeing and weeding turnips were considered jobs for women. Some impression of the increase in demand for female labour can be formed from the fact that whereas in 1780 turnips were virtually unknown in the Lothians, by 1853 there were over 16,000 acres in East Lothian alone.[72] Similarly, it was female labour which benefited from the extension to potato cultivation which began in the 1840s, when women outworkers had to be imported from the Highlands. The agricultural revolution thus created an imbalance in the demand for labour.[73]

Innovations after 1840 altered labour inputs still further. It is instructive to compare the impact of different innovations. The reaping machine, introduced in the 1860s, had surprisingly little effect on labour requirements. The replacement of the scythe by Bell's machine reduced labour inputs for reaping by just 0.5 mandays per acre, to 1.25 mandays per acre. Most of the increase in labour productivity after the agricultural revolution can be attributed to the period after 1880. In terms of labour productivity, obscure inventions like the horse fork, the rick lifter, and the dung spreader were more important than the innovations celebrated by historians.[74]

Mechanisation after 1840 did not create unemployment since after that date it was more probably a response to labour shortage. This was most noticeable at peak periods like harvest. The summer months in East Lothian saw an influx of migrant labour in the form of 'bands of blue-bonneted Highlandmen and hordes of gray-coated Irishmen who ... swarm into the county at the ripening of the corn'.[75] Irish harvesters outnumbered the Highlanders by the 1830s.[76] By the 1850s, it was estimated that 12,000 Irish were employed in the Lothians during the four-week harvest period.[77] Reaping machines were introduced only when this supply threatened to dry up.[78] By the 1880s, the 'hook fairs' where harvesters had been hired were a thing of the past.[79]

Overall, labour requirements for cereal crops fell by over 160 per cent between 1760 and 1914. The effects of innovation were far-reaching, reducing the need for casual labour throughout the year as well as the need for migrant labour at harvest. Only the hind escaped this tide of mechanisation, since the tractor did not replace the horse-plough until after 1914. A comparison of labour inputs in 1914 with those in the 1950s shows the scale of the change that was yet to come. Some, like the ploughman poet Andrew Dodds, foresaw its results. 'One could find it in one's heart to wish that the motor invention would soon go the same way as its predecessor, the steam plough, for as surely as it robs the hand of its craft, it takes from the heart its spontaneous tune. There is something in the monotonous repetition of machinery that stifles the effervescent song ...'.[80] By 1914, the days of the hind and the remnants of a peasant culture were numbered.

4. Labour's response to technological change: exit, voice and loyalty

Why labourers opposed the introduction of new technology and why they did not are questions which have received unequal attention from historians.[81] Broadly, three responses were open to farm workers whose livelihoods were threatened by technological and social change. They could voice their protest by destroying new machines, as happened in the Swing revolt in southern England in the 1830s, when some 400 threshing machines were wrecked in twenty-two counties.[82] Alternatively, labourers could opt for exit through migration or even emigration. Finally, labourers could accept the introduction of new technology. Loyalty then takes precedence over exit and voice.

Why did the labour force in the south-east, unlike its English counterpart, prefer exit and loyalty to voice or violent protest? After all, 'improvement' in this region was apparently more drastic than anywhere else. The results of wholesale enclosure horrified William Cobbett in 1832. 'Everything,' he wrote bitterly of the Lothians, 'is abundant here but people, who have been studiously swept from the land'.[83] Mechanisation was equally ruthless — by 1836 there were sixty-four threshing machines in East Lothian alone.[84] Yet the conservatism of the labour force was proverbial. 'Steady, temperate, honest, frugal, industrious and intelligent, their lives are useful and exemplary,' wrote an approving employer.[85] This apparent passivity can be explained in several ways.

Most important was the structure of the labour force which, as we have seen, contained remarkably few day labourers. This is vividly demonstrated by the parish Statistical Accounts penned in the 1790s. In

Prestonpans, for example, out of a total of 130 agricultural workers, only nineteen are listed as day labourers. Even if domestic servants are excluded from the total, farm servants outnumber labourers by twenty-nine to nineteen.[86] Similarly, on the large farm of Fenton Barns in East Lothian in the 1830s, out of seventeen male agricultural workers, only four were day-labourers.[87] As a result, the introduction of labour-saving technology affected only a small number of workers. Threshing machines, for example, did not create mass unemployment since threshing had traditionally been done, not by casual labour, but by farm servants and 'taskers' hired for the duration of the winter.[88]

Next, there was the more regular demand for labour in Scottish agriculture in relation to areas of cereal monoculture. This was the result of the six-course rotation (Table 6). As one farmer explained, 'the most prominent advantage certainly is, the equal distribution of farm labour, so that the sowing of each kind of grain follows another in regular succession, thereby enabling the farmer to execute all his operations in the best style'.[89] This regularity in the demand for labour is shown by the monthly labour inputs on a typical farm in the Stirlingshire carse (Figure 2). By evening out labour requirements the six-course rotation increased the need

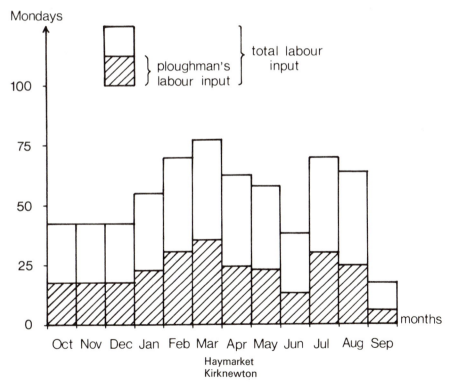

Fig. 2. Seasonal distribution of crop labour requirements with six-course rotation, Forth Valley carse.

for labour during the slack season, thus helping reduce underemployment. Simultaneously, by minimising fluctuations in demand, it reduced the need for casual labour: 'With regard to the class of labourers required, it will be at once seen from the rotation of crops that except at harvest time and on threshing days, there is but little need for odd hands or casual labourers'.[90] This was very different from southern England, where cereal monoculture required large numbers of casual labourers. In the south-east, both the structure of the labour force and the nature of labour requirements reduced the risk of voice or protest in response to technological change.

The nature of the labour market, on the other hand, encouraged exit. The practice of annual and six-monthly contracts for farm servants fostered migration by ruling out the possibility of work sharing which existed when labour was hired on a daily basis. Men who could not find work simply had to leave. Moreover, the ploughman's mobility applied to most of the labour force, since a substantial part of the single male and female farm servants were recruited from his household and so were dependent on his decisions. The bondager system and the custom of family contracts gave labour in the south-east a mobility it did not possess elsewhere. This reduced the risk of surplus labour. In addition, unlike their English counterparts, Scottish farmworkers were not guaranteed poor relief while unemployed. There was legal uncertainty as to whether the Scottish Poor Law granted the able-bodied unemployed the right to relief. After 1828 it did not.[91] This encouraged migration, since the social opportunity cost of eviction was zero.

Finally, loyalty may have been the result of the paternalistic labour relations on which Lothian farmers so prided themselves. 'Nowhere,' boasted one, 'does there exist more of that community of feeling and that friendliness of relation which ought to subsist between employers and employed, than in this county.'[92] However, such evidence is always difficult to interpret.

The relationship between the farmer and his servants was changed by the agrarian revolution. The 'gudeman' was transformed into the master ('a revealing change in terminology which needs no comment,' notes one historian).[93] The new relationship between master and man was demonstrated in a host of ways. It was symbolised by the new farmhouse, built with its back to the farmyard, 'as if ashamed of the connection.'[94] Work discipline became impersonal. As farm service became less common, farmers could no longer impose discipline through the household. Instead, the wages, hours and working conditions of farm servants were regulated by the courts. Magistrates tried heroically to uphold traditional relations of dependence. 'It was a mistake in servants, hired by the year or half year,' ruled a Kelso J.P. in 1807, 'to suppose that, after their ordinary work hours, they are at liberty to dispose of or absent themselves as they please without their master's leave; that, on the contrary, all such servants are bound to be at their master's call, at all times during their service, by day or by night, when occasion requires.'[95] Such edicts were powerless to prevent the breakdown of patriarchal discipline. By the 1860s, few farmers made any attempt to regulate their servants after working hours.[96] Again, farmers no longer toiled alongside their servants; they supervised.[97] As farms grew bigger, supervision was delegated to bailiffs or 'grieves'. Authority over the labour force was vested in the grieve, whose house guarded the entrance to the farmyard.[98] 'The overseer goes out with them in the morning; his watch regulates their time of rest, and the hour when they can cease from their labours at night.'[99] Since many farmers transmitted orders only through the grieve, direct contact with the labour force was reduced to a minimum. Such commercial relationships between master and man left little room for loyalty.

It was true that despite the passing of the patriarchal household, many farm servants in the south-east continued to live under their master's roof, and sheer physical proximity may have encouraged good labour relations. But the quality of the bond linking the labourer to the farmer was different from that which had linked him to the gudeman. Formerly, recalled one observer, 'The whole household constituted one family, which looked to the gudeman as their natural and patriarchal head, and considered his interest as in some degree connected with their own. The words, *our hairst* and *our crops,* were commonly used to express those of their master.'[100] Only a vestige of this relationship now survived in the tradition of the harvest supper or 'kirn', 'the symbol of human and class cooperation in labour.'[101] On many farms, this was now the only occasion in the year when master and servant ate together at the same table.[102]

Again, it is the case that on most farms the labour force was still relatively small. Table 8 shows the distribution of male labourers by holding in 1851.

Table 8   *Distribution of labourers per holding, and of holdings by number of labourers, South-East and Forth Valley, 1851*

Number of labourers per holding	Distribution of farms No.	%	Distribution of labourers No.	%
1–5	1006	64.4	2844	30.4
5–9	452	28.4	3685	39.4
10–14	54	3.4	810	8.6
15–19	42	2.6	840	8.9
20–29	20	1.2	600	6.4
30–39	5	0.3	200	2.1
40–49	5	0.3	250	2.6
50–59	2	0.1	120	1.2
Total	1586	100.0	9349	100.0

Source: *Census of Scotland, 1851.*

The majority of farms (64 per cent) employed less than five male labourers. Conversely, most labourers (70 per cent) worked on farms employing fewer than ten men. It might be argued that such small numbers permitted a personal relationship between master and man. However, the figures omit female workers, who constituted over 30 per cent of the hired labour force. Moreover, such a relationship was not reflected in any tradition of long service among hinds. Many farmers believed that long service remained the norm until the 1860s, when a spate of bankruptcies increased the rate of turnover among tenants.[103] Yet quantitative evidence from the 1851 census enumerators' schedules suggests that despite the custom of annual contracts, farm servants in the south-east were mobile and there was much short-distance migration.

Conclusion

It is evident that the model of the transition to capitalist agriculture hitherto used by historians does not always reflect rural realities. This transition is identified with the emergence of institutions like a free labour market, the cash nexus, and short-term labour contracts. No doubt some regions, like southern England, followed this pattern, but it was strikingly absent in the south-east of Scotland and elsewhere in the Lowlands. The persistence of traditional labour relations like service; the survival of forms of labour-tying, such as family contracts and bondage; the prevalence of the boll wage; the custom of long-term contracts for farm servants and labourers alike: all suggest that the conventional model is of limited relevance. This conclusion assumes wider significance in view of the current debate over the 'mode of production' in Third World agriculture, especially in India.[104] A feature of this debate is the identification, by economists, of 'capitalist agriculture' with certain institutional forms. This is to confuse form with substance.[105] The history of agricultural labour in the south-east demonstrates how old and familiar institutions could be made to serve new and revolutionary ends. The transformation of traditional agriculture was achieved through traditional institutions.

Appendix

'Servants' as a proportion of the agricultural labour force, 1831

County	Ratio
East Lothian (Haddington)	0.159
Berwick	0.193
Midlothian (Edinburgh)	0.239

Roxburgh	0.256
Selkirk	0.294
Ayr	0.294
Wigtown	0.307
Fife	0.327
Kincardine	0.347
West Lothian (Linlithgow)	0.349
Clackmannan	0.353
Forfar	0.377
Kirkcudbright	0.446
Dumfries	0.450
Peebles	0.454
Kinross	0.459
Lanark	0.562
Dumbarton	0.562
Aberdeen	0.572
Banff	0.574
Renfrew	0.646
Stirling	0.689

Source: *Census of Scotland, 1831.*

NOTES

1. Note that the area defined for the purposes of this chapter as the 'south-east' differs slightly from the region described elsewhere in this volume.

2. E. J. Hobsbawm and George Rudé, *Captain Swing* (Harmondsworth, 1973), p. 18.

3. Ann Kussmaul, *Servants in Husbandry in Early Modern England* (Cambridge, 1981).

4. This division of labour is evident from old estate plans, like that showing part of Hopetoun estate in West Lothian in 1754: of nineteen holdings, the largest was 106 acres, seven were below twenty acres, and the smallest just four acres. Arthur Geddes, 'The Changing Landscape of the Lothians (1600–1800) as revealed by old Estate Plans', *Scottish Geographical Magazine,* vol. 54, No. 3 (May 1938), pp. 130–1.

5. Anon, 'The Condition of the Agricultural Labourer', *Journal of Agriculture,* New Series, vol. XXII (March 1859–March 1861), No. LVI, p. 723.

6. George Robertson, *Rural Recollections, or the progresses of improvement in agricultural and rural affairs* (Irvine, 1829), p. 110.

7. Rev. Dr. George Barclay of Middleton, 'Account of the County of Haddington', *Trans. Society of Antiquaries of Scotland,* I (1792), pp. 40–120, Appendix no. 2. Assuming one ploughgate equals sixty imperial acres. *New Statistical Account,* vol. 2, p. 214 (Dirleton, Haddington).

8. Anon, 'Comparative View of East Lothian Husbandry in 1778 and 1810', *Farmer's Magazine,* vol. 12 (March 1811), No. XLV, p. 52.

9. T. C. Smout, *A History of the Scottish People, 1560–1830* (Glasgow, 1969), p. 313.

10. James Tait, 'The Physiological Distinctions in the Condition of the Scottish Peasantry', *Transactions of the Highland and Agricultural Society of Scotland* (*T.H.A.S.*), 4th Series, vol. XV, (1883), p. 11.

11. James Tait, 'The agriculture of the county of Stirling', *T.H.A.S.*, 5th Series, vol. XVI (1884), pp. 171–2.

12. *Royal Commission on Labour. The Agriculture Labourer. Parliamentary Papers*, 1893, vol. XXXVI (hereafter *R.C. on Labour, 1893*), p. 45, para. 34 (Clackmannan).

13. Robert Scot Skirving, *Landlords and Labourers* (Edinburgh, 1862), p. 75, note.

14. 'I have a strong suspicion that it has been through bondaging during the abolition of crofts, that the Lothians and other southern counties have escaped the bothy system...'. Henry Stuart, *Agricultural Labourers, as they were, are, and should be, in their social condition* (Edinburgh, 1853), p. 23.

15. *Royal Commission on the Employment of Children, Young Persons, and Women in Agriculture (1867) Fourth Report of the Commission. Parliamentary Papers*, 1870, vol. XIII (hereafter *Fourth Report on Women in Agriculture, 1870*), p. 50, para. 17.

16. *New Statistical Account*, I, p. 182.

17. John McCulloch, 'On providing a sufficient supply of labour during press of agricultural work', *T.H.A.S.*, 4th Series, vol. XII (1880), p. 231.

18. *Fourth Report on Women in Agriculture, 1870*, p. 53, para. 27.

19. McCulloch, 'Supply of Labour', p. 231.

20. G. Houston, 'Labour Relations in Scottish Agriculture before 1870', *Agricultural History Review*, vol. VI, Part I (1958), p. 40.

21. R. Hunter Pringle, 'The Agricultural Labourer of Scotland — Then and Now', *T.H.A.S.*, 5th Series, vol. VI (1894), p. 247.

22. A. Fenton, 'The Rural Economy of East Lothian in the 17th and 18th Centuries', *Transactions of the East Lothian Antiquarian Society*, vol. IX (1963), pp. 18–19. For fuller discussion of bondagers, see below, pp. 98–106.

23. 'We find joint contracts including some or all members of a family, in every county in Scotland, but they are exceptional outside the South-Eastern Counties, where they are the rule'. *Scottish Farm Servant*, vol. XIII, No. 146 (May, 1925), p. 17.

24. Patrick Graham, *General View of the Agriculture of Stirlingshire* (Edinburgh, 1812), p. 313.

25. E. H. Hunt, *Regional Wage Variations in Britain, 1850–1914* (Oxford, 1973), p. 172. For a discussion of women in Scottish agriculture, see T. M. Devine's essay below, pp. 98–123.

26. Skirving, *Landlords and Labourers*, p. 42.

27. *Fourth Report on Women in Agriculture, 1870*, p. 180.

28. E. L. Jones, 'The Agricultural Labour Market in England, 1793–1872', *Economic History Review*, New Series, vol. XVII, No. 2 (1964), p. 329.

29. Anon, 'Comparative View of East Lothian Husbandry', *Farmers Magazine*, vol. 12, No. XLV (March, 1811), pp. 67–8.

30. Anon, 'The Condition of the Agricultural Labourer', *Journal of Agriculture*, New Series, vol. XXII (March 1859–March 1861), No. LVI, pp. 722ff.

31. *Fourth Report on Women in Agriculture, 1870*, p. 47, para. 11.

32. *Report by Mr. Wilson Fox on the Wages, Earnings, and Conditions of Employment of Agricultural Labourers in the United Kingdom. Parliamentary Papers*, vol. LXXXII, 1900 (hereafter *Wilson Fox's Report on Agricultural Labourers, 1900*),

33. Compare the wages of ploughmen and 'ordinary labourers' (i.e. orramen) in *Ibid.*, p. 86; there was less distinction in the north-east.

34. Anon, 'Digest of Essays on the Bothy System of Maintaining Single Farm Servants', *Prize Essays and Transactions of the Royal Highland and Agricultural Society*, vol. XIV (1843), No. XV, pp. 143–4.

35. *R.C. on Labour, 1893, Part II*, p. 51, para. 95 (Fife, Kinross, and Clackmannan).

36. Hunter Pringle, 'The Agricultural Labourer', p. 262. For other examples, see Frederick Purdy, 'On the Earnings of Agricultural Labourers in Scotland and Ireland', *Journal of the Royal Statistical Society*, vol. XXV (December, 1862), p. 428.

37. Pringle, 'Agricultural Labourer', p. 262.

38. *Ibid.*, p. 263.

39. *Wilson Fox's Report on Agricultural Labourers, 1900*, pp. 77–9.

40. *Royal Commission on Agricultural Depression. First Report. Parliamentary Papers*, 1894, vol. XVI, Part 2, p. 420, Q. 26262.

41. *Report from the Select Committee appointed to inquire into the present state of Agriculture, and persons employed in Agriculture in the United Kingdom, Parliamentary Papers*, 1833, vol. V (hereafter *S.C. on Agriculture, 1833*), Q. 2656.

42. *Wilson Fox's Report on Agricultural Labourers, 1900*, p. 67.

43. Anon, 'Some Account of the Fairs in Scotland. No. III. East Lothian, or Haddingtonshire', *Quarterly Journal of Agriculture*, vol. VI (1836), p. 428. Few single women presented themselves for hire. Skirving, *Landlords and Labourers*, p. 44.

44. Skirving, *Landlords and Labourers*, pp. 42–3.

45. Pringle, 'Agricultural Labourer', p. 245. For a consideration of the reasons for the long-hire, see above, pp. 2–4.

46. G. Houston, 'Farm Wages in Central Scotland from 1814 to 1870', *Journal of the Royal Statistical Society*, Series A (General), vol. 118, Part II (1955), p. 224.

47. 'On Threaving', *Farmer's Magazine*, 6 (1805), XXIV, p. 466. See the discussion in Orr, 'Productivity and Innovation', pp. 114–15.

48. For a discussion of the labour market in East Lothian, 1815–40, see T. M. Devine, 'The Demand for Agricultural Labour in East Lothian after the Napoleonic Wars', *Transactions of the East Lothian Antiquarian and Natural History Society*, vol. 16 (1979), pp. 119–61.

49. 'Report of the Special Committee on the various Systems of Cultivating Land by Steam Power in East Lothian', *T.H.A.S.*, 4th Series, vol. 3 (1870–71), p. 282.

50. Anon, 'Comparative View of East Lothian Husbandry, part II', *Farmer's Magazine*, vol. 12 (June, 1811), No. XLVI, p. 217; G. Robertson, *General View of the Agriculture of Midlothian* (Edinburgh, 1795), p. 79.

51. *R.C. on Labour, 1893* Part II, p. 105, para. 55.

52. *Stirling Journal*, February 24, 1905.

53. Anon, 'The Scottish Farm Labourer', *Cornhill Magazine*, 1864, X, p. 613.

54. *Ibid.*, p. 615; McCulloch, 'Supply of Labour', p. 234. Attitudes to working wives varied locally. See below, pp. 104–5.

55. Hunt, *Regional Wage Variations*, p. 172; see below, pp. 244–7.

56. Skirving, *Landlords and Labourers*, p. 12.

57. Charles Stevenson, 'On the farming of East Lothian', *Journal of the Royal Agricultural Society of England*, vol. 14 (1853), No. XX, p. 295.

58. Pringle, 'Agricultural Labourer', pp. 296, 307.

59. Skirving, *Landlords and Labourers,* p. 5; T. M. Devine, 'Temporary Migration and the Scottish Highlands in the Nineteenth Century', *Economic History Review,* 2nd Series, vol. XXXII, No. 3., pp. 334–59.

60. *R.C. on Labour, 1893,* p. 99, para. 22 (Lothians).

61. *Report on the Decline in the Agricultural Population of Great Britain, 1881–1906. Parliamentary Papers,* 1906, vol. XCVI, p. 97 (Midlothian).

62. *The Scotsman,* 30 April, 1850, quoted in J. E. Handley, *The Irish in Scotland* (Cork, 1943).

63. *R.C. on Labour, 1893, Part II,* p. 99, para. 22 (Lothians).

64. *Fourth Report on Women in Agriculture, 1870,* p. 106.

65. *R.C. on Labour, 1893, Part II,* p. 97. For this period see Retta McLachlan, 'The Impact of the "Agricultural Depression" on the Life and Work of the Agricultural Labourer in Scotland', B.A. dissertation, Department of History, University of Strathclyde, 1979, and below, pp. 249–250.

66. For a detailed discussion of this point, see below, pp. 119–120.

67. C. Peter Timmer, 'The Turnip, the New Husbandry, and the English Agricultural Revolution', *Quarterly Journal of Economics,* vol. 83, No. 3 (August, 1969), p. 392.

68. Fanners were a Dutch invention, but were introduced in Britain by Scots. G. Buchan-Hepburn, *General View of the Agricultural and Rural Economy of East Lothian* (Edinburgh, 1794), p. 145.

69. For the two other measures of labour productivity in British agriculture after 1880, see Saburo Yamada and Vernon W. Ruttan, 'International Comparisons of Productivity in Agriculture', in John W. Kendrick and Beatrice N. Vaccara, eds., *New Developments in Productivity Measurement and Analysis* (Chicago, 1980), pp. 509–85.

70. Robert Scott Skirving, 'On the agriculture of East Lothian', *T.H.A.S.,* 4th Series, vol. V (1873), p. 27; Tait, 'The agriculture of the county of Stirling', p. 161; Anon, 'Comparative View, Part II', pp. 210, 214.

71. Hobsbawm and Rudé, *Captain Swing,* p. 321.

72. Anon, 'Comparative View, Part II', p. 204; *T.H.A.S.,* New Series (1853–55), No. XXI, p. 208.

73. Interestingly, the same is true of the introduction of labour-intensive high yielding varieties into rice-growing areas of India. John Harriss, *Capitalism and Peasant Farming: Agrarian Structure and Ideology in Northern Tamilnadu* (Oxford, 1982), pp. 97–9.

74. For example, C. Ó'Gráda, 'Agricultural decline 1860–1914', in R. C. Floud and D. N. McCloskey, eds., *The Economic History of Britain since 1700,* Vol. 2 (Cambridge, 1981), pp. 182–6.

75. Skirving, 'Agriculture in East Lothian', p. 37.

76. *S.C. on Agriculture, 1833,* Q. 2674.

77. Stevenson, 'On the farming of East Lothian', p. 305. This represented about one third of the Irish harvesters in Scotland, who numbered 36,514 in 1841. David Hoseason Morgan, *Harvesters and Harvesting 1840–1914: a study of the rural proletariat* (London, 1982), p. 82.

78. James W. Hunter, 'Paper on Machine Reaping', *T.H.A.S.,* New Series (1853–55), No. XIX, p. 190. For other complaints of labour shortage, see A. Farmer, 'The Present Position of Agriculture', *Journal of Agriculture,* New Series,

vol. XXI (July 1857–March 1859), p. 61; Anon, 'Condition of the Agricultural Labourer', p. 724; 'Condition of the Rural Labourer in Scotland', *The Scotsman*, January 10, 1861. Speech by Mr. J. F. Cadell of Lochenzie.

79. For example, *Stirling Journal*, 18 July, 1884 (Callendar Hook Fair).

80. *Scottish Farm Servant*, vol. VI, No. 66 (September, 1918), p. 214. For Andrew Dodds' verse, see *The Lothian Land: poems*, (Aberdeen, 1917), *Songs of the Fields* (Stirling, 1920), *Antrin Sangs* (Stirling, 1921), *Poppies in the Corn: verses in Lothian Scots* (Glasgow, 1924).

81. This section draws heavily on George Houston, 'Farm Labour in Scotland 1800–1850', *Bulletin of the Society of Labour History*, No. 11 (1965), pp. 12–13; T. M. Devine, 'Farm Servants and Labour in East Lothian after the Napoleonic Wars', *Journal of the Scottish Labour History Society*, No. 15 (1981), pp. 20–23; idem, 'Social Stability and Agrarian Change in the Eastern Lowlands of Scotland, 1810–40', *Social History*, vol. 3, No. 3 (October, 1978), pp. 331–46; and Paul Docherty, 'The Condition of the Rural Labourer in East Lothian, 1780–1840', B.A. dissertation, Department of History, University of Strathclyde, 1977.

82. Hobsbawm and Rudé, *Captain Swing*, pp. 166, 190.

83. William Cobbett, *Rural Rides in the Southern, Western and Eastern Counties; with tours in Scotland and in the Northern and Midland Counties of England; with letters from Ireland*, edited by G. D. H. and M. Cole (London, 1930), pp. 755–6.

84. *First Report from the Select Committee appointed to inquire into the State of Agriculture, Parliamentary Papers*, 1836, vol. VIII (hereafter *S.C. on the State of Agriculture, 1836*), p. 20.

85. Skirving, *Landlords and Labourers*, p. 99. For the political conservatism of the hinds, see Robertson, *General View of the Agriculture of Midlothian*, p. 27.

86. *Old Statistical Account*, XVIII, pp. 85–6.

87. *S.C. on the State of Agriculture, 1836*, pp. 120–1.

88. Robertson, *Rural Recollections*, p. 110.

89. Observator, 'On a Suitable Rotation of Crops; *Farmer's Magazine*, 5 (1804), p. 280.

90. *R.C. on Labour, 1893*, Part II, p. 45, para. 31 (Clackmannan).

91. See Rosalind Mitchison, 'The Creation of the Disablement Rule in the Scottish Poor Law', in T. C. Smout, ed., *The Search for Wealth and Stability* (London, 1979), pp. 199–217.

92. Stevenson, 'On the farming of East Lothian', p. 306.

93. Docherty, 'Rural Labourer in East Lothian', p. 12.

94. Robertson, *Rural Recollections*, p. 88.

95. *Edinburgh Evening Courant*, August 8, 1807, quoted in Houston, 'Labour Relations', p. 34.

96. E.g. 'Address on the Law of Master and Servant', Logie and Lecropt Farmers' Club, *Stirling Journal and Advertiser*, May 10, 1867.

97. Robertson, *General View of the Agriculture of East Lothian*, p. 51.

98. R. H. Greg, *Scotch Farming in the Lothians* (London, 1842), p. 6.

99. Anon, 'The Effect of Farm Overseers on the Morals of Farm Servants', *Blackwood's Magazine*, vol. III, No. XIII (April, 1818), p. 86.

100. *Ibid.*, p. 86.

101. Hobsbawm and Rudé, *Captain Swing*, p. 19.

102. See Thomas Atkinson, *Three Nights in Perthshire with a Description of the Festival of a 'Scotch Hairst Kirn', comprising Legendary Ballads etc. in a letter from Percy Yorke Jr. to J. Twiss Esq.* (Glasgow, 1821), p. 38.

103. Skirving, 'The agriculture of East Lothian', pp. 45–6; Patrick Shireff, *A Tour through North America, together with a comprehensive View of the Canadas and United States, as adapted for agricultural emigration* (Edinburgh, 1835), p. 337; George Brooks, *The Destruction of Scottish Agriculture. A Statement of Facts respecting the present position of agriculture in Scotland, especially in East Lothian, with some particulars of the case of Mr. James M. Russell* (London, 1885), pp. 29ff.

104. For a recent review of the debate, see Alice Thorner, 'Semi-Feudalism or Capitalism? Contemporary Debate on Classes and Modes of Production in India', *Economic and Political Weekly* (Bombay), vol. XVII, No. 49 (Dec. 4, 1982), pp. 1961–1968; No. 50 (Dec. 11, 1982), pp. 1993–1999; No. 51 (Dec. 18, 1982), pp. 2061–2068.

105. For a similar criticism directed at social anthropologists, by a social historian, see E. P. Thompson, 'Folklore, Anthropology, and Social History', *Indian Historical Review*, vol. 3, No. 2 (January, 1977), pp. 256ff.

4

Agricultural Labour in the South-West

R. H. Campbell

The sheer remoteness of the south-west may explain why it is often neglected in Scottish historical studies: the Mull of Galloway is as far from Glasgow as Kingussie, and Wigtown as far as Glencoe, while the area traded with the north-west of England and Ireland as readily as with the more populous parts of Scotland. It is hardly surprising, then, that some characteristics of agricultural labour in other parts of Scotland are not found there to the same extent as elsewhere: bothies, bondaging, hiring fairs, the domination by the hind — all critical to any examination of agricultural labour in other parts — were soon recognised by investigators of the nineteenth century to be of limited application in the south-west.[1] Recently historians have noted two features which may explain some of the area's differences:[2] first, its population growth was buoyant until the later nineteenth century, experiencing both high natural increase and immigration from Ireland, whence it derived some of the labour for its agricultural enterprises; second, it came to concentrate more on dairying than any other part of Scotland, and its small family farms proved peculiarly suited to it. Each aspect deserves fuller investigation. In doing so a more limited definition of the south-west, confined to Carrick, Nithsdale, Kirkcudbrightshire and Wigtownshire, is sometimes preferable to a wider one of the four counties of Ayr, Dumfries, Kirkcudbright and Wigtown, but the latter is essential for investigations which have to use county-based statistics, and useful to illustrate some aspects of agrarian practice.

I

Population grew between Webster's census of 1755 and 1901, but at different rates:

	1755–1801	1801–1851	1851–1901
	%	%	%
Carrick	27.2	127.6	−28.2
Nithsdale	28.7	40.1	−27.8
Kirkcudbright	37.8	47.6	−8.7
Wigtown	39.2	89.3	−24.7

E

No parish had a smaller population in 1851 than in 1801, but, because of the exceptionally high rate of increase in central Scotland, 47 of the area's 66 parishes had increases below the Scottish average between 1801 and 1851, compared with only 31 between 1755 and 1801. Eleven of the 47 increased above an assumed rate of natural growth of 10 per cent per annum.

Though the distribution varied, the increase shared some characteristics. The relatively greater growth in Nithsdale and Kirkcudbrightshire between 1755 and 1801 was concentrated in a few parishes: in Nithsdale in Morton and Sanquhar and in Kirkcudbrightshire in Crossmichael, Girthon, Kelton and Troqueer, which, with Kircudbright, increased above the assumed rate of natural growth. In the early nineteenth century, when the more buoyant increase was transferred to Carrick and Wigtownshire, Carrick's growth was concentrated in the three parishes of Girvan, Kirkmichael and Maybole, but Wigtownshire's was spread more evenly. With the exception of Wigtownshire, then, the highest population growth in the south-west — whether in Nithsdale and Kirkcudbrightshire in the late eighteenth century, or in Carrick in the early nineteenth century — was concentrated in a few parishes, which were noted for non-agricultural, even if agriculturally related, developments within their bounds. The parishes which lost population were in the hill country. The ministers of Carrick drew attention to the problem and its cause in the Old Statistical Account. The minister of Barr's report is representative of those from Ballantrae, Colmonell, Kirkmichael and Straiton, all parishes in Carrick with large upland areas, when he wrote that amalgamation of farms meant that in some 'there is not one inhabitant, and many where a shepherd man servant and his family alone occupy the farm...'.[3] Similar reports came from Durisdeer in Nithsdale, the Glenkens of Kirkcudbrightshire, and from Kirkcowan, one of Wigtownshire's two great hill parishes. Away from the hill country, and so in much of Kirkcudbrightshire and most of Wigtownshire, only a redistribution of population within the parish accompanied agricultural change in the late eighteenth century. In Wigtownshire comments were often made about the opportunities for new settlement following agricultural reorganisation, as at Kirkinner, scene of the well-known earlier initiative in cattle-grazing at Baldoon, and on the Monreith estates in Mochrum and on the Galloway estates in Sorbie. An awareness of the problems of the hill parishes led to the adoption of a more apologetic tone in the Stewartry, but from Balmaghie, Kirkbean, Kirkmabreck, New Abbey and Rerrick came reports that agricultural improvement 'has prevented any from leaving the place for want of employment, and has encouraged others to settle in it',[4] while at Kirkpatrick-Durham, always somewhat unusual in its experiences, the process of amalgamation was portrayed as going into reverse.[5]

It is no surprise, then, that the ministers who expressed little concern over loss of population following the agricultural changes of the late eighteenth century were still not doing so half a century later in the New Statistical Account, when population was increasing more rapidly still. Where ministers felt they had to offer an explanation of a reduction in population, the few who suggested, as at Kirkgunzeon or Tynron, that the cause was the reorganisation of holdings, were offset by those who suggested the reverse, as at Parton and Kirkconnel. More generally any loss of population was attributed to the collapse of some early industrial enterprise, as of the cotton mill at Castle Douglas in the parish of Kelton, or through the completion of some temporary work, as at Balmaghie, Closeburn or Twynholm. The impression left by the New Statistical Account is confirmed by the replies to the questions on emigration issued in the investigation into the poor laws in the early 1840s,[6] which show that in a number of parishes generally in Carrick and Wigtownshire, there were no emigrants, or 'almost none', and throughout the area the comments were typical: one or two cases but very few (Glencairn); one, who returned again (Ballantrae); two or three in each of the last three years (Kirkcolm); about two individuals per annum, chiefly young men (Balmaghie). Only five parishes, spread over the entire area excluding Wigtownshire, returned twenty or more emigrants in the three years previous: Borgue, Dalry, Kirkmichael, Penpont, Urr. The numbers, though never accurately stated, are sufficiently small to confirm that emigration from the south-west was not considered a general problem before the middle of the nineteenth century, but more the consequence of individual and personal circumstances. Even the hill parishes, which suffered most of the losses in the eighteenth century, gained in the early nineteenth, sometimes because of freakish non-agricultural developments. The only parochial loss in the whole south-west was Tynron's 14.4 per cent, which contrasted with its increase of 21.3 per cent between 1755 and 1801.

The demographic buoyancy changed sharply in the later nineteenth century, when all four areas recorded losses. The decline was constant, apart from slight increases in all except Nithsdale between 1871 and 1881 and a more substantial increase there in the early twentieth century, the consequences of coalmining in Kirkconnel. After Kirkcudbrightshire's substantial increase to 1821, its growth was modest, as was its fall after 1851, so that over the entire period to 1901 its increase was comparable to Wigtownshire's. Carrick's and Wigtownshire's more buoyant growth of the first half of the nineteenth century were offset by sharp falls in the later part.

During this period the information on places of birth and residence in the censuses shows that the south-west was not, and probably never had been, an area into which other Scots moved, even when the examination is based on the four counties and so includes parts of Dumfriesshire and especially of Ayrshire, which were not so strongly dependent on agriculture.[7] As the nineteenth century progressed, the four counties — individually and collectively — retained a lower proportion of their native-born who still lived in Scotland. For the south-west it fell from 85.9 per cent in 1851 to 76.0 per cent in 1891. The same reasons which discouraged natives from staying at home discouraged those born in other parts of Scotland from moving into a remote area, and so led to a high proportion of natives in the total population, over 80 per cent in the four counties taken together. The proportion of native-born to the Scottish-born population was even higher, at 92.1 per cent in 1851 and 88.6 per cent in 1891, because of Irish immigration. In 1851, 11 per cent of Ayrshire's population and 16.2 per cent of Wigtownshire's had been born in Ireland, compared with only 2.8 and 6.0 per cent in Dumfriesshire and Kirkcudbrightshire respectively. Only a relatively small proportion of the population had been born in other parts of Scotland. Though the south-west had a buoyant growth of population, especially in the early nineteenth century, it was still a self-contained area, with the injection of migrants from Ireland a major movement from outside. These characteristics influenced the supply of labour.

Of the importance of agriculture in the south-west, and of the employment it offered to the population before 1914, there is no doubt:

Table 1

	Ayr		Dumfries		Kirkcudbright		Wigtown		Scotland	
	1	2	1	2	1	2	1	2	1	2
1841	0.90	19.0	1.73	42.1	1.62	39.3	1.78	43.2	1.00	24.3
1851	0.85	21.1	1.49	37.1	1.70	42.3	1.71	42.5	1.00	24.9
1861	0.79	17.6	1.61	35.8	1.89	42.0	1.90	42.2	1.00	22.2
1871	0.77	17.1	1.72	38.1	1.90	42.1	1.92	42.6	1.00	22.2
1881	0.84	14.1	1.73	28.8	2.00	33.4	2.49	41.5	1.00	16.7
1891	0.83	11.9	1.93	26.9	2.42	33.8	2.79	39.0	1.00	14.0
1901	0.84	9.7	2.20	25.3	2.50	28.8	3.46	39.7	1.00	11.5
1911	0.89	9.4	2.30	24.3	2.87	30.4	3.88	41.1	1.00	10.6

1 = location coefficient of agriculture
2 = numbers employed in agriculture as percentage of total employment
Source: C. H. Lee, *British regional employment statistics, 1841–1871*, (Cambridge, 1979)
I am grateful to Mr. Lee for making available to me further information of employment on a county basis.

The location coefficient was stable in Ayrshire and increased steadily in each of the three other counties, particularly so in Wigtownshire. In Ayrshire the percentage of those employed in the industrial group of agriculture, forestry and fishing (of which the first was of overwhelming importance in the south-west) to the county's total employment fell steadily through the nineteenth century and was always slightly below the Scottish figure; those for Dumfries and Kirkcudbright were always substantially above and fell with it except between 1861 and 1871; Wigtownshire's proportion remained consistently high, so that in 1911, when those of the three other counties were smaller, Wigtownshire's was almost the same as it had been in the mid-nineteenth century. The difference between the counties in the absolute numbers employed were less marked. The share of agricultural employment in Wigtownshire was maintained because of a sharp drop in total employment between 1851 and 1911, compared with slight falls in Dumfries and Kirkcudbright and a large increase in Ayrshire, differences reflecting the changing demographic histories of the four counties.

II

When dairying became the special characteristic of the agriculture of the south-west, it gave rise to a social structure with unusual demands for labour. The neglect of its unique aspects by historians reflects its localised importance and the perpetuation of an obsession with other branches of agriculture which led to a complaint of neglect from Ayrshire in *The Farmer's Magazine* as early as 1803.[8] By then the specialisation was growing, although, as the Old Statistical Account shows, with considerable local variety. In Ayrshire the parishes of Cunninghame and Kyle had already passed the pioneering stage. In Dunlop 'cheese has been the great and almost the only business', with an estimate of 758 cows, producing 10,612 stones of cheese valued at £3,714 4s.[9] By the end of the century Dunlop cheese had such a reputation that all cheese from Ayrshire and Galloway was sold in Glasgow and Paisley markets under that name.[10] The interest spread through Cunninghame and into Kyle.[11] The specialism was less evident further south. In Carrick an occasional improvement in dairying was noted, but in Wigtownshire the few comments were confined to a recognition of Ayrshire's lead. By the time of the New Statistical Account dairying had penetrated Carrick and Wigtownshire even more thoroughly and was becoming common in Nithsdale, where the change was to become more notable than in other parts of Dumfriesshire.[12] Progress was less in Kirkcudbrightshire, where the rearing and fattening of livestock retained its prominence longer, though there too dairying spread rapidly by the later nineteenth century.[13]

Though it is not possible to distinguish beef and dairy animals, the south-west's specialisms are evident in the Agricultural Statistics.[14] All four counties taken together had a high proportion of all cattle in Scotland (21.5 per cent in 1855; 20.0 per cent in 1878; 20.7 per cent in 1886; 23.8 per cent in 1914) and of cows/heifers in milk/calf (for the same years, 24.6 per cent, 23.7 per cent, 24.1 per cent, 28.7 per cent). Ayrshire's share was substantially above the others in both categories and, with Wigtownshire in the later nineteenth century, had a high proportion of cows/heifers in milk/calf to its total cattle population — around 50 per cent compared with around 30 per cent in Dumfries and Kirkcudbright. By 1914, when cows in milk and in calf were distinguished, Ayrshire had a higher proportion of the latter than Wigtownshire (13.2 per cent of the total cattle against Wigtownshire's 5.0 per cent, though Wigtownshire had 44.6 per cent of its cattle in milk compared with 40.1 per cent in Ayrshire). The difference arose because Ayrshire supplied milk cattle for herds in Wigtownshire and much further afield.[15]

The increase in dairying was reflected in the changed pattern of arable cultivation, particularly in the high proportion of arable land under grass, both permanent and temporary, though the distinction between the two cannot always be made reliably.[16] Permanent grass rose in each county to 1914 to proportions of total arable substantially above the figure for Scotland. When temporary grass is included, Wigtownshire's proportion of 70.1 per cent was above Scotland's 62.1 per cent even though still below Ayrshire's 80.6 per cent, Dumfries's 74.7 per cent and Kirkcudbright's 79.1 per cent.

The most profitable outlet for the dairy was the sale of liquid milk, for which proximity to a large urban centre was necessary. Though not so well-sited as Lanarkshire and Renfrewshire, Ayrshire had the readiest access of all the south-western counties to the central belt. It had also its own small urban centres, a widespread industrial community — with the miners providing a characteristic demand for butter milk — and the special advantage of a demand from its coastal resorts in summer when supplies were more plentiful. Though the south-west's first reputation for cheesemaking originated at Dunlop, and Kilmarnock became a centre for marketing, showing and instruction, the greatest concentration on cheesemaking passed to the more remote parts in the south, especially to Wigtownshire, where it was estimated that the milk from six-sevenths of the cows was made into cheese.[17] In many cases the spread was initiated by those from the pioneering district of Ayrshire, from which a later move was to be made to Essex and to the eastern counties of England. Ayrshire was indeed the breeding ground for dairy farmers as well as dairy cows — 'a veritable congested district, which rears twice as many farmers than there are farms for', so pushing up rents in the south-western counties and beyond, which led John Spier to assert that 'At least 30 per cent of the farmers of Wigtownshire are Ayrshire men, or their descendants, and any farms becoming vacant in the counties of Wigtown, Kirkcudbright, or Dumfries are generally taken by dairymen, most of whom come from Ayrshire, with a few from the counties of Lanark and Renfrew'.[18]

The most notable expansion came from the middle of the century, helped, first, by the expansion of the railway network, which gave easier access for supplies of liquid milk to the urban areas, leaving the more remote parts to gain from the demand for cheese, and, second, by the improvement in the manufacture of cheese.[19] Cheddar replaced Dunlop cheese in the 1850s when the Ayrshire Agricultural Association established a two-way traffic in instruction with Somerset. By the 1880s, helped by grants from the Highland and Agricultural Society, extensive instruction in cheesemaking, and to a lesser extent in buttermaking, was given throughout the south-west. More permanent arrangements became available in the Kilmarnock Dairy School, started in March 1889.[20] The instruction on the farms was necessary to improve techniques because creameries were rare. The most important, at Dunragit, was started only in the 1880s. It processed the milk from 1,500 to 2,000 cows and fed the whey to some 300 to 500 pigs. Sending milk to the creameries was not initially a major method of disposal, but the introduction of the manufacture of Cheddar cheese, particularly in Wigtownshire from the mid-1850s, so changed dairy management and its profitability that the value of farms rose as their leases came to an end, and landlords had to provide better accommodation.[21]

The operational requirements of dairying determined the optimum size of holdings. In the south-west holdings remained small. In Ayrshire in 1836 one of 150 acres was considered large, and 'generally speaking they are from 50 to 100 acres or 150 acres'.[22] When the continuous series of agricultural statistics started in the mid-1870s, about two-thirds of the holdings in the south-west were less than 100 acres and not quite ten per cent about 500 acres. The large units, notably in Ayrshire, can be explained by the sheep farms in the hill area. The south-west did not have the high proportion of very small holdings common in some parts of Scotland, but had a higher proportion in the range of 50 to 300 acres, especially in the lower range (50.2 per cent in Ayrshire; 41.8 per cent in Dumfriesshire; 42.9 per cent in Kircudbrightshire; 46.7 per cent in Wigtownshire; 26.8 per cent in Scotland). This 'moderate size' — defined as from 100 to 300 acres — was considered most profitable in the late nineteenth century.[23]

Small holdings were appropriate for dairying when the physical difficulties of milking large herds twice daily limited the advantages of the larger units. In the main concentrations in Ayrshire and Wigtownshire the typical size of herds varied. Ignoring holdings of under 40 acres, the typical dairy farm in Cunninghame and Kyle was described in the 1860s as being between 100 and 120 acres, and perhaps about 50 acres or larger in Carrick, with a milking stock of 18 to 22 cows, and turning out one cheese daily during the season. The successful manufacture of Cheddar cheese was considered to require a larger herd of about 30 cows or more, so giving an advantage to the Wigtownshire farmer.[24] In Wigtownshire the size of herd was more dispersed: estimated in the 1870s variously at 20 or 40 to 100 and in the 1880s at 20 to 140, though commonly 60 to 80.[25] Even in Wigtownshire, near towns and villages, where the milk was sold fresh or made into butter, as in Ayrshire, herds were as low as 20. At the other extreme were some farms with up to 200 cows, but maintained in different dairies as 100 animals were thought the maximum which it was expedient to herd together.[26]

In the smaller units, especially those of Cunninghame and Kyle, the family provided most of the labour, often only one unmarried servant living in,[27] the traditional 'boy for byres' of later newspaper advertisements. Their dairies were too small to offer suitable employment to skilled persons, and responsibility for them devolved entirely on the wives and daughters of the farmers. The dairy farmers 'themselves, wives, sons, and daughters...' were 'all the year round, being worked like slaves'.[28] For them there was no rest, even after six days' labour: 'Dairying entails a seven day week, and the scene at Kilmarnock on a Sabbath morning when the milk is being shipped awakens considerable misgivings on the part of the onlooker'.[29] Some regular labour was employed except on the smallest units. The highly knowledgeable John Spier, whose origins were in the dairying districts of Cunninghame, suggested 'generally about two or three or four on each farm' in 1895; he also held that '...every family in most of them ... are by far too hard working ... The farmers in most cases do a great proportion of the work; even the wives in many cases do the bulk of the cheese-making ... They work, and work very hard'.[30] A decade later the editor of *The Scottish Farmer,* Andrew MacNeilage, again with his roots in the south-west, explained the conditions more fully. On a farm of 140 acres, which was one of average size, the typical labour force was 'one ploughman, one odd man ('orra' man in the north), who assists in the byre and delivers the milk, one harvester (in season), four women workers — i.e. two girls, one for house, and the other for dairy and byre, and these, along with other two milkers, constitute the female staff'.[31]

The heavy dependence on family labour was feasible only in the small dairy farms, especially those in Ayrshire which were more dependent on exploiting the market for liquid milk and less on the manufacture of cheese. In the larger dairies family labour remained important but inadequate. The result was the growth of the system of bowing, which persisted in a modified form in a few cases until after the Second World War.[32] The general principle behind bowing was that the farmer, who may well have been a tenant himself, supplied practically all the capital, working as well as fixed. The dairy herd was supplied with pasture in summer and feeding stuffs in winter, one writer of 1876 suggesting 'the usual allowance being five or six tons of swede and common turnips per cow, with $2\frac{1}{2}$ cwt. of beanmeal, and hay and straw'.[33] The bowers' agreements ran usually for a year from Martinmas, but were frequently renewed. Payment was in money or kind. If in money, the rate was based on each cow, ranging from about £8 to £15 in the 1870s to £12 to £18 before 1914. Payment in cheese was common in the larger Wigtownshire dairies, and in the 1870s was from 17 to 20 Ayrshire stones of 24 lbs each. The latter was an attractive arrangement when bowers were often unknown to the farmers and had no capital.[34]

As with many of the tenant farmers who spread dairying throughout the south-west, many bowers came from the small family farms of Ayrshire in which many of the dairying skills had first been developed.[35] The tenure provided the larger farmers with access to the skills of the bowers and gave the bowers, with skills but little or no capital, a way of acquiring some capital and an independent reputation, which enabled them to take full tenancies of farms later.[36] It was a striking method of social mobility.

Extensive bowing emerged in the dairying areas after the Napoleonic Wars,[37] and by the later nineteenth century was described as 'pretty common' in Ayrshire[38] and 'the almost universal custom' in Kirkcudbrightshire and Wigtownshire.[39] It remained common until the First World War but was gradually surrendered as farmers took dairies under their own control and employed a full-time dairyman or dairymaid, relatively highly paid, sometimes on the basis of sharing the proceeds above a certain sum. There were good reasons for the change. The successful operation of a bowing required harmonious relations between both parties, but relations were so close that they could easily lead to friction.[40] The agreement often specified the amount of cheese a bower had to supply and on the other hand detailed feeding and grazing arrangements. Difficulties could then easily arise from any attempt to change the provisions, perhaps necessary to exploit changing opportunities in the markets for dairy products. As creameries became more widely available, the need for the skills of the bower declined.

When a bower was employed, the result was often to pass the responsibility for the dairy to another family, and so to perpetuate the family structure of agricultural work in the south-west. Even when the method followed was to employ a full-time dairyman, he also provided the labour, especially of milkers, from his own family.[41] Dairying was, then, very much an extended system of family labour in the south-west.

III·

The influence on the demand and supply of labour of the distinctive demographic and agricultural history of the south-west helps to explain why many of the characteristics of social life and their changes offered to explain the determinants of the supply of labour to Scottish agriculture in the nineteenth century do not apply there.

Though the main increase in population from the mid-eighteenth to the mid-nineteenth centuries was concentrated in a few parishes, practically all gained. Irish immigration is a necessary part of any explanation of this buoyancy. By the end of the eighteenth century the minister of Wigtown, the county where the increase in population was most widespread, complained that the Irish 'are scattered over the whole of this county'.[42] Their presence grew in the next half-century and established a difference between the main areas of Irish immigration in Wigtownshire and Carrick, which registered the most rapid increases of population in the early nineteenth century, and in Nithsdale and Kirkcudbrightshire, a difference confirmed in 1841, when 15.3 per cent of those living in Carrick had been born in Ireland and 14.7 per cent of those in Wigtownshire, compared with only 3.7 per cent in Kirkcudbrightshire. Many of the Irish in these areas, and not necessarily ever enumerated in any census, were vagrants, whose potential calls on poor relief always engendered alarm, particularly in parishes on the roads from Portpatrick, such as Old Luce to the east or Ballantrae to the north.[43] The importance of the flow must not be underestimated, either because of its limited numerical strength — in 1851 only 32,736 Irish-born were living in the four counties of the south-west, less than ten per cent of their entire population — or because of its transient composition. The frequent complaints by ministers and others that the immigrants were seeking a parochial settlement attributes to many a degree of foresight they probably did not possess. Gaining one was an added bonus, but a more immediate and obvious reason for moving into some locality in Wigtownshire, Carrick or elsewhere was the existence of a special demand for the type of labour the Irish offered. Even when the demand passed, the immigrants often remained, so providing an unusually elastic supply of unskilled labour. Responding to the attractions of prosperous times, they 'swarmed' even to Dumfries,[44] but their more marked influence in Carrick and Wigtownshire was well illustrated in various investigations of the 1830s and 1840s. The views of contemporaries on the effects of the Irish immigration cannot be dismissed because the numbers revealed in the censuses were not great. Their influence spread more widely. The factors for the Earl of Stair and the Duchess de Coigny maintained in 1844 that eighty per cent of the population were Irish or of Irish extraction. The former believed that 'by working at less wages than the natives, they have, in point of fact, driven them away to other places, and have supplied the want of labour so caused', an interpretation he applied to all the extensive Stair estates, except those around Whithorn, where, however, the parish minister did not allow the exception. Vans Agnew of Barnbarroch agreed, and the minister of Kirkinner summed up for all: 'In a very short time the whole of the labouring population of his parish will be Irish'.[45]

Even when the numbers coming directly from Ireland were reduced in the late nineteenth century, they still provided the labour needed for special work in two ways. The first was by the emergence of a tradition of casual agricultural work among wives and daughters of Irish settlers, even when born in Scotland, so that where the Irish population 'predominated', female day labourers were 'abundant'.[46] The second way was in the provision of labour from Ireland for seasonal tasks, often by prior arrangement. Later in the nineteenth century such arrangements were notable in Ayrshire, where 'a considerable proportion are still to be found annually; they arrive early in the year for potato planting, taking next turnip singling, then early potato lifting, and lastly the corn harvest. It is stated that they usually return to Ireland with considerable funds'.[47]

On this supply of labour the agriculture of the south-west could rely. In 1836, even in the years of the most rapid increase of population, one Ayrshire farmer explained that 'we could not get on without them', and that, whatever other problems they created, if they did not come, 'we should have to pay higher wages and perhaps not get the work done so regularly'.[48] Because of the nature of its agricultural enterprises the south-west's demand for casual labour differed from some other regions. In the later nineteenth century the need was numerically significant for casual labour only in those areas which were not devoted to dairying: generally in parts of Kirkcudbrightshire, the Machers of Wigtownshire and the highly localised potato fields of Ayrshire. In these areas was found the nearest approach to agricultural gangs, usually of women and boys. They were not paid by the gangmaster, whose task was confined to collecting the gang and who worked as part of it, receiving an additional payment for his trouble. The gang was far from being in general use and was merely a minor convenience; its virtual absence in Wigtownshire did not lead to any difficulty in recruiting adequate labour. Generally a strong Irish influence, whether by descent, or by seasonal movement, ensured that labour was available and wages were kept down. Sometimes competition from industry restricted the supply of day labourers for green crops,[49] which were not, however, a leading interest in the south-west, least of all in north Ayrshire.[50] In any case the most general form of industrialisation in the south-west was mining in Ayrshire and Nithsdale, which provided its own useful reserve of miners' wives. The form of arable cultivation in the south-west limited its demands for casual labour, and in the Irish it had its own special supply, whether permanent or temporary. In these ways it was different from many other areas.

The Irish contributed much less, except as they became absorbed in the native stock, to meeting the special requirements of dairying. Its expansion required less labour, especially when dairying involved a reduction in green cropping. The change was so marked on the Ailsa estates in Carrick that the factor suggested that building cottages could be justified only 'by way of experiment', as 'the demand for Agricultural Labourers is now less than it once was'.[51] Dairying required skill in the south-west on a scale not comparable with elsewhere, and, whether the dairies were conducted chiefly by family labour, bowers or employed dairymen, female labour played an essential part. In Ayrshire 'every process connected with the milk, the butter, or the cheese, is conducted by women'.[52] Not surprisingly the inadequacy of female labour was noted in the late nineteenth century and could not be tackled by employing much of the casual labour available for seasonal fieldwork. Though employment in the dairy was often part-time, it was permanent, apart from seasonal fluctuations in milk production. The milkers, each of whom could deal with about ten cows in one and a half hours, were the leading part-timers. Married men were expected to provide workers, especially milkers. Though such provisions on engagement were often not enforced,[53] the main objective in one could be to obtain the milker rather than the ploughman, and the milkers could be the determinants of mobility. 'The great cause of removing in a dairy district is the milkers, every cotman being bound to supply a milker. This in many cases necessitates a second class man to be taken, on account of his supplying one or two good milkers, when it is found he is unfit for the work required of him, and has to be parted with. The milkers themselves too are often the cause of removal, as when so many women meet twice a day in a byre very often they quarrel amongst themselves, and some of them have to be removed in order to have quiet restored.'[54]

Apart from the milkers, dairies, especially where cheesemaking on any scale was carried out, necessitated skilled dairymaids. As early as 1802 Sir John Sinclair had suggested as the second of three requirements for extending a dairy farm: 'To procure an attentive and skilful dairy-maid, as the whole success of the undertaking must depend upon her good conduct'.[55] In the 1890s, 'A good chief dairymaid, especially in a cheesemaking district, is difficult to obtain, and the remuneration required is said to be constantly rising',[56] and John Spier was suggesting that this difficulty was leading to the use of milking machines,[57] though his faith in the march of scientific progress was not always realised.

It is instructive, then, to examine in detail the demand for female labour in the agriculture of the south-west in the nineteenth century. Male and female participation in employment was similar throughout the area and comparable to Scottish experience, but, as shown in Table 2, the ratios of male to female in the agricultural labour force of the four counties differed. In 1851 the proportions were similar, except in Wigtownshire, which had a lower proportion of females. Thereafter the proportion of females in Kirkcudbrightshire declined steadily. In Dumfriesshire it fell after 1871, and by 1911 the proportions for the two counties were almost the same. Employment in the agriculture of both was male-dominated. The experiences of Ayrshire and Wigtownshire provided a contrast. In the latter the proportion of females in the labour force rose from its low level in 1851 until 1881, though always below the Scottish figure, while in the former the proportion, though always above the Scottish figure, fell and rose again to its highest value of 23.8 per cent in 1881. The experiences of the two dairy counties converged from 1881. Ayrshire and Wigtownshire, then, were counties which offered relatively greater opportunities to females than to males in agriculture in the later nineteenth and early twentieth centuries, though not because of any significant change in participation ratios or, in the case of Ayrshire, because of an increase in the location coefficient of agriculture.

The same conclusion emerges from a consideration of the absolute

Table 2   *Percentage males and females employed in agriculture, forestry and fishing*

	Ayr		Dumfries		Kirkcudbright		Wigtown		Scotland	
	M	F	M	F	M	F	M	F	M	F
1841	96.1	3.9	75.0	25.0	90.4	9.6	93.4	6.6	90.7	9.3
1851	80.1	19.9	81.0	19.0	80.8	19.2	89.1	10.9	80.8	19.2
1861	82.5	17.5	78.2	21.8	80.8	19.2	85.1	14.5	83.5	16.5
1871	83.0	17.0	77.7	22.3	84.0	16.0	85.8	14.2	84.3	15.7
1881	76.2	23.8	80.0	20.0	83.4	16.3	80.9	19.1	79.3	20.7
1891	84.8	15.2	86.7	13.3	90.2	9.8	84.0	16.0	87.7	12.3
1901	80.1	19.9	87.6	12.4	90.7	9.3	82.1	17.9	87.5	12.5
1911	83.2	16.8	90.7	9.3	91.7	8.3	84.7	15.3	89.6	10.4

Source: as for Table 1. Much of the information on female employment in the censuses must be treated with care as it is not always reliable (see below, pp. 111–112). The figures for 1841 are open to very severe reservation in making comparisons with other years, but all are subject to a margin of error.

numbers employed. While male employment in the four counties fell more heavily than in Scotland as a whole between 1851 and 1911, and more heavily in Ayrshire and Wigtownshire than in Dumfriesshire and Kirkcudbrightshire, the number of females employed in agriculture fell slightly more extensively in Dumfriesshire and Kirkcudbrightshire than in Scotland as a whole, but less in Ayrshire and hardly at all in Wigtownshire. In the last the increase in the employment of females in 1881 compensated for much of the decline of males. Where agriculture was strongest in the local economy, as revealed in the location coefficient, female labour was in demand.

The labour requirements of the dairying districts of the south-west were very different from those of many other parts of Scotland. The small farms dependent on family labour, and the larger units let out to bowers or worked by hired dairymen, meant that an important source of labour was an extended family system. The social mobility afforded by bowing and the opportunities to females as skilled and well-paid dairymaids in addition to a wider demand for female labour in the byres were unusual characteristics of the social structure of the south-west. The additional demand for milkers was not for casual, but for permanent, though part-time labour, which provided a stable demand over long periods and was not simply the extraordinarily heavy demand for short periods required by activities confined to a much shorter season. To meet such contingencies Irish labour was present. In these conditions comparisons between the experience of the south-west and other parts of Scotland break down. The Irish migrant and the strength of dairying in the nineteenth century gave the area too many distinct characteristics.

NOTES

1. *Royal Commission on the Employment of Children, Young Persons and Women in Agriculture. Fourth Report. Appendix Part I. Parliamentary Papers*, 1870, XIII (hereafter *Fourth Report on Women in Agriculture, 1870*), *Reports of Assistant Commissioners*; *Royal Commission on Labour: the Agricultural Labourer, vol. III, Scotland, Part I. Parliamentary Papers*, 1893–5, XXXVI (hereafter *R.C. on Labour, 1893*).

2. Malcolm Gray, 'Migration in the Rural Lowlands of Scotland, 1750–1850', in T. M. Devine and David Dickson (eds.), *Ireland and Scotland, 1600–1850*, (Edinburgh, 1983), p. 105.

3. *Old Statistical Account* (hereafter *O.S.A.*), xii, p. 82.

4. *Ibid.*, xiii, p. 644.

5. The parish had a somewhat unusual parish minister.

6. *Royal Commission on the Poor Laws in Scotland. Appendix Part V. Parliamentary Papers*, 1844, XXIV (hereafter *R.C. on Scottish Poor Laws, 1844*). Answers to questions 30 and 32.

7. The availability of statistics for counties requires the south-west to be examined on that wider basis. Fortunately boundary changes of the four counties between censuses were trivial and can be ignored.

8. *Farmer's Magazine*, iv (1803), p. 381.

9. *O.S.A.*, ix, p. 538.

10. Robert Heron, *Observations made in a Journey through the Western Counties of Scotland in the Autumn of MDCCXCII* (Perth, 1799), ii, pp. 371–2.

11. *O.S.A.*, xx, p. 151.

12. John Gillespie, 'Report on the Agricultural of Dumfriesshire', *Transactions of the Highland and Agricultural Society (T.H.A.S.)*, fourth series, iv (1869), p. 270.

13. *Royal Commission on Agricultural Depression. Reports of Assistant Commissioners. Parliamentary Papers*, 1895, xvii (hereafter *R.C. on Agricultural Depression, 1895*). Report on south-western Scotland by John Spier, para. 8.

14. Early Scottish agricultural statistics, gathered nationally by the Highland and Agricultural Society, are in Parliamentary Papers. 1854–5. XLVII. 637; 1856. LIX. 369; 1857 (sess. 1) XV. 1; 1857–8. LVI. 33 and continuous from 1867. LXXI. 125.

15. *Farmer's Magazine*, xix (1818), p. 355; *British Farmers Magazine*, ii (1828), p. 366; *Royal Commission on Agricultural Interests. Minutes of Evidence. Parliamentary Papers*, 1881, XVII (hereafter *R.C. on Agricultural Interests, 1881*). Qs. 36,931 and 36,936. Evidence of George Cowan.

16. See *Agricultural Statistics, Parliamentary Papers*, 1884–5. LXXXIV. 16 and 1886. LXX. 18, 23.

17. John Spier, 'Dairying in Scotland', *T.H.A.S.*, fourth series, xviii (1886), p. 330.

18. *R.C. on Agricultural Depression, 1895*. Report by John Spier, para. 18; *Royal Commission on the Law relating to the Landlord's Right of Hypothec in Scotland. Parliamentary Papers*, 1865, XVII, Evidence of William Sproat, p. 278.

19. That improvement was needed was suggested in 1842 by a dealer from Preston, who purchased in Wigtownshire, and found Scottish cheese 'soapy', lacking firmness and 'a ripe sweet flavour'. *Farmer's Magazine*, second series, vi (June to Dec. 1842), p. 40.

20. *R.C. on Agricultural Depression, 1895*. Report by John Spier, appendix XV.

21. Scottish Record Office (S.R.O.). Cunninghame of Craigends MSS. GD 148/409/1/2 and 22. Reports on the value of the Dunragit estates, 1875 and 1888.

22. *Third Report of Select Committee on Agricultural Distress. Parliamentary Papers*, 1836. VIII (hereafter *S.C. on Agricultural Distress, 1836*). Q. 12, 103 (evidence of William Brown).

23. *R.C. on Agricultural Depression, 1895*. Report by John Spier, para. 101.

24. Archibald Sturrock, 'Report on the Agriculture of Ayrshire', *T.H.A.S.* fourth series, i (1866), pp. 89, 102.

25. John McCulloch, 'On Dairy Management as Pursued in Galloway', *T.H.A.S.*, fourth series, vii (1875), p. 267; Thomas MacLelland, 'On the Agriculture of the Stewartry of Kirkcudbright and Wigtownshire', *T.H.A.S.*, fourth series, vii (1875) p. 52; William H. Ralston, 'The Agriculture of Wigtownshire', *T.H.A.S.*, fourth series, XVII (1875), p. 120.

26. McCulloch, 'Dairy Management', p. 267.

27. *Fourth Report on Women in Agriculture, 1870*. Report of the Assistant Commissioner on Ayr etc. Evidence, Ayrshire, pp. 7, 10, 12, 13.

28. Sturrock, 'Agriculture of Ayrshire', p. 81.

29. Archibald MacNeilage, 'Farming Methods in Ayrshire', *T.H.A.S.*, fifth series, xviii (1906), p. 6.

30. *R.C. on Agriculture Depression, 1895. Parliamentary Papers*, 1896, XVII. Qs. 46, 986 and 47,001–3 (evidence of John Spier).

31. MacNeilage, 'Farming Methods in Ayrshire', p. 7.

32. *Report on the Present State of the Agriculture of Scotland* (Edinburgh, 1878), p. 168.

33. Thomas Farrell, 'On the Ayrshire Breed of Cattle', *T.H.A.S.*, fourth series, viii (1876), p. 141.

34. Payments in kind were not always adequate security (*Select Committee of the House of Lords on the Law of Hypothec in Scotland. Parliamentary Papers*. 1868–9. IX. Q. 1894–5). Though described as 'sharp fellows' (Sturrock, 'Agriculture of Ayrshire', p. 84), few absconded with the proceeds of their sales.

35. Gillespie, 'Agriculture of Dumfriesshire', p. 308.

36. *Select Committee of House of Lords on Hypothec. Parliamentary Papers*. 1868–9. IX. Q. 1890–2 (evidence of A. M. Caird); John Drysdale, 'The Management of a Dairy Farm', *T.H.A.S.*, fifth series, xxv (1913), p. 72.

37. *Farmer's Magazine*, xix (1818), p. 501.

38. Sturrock, 'Agriculture of Ayrshire', p. 83.

39. MacLelland, 'Agriculture of Kirkcudbright and Wigtown', p. 52.

40. Drysdale, 'Management of a Dairy Farm' p. 72; MacNeilage, 'Farming Methods in Ayrshire', p. 7.

41. *R.C. on Labour, 1893*. Report by H. Rutherford on Wigtown, etc., para. 40 and appendix C.

42. *O.S.A.*, xiv, p. 480.

43. *R.C. on Scottish Poor Laws, 1844*, pp. 515 and 517. *Parliamentary Papers*, 1844, XXII.

44. *Farmer's Magazine*, xxiii (1821), p. 246.

45. *R.C. on Scottish Poor Laws, 1844*, pp. 444, 525, 533, 535. *Parliamentary Papers*, 1844, XXII.

46. *Fourth Report on Women in Agriculture, 1870*. Report of Assistant Commissioner (Tremenheere) on Ayr, etc., para. 81, also para. 78 and Evidence, Wigtown, 5, 8.

47. *R.C. on Labour, 1893.* Reports of Assistant Commissioner (Rutherford) on Ayr, etc., para. 16 and on Wigtown etc. para. 15.

48. *S.C. on Agricultural Distress, 1836.* Qs. 12, 254–5.

49. *R.C. on Agricultural Interests, 1881.* Qs. 38761–2; 38766–8 (evidence of John Cunningham).

50. When the first set of agricultural statistics for Scotland were collected in 1854, the four counties had 62,339 or 14.4 per cent of the Scottish acreage under turnips and 23,767 or 11.2 per cent under potatoes. Ayrshire's position was different. It had a higher percentage of the south-western counties' acreage of potatoes than of turnips, though concentrated in a few districts: 24.3 per cent of the turnip acreage and 35.3 per cent of the potato acreage in 1854 and 14.5 per cent and 59.0 per cent respectively in 1914. Its lower acreage under turnips is conspicuous. In 1854 it had 15,158 or 3.5 per cent of the Scottish acreage and 7,079 or 1.6 per cent of the Scottish acreage in 1914. The practice in north Ayrshire was especially unusual. It had a 'rotation without roots'. By the 1860s the upland farms, particularly around Kilmarnock, concentrated on a special seven years' rotation: two white crops of oats in succession, then two of hay, followed by three years in pasture. A feature of the first hay crop of ryegrass was that it was seeded and threshed, a practice which brought strong condemnation from agricultural writers of the 1860s, was tolerated in the 1870s, and then accepted as a system which worked where it was practised. Even the critics did not advocate a large crop of roots.
It is not possible, then, to apply to the south-west the judgement made of the east and north-east, and vitally important for labour requirements, that turnips were 'the crop which more than any other rules the fortunes of our whole system of Scottish agriculture'.

51. S.R.O., Ailsa MSS. GD 25/9/78/7/5/5. Information for Lord Ailsa on the subject of Cottages for Agricultural Labourers on his Lordship's Estates, 30 Jan. 1867, pp. 5–6.

52. Sturrock, 'Agriculture of Ayrshire', p. 89.

53. *R.C. on Labour, 1893.* Report of Assistant Commissioner (Rutherford) on Wigtown, etc., paras. 22, 23, 40, 60 and on Ayr, etc., para. 18.

54. Ralston, 'Agriculture of Wigtownshire', p. 129.

55. Sir John Sinclair, 'Hints regarding cattle', *Farmer's Magazine,* iii (1802), p. 161.

56. *R.C. on Labour, 1893.* Report of Assistant Commissioner (Rutherford) on Ayr, etc., para. 26 and on Wigtown, etc., para. 34. Fourth Report of Women in Agriculture, 1870. Report of Assistant Commissioner (Tremenheere) on Ayr, etc., para. 64; evidence, Wigtown, 10.

57. *R.C. on Agricultural Depression, 1895. Parliamentary Papers,* 1896, XVII. Qs. 46, 884–5 (evidence of John Spier).

5

The Border Farm Worker

Michael Robson

'But dear aunt,' replied Miss Sophia, 'who cares
to hear about cottagers, and shepherds, and all
those sort of people.' 'Those sort of people, my
good girl, are to me the most interesting to hear
about.'

(*The Spy*, No. 32, 6 April 1811, p. 249)

I

From a high point such as Carter Bar or the Eildon Hills there is an
almost comprehensive view of the Borders. To the north-east the low,
colourful arable country around Kelso spreads away to the Berwickshire
Merse and the haze over the North Sea, while in all other directions the
land rises, the river valleys become more pronounced, and solitary peaks
such as Ruberslaw lift abruptly out of the woods and fields. Then the eye
moves to horizons, where lie the long banked ranges of the higher moors
and hills. The hill-ground and river systems define the districts into which
the area is divided and which includes such different valleys as Lauderdale,
Glendale, Yarrow, and Liddesdale and Eskdale which turn their backs to
the rest of the Scottish Borders. There are basically two types of farming,
sheep on the hills and crops in the fields, with cattle finding a place in
both; created by the natural environment and by centuries of human
activity, upland and lowland divisions of agriculture are much more
distinct from each other than are the two countries on either side of the
Border. In considering the life of those who have worked on the land, the
shepherds and the ploughmen, dykers, drainers and many others, it is of
greater use to treat the English and Scottish sides as all part of the Border
country.

Two hundred years ago the traditional structure of Border farm
communities had already reached a stage which could be called modern as
opposed to mediaeval. Farmers were commercially minded, experiments in
methods were increasingly frequent, and even the diehard enthusiasts for
long-established custom were adapting to new breeds of stock, new

F

ploughs, and novel approaches to old familiar problems. On the other hand the work pattern of the farming year was founded upon seasonal inevitabilities which gave stability in the midst of innovation, and even the more rapid pace of change which came after 1800 did not so disrupt life on the farm as wholly to deserve the name of a revolution in agriculture.

In 1780 the people were more evenly scattered over the whole area than they are today, for although there were several old burghs and villages, the population of such centres was very small, and places like Galashiels and Hawick were still at the beginning of their lives as manufacturing towns. Kelso, which never developed industrially, was the largest. Agriculture provided employment for the majority, either directly through labour on the farms or indirectly by means of the servicing trades, and the villages with their predominantly tradesmen population must be seen as part of the wider farming community.

In the eighteenth century and earlier not all those carrying on a trade or craft lived in villages and towns. Many did, but it had always been common for weavers, tailors, gardeners, dykers, blacksmiths and others to live on or close to the farms and country estates so that they were certainly rural if not strictly agricultural employees. The small villages of the Borders were the principal locations of these people, and in addition to those trades already mentioned it was usual to find in places like Newstead or Lilliesleaf, and even lesser settlements such as Lanton, the coopers, shoemakers, litsters, glovers, masons, joiners, saddlers and skinners whose skills were just as necessary to the wellbeing of country life. The range of provision at a local level was therefore almost enough to make a country family in this respect independent of the burghs and towns unless these were nearer than any village. But if, for instance, the better off farmer needed some legal advice or a cure from the doctor, or if he had ambitious ideas about educating his children, he had most probably to resort to the town, which in any case provided the outlets for his farm produce.

This pattern of service crafts is clearly presented by the parish ministers writing for the first Statistical Account in the 1790s. Up among the hills at Cranshaws two masons, four joiners, two weavers, a blacksmith and a tailor were 'chiefly employed in working to the people of the parish and neighbourhood, seldom manufacturing any articles for sale'.[1] At Langton near Duns, where the village had recently been rebuilt on a new site and called Gavinton after its founder, there were hedgers, thatchers and ploughwrights as well as the more familiar trades, and at Mertoun there were two 'Egglers' who earned a living by marketing eggs. Swinton and Simprin offered more unusual refinements in the shape of a surgeon, a fiddler and a dancing master.

These illustrations are all from Berwickshire (the old county names are used throughout), but a very similar situation existed everywhere in the Borders. Weavers were often the most numerous of the tradesmen, particularly in villages that did out-work for town-based manufacturers, and in the hilly areas where wool, spun by the women at home in the cottage or farm-house, was readily available. In their account books farmers made frequent reference to the local tradesmen, naturally recording transactions with the wide range of suppliers to the domestic household and the farm, from the tailor who produced a Sunday coat to the smith and wright who between them supplied the new plough or repaired the old one. Farmers obviously benefited from these services more than the ordinary poor labourer, who must have had to make do usually with home-made or second-hand clothes and was not otherwise much involved.

Here and there throughout the Borders there were, in the late eighteenth century, other forms of occupation which depended upon a variety of local resources. Apart from the developing manufacturing industries in towns, there were in the countryside small-scale enterprises of a similar kind. In Newlands parish, Peeblesshire, twenty people worked in the lime quarries, and there were four 'Coal Hewers'.[2] Limestone and coal were also mined in the hills on the northern edges of Liddesdale, and at Canonbie. Along the North Sea coast communities such as Cockburnspath depended greatly upon fishing. Local concerns often became established as a result of initiatives taken by particular individuals. At Lamancha the Honourable Captain Cochrane had launched 'A manufactory for converting ochre into paint',[3] while at Hassendeanburn near Minto the Dicksons ran the tree and garden nurseries started by their grandfather sixty years earlier. Ednam benefited temporarily from the public-spirited efforts of James Dickson who had introduced cloth manufacture and a successful brewery. In addition an almost universal possibility of work existed at the time in the form of labour on the roads, which having been hitherto widely lacking, were under construction in many districts. These various activities gave opportunities for work outside agriculture and the usual range of trades, so that it was possible for a ploughman's children, at least in some places, to seek a job other than on the farm. The general impression given by the parish accounts of the 1790s is that there was little unemployment in the rural areas, but some labourers certainly did have to look for work outside the area, and the minister of Coldingham noted that 'Our supernumerary young men go partly to England, and partly to Edinburgh, and other populous towns in Scotland, in quest of employment'.[4] In a few parishes military service took up some young men. Mobility among farm-workers was probably dictated chiefly by the chance of a slightly higher or just a regular wage, and, since there is no indication prior to 1800 that the labourer enjoyed a choice of local work, a journey to Edinburgh might well have been a better option than staying at home to scrape a bare pittance.

The differences between one locality and another in the kind of occupations available, whether on the farm or of some other kind, underline the risk in generalising about the situation of labourers. When it comes to describing specifically agricultural workers, a much broader difference arises between upland and lowland areas. The workforce on a hill-farm bore only a slight resemblance to that on an arable holding, a fact which, united with the variety of minor local characteristics, meant that western Roxburghshire and nearly all Selkirkshire contrasted greatly with the Merse, and if 'To pass from the Borders of Scotland into Northumberland was rather like going into another parish than into another kingdom',[5] then to go from, say, Eccles parish to Yarrow was to move from a kingdom of the ploughman with his women out-workers and harvest bands to that of the shepherd, ewe-milkers and smearers.

The traditional labourers on an upland or even on what was later considered a marginal farm were predominantly concerned with sheep. The shepherd was the leading figure, equivalent in rank to a farm steward. He had charge of a 'hirsel' of sheep all the year round, and was often assisted by a 'young herd', who was either a less experienced man or a kind of apprentice, and, like other apprentices, was sometimes given the more difficult and uncomfortable tasks. In the hill country the shepherd had to be an all-rounder; there were skills involved in his own ordinary duties like castrating lambs, dressing sheep for market, and smearing and clipping, but he had also to turn when necessary to 'repairing stone dykes, cleaning out drains, mowing grass, making hay, casting or winning turf or peats, and, in short, every little odd kind of work'.[6] In July and early August he was joined by a company of girls hired for nearly two months of ewe milking and for the subsequent butter and cheese-making, and in the late autumn men were taken on for the arduous process of smearing the sheep to protect them against parasites and the weather. The other regular labourers on this kind of farm were the ploughman, with the goadman who 'called the plough', and a barnman who threshed corn with a flail. Work in the house and byre was given to the women, usually wives, daughters or female relatives of the male employees, and boys and girls aged seven or above had simpler duties like looking after lambs and cattle as they grazed or helping in someone else's household.

In complete contrast to this arrangement, the lowland farm down towards the Solway or in the eastern parts of Northumberland and Berwickshire was the setting for the hind. While there might still in 1780 have been a piece of rough unploughed ground on which, along with a field or two, a small number of sheep could pasture under the care of a shepherd, work with a flock was of relatively minor importance, and attention was focused on the arable where the hind was the most important farm-worker. His task was to look after a pair of horses and to use them in ploughing, harrowing, carting and leading. Otherwise called ploughman, the hind had generally to supply a woman or boy worker, usually the former, and the arrangement being more formalised than in the world of shepherds' wives, this person, not always a wife or relative, had the title of bondager. Along with the hind and the bondager went the goadman, barnman and all the seasonal and day-labourers, mainly harvest workers who were employed for a month or more to shear the corn with reaping hooks, bind the sheaves, and load the carts at leading-in.

Of the sixty-six houses in the upland and marginal parish of Hounam about 1790, twenty-three were inhabited by 'cottagers', a group said to consist of hired servants, day-labourers and women, but excluding shepherds and tradesmen.[7] The term was used widely for those living in the scattering of cottages found on most farms, apart from those occupied by the shepherd, the hind, and the steward, in other words, the inhabitant of a farm who was not hired for a year or six months, but was at hand as casual labour. Some of these cottagers, of whom a few were in practice tradesmen, were 'cottars', that is to say people who were, in return for their cottage, more or less bound to be at the farmer's beck and call throughout the year but had the independence given by possession of a small-holding set off from the farm. As defined at Whitsome, 'the cottar, instead of paying rent for the house and 'kailyard', engages to do the harvest work; at every other season, a payment in money, of from 8d. to 10d. per day, is received for each day employed; the cottar also reaps the benefit of as much ground as two bushels of potatoes will plant, together with the carriage of coal'.[8] This was written in the 1830s in Berwickshire; in more hilly areas, with less harvest work to be done for the house, the cottar paid a rent, and a rare agreement between a farmer and two cottars in such an area, surviving from 1764, shows the nature of the relationship. The farmer set, in tack, for four years to the cottars a piece of ground on his farm, enclosing part of it with 'a strong feal dike'. He also had built at his own expense 'a stone and feal' walled dwelling for them. They were allowed to plough land enough to sow two bolls of corn, and the farmer would give them 'two yoking of his pleugh' each year. In return they had to pay £3.10s. rent in March, make a boundary dyke 'fencible' by putting whins along each side, cast the feal for the house walls, and 'cast, win and lay on' the divots for the roof. During the course of the tack they had to uphold the dykes and house in good repair, and 'are yearly to work two or three days at the moss as the rest of the Coaters'.[9] The benefit to the farmer in having these cottars on his land was a little extra income from their rents and probably the convenience of having a source of day-labourers when needed.

A dozen 'small tenants' in the village of Roxburgh were known as 'cotlanders'. They each held about two acres of land, with a house, yard, and the liberty of pasturing their cows in the nearby 'loaning', all of which 'along with their own industry in some trade' gave them a living.[10] Elsewhere such people were called 'cot-men', and it is not easy to detect the difference of meaning between these terms. In some cases the cottars were women, possibly widows with children, who still did outside work when they could. In Roxburgh parish, where about 1790 there were 540 females and only 360 males, the disproportion between the sexes seemed to arise 'from a number of cot-houses being possessed by women, whose husbands or sons are employed elsewhere';[11] and a similar situation existed at Yetholm because, as was surmised, following depopulation in the country parts, 'single women unfit for farmers service, or an old widow with a daughter or two, most of them equally unfit, took refuge in these villages, and earned their livelihood by spinning, perhaps some one of the family by hoeing turnips by the day, and hiring themselves in harvest; whilst the males hired themselves as herds, hinds, and farmers servants, and were in other parishes'.

Such were the people who worked among the farms of the Borders in the late eighteenth century.

II

A Berwickshire farm had a large group of buildings, the farm-house, the steading and the cottages of the hinds and other labourers hired for a whole or half a year together forming a substantial settlement. West Laws, south of Duns, was typical, forming 'a little village' on top of a long ridge.[13] All over the Borders this little village was known as the 'town' or 'toun', a term that still survives, even in application to the one remaining house on a site from which the rest of the buildings have long ago vanished. There was not much difference in size and appearance between this 'town' and a country village, except that the latter probably also included the school and the church and perhaps some plots of feued land with houses. In the hills and wild moorlands further west, without the hinds, farm towns were smaller, with fewer cottages and much less imposing 'onsteads' of office buildings. At Nether Horsburgh, not far down the Tweed from Peebles and rather more imposing than a farm at the head of the river, the town consisted of the dwelling house, stable, two barns, two byres, two 'Coat houses' and a 'Chaff House', with the mill, kilns, and a miller's house not far away.[14] The isolated upland farmstead was smaller still, more compact, and with a grey rather mysterious atmosphere, especially in the wastes along the Border in Cumberland, where 'Every farmhouse forms a little community within itself, and the sight of a passing stranger never fails to attract the undivided attention and conjecture of the inmates so long as he is within the reach of vision'.[15]

The generality of labourers' cottages had walls of stone and feal, with a thatched roof, clay and dung 'plaster', and clay floor. Some were constructed entirely of divots; a few old 'turf-walled cottages' survived in Peeblesshire in 1800, but these were exceptionally poor dwellings.[16] Since the cottage of that time was certainly a mean affair, it was with no surprise that a farmer recorded in his diary on January 12, 1796 that 'Davie's House fell last night — no damage done to his furniture or ought else'.[17] But if the house could easily fall down, it could with equal ease be built up again, and there was not much furniture needed for the single room. The living space was divided by box beds, yet remained extremely inconvenient when anyone was ill. Some cottages had no chimneys, others had constructions of wood and clay set against a gable wall. About 1840 the chimneyless variety was still prevalent in Westruther, and with no outlet for smoke except a rough crevice in the roof the interior was 'almost constantly filled with a dense cloud' hanging about six feet above the floor and giving a strong peaty smell to clothes.[18] Not far from Hawick on farms all the way up Borthwick Water there were labourers' cottages of this kind. Cruck-framed dwellings survived in some localities as at Great Ryle in north Northumberland, where in 1850 there were still 'several long, low-roofed thatched houses' with oak beams carried down into the earth so as 'to prevent the thrust on the mud-built walls'.[19]

In simple conditions, where damp, smoke, and cramped space were more common than snug comfort, the farm labourers raised large families and endured the loss of many children from disease before they had reached school age. In a frugal diet meal, potatoes, kale and milk were the basics, but there was variety depending on the season and the district, and nearly everywhere people salted away parts of the pig and of the 'mart' ox or sheep killed in November. The normal fare could also be supplemented with fish from the sea or the rivers, wild fruit, black-headed gulls' eggs, rabbits, and vegetables. Even so, in bad years the threat of starvation loomed, and the poorer folk were reduced to eating plants and other things which they would not normally touch.

Education was still a haphazard affair, although it was possible, as the story of the Denholm cottager's son, John Leyden, shows, for a labourer's child to progress to university. In the 1830s the inhabitants of the Borders were supposed to be 'alive to the benefits of education', a rather meaningless expression used by nearly every minister in writing up his parish for the second Statistical Account. In spite of the unoriginal character of the words, it does seem to have been the case that parents made sure that their children received at least a little schooling. There was in every parish a 'parochial school', and in many others a privately endowed school as well. Special provision was made in wilder areas, such as Eskdalemuir, Tweedsmuir and Ettrick, where 'distance from the school not unfrequently induces several families to unite in hiring a teacher for the winter half year'.[20] The miscellaneous collection of teachers employed privately, ranging from boys and girls to old men, meant considerable variety in the quality of education, but at the parish schools the standard was high. The range of subjects offered included the usual English writing, reading, arithmetic and book-keeping, and less often, but still quite commonly, Latin, geography, French, mathematics and Greek. Every minister claimed that all but one or two of his parishioners could read and write by the age of fifteen, and some emphasised that education transformed the conduct and morals of the people.

Some of the money received by teachers came in the form of fees paid by parents, which might amount to 3s. a quarter for the three main subjects and more for others. Clearly school costs were a burden to the poorer labourers, whose children were never likely therefore to venture further than basic reading, writing and counting. Attendance might have been much diminished had no parish funds come to the rescue in the cases of real need, and here and there special help came from a private source, as at Stobo where, 'As an encouragement to the people to attend, Sir James Montgomery pays the school fees of every boy or girl of a family where the numbers that attend the school out of each family exceed two'.[21] Even so the pinched circumstances of the labouring community meant that on occasions 'the humbler families find it extremely dificult to procure the necessary books',[22] and that 'their anxiety to put their children soon to work for themselves, frequently induces them to take them from school before their education has been at all properly advanced'.[23]

However enthusiastic parents might be about education and the chance it offered to 'better oneself', school life for most country children was irregular and the John Leydens were very few. George Scott, recollecting his Borthwick Water childhood, pictured the little side school at Deanburnhaugh as he had known it about 1840. At the age of five he went to school for the first time, smartly dressed in corduroy trousers and waistcoat with brass buttons. In his pocket he had a penny or two, for on Monday mornings each 'scholar' paid from a penny to threepence as an advance fee. Some of the children came from miles away, and the teacher, Mr. Amos, who strictly enforced discipline with 'saugh wands' for boys and the tawse for the girls, lodged at the parents' houses in turn, the nearest to the school in winter. Holidays occurred on the Hawick fair days in May and November, and on festive occasions such as Hansel Mondays at the beginning of January and Barring-Out Day on 21st December.[24] The main holiday period was at harvest, five or six weeks off which could be adapted to the readiness of the corn, and the children spent much of the time with the shearers in the fields. In winter bad weather might keep children at home, and in any parish having a long reach into the hills, many children could only attend school for a short spell in the summer. So exposed was the Megget district that the school there only functioned between Whitsunday and Martinmas.

Usually, however, attendance in winter was higher than at other seasons when children stayed off or were kept at home to work. In Westerkirk, where forty or so attended in summer and seventy in winter, a school was sometimes opened for the winter months only.[25] It was summer that provided most distraction; in Abbey St. Bathans parish about 1840, it was remarked that 'the progress of children at school is much impeded during the summer and autumn by their being so frequently called out to work in the fields'.[26] Teachers were complaining of the same practice fifty years later, when more schools had been built in remote districts to cater for those previously out of reach, and when a log-book was kept to record events and general progress. These books show that children were absent regularly each year for hay-making, potato-lifting, clipping, peat work, lambing, winter foddering, driving sheep, keeping house, beating for shooters, pig killing, and for such reasons as illness, lack of boots, watching a ploughing match, floods, and being afraid of the bull. Country life and the needs of the farm had always overruled the teacher, whatever timetable he tried to enforce.

Work became a six day week reality during later childhood, and for many started with a hiring-fair. For shepherds these occasions were largely irrelevant as they either remained on a farm year after year or else made their own arrangements for a new situation in the course of the year's work. Hinds and shearers on the other hand were regularly hired at the fairs, although as with the shepherds it was possible for the farmer to reach private agreement on conditions for a further year with those already working for him whom he wished to keep on. This might be done at any time but was usually a subject raised about January when the employee expected to be 'spoken to' by his master with regard to future work.

The hiring fairs were held at fixed times of the year in the towns and large centres of population, and many of them originated no earlier than the eighteenth century. They were essentially markets at which the level of wages was fixed by demand, and where the labourer found a new master or the master completed his requisite number of employees. The 'Great Hiring Days' were related to the Whitsunday and Martinmas terms and thus fell during the spring and autumn, but there was also a hiring day for shearers in late July or August and sometimes another, nominal day given over largely to recreation. Of the twelve 'high markets' occurring in Kelso in the 1790s, two were held before and one after the term days; 'the two first are for hiring male and female servants; the last is generally employed by servants in mirth, and in laying out their wages before they enter again into service'.[27] Most older fairs were originally intended to offer marketing opportunities for specific produce, and this aspect continued, though in altered form. At Broughton, Peeblesshire, by the late eighteenth century, a fair which had once been associated with the marketing of black cattle was used for hiring servants and by storemasters for selling cheese. Held on 30th October, it took place on the village street, 'where the stalls are overloaded with the produce of the orchards of Clydesdale and other merchandize', and, despite the location, it was 'distinguished by horse and foot races'.[28]

If it coincided with a long-established traditional fair, such as the St. James' Fair, at St. James' Green by Kelso on 5th August, the hiring day was at least as much an event of pleasure as of business, with stalls and races among the main attractions. These old festival occasions were however outside the main hiring seasons and were relevant only to incidental employment bargains and to the temporary labour needed for harvest. Those who went to them were usually in a sporting mood, and the young men who worked around St. Boswells treated the fair there on 18th July as the recreational highlight of the year, escaping for once from the ordinary labouring round on the farm. Tents and stalls covered the fair ground, filled with goods for sale, including 'linen, hardware, toys, crockery, shoes, books, etc.'.[29] The variety of entertainment at Whittingham Fair near Wooler, held on St. Bartholomew's Day, 24th August, made it at least as noteworthy as St. Boswells, 'with its rows of refreshment tents and gingerbread stalls, troops of mountebanks, strolling players and boxing booths; gangs of hucksters and muggers displaying their varied assortment of merchandise, ... its crowds of fresh-coloured country lads and lasses, enjoying their annual holiday'.[30]

It is not surprising that at least the refreshment and trading side of the great summer fairs also appeared at the more serious hiring days. Stall owners took up regular positions in the customary street or market place where the farmers and labourers gathered. The beginning of March was the hiring time for hinds: the first Friday at Kelso, the first Tuesday at Jedburgh, Duns and Lauder, and so on. Shepherds, if hired in this way at all, came forward towards the end of the month, the last Wednesday at Thirlestane in Ettrick, the 25th March at lonely Pennymuir where 'a tryst or market for hiring shepherds' was introduced in 1830. Hiring days for other men and women labourers, usually for a 'half year', took place nearer the towns.

In the market place, or the immediate streets around, the farmer or his steward bargained either with new men or with old employees with whom new arrangements were necessary. The haggling, if there was any, was generally over a penny or a small proportion of the grain, meal or potatoes paid in kind. When the bargain was struck, the parties shook hands, the hired employee was given his or her 'arles', usually a shilling, as a final mark of agreement, and the parties went off to the pub to put a glow upon the proceedings. Hinds themselves also did some hiring: 'There was a large gathering of male and female workers from the whole of Glendale. The hinds wore a spring of hawthorn in their hats, the carters a piece of whipcord, and the shepherds a tuft of wool, as emblems of their respective callings. Among the crowd mixed the farmers, who were looking around for likely hands to replace those who were leaving, and those hinds, who could not find a place without a bondager, were there to engage one'.[31]

This was Wooler, one March about 1845. Hiring fairs were not always so cheerful, however, and there were years when many went home without a hiring. Alexander Somerville, in his autobiography, described how as a youth he went to the hiring market at Duns in 1827, 'with a piece of whipcord in the ribbon of my hat, and a piece of straw in my mouth, as signals that I wanted to be hired. But with the exception of one person, nobody even asked how much wages I expected. Men were more plentiful than masters'.[32]

Being a market, the hiring was sometimes a good one, sometimes not, and wages went up and down, much like the price of a stone of wool. With fluctuation the rule, a trend is difficult to detect, particularly as so many different aspects of the pay system have to be considered. Bare statements of money amounts or of payments in kind do not always show the full picture, excluding as they do the little adjustments and qualifications that individual farmers could make over and above the market levels, and to isolate a cash sum from the full array of possible forms of wage may mislead.

Among the tradesmen in 1790, tailors, who worked in the houses of their customers and 'who always get their meat where they work',[33] received 8d a day; but in some districts they worked differently and did not get their food supplied, so that their pay went up to a shilling. A similar variation applied to all those who were hired by the day or by the piece, and the value of the 'meat' or 'victuals' could likewise rise or fall according to area so that a labourer, to whom a penny or two meant a great deal, had always to look about and find where the best rates were. Wrights and masons might average 1s 6d a day without victuals, and a shilling with, but a glance across all the Border country in the years around 1800 would show that if a wright went off to Greenlaw or Langton near Duns he might get 1s 8d without victuals, whereas in Eckford he would only be paid 10d with his meat, which, since 'victuals' at that time were valued at 6d to 8d, was a significant difference.

Day labourers, who were hired for all sorts of work like mowing grass, strengthening a river bank, and gardening, received pay at much the same level as the tradesmen, but there were adjustments according to the work and time of the year which applied to the tailor and mason much less often. At Duns in 1793 a male labourer received 1s a day in summer, 9d or 10d in winter, 1s 6d in hay time without victuals but 'a bottle of ale at noon, and another in the afternoon, with $\frac{1}{2}$d worth of bread', and in harvest 1s or 1s 6d with victuals.[34]

The system of wages for shepherds and ploughmen was quite different and less complex. These workers were needed all the year round, so daily rates were not involved and accommodation was. An unmarried man, herd or ploughman, normally received his board in the farmhouse, had his washing done for him there, and slept in a steading loft or attic room. He was paid between £6 and £10 a year around 1800, according to the district. The hind, an older, married man, with his family, occupied one of the cottages on the farm town, which he was allowed free so long as his wife, or another female worker provided by him, worked unpaid during harvest. With the house went a yard or small garden for vegetables, grazing for a cow, and ground for planting a firlot of potatoes and a peck of lintseed. The potato ground was sometimes stated as 1000 yards of drill or thereby. He was also given quantities of oats, barley, and peas measured in bolls, the number of which varied between the different kinds of produce but usually turned out to be in the region of ten bolls of oats, two of barley and one of peas. He was able to keep a pig and poultry, and was supplied with coals for which he paid the price at source and the cost of the tolls, but had them led free. In some places he received a small sum of money which included a pound or two in place of pasture for a sheep. The wages paid in kind were collectively called the hind's 'boll' or 'gains'. In total value the hind's wage was judged to amount to about £13 to £15 around 1800, but at Legerwood for instance it was as high as £20,[35] which meant that the hind then earned more than many a parish schoolteacher. In the western and upland parts of the Borders, where the ploughman was a far less significant figure, much of the grain was replaced by a sum of money, about £6 to £8. Instead of the hind the hill shepherd was here the best paid servant; as a married man he also occupied a cottage on the farm, anywhere from near the steading to some hidden corner far into the hills, and under the usual 'conditions', as terms of employment were generally called, he received the same mixture of payments in money and kind. Like the hind's gains, the shepherd's 'perquisites' included oatmeal, potatoes and lintseed, but instead of the great quantities of oats, barley and peas, he was allowed the grazing of about 45 sheep of his own, a small flock known as his 'pack'. A shepherd who lived on a led farm and acted as manager for the absentee tenant could have as many as 100 sheep, but half of these were for an assistant whom he had to employ.

The daughters of hinds and shepherds began work when children, like Janet Bathgate who was hired by a shepherd when she was only seven 'tae herd the cow an' be company for my mother' during summer.[36] Her tasks included fetching and carrying peats, digging up potatoes and washing them in the burn, cleaning out the byre, sweeping out the house, taking warm milk to the lambs, washing dishes, all for the promised total sum of twelve shillings for the six months. This was exceptionally harsh treatment for a small girl, but it was good training for the heavier duties of a young woman worker. In the 1790s a maidservant in the farmhouse received lodgings, victuals, and between £3 and £5 a year depending on where she worked. Girls undertaking labour by the day, such as turnip weeding or hay-making, earned between 6d and 1s a day with victuals provided, and in harvest up to 1s 6d, while those who became ewe milkers were paid just over £1 for two months with board and lodging. According to the minister of Glenholm parish in Peeblesshire, 'The reason why the summer wages do so much exceed the winter, is the labour of ewes milking, which is reckoned a severe task, which nothing but high wages can induce them to engage in; and part of that wage having been by long use paid in wool, the rise in the price of that commodity has contributed to raise their wages'.[37] Once married the servant girl became a 'female worker', whose main task was to earn the 'free' house by shearing in harvest.

In the lower, eastern districts a girl, whether married or not, commonly spent some years as a bondager, a colourful and distinctively Border farm-worker whose duties required considerable strength and endurance. The accepted arrangement was that 'each hind, possessing a cottage, is ...

obliged to furnish to his landlord and employer, a female-labourer, his wife, daughter or servant, to work occasionally throughout the year for the hire of 8d a-day'.[38] Though there were people who thought that the term 'bondager' for this provided female labourer denoted something approaching a form of slavery, the 'bond' and 'bondage' seem to have applied rather to the condition laid upon the hind that he should produce a woman worker in this manner. The point was made in the 1830s by the minister of Westruther, who noted that 'The class of servants here called *bondagers* are not less free and independent than other labourers, but they are distinguished from others by being engaged by the hinds or ploughmen to perform upon their master's farm the ordinary work of weeding, hoeing, barn-work etc'.[39] They were also distinguished by their mode of dress. If she was not one of the family, the hind paid the bondager half-year wages at the level of those of a house-servant, for she received board and lodging in his house, and he received from the farmer the day wage earned by her, which might just leave him with a penny profit. The young ploughman, just married with perhaps young children, was the worst off under the system, for he had to supply a bondager at a time when his wife was busy at home and no daughter was able to work.

Women out-workers in the turnip and hay fields, most of them bondagers, counted as day-labourers, who formed a high proportion of the working population in any country parish. It was possible for a day-labourer to engage to work with a farmer for a whole or half-year, at a daily rate which in 1790 was about 9d or 10d with victuals in summer, less in winter, more in harvest. As in all other employment, terms and conditions depended on the locality, but women generally were paid at a lower rate; at Swinton and Simprin 'the day-labourers are often a set of neat, clean young girls, who feed in their parents' houses, and employ themselves in that easy and wholesome exercise, for 4d, 5d or 6d, according to their age and skill, without victuals from their employers, and who deck themselves out with their purchases in Swinton October fair by their gains'.[40] An unusual term was used near Chirnside, where were 'Mr. Hall's day-labourers, called *groat-men*: of which a considerable number was retained throughout the year, for the purposes of ditching, hedging and fence-building, and other works carried on in the extensive plantations of Whitehall'.[41] It was open to all day-labourers to work by the piece, and farmers tended to prefer this since 'Men working by the piece do at least $\frac{1}{4}$th, if not $\frac{1}{3}$rd more than on day's wages'.[42] Labourers engaged to mow hay, for instance, might get 1s 6d a day without victuals, but 'they often undertake it at 2s or 2s 6d per acre',[43] so that earnings in a day might be higher and the farmer have more work done.

III

Flexibility against a background of local circumstances and individual discussion was the basis of employment. Entries in farm day-books show that adjustments were always possible, particularly when payments in kind were involved, as they usually were. The actuality of being hired in the later eighteenth century is not conveyed by instances of averaged money wages, as if a modern standardised rate was already in being. Immediate local circumstances and the attitude of the individual farmer played across the market level, which was itself something which could alter within one season several times. Examples from a marginal farm near Hawick will serve as illustration.

Through the 1770s Walter Grieve, tenant in Branxholm Park, employed a typical range of farm labourers in a manner that was still usual twenty years later. The herd, Thomas Rutherford, was retained each year under unstated conditions fixed long before and never altered. James Laidlaw was ploughman in 1774. On 18th May the farmer recorded that 'I said I would take his wage down but not so much as to the rate of the Market, Tho the Men's wage fell greatly yesterday. I intend to take his down only 5sh., which is much within what the Common rate was, So that his wage by that rule will be £5str. in cash, a pair double soled shoes, and 1 sheep's grass at Linhope'. The following year Laidlaw's successor received £4.5s and a pair of shoes, a further 5s being left at the farmer's option to give if he felt it was deserved. By 1778 the same ploughman's wage had risen to £4 15s, a pair of single soled shoes and three sheep's grass, one till Martinmas and two all the year. At the same time two barnmen worked all the year for £4 4s and a pair of shoes, though in 1778 Archibald Henderson, barnman, was allowed in addition to the money a pair of double soled shoes, two pairs of single soled shoes, and grass for three sheep, and he also asked for some old clothes. A young lad was taken on in 1774 without clear conditions: 'Walt Tailor I intend to keep all the year and give him cloaths of every kind, and some wage for herding the Cows. But am not resolved what to make it yet, But being an Orphan, will not putt him to the worse'. Tailor was made cow-herd in summer, goad-man in winter, for which in the spring of 1777 he was given £1.10s, a lamb, grazing for another, and a pair of shoes; but when he left at Martinmas John Nichol received the shoes and 15s for succeeding him as goadman. In addition to these men four or five girls were hired as milkers, kitchen woman and byre woman, for around 18s and a pair of shoes, though miscellaneous extras and substitutes were occasionally included.[44]

In April 1800 Walter Grieve's son, James, followed the same method of hiring in the case of two existing workers whom he wished to keep on.[45] They lived in the old abandoned farmhouse on Branxholm Park hill. Jock Tait was the hind: 'He is to have the Parlour for his House, The South East quarter of the Garden for his yeard, a Cow's Milk — One stone of Meal per week, Five sheep — one Full of Barley sowen with mine on the Turnip Land. Two fulls of Tatoes 2 Caps of Lint sowen. And six pounds sterling in money. Also half a boll of Barley for Bread this year only. And leave to lead home a cart of coals he loosing them. Also a pair of old breeches to save his own in bigging the corn'.

And the shepherd was George Helm: 'To get a Cow's milk and one st. of Meal p week or 3 Bolls 4 stone a year and Thirty sheeps gras[s] and five summer sheep. The easter room upstairs and one end of the garret for his House, and the North west quarter of the Garden for his yeard, Two fulls of Potatoes sett and one Cap of lintseed sown. For which he herds the sheep'.

Such arrangements enabled the employee to hold out for a little extra, and the farmer could be generous to a good servant. Market conditions, however, were always in the background, and there were times when, with unfavourable economic conditions prevailing, farmers were unwilling or unable to afford all the labourers they needed. Thus the price of grain or wool could dictate the fate of the farm worker, as evidently happened in November 1800: 'The Hiring for Servants uncommonly bad few very few hired indeed and those at very low wages. Men £3 almost none more and a great many not so much. Women from 12/- to 15/- and some 20/- none more than 20/- and a great many was never asked to hire at all. Some even offered to serve without any wages and could not be taken Victual is so high'.[46]

Those who were hired for the whole or half-year, the true farm employees, on terms such as Tait or Helm, were not much concerned with money payments, whereas the day-labourer was. If the latter was like Alexander Somerville, he might travel all over the countryside looking for a sequence of work, and was paid as he went. In 1825, aged 15, Somerville spent the spring ploughing, and the early summer in hoeing turnips. He then moved on to the harvest as binder and shearer, getting a cart for leading in. That over, he took up piecework draining which produced 9s a week, and in the winter and spring of 1826 he broke stones for the public road at 1s 4d a cartload, which meant 1s a day. He did some gardening in the spring, worked for a Cockburnspath joiner in May at 1s 6d a day, and continued through the summer mowing grass, first on a lower farm, latterly on the uplands of Herriot.[47] This continuous movement was necessary to find work at all. On the other hand the day-labourer who was a cottar or otherwise locally based spent most of his days on one farm, and was paid periodically, like Robert Miller in 1830:

	£ s d
10½ days 'before mowing began'	1. 1. –
18½ days mowing at 1s 8d a day	1.10.10
Days 'twixt mowing and shearing'	1. –. 3
Harvest wages and odd days	2. 9. –
Other days	1. 1. 6
'days at the Walks in the wood'	1. 3. –
Coping a dyke — 78 Roods at 8d	2.12. –
Rebuilding old garden dyke 17 roods at 2s	1.14. –
Building a low feal dyke 88 roods at 1½d	– 11. –
'3 days o' his wife at turnips'	– 2.11
	£13. 5. 6

For this work Miller had received £6.18s.6d in advance on 1st April 1830, £1 on 16th October and on 30th December, £2 on 28th January, and two loads of potatoes valued at 10s. Due him on 29th March 1831, therefore, was £1.17s.–; the farmer paid him £2, and since he had also received 5 bolls of oats at 17s a boll, he owed his master £4.8s.0d. This debt was probably worked off, as he remained with the same farmer for several years.[48]

For both the hind and the day-labourer the normal working day lasted from 6 a.m. to 6 p.m. in summer, and as daylight allowed in winter. With two hours off for meals, it was in practice a ten-hour working day in the summer season which, according to the minister of Bowden, began for day-labourers on 13th February and lasted eight months.[49] The winter season was otherwise devised as the period between Martinmas and Candlemas, during which the average wage was reduced by about 2d, but it was more usual to see the change from summer to winter as occurring 'when the days shorten'.[50] Harvest time was exceptional; then, 'While the corn is carrying in, farm servants are ready to work at all times, labouring sometimes the greater part of the night'.[51] On 15th October 1795, towards the end of a very wet harvest, one farmer observed that 'it was well bestowed Labour indeed working all night on Wednesday last — Whenever corn is in a state fit to be stacked, that ought to be done ... And whenever there is any moonlight and corn fit to inn always to make use of it at any expence — Twice a week it would be no hardship to get servants to do the same during the Harvest and give them an allowance of Strong Beer'.[52]

In practice the farm worker rose much earlier than 6 a.m., in time to prepare the household and equipment for the day. Instructions given Jamie Riddell on 26th May 1845 illustrate not only the early start, but also the miscellaneous ordinary tasks and general principles involved in the summer farming day:

> Ring Wemen up every morning at 5.
> Be ready to begin work at 6. Go to Bed at *10*, And endeavour to prevent noise in Kitchen. Take a general *Charge* an[d] Care of everything about the Place. *Never wait to be told* to put anything Right.
> Be patient and Kind with Horses. Never overload them. Shoes removed and in 5 weeks.
> No Skin broke for want of Stuffing Harness.
> Swine cleaned *every week* and Dung led off.
> Keep all Implements not in daily use, In one place. Such as Spades, Picks, Grapes, Ropes, Rakes, Forks, Scythes, Corn Sacks, Pack Sheets etc. Carts washed and Kept in Shed. Roller, Drill etc Kept under cover.
> In wet days Red up and clean every corner. Grass cut for Cows every night.
> Prevent Names being Cut on Doors. No Branches broke off Trees at Whitegate for Riding or Driving. One man at home every Sunday. Be at all times Good Tempered, Ready, and obliging.

Your Strict attention to the above Shall not pass unrewarded.
Keep Gates Shut — Greasing Carts — Oiling Harness. Breaking Sticks. Carts in Repair. Sacks Ditto. Never leave Horses in Carts standing at Doors without a person at their head.[53]

Over and above all this, of course, was the main work of the day!

It may be easily seen that the steward overseer, a promoted worker, who received a wage equivalent in value to that of the best paid hind or herd, saved the farmer a great deal of disciplinary worry as well as taking care of general maintenance. His job, rather like that of the factor, was not a popular one: 'The steward was the man between the farmer and the worker, and he had to take the impudence of both'. Having received his orders from the farmer, he met the hinds and women every morning, assigned them their duties, and kept firm control. Leading the hinds was the 'first ploughman', sometimes called 'ploughman-steward', and a first or 'heid wumman' led the bondagers, each of these principal figures going in front of the work team and setting the pace.[54]

If the parish ministers are to be believed, the work and conditions of a farm labourer were such as to enable him to bring up a family in reasonable circumstances as long as there were no disruptions. 'Sober', 'frugal' and 'industrious' were terms often applied, 'content' and, as at Channelkirk, 'happy' more rarely. With a good manager for a wife a worker was supposed to be able to save a little and perhaps even prosper on occasion. Indulgence was not much approved of; servants enjoying a break at one of the Kelso fairs were said 'to lay out incredible sums of money, principally for wearing apparel, and female ornaments',[55] but a more thrifty spirit prevailed among most people, and money saved could be put into a bank. There had been some suspicion about the savings banks at first in case they were a device, on the part of the masters, to find out by how much a wage could be reduced, but the suspicion faded, and the servant girls in particular stored small amounts so that they could withdraw about £10 on getting married. In addition to the banks, most parts of the Borders in the early nineteenth century had a Friendly Society, into which workers paid a small contribution of about 5s or 6s a year to insure themselves against sickness or similar disaster. In some places a further form of insurance existed in the form of a Cow Club, which was a means of covering the loss of the labourer's cow. Those living in upper Lauderdale must have had rather grander notions of such a club since theirs was called the Oxton Bovial Society.

For Border farm workers it was possible to live 'decently', although close to the edge of poverty, save a little, spend a little on education, Sunday clothes, fair day entertainments, and occasionally on books and foodstuffs. There were also times when the hardship of work was relieved by cheerfulness, if not quite by a real holiday. Apart from the fair days, there was in particular the festivity marking the end of shearing and the end of leading in. The latter was known as the 'Kirn'; on 12th October 1796 a

G

farmer noted that 'The Servants keeps their Harvest home tonight. Gave them 4 pints o whiskie value 20/- and they had a Roasted goose for supper. And Dance as usual'.[56] The same man, a careful master, was liberal when circumstances suggested he should be. Four years earlier in 1792, the shearing was not finished until 26th October, and to mark the end of it he gave his servants six bottles of whisky to make into punch and killed a sheep — 'not a good one indeed' — which he thought would be needlessly extravagant if the corn was all cut in eight days as ideally it might be, but 'Where there is a long tedious Harvest such a Fete is quite necessary and an object to look to to cheer their spirits in a damned long wet Harvest as all ours are'.[57] More impromptu and everyday pleasures, like the smell and taste of oatmeal porridge bubbling ready for the hungry labourer, an evening dance in the farm kitchen to the music of the hind's fiddle, the fresh milk produce, or just a fine spring morning in the country, made life much more tolerable, and it is certainly not possible to accept that the life of a Border farm worker prior to, say, 1850 was one of downtrodden misery, drudgery and squalor.

IV

G. E. Evans, writing in 1968 of East Anglian farming, referred to 'the relatively unchanging rhythm of farming during the whole of the time prior to modern mechanization', and of the important recollections of old people whose 'experience on the farm during their boyhood days was not much different from that of a boy who lived on the same farm during, for instance, the fourteenth century'.[58] Continuity of long-established practice was certainly still an important element in the life of those living in the Borders at the beginning of the twentieth century, and hinds and shepherds born about 1890 were brought up at a time when there were still many features of the farm environment that had been familiar to their ancestors of two centuries earlier. At the same time they also grew up in a quite different world, and the features which stand out as the symptoms and agents of change often seem more prominent than those indicating the continuity and stability in a traditional society.

It would indeed be hard to think of any period without change. Farming practice might not have altered much over centuries, but in 1780 Border farm workers were already living in circumstances very different from those of their grandparents. The old runrig farm towns had disappeared only forty or fifty years before, and many of the small tenants had become labourers, especially in the lower arable areas to which they had moved from the uplands in the hope of work on the new large farms where plough teams, dykers, drainers and others were ever more in demand. Hill farmers at first did not rebuild vacated cottages when they fell down, for their labour needs were less, but by 1800 this trend was being reversed in places where demolition had gone too far. Tradesmen cottagers received encouragement to move as landowners enthusiastically established new villages, and the introduction of manufacture was such a popular idea that the ministers of quite unlikely places, including Channelkirk, Edrom, Eckford, and Hounam, all thought it would be worthwhile. The Duke of Buccleuch had approved the creation of a new town at Langholm, another at Copshawholm in Liddesdale, and groups of feus in almost every district of his Border estates. To these and other centres the country tradesmen flocked in the hope of a successful industrial future, and New Castleton had been established following a petition from them, with the expectation that a village would quickly develop into a manufacturing town — which in that case, to the disappointment of their descendents, it never did. The value of these new settlements, like that of the old villages, was that tradesmen were held in the locality who might otherwise have moved to remoter towns, and to them also came some more modern services such as post offices, banks and shops. Country tailors and weavers eventually became confined to the villages, where they set up small businesses. The tailor gave up travelling round the farms, a practice called 'whipping the cat', and, in the face of manufactured goods, both found less work, so that Neville, in 1909, noted of Ford parish that only one or two tailors existed where once there had been six or seven,[59] and the minister of Drummelzier recorded that in 1844 the one dyer and six of the seven weavers had gone. The latter also remarked that 'The giving up of weaving and dyeing is one of the greatest changes that have taken place in parochial economy'.[60]

There had long been feued or rented holdings on the farms and in the old villages, and the new settlements added more. Those on farms varied in size; for example at East Newton, Whitsome, they ranged from 'a very small feu of much less than an acre' to the 60 acres possessed by John Herriot.[61] Village feus were generally about two acres, but, if the ground was reasonable, even this amount was not to be scorned; at Chirnside, 'Out of an acre, although rented at 30s, a day-labourer, without any other expense but that of the ploughing, and without abstracting above 2 or 3 days of his earnings throughout the year, can raise, in crops of corn, potatoes, turnips or clover, what is, at least, of £5 value to him ...'. Such small holdings, and the lesser farms scattered throughout the Borders, offered to the farm labourers an opportunity to better their circumstances, and were in a way a replacement for the vanished joint tenures of old. Some of these stepping-stones to farming, never anything like as numerous as in the Lake District for instance, still exist, but in the later nineteenth century the agricultural depression rendered a two-acre holding insufficient as a farming unit, and the process of combining farms has seen the disappearance of the majority. This was a change that widened the gap between labourer and tenant or landowner.

Socially also that gap widened. The period of the Napoleonic wars, with its artificially raised prices, saw farmers prosper and become gentlemen, who spent their money on their farms, on new, substantial houses, fine clothes, travel and entertainment, boarding education, and investments, all of which were outside the world of the labourers. No longer did farmers mix with the workers and servants housed in the farm, and 'the universal practice' of sharing the same table in the kitchen was given up.[63] The difference between the kitchen and the dining room became definite in many a farmhouse, and it was perhaps an inevitable result that the farm servant should learn, as he had done before 1900, to doff his cap to the farmer in the morning.

The well-to-do farmer, more experienced commercially than he had ever been, was constrained to manage his farm as a business, and so reviewed his labour requirements, cutting back where necessary. Cottars were increasingly turned off the land in large numbers. Similarly the sheep farmer around 1820 was finding that milking ewes was not worth the loss of condition that followed, so the girl milkers were no longer needed; and at much the same time new dipping substances were coming on the market which rendered the laborious and expensive task of smearing unnecessary, with the result that no smearers were hired. As in urban manufacture, machinery was increasingly rendering certain forms of manual labour unnecessary. By the 1790s threshing machines were beginning to be used in the Borders, and though they could cost between £60 and £100 to set up, it was recognised that 'this expence is quickly repaid by the saving of labour'.[64] In spite of some reserve about the machine, the barnman, who often received a boll for every twenty-five bolls threshed, soon found himself redundant, and in Berwickshire by 1905 this 'quite distinct class of agricultural workers' had long been extinct.[65] The goadman too was a casualty of mechanical change, since the improved two-horse ploughs did not require him. Machines needed operators, but on balance, as the nineteenth century proceeded, there was a reduction in labour which was remembered as something of a revolution by a Cockburnspath farmer of the early 1900s.[66] The reaper and the later self-binder replaced the large bands of mowers and shearers, especially those Highland and Irish labourers who came every season, and the more efficient drills, lifters, dressers and so on all helped to reduce labour costs by speeding up the agricultural processes. More could be achieved by one man in a given time, and the harvest could be completed in days rather than weeks.

All this did not happen without distress. The depression of the 1820s which bankrupted many farmers came as a shock to those labourers who had grown used to higher wages, and the indications are that employment around 1830 was in some districts difficult to come by. In a letter to the Duke of Buccleuch, dated 5th October that year, William Oliver wrote of 'the necessity of devising employment for the Labouring Classes' in Liddesdale, since, following the depressed state of the markets, tenants were not financially in a position to make improvements which would require labour, and the incessant rains of the past summer had severely damaged the potato crop and made the peat fuel almost useless. He continued: 'I am therefore convinced, that unless your Grace concur in commencing some Public Work, they and their Families must be reduced to Misery and starvation. I feel that it would be suffient to appeal to your Grace's Humanity and Charity, but when I contemplate the spirit of Discontent and Insubordination which has gained such an ascendancy abroad and is spreading so rapidly in our own Country, I would further urge that self-interest makes it imperious that we should endeavour to stop its Progress by giving Employment at fair wages, and thus remove any ground for murmuring and the other Consequences which are too likely to result from Misery and Idleness'.[67]

Oliver thought road work was the answer. Elsewhere reclamation of land and enclosure of fields was being carried on at the instance of landowners and better-off farmers, which meant a greater demand for dykers, hedgers, ploughmen and carters of lime, and as the pace quickened, rescuing labour from its predicament, the abundant drainage operations, accompanied by the erection of tile works on many estates, also provided extensive employment. A further limited period of relief was provided by the construction of the various Border railways in the 1850s and early '60s. The countryside, however, could not, in spite of these enterprises, take up and hold all the available labour, and, as with the other rural areas of Britain, the second half of the nineteenth century saw, in the Borders, a population decline and migrations to the towns and abroad.

The inhabitants of a Border parish, like those elsewhere in the Lowlands were perhaps more mobile than might be imagined. About 1790 the remote district of Glenholm in Peeblesshire had a population of 350, of whom 158 had been born in other parishes. A survey of Ettrick parish in 1832 shows that among adults far less than half were natives, the majority coming from anywhere between lower Eskdale and Peebles, with one or two wanderers from Ireland and the Highlands.[68] The same survey also records a few departures to America, for already emigration overseas was occurring in several parts of the Borders. Encouraged by seductive advertisements in local newspapers, the younger sons of farmers, village tradesmen, cottars and day-labourers took themselves off abroad in ever-increasing numbers, many going in response to letters from the advance guard of relatives. As early as the 1830s the minister of Foulden, not far from Berwick, noticed that emigration had become common, especially of the robust, enterprising and provident.[69] On 2nd December 1880, a native of Hawick, Mr. Lancelot Watson, agent for the Iowa Islands and Loan Company, read a paper on Emigration to the Teviotdale Farmers' Club, emphasising 'that it was the very best thing for men with limited means, strong arms, and determined energies and brains, to engage in'.[70]

Emigration of any kind, whether locally or abroad, was the outcome of dissatisfaction with the state of things at home and of temptation by possibly better conditions elsewhere. In the Borders the progress of woollen manufacture in the towns, with higher wages, was the most immediate draw. Material progress in the countryside was uneven, bringing improved housing and diet in some places, and an unsatisfied desire for these improvements in others. By the mid-1830s sturdy new cottages with three rooms and a loft, slated or pantiled roofs, and stone and lime walls, were being provided for the labourers in many districts, especially by such enlightened landowners as Lady Helen Hall at Cockburnspath, and later in the century a further generation of dwellings was built, also in rows but this time with two storeys. Farms today can show three stages of improved workers' houses, the most substantial building always being the steward's or head shepherd's which stood separately from the rest. But mingled with all the new were the ramshackle, sagging habitations, rotten in the walls and thatch, of the less fortunate labourers, illustrated by Gilly in his *Peasantry of the Border*.[71] In 1861 the majority of dwellings in a Border parish had only one or two windows, and here and there were a few with none at all, though the explanation for this was usually that the inhabitants were railway construction workers living in huts, or vagrants sheltering in a barn.[72] It was at least 1900 before most of the old cottages had disappeared, and the last thatched cot in Yarrow was still occupied by a retired farm worker in 1904. Housing in itself, however, was not the greatest complaint.

Wages, fluctuating in the short term, and varying from place to place all over the Borders, tended to move slowly upwards. Day-labourers gained the least, and the range of 8d to 1s 6d a day earned by workers at Kirndean, Liddesdale, in 1883 seems to be little better than that available a century earlier.[73] On the other hand, male workers on the Manderston estate in Berwickshire in 1896 were paid fortnightly at a daily rate of between 1s 8d and 3s 8d while women received 1s 5d or 1s 6d.[74] Since money wages did not rise greatly in the intervening thirteen years, it may be that these two sets of figures represent low and high levels of pay, differing in part at least according to the district and type of farming. The shepherd and hind were rather better off. In the Hawick area, for example, the hind was paid £7 excluding board or gains in 1793,[75] £12 'besides victuals and lodging' in 1839,[76] and £25 along with gains and allowances for workers to be hired by him in 1874.[77] By 1901, the money element stood at £31. Around Greenlaw the hind's wages with gains increased from about £26 in 1834 to £30 in 1847, £33 10s in 1867, £48 in 1872, £40 in 1887, and £50 in 1902.[78] In relation to the fairly static and in some cases diminished prices of merchant goods between 1845 and 1900, a much improved standard of living was achieved by the end of the nineteenth century.

Perhaps the most profound change, taking place gradually but relentlessly throughout the period, was not that in living standards, or even that brought about by the introduction of machinery, but the alteration in attitudes and customary arrangements which helped to detach the farm worker from his traditional past. Life fell increasingly under the control of those who thought they knew best. Individuals like the great improving laird, Sir John Buchanan Riddell of Riddell, and farmers' societies which were instituted in every district, established meetings, shows, and competitions at which the farm-labourer was expected to show off his pack sheep, his ploughing skill, or his number of children, with the aim of winning a medal. About 1845, after 'a great commotion' in the market square at Wooler, the 'bond' was broken when a farmer hired ploughmen, leaving out the bondage condition.[79] Thereafter the system died out in north Northumberland, while after a period of attack in the newspapers and by men like the Rev. John Thomson in Hawick, who in 1869 published letters and speeches denouncing the 'bondager' condition, it faded away in the Scottish Borders as well, though everywhere the female out-worker, retaining her old name, continued on the farm as a direct employee of the farmer. Similarly the hiring fairs were denounced by ministers and papers as occasions of drunkenness and immorality; the *Peeblesshire Advertiser* for 25th October 1879 declared that the fairs were 'a positive disgrace to our boasted civilisation' and 'simply vehicles for propagating untold evils'. In spite of the disapproval the old hiring days survived until the 1930s, but long before 1900 private communication and newspaper advertisements were taking over. From the 1860s onwards farmers called into question the gains and pack systems because of the inconvenience they caused and their 'primitive' nature, so that by 1914 money wages only were taking over, a desirable change in times of prosperity when workers might wish to buy the increasingly varied goods available in shops or on carriers' carts, but the reverse when prices were high and the labourer found himself without the shelter from bad times afforded by gains.

Religion and education added the final touch to all these material changes. Customary amusements and superstitions were dismissed as relics of barbarism. Songs and stories were no longer the popular entertainment, a change that James Hogg thought the most striking in the world of the Border peasantry,[80] and even the language was becoming different. The minister of Eddleston wrote in the 1830s of the 'corrupt Scotch, with a barbarous admixture of English', spoken in his parish, and observed that only a few very old people retained 'the Scottish dialect in its purity'.[81] The teachers in the country schools scorned what was seen as the ignorance of former times, introducing their pupils to a greater awareness of the world and substituting, as the minister of Yarrow put it, general knowledge for local attachments.[82] Such separation from the immediate surroundings made it easier to think of moving away, and easier to do so.

The Border farm worker had not been quite so well off as his neighbours of East Lothian, mid-Northumberland, and Cumberland, but family letters, inventories of a girl's 'providing' upon her marriage, glimpses of the cottage interior through the eyes of a visitor, and reminiscences by the workers themselves indicate that at least from about 1840 onwards there was a measure of comfort at home and of satisfaction at work. It is never possible to quantify contentment and happiness, but in this connection it is as well to bear in mind that it is the ministers and writers from the early nineteenth century onwards who speak of the mean hovels and harsh conditions of the poor labourers,[83] and Janet Bathgate who greeted the completed new hovel at Hartleap with 'How fine all things look now',[84] and the servant maid of 1910 who, with a washing day that started at 2 a.m., recollected it with 'But we were happy in thae days'.[85]

NOTES

1. Old Statistical Account of Scotland. New edition. Vol III. The Eastern Borders (hereafter *O.S.A.*), p. 123.

2. *O.S.A.*, p. 841.

3. *Ibid.*, p. 832.

4. *Ibid.*, p. 104.

5. *Ibid.*, p. 491.

6. J. Little, *Practical Observations on the Improvement and Management of Mountain Sheep and Sheep Farms* (second edition, Edinburgh, 1818), p. 85.

7. *O.S.A.*, p. 483.

8. New Statistical Account of Scotland (Edinburgh, 1842), (hereafter *N.S.A.*), Berwickshire, p. 174.

9. Border Country Life Museum (B.C.L.M.), Grieve Papers.

10. *O.S.A.*, p. 625.

11. *Ibid.*, p. 616.

12. *Ibid.*, p. 668.

13. *Ibid.*, p. 307.

14. Traquair House Muniments.

15. W. Steele, *Beauties of Gilsland* (London, 1836), p. 131.

16. C. Findlater, *General View of the Agriculture of the County of Peebles* (Edinburgh, 1802), p. 47.

17. B.C.L.M., Grieve Papers, Diary No. 10, p. 119.

18. *N.S.A.* (Berwickshire), p. 77.

19. D. D. Dixon, *Whittingham Vale, Northumberland* (Newcastle-upon-Tyne, 1895), pp. 71–72.

20. *N.S.A.* (Dumfriesshire), p. 413.

21. *N.S.A.* (Peeblesshire), p. 126.

22. *N.S.A.* (Berwickshire), p. 178.

23. *Ibid.*, p. 346.

24. G. Scott, 'Reminiscences of Borthwick Water Sixty Years Ago', *Transactions of Hawick Archaeological Society* (1909), pp. 76–77.

25. *N.S.A.* (Dumfriesshire), p. 435.

26. *N.S.A.* (Berwickshire), p. 114.

27. *O.S.A.*, pp. 513–14.

28. *N.S.A.* (Peeblesshire), p. 97.

29. *N.S.A.* (Roxburghshire), p. 113.

30. Dixon, *Whittingham Vale,* pp. 182–87.

31. H. M. Neville, *A Corner in the North* (Newcastle-upon-Tyne, 1909), p. 13.

32. A. Somerville, *The Autobiography of a Working Man* (London, 1848, 1967 edition), p. 68.

33. *O.S.A.,* p. 297.

34. *Ibid.,* pp. 137–38.

35. *Ibid.,* p. 244.

36. J. Bathgate, *Aunt Janet's Legacy to her Nieces* (fifth edition, Selkirk, 1901), p, 53.

37. *O.S.A.,* p. 759.

38. *Ibid.,* p. 247.

39. *N.S.A.* (Berwickshire), p. 78.

40. *O.S.A.,* p. 297.

41. *Ibid.,* 53.

42. *Ibid.,* p. 374.

43. *Ibid.,* p. 297.

44. B.C.L.M., Grieve Papers.

45. B.C.L.M., Grieve Papers, Diary No. 12, pp. 116–17, 121.

46. *Ibid.,* p. 183.

47. Somerville, *Autobiography,* pp. 64–65, 67.

48. B.C.L.M., Grieve Papers, Diary No. 25, p. 174.

49. *O.S.A.,* p. 374.

50. *Ibid.,* p. 654.

51. *N.S.A.* (Berwickshire), p. 239.

52. B.C.L.M., Grieve Papers, Diary No. 10, p. 90.

53. B.C.L.M., Grieve Papers.

54. Oral information, Mr. P. Jeffrey, Jedburgh, July 1975.

55. *O.S.A.,* p. 16.

56. B.C.L.M., Grieve Papers, Diary No. 10, p. 197.

57. *Ibid.,* Diary No. 8, p. 140.

58. G. E. Evans, *The Farm and the Village* (London, 1969, paperback edition 1974), pp. 14–15.

59. Neville, *A Corner in the North,* p. 80.

60. *N.S.A.* (Peeblesshire), p. 77.

61. *O.S.A.,* pp. 307–08.

62. *Ibid., pp.* 59–60.

63. *N.S.A.* (Peeblesshire), p. 148.

64. *O.S.A.,* p. 243.

65. R. Gibson, *An Old Berwickshire Town* (Edinburgh and London, 1905), p. 222.

66. J. Wilson, 'Half a Century as a Border Farmer', *Transactions of the Highland and Agricultural Society* 5th ser., XIV (1902), pp. 35–48.

67. Scottish Record Office, Buccleuch Muniments, GD 224/503.

68. B.C.L.M., MS Survey of Ettrick Parish 1832, pp. 89–90.

69. *N.S.A.* (Berwickshire), p. 263.

70. *Résumé of the Discussions of the Teviotdale Farmers Club 1859–1909* (Hawick, 1909), i, p. 162.

71. W. S. Gilly, *The Peasantry of the Border: An Appeal on their Behalf* (Berwick upon Tweed, 1841, new edition, 1973). Facing, p. 15.

72. *The Southern Counties' Register and Directory* (Kelso, 1866).
73. B.C.L.M., Kirndean Wages Book.
74. B.C.L.M., Extracts from Manderston Estate Records, Berwickshire.
75. *O.S.A.*, p. 449.
76. B.C.L.M., Grieve Papers, Wages Books.
77. *Ibid.*
78. Gibson, *An Old Berwickshire Town*, pp. 208–09.
79. Neville, *A Corner in the North*, p. 13.
80. J. Hogg, 'On the changes in the Habits, Amusements, and Condition of the Scottish Peasantry', *The Quarterly Journal of Agriculture* (1831–32), iii, pp. 256–264.
81. *N.S.A.* (Peeblesshire), p. 149.
82. *N.S.A.* (Selkirkshire), pp. 57–58.
83. J. Russell, *Reminiscences of Yarrow* (Edinburgh and London, 1886), p. 76.
84. Bathgate, *Aunt Janet's Legacy*, p. 79.
85. Oral information, Miss A. Storie, Yetholm, 1967.

Part II. Working Groups

6

Women Workers, 1850–1914

T. M. Devine

An important characteristic of the Scottish agricultural labour force in the nineteenth century was the widespread employment of women in the daily and seasonal routine of lowland farms. Of the 165,096 persons enumerated as farm grieves (or bailliffs), agricultural labourers, shepherds and farm servants (indoor) in 1871, 42,796, or 26 per cent of the total, were women.[1] This, however, was an underestimate of the entire female contribution because the census figure did not include the army of seasonal labourers who came during the spring, summer and autumn months to sow, harvest and gather Scotland's grain, green and fruit crops. Moreover, since the census total referred only to 'number employed', it took no account of the wives and daughters of smaller farmers and crofters who were a vital, though normally unpaid, component of the work force of the dairying districts of the south-west and of the north-east counties of Aberdeen, Banff and Kincardine.[2] In relation to the employment structure in the English countryside, the general engagement of women in Scotland was distinctive. As defined by the classes mentioned above, female wage earners in agriculture in England and Wales formed 5.8 per cent of the total number employed, and only one county, Northumberland, where 25 per cent of wage earners were female, approached the Scottish average.[3] As George Culley, the agricultural reporter for south-east Scotland, noted in 1870, 'The Scotch practice differs from the English in the much more extensive employment of women. Throughout the whole of my district women are employed in all the lighter and in not a few of the heavier operations of farm labour'.[4]

Here Culley was merely echoing the comment of Henry Stephens thirty years before: 'field workers consist mainly of young women in Scotland but mainly of men and boys in England'.[5] Women carried out virtually every task on the farm except those which directly involved the management of horses. Their duties were to perform all the 'normal operations' of the fields and those concerned with the use of 'smaller implements' not worked by horses. The former included sowing potatoes, gathering weeds, picking stones, collecting potatoes and filling drains with stones; the latter embraced such varied jobs as pulling turnips and

98

preparing them for feeding stock, barn-work, carrying seed corn, spreading manure on the land, hoeing potatoes and turnips, and weeding and reaping corn-crops. In addition, they had a monopoly of milking and cheese-making. Thus in 1812 it could be said, 'there are few operations in husbandry in which women are not employed, except those of ploughing and threshing'.[6] The purpose of this essay is to survey the reasons for this characteristic pattern of female employment in Scotland, then to attempt to categorise and describe the varied types of female work-groups, and finally to examine why regular farm employment for women was becoming increasingly unpopular in the later nineteenth century.

I

Before the late eighteenth century some farm tasks had, by custom and tradition, become accepted as the special province of women, and their role in these areas survived throughout the nineteenth century. It was, for example, the invariable custom in Scotland that women attended to the cows. In Ayrshire, 'unlike England, every process connected with the milk, the butter or the cheese is conducted by women and rightly too'.[7] Moreover, in the smaller farms of the era before the 'Agricultural Revolution', wives and daughters had inevitably formed an important part of the family work team. Between 1750 and 1830, this small farm sector did not disappear but survived strongly in modified form in the south-west and north-east lowlands. The women of the family continued to make a major contribution to its labour needs.[8] Also, in the old world, wives of married ploughmen were regarded by farmers on larger units as a useful source of additional labour at the grain harvest. The wives of Berwickshire hinds were obliged to work during the harvest without wages as part of their husband's labour contract in lieu of payment for the rent of the family cottage.[9] This system prevailed throughout the south-eastern district of arable farming and reflected its particular needs for extra labour at harvest time. Over the centuries the sickle was the tool for cutting cereal crops and it was employed chiefly but not exclusively by women. The stalks were cut low down, and 'for this reason it was especially used by women, who are said to be physiologically better adapted to bending than men'.[10] These social attitudes on what constituted male or female tasks continued to influence the labour market for women workers throughout the period covered by this essay.

Demand for female labour was also powerfully affected by the changing economic and social structure of Scottish farming between 1780 and 1830. It was in that period that specialist horsemen emerged on the medium and larger farms. Ploughmen were increasingly withdrawn from the range of farm tasks and instead devoted their time to working with a particular pair of animals in ploughing, carting and related activities.[11] As George

Robertson noted in his *Rural Recollections,* it was 'employing professional men to professional objects'.[12] The tendency was already apparent in the Lothians in the middle decades of the eighteenth century. Ploughmen were no longer used directly in the harvesting process but instead worked with their horses 'directly behind the shearers as fast as they could get out of their way, tilling the ridges that were in the intervals betwixt the rows of stalks'.[13] The result of this new specialisation was to enhance the status of the male farm servant, contribute to the development of his skills and to a sense of pride in the job and, in the long run, increase labour productivity. Necessarily, however, it also meant the recruitment of other regular employees. The extensive employment of female outworkers was one response to this growing differentiation of labour within the new farm structure. In essence, the old blurred distinction between male and female tasks was preserved and strengthened within the new agriculture. Thus in the north-east lowlands in the second half of the nineteenth century 'the cultural prescription against women working with horses was absolute', while before the First World War 'a Lothian ploughman would feel insulted if asked to pull turnips and most ploughmen would refuse to do byre work'.[14]

The employment of female labour reflected other economic and social trends in the late eighteenth century. In that period sub-tenancy was under widespread attack throughout the rural lowlands. The small plots of land which cottagers and sub-tenants had held in return for labour services on adjacent larger farms were now increasingly absorbed within bigger and more compact units. Sub-tenancies were more valuable after c. 1770 to main tenants as food prices rose in the final decades of the eighteenth century, while the achievement of higher levels of labour productivity required the recruitment of full-time workers over whom farmers could exert more discipline and control.[15] Yet the sub-tenant class had been a crucial source of seasonal labour and, as their ranks were thinned, farmers in some areas consolidated the family system of hiring by which married male servants were employed on condition that they could produce a woman to work whenever needed. Seasonal migrants from towns and villages, from the Highlands and Ireland but also members of the families of the married ploughman class, were seen as a reserve army of labour which remained vital in the new farming.[16] Tied female labour, available for seasonal tasks, was especially crucial in the south-east because that area was thinly peopled, with large, isolated farms and limited access to town labour because of the poorly developed industrial structure of the region. Inevitably, farmers were forced to depend on the female dependents of their married workers if for no other reason than that it was difficult to obtain an alternative supply which was both cheap and reliable: 'the practice is good, because it enables the farmer to command a certain number of hands at all times, and also to accomplish his ends by his own resources, independent of extraneous aid. It is no answer to say that women may be hired out of villages when their services are required, because many large farms are situated far from any village and when trade is brisk women are encouraged to desert the fields ...'.[17]

The problem was not simply or directly associated with the traditional grain harvest, because that lasted for only three to four weeks and its labour requirements, though great, were essentially of short duration. The difficulty was the needs of the new agriculture differed radically from those of the old. More land was absorbed into production and the existing arable was worked more intensively. The development of new field systems, based on turnips and sown grasses, and the cultivation of new crops such as potatoes, stretched the farmer's busy time both backwards and forwards in the year. It therefore became necessary to recruit labour for the new cycle of tasks of weeding, sowing, thinning and gathering which endured from spring to early winter.[18]

Female labour had considerable attractions for those farmers who were developing the new rotations. These systems were highly labour-intensive. Root crops were the most demanding of labour, requiring as many as ten to fifteen worker-days per acre, compared with between four to five worker-days in corn harvesting with the sickle.[19] Robert Hope of Fenton Barns, near Haddington, employed thirteen ploughmen in the early 1830s, a further six seasonal workers in winter but an additional eighteen over a period of 24 weeks for weeding and hoeing turnips. There was, therefore, an incentive to exploit cheap sources of labour if at all possible.[20] Valerie Morgan has shown that female cash wages in Scottish agriculture in the 1790s were approximately half the pay of men.[21] Society regarded women as dependents, whether as wives or daughters, who were not entitled to the same rate for the job as their male counterparts. These differentials were strongly influenced by custom and by what was deemed an acceptable proportion of the male rate.[22] Despite the growing shortage of female labour after 1870, in many areas, these traditional distinctions were preserved with only partial erosion. The advantage of hiring women was obvious. One observer in 1867 put it bluntly: 'Farmers employ women because their wages are about half *what is expected* by men'.[23] There were significant economic benefits in a hiring policy which combined in an effective working partnership, a corps of skilled ploughmen and large numbers of low-paid women. As the Royal Commission on Employment of Women in Agriculture put it in 1870: 'It is no doubt owing to the comparatively lower wages at which female labour can be obtained that Scotch farming in an economical point of view owes a considerable portion of its success'.[24]

It was also recognised that women often gave better service than men. They were regarded as particularly adept at hand-weeding, reaping with the sickle and, when the scythe, a man's tool, was widely adopted, gathering at the grain harvest. In the early nineteenth century, when the sickle was still the most important hand-tool at harvest, several commentators acknowledged the special skill of women and asserted that when work was done by the piece, they regularly earned more than men.[25] Their expertise in turnip-picking was a tribute to their manual dexterity: 'for a woman, though not so *strong* is *more alert,* and generally, *more neat* in picking the young turnips with her fingers, when they are so close that the hoe cannot separate them'.[26] Early training maximised these physical advantages, as the young daughters of farm servants were reared from their earliest years in the handling of the hoe and other tools.

It would be wrong, on the other hand, to conclude that the widespread employment of women in Scottish agriculture was only conditioned by the nature of the farming system itself. Of considerable additional significance was the nature of industrial demand for rural labour. Scottish farmers had to compete with industrial employers to a much greater extent than their fellows in most parts of England, outside the northern region. Industrial and urban development, though most rapid and vigorous in west-central Scotland, occurred widely throughout the lowland zone. Few rural areas were remote from the pull of alternative employment in towns, cities and industrial villages.[27] Yet, after c. 1830, Scottish economic expansion depended on the growth of the heavy industries of coal, iron, steel, engineering and shipbuilding. Overwhelmingly, therefore, the manufacturing sector had most need of adult male labour, and the evidence suggests that the bulk of its requirement were satisfied by male migrants from the lowland countryside.[28] This sexual bias in the industrial labour market helps to explain why cash wages for men in agriculture were rising in the 1830s and 1840s when female rates were stagnant.[29] Farmers were having to bid higher to retain their male workers as competition from industry increased. In some areas, this may have provided a further incentive to hire women. Thus, in the industrialised county of Lanarkshire, young men were drawn to coalmining in the 1870s and 1880s, a trend which caused heavy reliance on female labour.[30]

Yet, the point, though relevant, should be kept in perspective. Women were widely employed on Scottish farms long before the major expansion of the heavy industries. Some areas, such as East Lothian and the counties of Berwick and Roxburgh, were among the most significant employers of women in agriculture though they experienced only limited industrial development. Moreover, as the economy expanded on the basis of investment in manufacturing and mining, it generated a larger service sector in which women found employment in increasing numbers. By the final three decades of the nineteenth century, then, urban areas were attracting *both* men and women from the land at a faster rate, and this was reflected in a secular increase in female agricultural wages.[31] To fully explain, therefore, why women were such an important part of the farm labour force in Scotland, due attention must be paid to the influence of custom and agrarian structure, already discussed, as well as to the effect of industrial demand for male workers.

II

It is exceedingly difficult to place female workers in precise classifications which have enduring validity both over time and space. However, between 1850 and 1914 roughly four broad groups can be identified: (a) regular and full-time employees, mainly outworkers in the south-east and dairymaids and byrewomen in the dairying districts of the south-west; (b) family workers; (c) 'in-and-out' girls whose work was partly domestic but also involved field labour; (d) part-time, seasonal or casual workers.

(a) *Regular workers*

Two sub-groups can be discerned here. First, there were women servants employed in the dairying districts of Dumbarton, Lanarkshire, Renfrewshire, Ayrshire and Wigtownshire. They were unmarried and hired to carry out all the dairying work of the farm. Normally they were boarded and lodged by the farmers. They were among the highest-paid group of women workers because of the long hours and hard labour associated with dairying. Byre women were also kept to clean the stalls and tend cattle. The position, however, was complicated because only large and medium-sized farms could afford to hire specialist dairywomen.[32] Often, the work was done by female members of the farmer's family, and when extra labour was hired, the girls were expected to do field work and domestic chores as well as help in milking. Such women were exposed to a particularly arduous regime. One dairy woman in Dunbartonshire in the early 1890s described a typical day: '...we start at 5 a.m. and then we milk till 7. We have breakfast, porridge at 7 and a further breakfast at 8. In the house we start at once to work after meal, which occupies scarcely half an hour. Dinner is at 12; start as soon as finished to go and feed the cows; we work away with straw, turnips and other jobs till 4, when we have tea. Then feed cows again; rest from 5-30 to 7, then milk till 8; then fodder cows which takes half an hour'.[33] Perhaps, not surprisingly, skilled dairy workers, despite their high wages, were in short supply in many districts by 1900.[34]

The second group were full-time regular outworkers principally employed in the south-eastern counties of Fife, the Lothians, Berwick and Roxburgh and to a much lesser extent elsewhere. According to the census of 1871, females classed as whole-time agricultural labourers comprised 33 per cent of females employed in Haddington, 32 per cent in Berwick, 30 per cent in Roxburgh, 28 per cent in the county of Edinburgh and 24 per cent in Fife.[35] These ratios can be compared with the north-east counties where, in Aberdeen, only 3 per cent of females employed were full-time agricultural labourers, in Banff 5 per cent and in Kincardine 6 per cent. In

H

the farms of the south-east, therefore, there was very heavy use of regular female workers. In Linlithgow, women were reckoned to be employed to the extent of four to every 100 acres of cultivated land, while in Berwick and Roxburgh in the 1860s, about half the adult labourers and farm servants were women.[36] Table 1 demonstrates the extensive employment of women in the Lothians.

Table 1   *Particulars of Horses and Labourers to Acres in 25 Farms in Mid and East Lothian, 1893*

	Per 100 acres	Per 100 acres arable	Per 100 acres under crops
No. of horses	2.27	2.8	3.57
Labourers (regular)			
Men and strong lads	2.33	2.9	3.67
Women and young boys	1.75	2.21	2.76
	4.08	5.11	6.44

Source: *R.C. on Labour, 1893*, Part II, p. 131.

This dependence on women was partly associated with the cropping structure of these areas, with their great emphasis on the cultivation of green crops within the rotation systems. As Table 2 illustrates, the south-eastern counties had the largest proportion of land laid down to these crops of any in Scotland. Turnips were the ones most demanding of female labour. Just as significant was the larger average size of farm in the region: 'a farm of less than 100 acres would not afford constant employment for women'.[37] Regular outworkers were hardly used at all in the small farm districts of the south-west and north-east.

The nature of the supply of female labour in the area varied over time. In the later eighteenth century married ploughmen were hired on condition that they could supply a woman worker when required. Originally this was probably the ploughman's wife, at least in some districts. Thus in Berwickshire, 'wives of hinds are generally bound to shear in harvest without wages, but with full harvest food, and must work at all outdoor labour especially sowing and hay harvest, for the customary wages of the country'.[38] However, the new farming demanded more regular work throughout the year, and this inevitably conflicted with a wife's domestic responsibilities. In addition, it was usual for the hind's wife in the Lothians to keep a cow whose milk and butter were not only an

Table 2   *Percentage of Total Area of Land in Lowland Scottish Counties under Green Crops, 1891*

Aberdeen	8.0	Kincardine	8.8
Ayr	2.2	Kinross	6.2
Banff	6.7	Kirkcudbright	2.9
Berwick	*10.8*	Lanark	2.7
Clackmannan	3.8	*Linlithgow*	*7.8*
Dumbarton	2.3	Nairn	3.8
Dumfries	3.7	Peebles	2.3
Edinburgh	*8.2*	Perth	2.8
Elgin	6.0	Renfrew	3.6
Fife	*13.4*	*Roxburgh*	*6.0*
Forfar	8.8	Selkirk	2.0
Haddington	*14.0*	Stirling	2.8
		Wigtown	5.8

Source: *Board of Agriculture, Agricultural Statistics for Great Britain for 1891, Parliamentary Papers* 1890–1, (c. 6524), LCI. South-eastern counties in italics.

important element in family diet, but which, when sold in local markets, provided a vital source of cash income for households mainly rewarded through payment in kind to the father. Significantly, therefore, the extent to which *married* women worked regularly in the fields in the south-east tended to vary according to the local custom of keeping a cow. So in Linlithgow, 'because the hind's cow is absent, the proportion of married women employed is greater than further south'.[39] The labour returns from 10 farms in that county for the spring and winter quarters of 1867 indicate that 55 married and 99 single women worked during spring and 35 married and 74 single were hired during winter. On the other hand, in Haddington, a 'cow county', on 12 farms, 5 married and 150 single women were employed in spring and only 2 married and 149 single in winter.[40]

It followed, therefore, that except in Linlithgow and also in Fife, increased demand for female labour in the south-east could only be satisfied through the recruitment of single women. Married ploughmen were obliged to supply a female worker whenever called upon. Normally this would be a daughter or sister, but when none was available a 'bondager' was hired from outside. The ploughman was required to board and lodge her and received from the farmer an allowance in money for every day she was employed on the farm: 'The hind is obliged to pay whatever wage the woman can command, according to the current wages of the season, besides finding her lodging, food and washing; from the farmer she receives only so much a day for every day she works, and the number of days she works depends on the will of the farmer'.[41]

By the 1850s there was open resentment of the bondage system throughout the south-eastern lowlands, and a major campaign began to force its abolition.[42] The ploughman had to hire and feed the bondager, but he was only paid when her services were required. The hind therefore preferred to recruit labour from his own family than employ a stranger, and this was an obvious constraint on family freedom and opportunity. One critic of the system pointed out in the 1850s: '. . . rather than be teased with them, hinds often kept their own daughters at home as bondagers, when either they ought to have been earning better wages as principal servants, or at some other occupation'.[43] This was perhaps the crux of the matter. Hostility to bondage was an integral part of a wider change in attitude among farm servants in the south-east. Expectations were rising after 1860 as wage levels increased; the development of more attractive town occupations made it all the more difficult to keep daughters at home working in the fields; migration from the countryside served to increase the bargaining power of the labouring classes. Significantly, the campaign against bondage in the 1860s was the central element in a general attempt to raise wage rates and improve conditions.[44]

Bondage in its original form was therefore in decline in the 1860s, but it did not disappear everywhere at the same pace, and some aspects of it survived down to 1914 even when the formal requirement to hire a stranger 'to work the bondage' fell into abeyance. The system had practically disappeared from the Lothians by 1870 but persisted in Berwick and Roxburgh.[45] Farmers throughout the region, however, still required female labour and responded in a variety of ways to the decay of bondage. Increasingly men who could supply women from within their own families were given preference at the hiring fairs.[46] This gave an advantage to older workers but penalised the younger ploughmen. Another result was the maintenance of the family as the working unit in Berwick and Roxburgh long after the disappearance of formal bondage. As late as the 1920s in these counties women workers were still normally the daughters of men employed on the farms, their engagements were made through their father and they were 'bound' to work for the usual period of engagement of a year. The weekly wage was not paid to each individual separately but in a lump sum to the father or mother. In this way, the dependent position of female labour was perpetuated.[47] Elsewhere in the south-east, notably in the counties of Haddington and Linlithgow, the decay of bondage was accompanied by an increase in the migration of hinds' daughters to seek positions in domestic service in Edinburgh.[48] Farmers in these districts reacted by building bothies for women and boarding in them girls from the Highlands and Ireland. Cottages were also let to single women or to widows with daughters in return for providing work when required at day's wages.[49] Employers sought to maintain a reliable supply of cheap labour which did not have to be paid or maintained when climate deteriorated or seasonal work slackened. Once again, there was a certain continuity between the old days of the bondage system and the new era of 'free' labour.

(b) *Female labour in family farms*

The large farms of 300 acres and above were only dominant in a few areas, such as the Lothians. Each region, however, particularly outside the south-east, had its share of small holdings mainly or entirely worked by family labour. Table 3 provides an insight into the scale of this small farm sector. The figures are derived from the published censuses where occupiers of land were asked to state the acreage of their farms. The totals in each period have been reduced to 1000 to indicate the relative number of farms of different size in each decade.

Table 3   *Size of Farms in Scotland, 1851–1881*

Size of Farm	1851	1871	1881
Under 10 acres	345	120	160
From 10–50 acres	297	299	288
From 50–100 acres	149	192	174
From 100–200 acres	125	195	188
From 200–300 acres	39	76	71
From 300–400 acres	17	38	39
From 400–500 acres	9	18	18
From 500–600 acres	5	13	13
Over 600 acres	14	49	49
	1000	1000	1000

Source: John W. Paterson, 'Rural Depopulation in Scotland: Being an Analysis of its Causes and Consequences', *Trans Highland and Agricultural Society of Scotland*, 5th ser., IX (1897), p. 261.

The majority of those farmers working 100 acres or less relied heavily on the labour of their own families. One informed contemporary estimate suggested that in 1913 there were about 167,000 full-time and casual workers in Scottish agriculture. About 78,000 of this grand total were considered members of the occupier's family.[50] The importance of female labour within the family system varied both with the size of the enterprise and the emphasis of production. On the small farms of the north-east, 'the success of the holding depends as much upon the skill and industry of the housewife as upon that of the holder'.[51] The female members of the family were especially important in the operation of the crofts in Aberdeen and Banff. Sons apparently went to service on neighbouring larger farms almost as soon as they could, leaving their sisters and mothers to help run the croft. Thus, in 1911, even when wives are not included in the total, women comprised 54 per cent of the labour teams in crofts in Aberdeenshire, 49 per cent in Banff and 57 per cent in Nairn.[52] Similar patterns existed in the dairy farming districts in the south-western counties of Renfrew, Lanark and Ayr. In Ayrshire in the 1860s, 'most of the cheesemakers were the wives and daughters of the farmers, only a few of the larger farms engage dairy-women'.[53] Again, along the southern parishes of Lanarkshire, 'farms are generally about 100 acres in size, many of them are worked entirely by the farmer and his family, the farmer himself handling the plough and the wife making the cheese'.[54]

When a farm was worked in this way there was normally no wage exchange. The son might aspire one day to succeed to the farm but there was no such hope for the daughters. Yet it was recognised that theirs was a life of drudgery and toil, what one commentator called 'the slavery of family work'.[55] Dairying near centres of population involved very early rising, at about 2 to 3 a.m., because of a popular prejudice in favour of warm milk. Similarly, dairy women in upland farms needed to milk early to ensure that milk could be sent to town by early morning trains. In other cases the milk was manufactured into cheese, which entailed 'an enormous amount of continuous labouring, seven days a week during six to seven months in the year ... I have seen the women-folk on such farms at 3 o'clock in the afternoon in the same garb they had hurriedly donned between 3 and 4 o'clock in the morning, having been constantly toiling, one duty succeeding another — milking, preparing breakfast, cheese-making, calf and pig-feeding, preparing dinner etc. It is usual for women on dairy farms to work sixteen hours per day, time for meals only being allowed for'.[56]

The widespread use of family labour attracted both apologists and critics.[57] Some contended that it had obvious advantages from the point of view of both costs and productivity: a family working together as a productive unit, each individual feeling that he or she had a direct personal interest in the work and its result, was likely to be an efficient instrument of production. When farm prices declined in the last quarter of the nineteenth century, these farms, particularly in the south-west, met the challenge at least partly because of their minimal cost of labour. Others suggested that family labour was one cause of the general low wage-rates for women in agriculture. As one critic put it: 'a fundamental condition of the employment of paid female labour is that it competes with family labour employed without regular wages and actually as sweated or parasite labour'. There was also growing concern in the early twentieth century that the exploitation of young women inherent in the family system was one factor in the movement of women from the country to town which was causing labour scarcity in some sectors of Scottish farming by 1900. Carter, for example, has argued that the first group to leave the peasant agriculture of the north-east after 1880 were young women 'for whom there was no hope of ever replacing domestic servitude with the independence of the peasant farmer'.[58]

(c) 'In-and-out' Girls

According to the census of 1871, of the 42,789 females regularly employed for wages in Scottish agriculture, 52 per cent were described as 'agricultural labourers', by which was probably implied regular, full-time field workers, and the remaining 48 per cent as 'farm servants' (indoor). This latter group was most numerous in Lanark, Dumfries, Stirling, Dumbarton, Aberdeen, Banff, Kincardine and Ayr and least common in the south-eastern counties of Haddington, Fife, Berwick and Roxburgh.[59] They were therefore rare in districts where large farms were the norm and more significant in areas of small and medium-sized holdings. On these farms the female worker had to be versatile because no single task could absorb labour on a continuous basis in the fashion characteristic of the regime in the Lothians. The 'in-and-out' girls, as their name implied, did housework, milked cows, helped in the fields and generally turned their hand to any task in the steading. They had no fixed hours nor, as late as 1914, any generally recognised holiday customs.[60] But it is difficult to generalise about their conditions because much depended on the attitude of the individual employer and local custom. So, in the larger farms of the south-west dairying counties, they tended to spend most of their time in milking and tending the cows. On the smaller farms, they worked alongside the family, doing anything required.[61] In Aberdeenshire and Banffshire, however, the special function of the 'in-and-out' girl was to work in the kitchen, as most farm employees in the north-east were single males who took their meals in the farmhouse.[62] However, their outside duties also included milking, attending to poultry and occasional help in the fields.

It was generally agreed that the 'in-and-out' girl, especially if she was the only hired servant on the farm, worked longer and harder than any other female employee in agriculture. They became increasingly difficult to obtain in the years before 1914, and contemporaries attributed this to their poor working conditions: 'this state of matters must be attributed to the nature of the employment of these girls and chiefly to the length of their working day and the lack of fixed and regular leisure time'.[63]

(d) Seasonal, casual and part-time workers

The cycle of sowing, growth, maturity and harvesting in agriculture inevitably meant that demand for labour fluctuated throughout the year. There were different work-peaks associated with grain crops, turnips, potatoes and with the new soft fruit industry in Clydeside and the Carse of Gowrie. An indication of the seasonal movement in demand for labour comes from the example of a 'large cropping farm of 250 acres near Glasgow' in the 1880s.[64] The regular staff consisted of three to four ploughmen and two women servants. In winter only a few additional workers were needed about the threshing-machine or for filling sacks with potatoes. For the earliest spring work, planting potatoes in April, 20 to 24 more women were hired. Weeding potatoes at the end of May required 30 to 40 women, as did thinning turnips in late May and June. In August, September and October three major seasonal tasks followed in sequence: grain harvesting, potato lifting and turnip pulling. The gathering of the turnip crop was the most demanding of extra labour on this particular farm and required the hiring of between 60 and 70 extra women workers.

Mechanisation did have a significant impact on the market for grain harvest labour, firstly with the development of the machine reaper and then as a result of the adoption of the reaper-binder in the 1890s. But not all farmers could afford these services and they tended to be most common in regions of larger holdings which could sustain the capital costs involved. The other seasonal tasks remained labour-intensive in the later nineteenth century.[65] Indeed, it is possible to argue that there was an increased need for seasonal workers between 1880 and 1914. Rising wages among regular employees and a growing scarcity of certain grades of full-time labour, as a result of migration, forced farmers in some areas, notably the Lothians, to recruit more workers on short-term contracts.[66] Moreover, in the last three decades of the century, the heavy emphasis in the western parishes of Ayrshire on early potato cultivations and the developments of market gardening in Lanarkshire and Perthshire boosted demand for seasonal labour in these districts.[67]

Scottish farmers maintained their supplies of seasonal workers from three main sources. First, there was increasing dependence on Irish male and female labour, recruited either from permanent migrants, resident in the Scottish towns, or from Ireland itself. The Irish were extensively used in the Lothians for both the potato harvest and turnip thinning, filling the gap left by the ploughmen's daughters who sought opportunities elsewhere. The early potato crop in Ayrshire was gathered by gangs of Irish women who came over from Ireland from June to November, and moved from farm to farm as the work required.[68] Second, outside the Lothians, wives of ploughmen were extensively employed as additional sources of casual labour. Farmers in areas as far apart as Aberdeenshire and Dumfries often engaged a man on condition that his wife would milk or do seasonal work as required. In the dairying districts of the south-west 'a large number of women' were employed in part-time work on the basis of these informal contracts.[69] Thirdly, there was often heavy reliance on workers recruited for the season from neighbouring towns and villages. Casual workers from the towns, the urban unemployed and the wives and daughters of men working in industry were all represented. Women from Aberdeen and Edinburgh were hired to hoe turnips on adjacent farms.[70] In parts of Lanarkshire in the 1860s, 'women do nearly all the working of potatoes and turnips ... they come to work from towns and villages'.[71]

This reflected the industrial structure of the county as wives and daughters of miners and steelworkers sought work in the fields to supplement family income: 'These farms with the exception of the ploughman and an occasional extra hand worked almost entirely by women taken on as extra hands from the mining villages around '.[72] A similar pattern prevailed in the mining areas of Ayrshire and the industrial parts of Fife. Women employed in Dunbar at the herring curing laboured at other times on neighbouring farms.[73] So also around Paisley, the wives and daughters of industrial workers were important components of the seasonal labour force.[74] Ironically, the growth of the towns, which helped to increase the movement of regular employees from the land, also provided a pool of underemployed labour which could be used to carry out the vital tasks of the farming year. This advantage, of course, applied only to those areas close to urban locations.

III

The inadequacies in the census data make it difficult to carry out a precise analysis of the extent of female participation in lowland agriculture between 1850 and 1914. There was a persistent tendency for enumerators to exclude relatives assisting in agriculture, thus virtually ignoring the important contribution made by female family labour. In the 1871 census all children, even those under the age of five, were counted as part of the farm work force, but in 1881 and 1891 only male relatives of fifteen and above were included. This omission of wives, daughters, grand-daughters and nieces helps to explain the apparently massive fall in 'females engaged in agriculture' from 128,500 in 1871 to 51,657 a decade later. Furthermore, there was little uniformity over time or between different regions for some categories of women workers. 'In-and-out' girls were classed in the censuses of 1891, 1901 and 1911 as 'domestic servants' rather than 'workers engaged in agriculture'. This was probably more likely to happen in the north-east counties where outdoor employment was subsidiary to domestic service, but there is no way of knowing this for certain.[75] Finally, the census categories cannot provide any guidance about seasonal, casual and part-time women workers, a group which impressionistic evidence suggests was assuming an even greater importance in some rural areas in the later nineteenth century.

The main result of these weaknesses is that the census cannot supply even a rough indication of the total numbers of women engaged in agriculture over time. The massive fluctuation in the female labour supply from census to census is to be explained in large part by changes in the census modes of enumeration rather than by any fundamental alteration in numbers in real terms. Reliance on the crude census data obscures more than it reveals. Necessarily, therefore, the historian is compelled to employ only those parts of the census which are least deficient and complement this material with more qualitative evidence in order to gain an insight into female labour supply in the period of study.

While it is impossible to chart the movement of total numbers over time it is still feasible to survey the experience of particular groups of female workers. One such category is that of 'female wage earners in agriculture', i.e. women engaged as full-time regular labour on Scottish farms. Even this class is subject to the distortion caused by the ambiguous status of the 'in-and-out' girl, but that problem is probably mainly confined to the counties of Aberdeen, Banff and Kincardine, where there was undercounting, and, to a lesser extent, the south-west region. Table 4 presents census figures for 'female wage earners' in agriculture, 1861–1911. Table 5 provides a more refined view of regional conditions over the shorter period, 1871–1891.

Table 4   *Female Wage Earners in Agriculture in Scotland, 1861–1911*

Year	Total
1861	40,653
1871	42,773
1881	44,172
1891	22,055
1901	19,810
1911	15,037

Table 5   *Female Wage Earners in Agriculture in each Civil Division of Scotland, 1871–1891*

Civil Divisions	*Wage Earners in Agriculture*					
	Numbers			Increase(+) or Rate of Decrease (−)		
	1871	1881	1891	1871–1881	1881–1891	1871–1891
Northern	3184	3555	1221	+11.6	−65.7	−61.6
North & Western	4655	5742	3004	+23.3	−47.7	−35.5
North & Eastern	7642	5689	826	−25.5	−85.5	−89.2
East Midland	6186	7346	3292	+18.7	−55.2	−46.8
West Midland	3889	3941	1676	+1.3	−57.5	−56.9
South Western	5952	6373	3884	+18.5	−39.0	−32.8
South Eastern	5781	6850	4935	+18.5	−28.0	−14.6
Southern	5501	4676	3217	−15.0	−31.2	−41.5
Scotland, Total	42790	44172	22055	+3.2	−50.2	−48.4

Source: *Census of Scotland,* 1861, 1871, 1881, 1891, 1901, 1911.

No confidence can be placed in these data either as precise measurements of reality or as indicators of short-run movement between census years. As the Royal Commission on Labour of 1893 commented of the very heavy drop in female wage earners between 1881 and 1891: 'These results are so extraordinary as to suggest that there must have been some difference in the system of enumeration at the two periods'. Nevertheless, the overall, long-term pattern of decline which they reveal is confirmed by other evidence. In the 1890s, in Ayrshire and Renfrewshire, there was a shortage of full-time dairy-women.[76] In the north-east counties of Moray, Banff and Nairn 'women are hardly known as labourers now at all, unless at harvest'. Increasingly, young men were being employed in tasks formerly the preserve of women.[77] Regular female labour was more plentiful in the south-east, notably in Berwick and Roxburgh, but deficiencies were complained of in the Lothians.[78] After its exhaustive enquiries, the Royal Commission of 1893 reported: 'There were few, if any, places where women were available in sufficient numbers for field work, and where the rare instance of their being sufficient occurred, the supply was largely from the neighbouring villages, and not entirely from the staff of the farm or their families'.[79]

In fact, as the Commission's statement implied, while there was a general problem of scarcity, it varied between localities and different grades of worker. In the 1890s in the eastern parishes of Fife, there was a broad balance of supply and demand for women as the county's industrial towns and villages normally produced an adequate flow of seasonal labour when required.[80] Similarly, there was no serious problem in Selkirk, Peebles and Dumfries, because their concentration on pastoral husbandry created little demand for much regular field labour.[81] These areas apart, however, the shortage of women workers was virtually a universal complaint throughout lowland Scotland in the last decade of the nineteenth century. It was the growing scarcity of *regular* female labour which caused particular concern: the supply of seasonal workers was deemed adequate in some localities and plentiful in others which had access to town labour.[82] However, in the south-west 'the cry of the dairying districts is loud, that dairy-women were difficult to get at all and fully qualified dairy-women are very rare indeed'.[83] 'In-and-out' girls were becoming scarce in the years before 1914, and in the Lothian counties daughters of the hinds were increasingly seeking employment off the land as early as the 1850s and 1860s; thus, in the 1890s 'women are scarce in Haddington and in Clackmannan they are almost unprocurable'.[84]

The problem stimulated a considerable contemporary debate, and a number of theories were advanced in the later nineteenth century to explain why it was more difficult to obtain women for regular agricultural employment.[85] Some saw it as the inevitable consequence of improving technology displacing unskilled female labour. Others saw a connection with the depression in agricultural prices in the 1880s and 1890s which, in their view, reduced demand for all categories of agricultural labour. A further opinion suggested that conditions of employment for women in agriculture were bad and it was scarcely surprising that they were deserting the land and seeking better opportunities in the towns.

The pace of mechanisation did accelerate in the second half of the nineteenth century. The number of agricultural implement makers in Scotland rose from an estimated 58 in 1861 to 222 in 1891.[86] By 1900, on larger farms, the mechanical reaper-builder had much reduced the old labour requirements of the grain harvest. Even the reaping-machine, introduced into general practice from the later 1860s, in one estimate 'enabled the farmer to harvest his corn crop with half the number of hands'.[87] The horse-rake gave a similar advantage with the hay crop, and the grubber, the chain-harrow, the horse-hoe and the steam threshing-machine all contributed to a reduction in manual labour. But the adoption of these devices was irregular and patchy, and the traditional female tasks of milking, potato picking, turnip harvesting and fruit picking remained, for the most part, unmechanised until 1914 and later.[88] Moreover, there was no evidence of a general fall in demand for women as a consequence of improved technology; on the contrary, there were indications that innovation in labour-saving devices derived from labour shortages and rising labour costs caused by migration of workers.[89] As late as 1920, the Committee on Women in Agriculture in Scotland concluded: '... in nearly all districts the agricultural industry could still employ more women if women with country experience were willing to do the work'.[90] In addition, most of the improved technology before 1914 saved on seasonal labour: the more widespread use of machinery could not in itself explain why *regular* women workers were leaving agriculture. The problem was apparently not one of a major reduction in demand for female services but rather one where supply was not being maintained at the level required by employers.

There are similar difficulties associated with any attempt to explain the scarcity of women workers in terms of 'Agricultural Depression'. C. S. Orwin and E. H. Whetham have argued that 'the main reason' for the decline in rural population after 1870 was 'the restricted opportunity for employment, as farmers cut down their labour force during the depression'.[91] But this is hardly a convincing explanation in the Scottish context. Prices did fall for all the major cash crops between 1870 and 1900. However, as Tables 6 and 7 demonstrate, this led to alterations in the balance of the farming system but no drastic reduction in grain or green crop acreage on a scale which would have caused widespread redundancy of labour. Overall, Scottish grain acreage declined by about 15 per cent between 1870 and 1914, but much of the fall was concentrated in that 'cold, infertile plateau' from Midlothian in the east to Dumbarton in the western lowlands.[92] Even in the arable Lothians, as Table 8 illustrates, decline in the demand for regular female labour was confined to areas

Table 6 *Acreage under different crops in Scotland, 1867–1892*

	1867	1872	1882	1892
Total area under crops, bare-fallow and grass	4,379,000	4,537,000	4,784,000	4,896,928
bean crops	1,364,000	1,435,000	1,425,000	1,297,231
green crops	668,000	701,000	687,000	638,794
bare-fallow	83,000	28,000	21,000	8,584
rotation grass	1,211,000	1,320,000	2,467,000	1,614,070
permanent pasture	1,053,000	1,053,000	1,184,000	1,338,249
horses (farm only)		177,000	191,000	200,109
cattle	979,000	1,121,000	1,081,000	1,221,726
sheep	6,894,000	7,141,000	6,854,000	7,543,447

Table 7 *Acreage under different crops in Scotland, 1867–1892.
Calculated on the basis that the Returns for 1867 equal 100*

	1867	1872	1882	1892
Total area under crops, bare-fallow and grass	100	103	109	112
bean crops	100	105	104	96
green crops	100	105	103	98
bare-fallow	100	34	25	19
rotation grass	100	109	121	133
permanent pasture	100	100	112	127
horses (farm only)	100	100	108	113
cattle	100	114	110	125
sheep	100	103	99	109

Source: Paterson, 'Rural Depopulation', p. 268.

Table 8 *Demand for Labour in the Lothians, 1872–1892*

Class of Labourer	Type of Land		
	Purely Arable Per Cent	*Mixed Husbandry* Per Cent	*Hill and Arable* Per Cent
Hinds	No Change	−20	−35 to 40
Orra Men	−20		
Regular Women	No Change	−5 to 10	−30
Casual or Day Labourers (Male and Female)	+30	+5 to 15	No Change

Source: *R.C. on Labour, 1893*, Part II, Report by R. H. Pringle on Edinburgh and Haddington (the Lothians), p. 97.

fringing the hills and was partly compensated for by an increasing need for seasonal female workers elsewhere in the district.

The impression that demand for female workers was maintained or only fell marginally in most localities throughout the 'Agricultural Depression' is confirmed by the wage data presented in Tables 9 and 10. These suggest a buoyant market for women in general between 1860 and 1890 and indicate, as earlier discussion implied, that only at the grain-harvest, because of improved technology, was there a significant reduction in the need for female services.

Table 9   *Average weekly wage of a Woman-Worker (regularly employed) in Scottish Counties, 1867, 1879, 1893*

N.R. = No Returns;   N.C. = No Change

County	Rate of Wage Per Week					
	1867		1879		1893	
	Ordinary	Harvest	Ordinary	Harvest	Ordinary	Harvest
	s. d.	s. d.	s. d.	s. d.	s. d.	s. d.
Aberdeen	6 0	20 0	7 6	22 6	9 0	N.R.
Ayr	6 0	15 0	7 6	15 0	9 0	N.R.
Banff	6 0	20 0	7 6	15 0	7 6	22 0
Berwick	7 0	20 0	9 0	20 0	10 0	15 0
Clackmannan	N.R.	N.R.	N.R	N.R.	9 0	21 0
Dumbarton	N.R.	N.R.	N.R.	N.R.	9 0	21 0
Dumfries	6 6	15 0	9 0	18 0	9 0	18 0
Edinburgh	7 0	21 0	8 6	15 0	8 6	13 6
Elgin	5 0	N.R.	7 6	15 0	7 6	22 0
Fife	6 0	18 0	N.R.	N.R.	8 3	18 0
Forfar	6 0	18 0	N.R.	N.R.	8 3	24 0
Haddington	6 0	15 0	9 0	13 6	9 0	16 0
Kincardine	N.R.	N.R.	7 6	20 0	9 0	N.R.
Kinross	N.R.	N.R.	N.R.	N.R.	7 0	18 0
Kirkcudbright	N.R.	N.R.	N.R.	N.R.	8 0	15 0
Lanark	7 6	15 0	9 0	N.R.	9 0	18 0
Linlithgow	7 0	21 0	7 6	15 0	8 0	14 0
Nairn	5 0	9 0	7 6	15 0	7 6	22 0
Peebles	7 6	N.R.	10 0	N.R.	N.R.	N.R.
Perth	6 0	15 0	7 6	18 0	8 0	24 0
Renfrew	8 0	N.R.	9 0	18 0	12 0	21 0
Roxburgh	7 0	20 0	9 0	20 0	10 0	15 0
Selkirk	N.R.	N.R.	9 0	16 0	N.R.	N.R.
Stirling	7 6	15 0	N.R.	N.R.	9 0	21 0
Wigtown	N.R.	N.R.	7 6	15 0	8 0	15 0

Table 9 *continued*

| Remarks | Increase or Decrease Per Cent | | | | | |
| | 1867–79 | | 1879–93 | | 1867–1893 | |
	Ord.	Harv.	Ord.	Harv.	Ord.	Harv.
A 1893 No harvest wage stated	+25	+12.5	+20	...	+50	...
A 1879 Potato-lifting 2s per day	+25	N.C.	+20	...	+50	...
B 1893 £1 for harvest food	+25	−25	N.C	+46.6	+25	+10
B ...	+28.5	N.C.	+11.1	−25	+42.8	−25
C 1893 Potato-lifting 12s per week	...	...	...	...	...	...
D 1893 Potato-lifting 12s per week	...	...	...	...	...	...
D ...	+38.4	+20	N.C.	...	+38.4	+20
E 1893 Potato-lifting 12s per week	+21.4	−28.5	N.C.	−10	+21.4	−35.7
E ...	+50.0	...	N.C.	+46.6	+50.0	...
F 1893 Potato-lifting 12s per week	...	...	...	...	+37.5	N.C.
F 1893 Potato-lifting 12s per week	...	...	...	...	+37.5	+33.3
H 1893 Potato-lifting 12s per week	+50.0	−10.0	N.C.	+18.5	+50.0	+6.6
K ...	...	...	+20.0	...	...	...
K 1893 Potato-lifting 12s per week	...	...	...	...	...	...
K ...	+20.0	...	N.C.	...	+20.0	+20.0
L ...	+7.1	−28.5	+6.6	−6.6	+14.2	−33.3
L ...	+50.0	+66.6	N.C.	+46.6	+50.0	+144.4
N ...	+33.3	...	...	...	...	...
P 1867 Turnip-singling 9s	+25.0	+20.0	+6.6	+33.3	+33.3	+60.0
P 1893 Potato-lifting 12s per week						
R 1879 Near towns a higher wage	+12.5	...	+33.3	+16.6	+50.0	...
R 1893 Hay-making 2s 6d per day						
S ...	+28.5	N.C.	+11.1	−25.0	+42.8	−25.0
S ...	...	...	...	...	+20.0	+40.0
W ...	...	...	+6.6	N.C.	...	...

Source: R. H. Pringle, 'The Agricultural Labourer of Scotland: Then and Now', *Trans. Highland and Agricultural Society*, 5th ser. VI (1894) p. 31, based on returns from Royal Commissions, 1867, 1881 and 1893.

Table 10   *Average Female Cash Wages Offered At Spring Hiring Fairs,*
Aberdeenshire, 1870–1900

Year	Average Cash Wage
1871	4.9
1872	5.9
1873	6.6
1874	6.8
1875	8.7
1876	8.8
1877	7.8
1878	7.4
1879	6.1
1880	6.1
1881	5.8
1882	6.2
1883	6.6
1884	7.4
1885	6.9
1886	6.6
1887	6.0
1888	5.9
1889	6.3
1890	6.1
1891	7.1
1892	7.1
1893	7.5
1894	7.3
1895	7.1
1896	7.6
1897	6.9
1898	7.3
1899	8.0
1900	10.0

Source: R. Molland and G. Evans, 'Scottish Farm Wages from 1870 to 1900',
Journal Royal Statistical Society, Series A (general), CXIII (1950), p. 226.

The detailed series from Aberdeenshire reveals a rise of about 60 per
cent in spring wages between 1870 and 1876. This was then followed by a
fall almost as rapid down to 1881 but, even at the lowest figure, the rate
was still above that of 1870. The years 1881 to 1888 were a phase of
relatively stable wages, culminating in a significant increase between 1887–
88 and 1891–2 and from that point on a general rise to 1900. In brief,
spring cash wages paid to women workers increased two to three times
over the period 1870 to 1900. It is doubtful if rises of the same order
occurred in other areas because, as noted earlier, there was particular

difficulty in recruiting female labour in the north-east region. Nonetheless, both the evidence collected by R. H. Pringle (presented in Table 9), and contemporary comment, suggest that farmers in most areas were forced to bid higher in the long run for regular women labourers. Certainly there is no indication that shortage of employment was a factor causing women to leave the land.

It is more likely that the nature of pay and conditions in farming and the pull of alternative employments and opportunities elsewhere were decisive in explaining the migration of female agricultural servants. Some commentators stressed that the central factor was low wages, that women were paid much less than the male rate for doing the same work: 'At many branches of farm labour, a good girl will do more than an average man, yet she had to be content with half his wages. No doubt women's wages have doubled within the last 40 years, but the fact remains that often when working side by side with the orra men and hinds she is doing as much as a man, and yet only getting half a man's wages'.[93] The differential in rates was preserved, despite the difficulty of recruiting women workers, because by custom women's wages were measured as a traditional proportion of the male wage. An additional factor was that many farmers were able to recruit low-paid seasonal workers to replace regular employees, and this reserve may have helped to depress rates for full-time servants. Female labour was often hired through the father, who undertook to ensure that his women relatives would work when called upon. Joseph Duncan, the Secretary of the Scottish Farm Servants' Union, argued that in Berwick and Roxburgh, '... the men have used their women-folk as a lever, for getting better wages for themselves and the women's wages have in consequence suffered'.[94] On the other hand, there had always been a traditional difference between male and female wages. What is significant in the later nineteenth century was not so much the survival of low pay but the fact that it was attracting comment and criticism from women themselves.[95] The controversy over low pay for female labourers, therefore, reflected rising expectations and a growing hostility to farm work which was probably much wider than the problem of inadequate rewards.

Increasingly, agriculture was seen as an 'unwomanlike' occupation. Domestic service in the towns, whether or not it offered higher pay, was regarded as more genteel than labouring on a farm. Life on the farm was regarded as 'dirty and rough' compared to some town occupations and was widely criticised for its long and irregular hours, lack of holidays and absence of social attractions.[96] What contributed to these changing attitudes cannot be examined in detail here. Contemporaries explained it in terms of the wider availability of education from 1872, the impact of the railway in forging closer connections with the towns and the rise in earnings of the married farm-servant class, contributing to higher social expectations both for themselves and their families.[97] Whatever the reason, the movement from agriculture was sustained by the development of

J

alternative opportunities outside the farm. As R. H. Pringle argued cogently in 1894: 'Forty years ago, women working on farms had to take what they could get or go idle, for other employment was scarce and factory life was in its infancy. Now the scene is changed, and no educated country girl with a spark of ambition and pride about her need toil among the "tatties" for lack of opportunities to better herself in a different branch of employment'.[98] The structural change of the Scottish economy ensured that farmers in the later nineteenth century faced greater competition than ever before from urban and industrial employers for women workers. The days of cheap and abundant supplies of women, eager to labour in the countryside for paltry earnings, were gone for ever.

NOTES

1. *Census of Scotland, 1871. Report and Tables Vol. II, Parliamentary Papers,* 1873 (C841), LXXII (hereafter, *Census of Scotland, 1871*).

2. See above, pp.

3. *Census of Scotland, 1871.*

4. *Royal Commission on the Employment of Children, Young Persons and Women in Agriculture. Fourth Report. Appendix. Part I and II. Parliamentary Papers,* 1870 (C221), XIII (hereafter *Fourth Report on Women in Agriculture, 1870*), p. 47.

5. Henry Stephens, *The Book of the Farm* (Edinburgh, 1844), I, p. 227.

6. Patrick Graham, *General View of the Agriculture of Stirlingshire* (Edinburgh, 1812), p. 313.

7. Archibald Sturrock, 'Report of the Agriculture of Ayrshire', *Prize Essays and Transactions of the Highland Society of Scotland (T.H.A.S.)*, 4th series, I (1866–67), p. 89.

8. *Board of Agriculture for Scotland: Report of the Committee on Women in Agriculture* (1920) (hereafter *Report of Committee on Women in Agriculture, 1920*), p. 19. See below, pp. 107–9.

9. Robert Kerr, *General View of the Agriculture of the County of Berwick* (London, 1809), pp. 414–415.

10. Alexander Fenton, *Scottish Country Life* (Edinburgh, 1977), p. 54.

11. James Headrick, *General View of the Agriculture of the County of Angus* (Edinburgh, 1813), p. 492.

12. G. Robertson, *Rural Recollections* (Irvine, 1829), p. 239.

13. *Ibid.*

14. Ian Carter, *Farm Life in Northeast Scotland, 1840–1914* (Edinburgh, 1979), p. 101; D. T. Jones, Joseph S. Duncan *et al.*, *Rural Scotland during the War* (London, 1926), pp. 194–5.

15. T. M. Devine, ed., *Lairds and Improvement in the Scotland of the Enlightenment* (Dundee, 1979), p. 60.

16. Kerr, *Agriculture in the County of Berwick*, p. 415.

17. Stephens, *Book of the Farm*, II, p. 386.

18. J. Cunninghame, 'On the Cultivation of Lucerne', *T.H.A.S.*, new series, II, p. 115.

19. E. J. T. Collins, 'The Age of Machinery', in G. E. Mingay, ed., *The Victorian Countryside* (London, 1981), I, p. 201.

20. *Third Report from the Select Committee appointed to inquire into the State of Agriculture and into the Causes and Extent of the Distress which still presses on some Important Branches, Parliamentary Papers,* VIII (1836), Evidence of Robert Hope, pp. 20–21, QQ 9693–4.

21. Valerie Morgan, 'Agricultural Wage Rates in late Eighteenth-Century Scotland', *Economic History Review*, 2nd ser., 24 (1971), pp. 181–201.

22. E. H. Hunt, *Regional Wage Variations in Britain, 1850–1914* (Oxford, 1973), pp. 117–118; E. Richards, 'Women in the British Economy since about 1700', *History,* 59 (1974), p. 353.

23. *Fourth Report on Women in Agriculture, 1870,* Appendix C, p. 121.

24. *Ibid.*

25. Rev. J. Farquharson, 'On Cutting Grain-Crops with the Common Scythe as practised in Aberdeenshire', *T.H.A.S.,* IV (1835), pp. 189–193; Andrew Whyte and Duncan Macfarlane, *General View of the Agriculture of the County of Dumbarton* (Glasgow, 1811), p. 247; Headrick, *Agriculture of Angus,* p. 495.

26. George Skene Smith, *A General View of the Agriculture of Aberdeenshire* (Aberdeen, 1811), p. 521.

27. Malcolm Gray, 'Migration in the Rural Lowlands of Scotland, 1750–1850', in T. M. Devine and David Dickson, eds., *Ireland and Scotland, 1600–1850* (Edinburgh, 1983), pp. 104–117.

28. *Ibid.*

29. See below, pp. 166–168

30. James Tait, 'The Agriculture of Lanarkshire', *T.H.A.S.,* 4th series (1885), p. 77.

31. See below, pp. 117–119.

32. Sturrock, 'Agriculture of Ayrshire', pp. 81–89; *Royal Commission on Labour: the Agricultural Labourer, vol. III, Scotland, Part I. Parliamentary Papers,* 1893–4 (C6894–XV), XXXVI (hereafter *R.C. on Labour, 1893, Part I*), pp. 53, 68.

33. *R.C. on Labour, 1893, Part I,* p. 68.

34. See below, p. 113.

35. *Census of Scotland, 1871.*

36. *Fourth Report on Women in Agriculture, 1870,* p. 52.

37. *Ibid.,* p. 34.

38. Kerr, *Agriculture of Berwick,* pp. 414–15.

39. *Fourth Report on Women in Agriculture, 1870,* p. 52.

40. *Ibid.,* Appendix F, pp. 185–6.

41. *Ibid.,* p. 53; *New Statistical Account of Scotland* (Edinburgh, 1845), I, p. 78.

42. Anon., 'Social Condition of Our Agricultural Labourers', *Journal of Agriculture,* new ser., 1853–55, p. 152; *New Statistical Account of Scotland,* III, p. 453; Rev. Harry Stuart, *Agricultural Labourers as they Were, Are and Should Be* (2nd ed., Edinburgh, 1854), p. 23.

43. Stuart, *Agricultural Labourers,* p. 23.

44. J. P. D. Dunbabin, *Rural Discontent in Nineteenth Century Britain* (London, 1974), pp. 137–142.

45. *Ibid*; B. W. Robertson, 'The Border Farm Worker, 1871–1971', *Journal of Agricultural Labour Science* (1973), II, pp. 65–93.

46. *R.C. on Labour, 1893, Part II,* p. 196.

47. *Report of Committee on Women in Agriculture, 1920*, p. 13.

48. *Fourth Report on Women in Agriculture, 1870*, pp. 52–3, 102, 105.

49. R. S. Gibb, *A Farmer's Fifty years in Lauderdale* (Edinburgh, 1927), p. 30; James Robb, *The Cottage, the Bothy and the Kitchen* (Edinburgh, 1861), p. 15; T. M. Devine, 'Temporary Migration and the Scottish Highlands in the Nineteenth Century', *Economic History Review*, 2nd ser., XXXII, No. 3., pp. 344–59.

50. Jones, Duncan *et al.*, *Rural Scotland during the War*, p. 197.

51. *Report of Committee on Women in Agriculture, 1920*, p. 19.

52. *Census in Scotland, 1911. Report and Tables, Parliamentary Papers*, 1912–13 (Cd. 6097), CXIX–CXX; Carter, *Farm Life*, p. 106.

53. Sturrock, 'Agriculture of Ayrshire', p. 89.

54. *Fourth Report on Women in Agriculture, 1870*, Appendix F, p. 237.

55. *Report of Committee on Women in Agriculture, 1920*, p. 59.

56. *Ibid.*, Evidence of John Drysdale, Scottish Agricultural Compensation Society, p. 59.

57. The debate can be followed in the *Report of Committee on Women in Agriculture, 1920*.

58. Carter, *Farm Life*, p. 95.

59. *Census of Scotland, 1871*.

60. *Report of Committee of Women in Agriculture, 1920*, pp. 15–16.

61. *R.C. on Labour, 1893, Part II*, pp. 11, 14.

62. *Fourth Report of Women in Agriculture, 1870*, p. 34; A. Macdonald, 'On the Agriculture of the Counties of Elgin and Nairn', *T.H.A.S.*, 4th ser., XVI (1884), p. 119.

63. *Report of the Committee of Women in Agriculture, 1920*, p. 94.

64. James Tait, 'The Agriculture of Lanarkshire', *T.H.A.S.*, 4th ser., XVII (1885), p. 79.

65. Sturrock, 'Agriculture of Ayrshire', p. 59; John Speir, 'Changes in Farm Implements since 1890', *T.H.A.S.*, 5th ser., XVIII (1906), pp. 47–62; *Royal Commission on Agricultural Interests, Reports of Assistant Commissioners, Parliamentary Papers*, 1881 (C2778–II), XVI (hereafter *R.C. on Agricultural Interests*), pp. 567–8; John Wilson, 'Half a Century as a Border Farmer', *T.H.A.S.*, 5th ser., XIV (1902), pp. 39–40; C.S. Orwin and Edith H. Whetham, *History of British Agriculture, 1846–1914* (Newton Abbot, 1971), pp. 256–7.

66. *R.C. on Labour, 1893, Part II*, pp. 9, 49, 51, 89–90.

67. Jones, Duncan *et al.*, *Rural Scotland during the War*, p. 200; *Fourth Report on Women in Agriculture, 1870*, p. 95.

68. *Fourth Report on Women in Agriculture, 1870*, pp. 50–53; *R.C. on Labour, 1893, Part II*, pp. 64, 112, 134–5; *R.C. on Agricultural Interests, 1881, Minutes of Evidence, Part II, Parliamentary Papers*, 1881 (C3096), XVII, p. 318.

69. *Report of Committee on Women in Agriculture, 1920*, pp. 16–17.

70. *Fourth Report on Women in Agriculture, 1870*, pp. 34, 53.

71. *Ibid.*, Appendix C, p. 225.

72. *Ibid.*, p. 107.

73. *R.C. on Labour, 1893, Part II*, p. 209.

74. *Fourth Report on Women in Agriculture, 1870*, Appendix C, p. 250.

75. *Census of Scotland, 1911. Report and Tables: the Counties in Alphabetical Order, Parliamentary Papers*, 1912–13 (Cd. 6097).

76. Archibald McNeilage, 'Farming Methods in Ayrshire', *T.H.A.S.*, 5th ser., XVIII (1906), pp. 11–15.

77. *R.C. on Labour, 1893, Part I,* p. 109. See also *Royal Commission on Agricultural Depression, Minutes of Evidence, III, Parliamentary Papers,* 1896 (C7400), XVII, Q.51, 696, IV, *Parliamentary Papers,* 1896 (C8021), XVII, Q. 51, 829.

78. *Report by Mr. Wilson Fox on the Wages, Earnings and Conditions of Employment of Agricultural Labourers in the United Kingdom, Parliamentary Papers,* 1900 (Cd. 346), LXXXII (hereafter *Wilson Fox's Report on Agricultural Labourers*), p. 68.

79. *R.C. on Labour, 1893* Part I, p. 52.

80. *Ibid., Part II,* p. 52.

81. *Ibid.,* p. 190.

82. *Wilson Fox's Report on Agricultural Labourers,* pp. 68–69.

83. *R.C. on Labour, 1893, Part I,* p. 52.

84. *Ibid., Part II,* p. 9; *Fourth Report on Women in Agriculture, 1870,* p. 53; *Report of Committee on Women in Agriculture,* 1920, pp. 17–18; *Wilson Fox's Report on Agricultural Labourers,* p. 68.

85. The debate is summarised in Paterson, 'Rural Depopulation', pp. 237–279, but can also be followed in the comments of witnesses to the various Royal Commissions, 1867, 1881 and 1893 mentioned in earlier references in this essay.

86. Paterson, 'Rural Depopulation', p. 265.

87. *R.C. on Agricultural Interests, 1881, Part II,* pp. 567–8; Wilson, 'Half a Century as a Border Farmer', pp. 39–40; Speir, 'Changes in Farm Implements since 1890', pp. 47–62.

88. Orwin and Whetham, *British Agriculture,* pp. 257, 346–8.

89. *R.C. on Labour, 1893, Part I,* pp. 96–7.

90. *Committee on Women in Agriculture in Scotland, 1920,* p. 8.

91. Orwin and Whetham, *British Agriculture,* p. 317.

92. J. A. Symon, *Scottish Farming, Past and Present* (Edinburgh, 1959), p. 197.

93. *R.C. on Labour, 1893, Part II,* p. 117

94. *Committee on Women in Agriculture in Scotland, 1920,* p. 60.

95. *R.C. on Labour, 1893, Part II,* pp. 9, 32, 117.

96. *Fourth Report on Women in Agriculture, 1870,* p. 53, Appendix B, p. 98; *R.C. on Labour, 1893, Part II,* pp. 99–110, 117, 197; *Committee on Women in Agriculture, 1920,* pp. 38, 61, 75, 110.

97. *Ibid.*

98. Pringle, 'The Agricultural Labourer of Scotland', p. 248.

7

Grain Harvesting and Harvesters

William Howatson

The effects of the excessive heat of the present season is severely felt by the reapers in the field. In a park near Gorgie, within two miles of Edinburgh, where a number of shearers were employed on Tuesday last, some of them were induced to drink a quantity of cold water, and immediately afterwards no fewer than five fainted and dropt down, but fortunately soon after recovered. This ought to operate as a caution to others as the consequences might have been fatal.

Perth Courier, 26 August 1819

... lang hairst and little corn.

George Robertson, *Rural Recollections*

Ye mind the year whan the Auld Kirk was dung doun? It was a late hairst that year, an' a michty puir ane. First there cam a muckle daddin wind, juist whan the stuff was a' stan'in deid ripe, an' we'd gotten the roads cut an' a' ready to start, an' it threshed abune half the crap on the grund. An' syne it begoud to poor, an' it poored on maist o' the month o' September, wi' awfu' jaws an' skelps o' rain, an' no' a blink o' the sun frae the tae end o' the week to tither. There was a pouther O' snaw lyin on the stooks i' the upland fields afore a' was dune, an' the barley was jimp worth leadin in —'

P. Hay Hunter, *James Inwick, Ploughman and Elder*

No period in the farming year has caught man's imagination as much as the grain harvest. The arable farmer's survival rested on its successful conclusion; it fed his stock and paid his rent and caused the largest single input of labour in the farming year. The recognition afforded it by Church and State and its attraction to the seasonal labourer and the regular farm servant alike gave the harvest a special place in rural culture. Throughout the eighteenth and nineteenth centuries the harvest operation of cutting and gathering the grain crops underwent a complete transformation, and harvest labourers were faced on more than one occasion with a new technological world. This essay looks at the different tools used by harvesters, chronicles the main technological changes in the harvest field, and assesses the different methods of organising the harvest labour force during the nineteenth century. It also examines the importance of harvest diet and payment to harvesters.

124

I

The traditional method of cutting the grain crops in Scotland was with the serrated-edge sickle. Its light weight allowed the reaper to hold the sickle in one hand and grip the grain stalk with the other. Its gentle sawing motion permitted the grain to be held in the ear of the corn with the minimum loss of grain.[1] In Scots it was the 'heuk', as in English, and by metonymy it referred to the reaper himself.[2]

From the middle of the eighteenth century another sickle type began to be used in Scotland. This the smooth-edge sickle or the scythe hook, differed from the heuk in two ways: it was broader and longer and was ground on both sides of the blade.[3] It was the same basic shape as the earlier type but its use involved a different kind of cutting action. Instead of the gentle sawing movement of the heuk, a sweeping action was used with the scythe hook and it made the blade faster to operate. It could cut more at one stroke than the heuk.[4] A contemporary description of the scythe hook gave the breadth of the blade as one and a half inches with a cutting edge of twenty inches. The wooden handle was six inches long and four and a half inches in circumference. It weighed one pound and cost in the 1840s between one shilling and one shilling and ninepence. By contrast the heuk weighed only nine ounces and cost one shilling.[5] In Shetland, harvesters used a smaller rounded sickle type with a smooth cutting edge. There the sickles had semi-circular blades and were described as broad, blunt hooks that took much time to sharpen.[6] The locally produced sickles in the parishes of Sandsting and Aithsting were extremely small and required the reaper to make between thirty-five and forty cuts before he filled his hand with corn.[7]

There are frequent references to the existence of sickles in the eighteenth and nineteenth centuries. An inventory of the Castletown farming utensils in Fordoun contains a reference in 1792 to 'six corn hooks',[8] and sickles were easily purchased through shops. The Ayrshire minister, the Reverend John Mitchell, recollected that there were two clothiers in the Ayrshire village of Beith at the end of the century, 'and one of those, I recollect right, also sold flax seeds, with hooks and scythes'.[9] In Fife toward the end of the eighteenth century, reaping hooks and scythes were commonly to be had over the counter.[10]

Full-time sickle makers were recognised members of the community and they obviously supplied much of the demand that existed. In the Stirlingshire parish of Kilsyth the village was populated 'chiefly by miners, colliers and sickle makers...'[11] Sickle making was a thriving industry there in 1796 and was one of the few successful industrial enterprises in the locality. It employed up to six hands in 1796,[12] and by the later 1830s sickle making was still undertaken there.[13] This solitary factory produced annually about 1600 dozen sickles, and the bulk of the output went to the north of Scotland.[14]

The smooth-edged sickle had been in use on the European mainland for some time but only completed its conquest of south and western France in the nineteenth century.[15] In 1794 it was noted in Galloway: 'A reaping hook has been recently introduced. It is said to be better than the one generally in use in Scotland. It is smooth edged like a knife and is said to cut cleaner and easier. It is a little larger and is apt to blunt'.[16] By the first decade of the nineteenth century it was challenging the ancient serrated heuk in Dumfriesshire,[17] and Robert Somerville noted that it had gained ground in East Lothian by 1805.[18] Its progress was confirmed in that area by the early 1820s, and commentators there were pointing to a clear difference between the heuk and the scythe hook.[19]

In fact the scythe hook was rapidly falling into the vocabulary of improved agriculture in the first decade of the nineteenth century. Its use was recorded in the rich carse lands of Stirlingshire where the preference for the scythe hook was strong but the old heuk was still most frequently used by harvesters.[20] Moreover, throughout the opening years of the nineteenth century sickle technology was active. Scotland imported English, American and Russian sickles, and developing technology produced a sickle type that was an intermediate stage between the old heuk and the scythe hook. In the 1820s Hutton's improved reaping hook was recommended for thin, short crops of grain because it could do between one third and one quarter more work than the heuk.[21] However, plotting the precise distribution of hand tools at this time is made difficult by a lack of accurate descriptive material from the sources. Writing about Midlothian, for example, in 1794, George Robertson merely noted the use of the sickle and said that it was mostly used by women.[22] Similarly, identification is not easily possible in Angus and Aberdeenshire in the first decades of the nineteenth century, and it was not until the 1840s that the scythe hook made headway in Fife.[23]

II

The harvesting of the grain crops in the pre-mechanical age with the sickle was highly organised. Men and women were allocated separate and clearly defined tasks, and while methods varied according to the size of the farm, crop type and the availability of labour, clearly distinctive systems of organising harvesters emerge. The most sophisticated was undoubtedly the bandwin system which has its roots in the early seventeenth century. It survived intact as an expression of the organised use of the sickle in some areas until the arrival of the mechanical reaping machine. The system, for example, prevailed in Berwickshire, where Robert Kerr noted in 1809: 'Two parties of three reapers in each, called a rig or ridge, as three cut the grain of one ordinary ridge, or land, of fifteen feet broad'.[24] Ridges varied in breadth and width, but they were related to the functional requirements of sowing and reaping and were fundamental in regulating labour input in the harvest fields on the large arable units of the grain-producing counties.[25] Kerr observed the ensuing harvest operations at first hand: 'the harvest strength is distributed into bands, each consisting each of six reapers, provincially shearers, with the binder or bandster, which squad is provincially termed a bandwin, quasi winning or gaining a band or binding of the sheaves. The bandwin is subdivided into two parties of three reapers in each called a rig or ridge as three cut the grain of one ordinary ridge, or land of fifteen feet broad. The middle shearer of each ridge makes all the bands, composed of two handfuls of corn in the straw, tied or twisted together at the ear ends, called the corn knot and spread out on the ground ... The bands are successfully filled by the shearers and bound into sheaves by the bandster, who likewise sets up the stocks, all the sheaves of his two ridges in stooks or shocks'.[26]

Other commentators of the period agree with Kerr's description, and both Stephens[27] and Robertson assign the system to south-east and east-central Scotland in the nineteenth century.[28] Additional evidence suggest that the arrangement functioned in north-east England in the eighteenth and nineteenth centuries.[29]

The bandwin was one of the methods used to harness harvest labour effectively and its use was confined to the larger arable grain-growing units which required a massive and disciplined input of harvest labour. It was not common in the smaller arable farms of the north-east or south-west, where, on the whole, family labour was used to harvest the grain crops and where a different technology prevailed from the early years of the nineteenth century. A contemporary description from another of the Scottish corn counties and a rich agricultural area, Moray, illustrates not only the disciplined nature of this particular method of harvesting but indicates the large numbers involved in harvest work in the early nineteenth century. The description comes from a series of letters written by a young farm student to his father. They relate to the 2000-acre unit of Barnhill near Elgin where, in 1809, 250 acres of wheat were grown in addition to 150 acres of barley, 300 acres of oats and 200 acres of beans and peas. The extracts are worth quoting because they also demonstrate the quasi-military nature of the harvest operation on a large farming unit. The description of the bandwin differs from other accounts only in that each unit comprised nine people:

> September 2: On Monday morning our forces were mustered for harvest work and were divided into twelve bands of 12 shearers and two bandsters each, four of which were committed to the charge of Fairbairn, the like number to me, and the remainder to Howard, our head shepherd.
>   The ranking or sorting of the people was done with expedition by Mr. Jamieson [the farm owner], who seems quite up to that nature; and though half an hour or thereby might be lost before the ranking was completed, yet all that hurry and confusion which, without it, would inevitably have ensued,

were altogether kept clear of, and the whole regiment entered to work at once upon a horn being sounded by Fairbairn, who is first in command below Mr. Jamieson.

The arrangement was made in this manner — Mr. Jamieson having ascertained his numbers, selected twelve of those considered to be the best shearers and provided them with two able bandsters for tying and stooking the corn; ordered Fairbairn off with these and to place them at the left or open side of the field, four shearers upon each ridge, with their bandsters behind them. The second, third and fourth bands followed in their course, a ticket being given to each bandster mentioning the name of the band to which he belonged.

When the fifth band was formed, I marched at their head, and placed them on their respective ridges, and so on, as the sixth, seventh and eighth band arrived. Howard came with the ninth, and arranged them in likeway and Mr. Jamieson followed with the rear guard. After riding across the field and being satisfied that all were rightly arranged, he halted in the centre of Fairbairn's bands, and calling attention he stated in a few words, that these people were committed to his management and that full power was delegated to him to do everything which as a master he could do himself; that it was his desire to have the corn cut clean and low; and that while sufficient time was allowed to execute the work, idleness was in no account permitted. He came to my station, and repeated these orders and concluded with the same in the centre of Howard's division. After this, upon a sign being given, Fairbairn sounded the horn, and immediately the whole body fell to work. The total number were 144 shearers and 24 bandsters. Three fourths of the former are women, who, in fact, are our neatest cutters'.[30]

The bandwin's success, therefore, rested on its collective strength: it was paid as a unit, by the amount it cut, and it could not afford a weakling as one of its constituent parts. It comprised both men and women but not young children or elderly folk. The timeless dictum laid down for Dalhousie estate workers in 1658 held good until the bandwin ceased to be part of harvest labour organisation in the later nineteenth century: a bandwin must have 'nather boy nor lasse but such as are sufficient to be ane hewke'.[31] The system was geared to speed and efficiency and related purely to the use of the sickle.

Another method of organising harvest labour was employed and related to the use of the sickle — threaving. By contrast to the bandwin system, threaving was designed to allow individuals of various strengths to work as individual units. It was piece work and harvesters were paid accordingly. Threaving takes its name from threave, a measure of cut grain containing two full stooks, either 24 sheaves of oats or barley or 28 of wheat. Each threave measured three feet in length and twelve inches in diameter.[32] Threavers were paid on the basis of individual productivity, and each one worked along the ridge. In the 1830s threavers were paid 3d for a threave of oats or barley and 4d for a threave of wheat.[33] Their efforts were logged carefully by the farmer, and an accurate account was kept of individual performance.

Outwith the highly organised farming units of the large grain-growing districts, threaving was generally employed, particularly in Forfarshire.[34] It allowed seasonal labour to be recruited over brief periods and it suited rural folk and townsfolk alike who could only spend short spells away from their regular tasks. For the farmer it offered a flexible system of employing labour and paying them only on the basis of their output. Threavers, unlike regular bands of harvesters, were not hired for the season. The system provided work for the old, infirm and children.[35] It was argued that it allowed children to gain valuable experience of harvest work which they could not otherwise obtain, and women were able to earn wages comparable to a male, depending on their output.[36]

In the bandwin system the bandster, so crucial to the effectiveness of the team and invariably a skilled and experienced harvester, was part of the team, but in the threaving system he was engaged separately from the other harvesters and was employed on a full-time basis throughout the harvest to tie and stook the sheaves on the individual ridges.[37] With an army of harvesters of various ages, experience and aptitude at work in his field, the bandster represented a high degree of professionalism. However, the major criticism levelled at the threaving system was its relative slowness, despite the careful attention shearers paid to their work.[38]

The change from the serrated heuk to the scythe hook created fundamentally different work patterns for harvesters. The heuk with its limited cutting power was used by both men and women. They worked in groups along the ridge either in the bandwin or threaving system. The introduction of the scythe hook tended to deprive the female of her role as a shearer of corn. It was used extensively by male shearers, especially by migrant Irish harvesters who played an increasingly important, but geographically limited, role in the harvest fields of southern Scotland from the turn of the eighteenth century. Despite the high rate of seasonal harvest migration from Ireland, their numbers were concentrated in the west and south-west of Scotland, and from there they fanned out into Berwick and the Lothians and up into Fife and Kinross. There is little evidence of Irish harvesters spreading north of the Tay. The rate of Irish migration was impressive: at the height of the season in the 1820s, between 6000 and 8000 Irishmen landed on the Clyde coast each week during harvest, and by the 1840s numbers had risen considerably with, on one occasion, 14,000 reapers at the Broomielaw in one August week.[39]

In terms of productivity, the scythe hook could cut more than the heuk.[40] With the heuk only a small amount could be cut at each stroke, but as a sawing motion was employed it was easier to shear the stalks low down where they had greater firmness and resistance. As a result it was easily used by women who were said to be physiologically better equipped to bend low than men.[41] The pattern of cutting changed with the scythe hook and a more slashing motion was used in cutting. It was not necessary for the shearer to bend so low to cut the grain and, given also its speed, it was more suited to use by men.[42] The employment of the scythe hook also required a new application on the harvester's part. It was noted in East Lothian in 1821 that 'The scythe hook has been gradually gaining ground with the shearers in the harvest, for some years past ... but as it requires some experience in the use of it, before those who have been accustomed to the common sickle can handle it properly, many without taking time to appreciate the merits of the newly introduced implement, have keenly expressed their reluctance to the use of it'.[43]

In general terms, then, the use of sickle types can be related to Irish male harvesters who tended to use the scythe hook and Highland female harvesters who favoured the heuk. Both formed the main elements in the flow of seasonal harvesters to the corn fields of the Lothians and south-east Scotland.[44] The appearance of two different groups of harvest labourers often resulted in open competition between Highlanders and Irish.[45] But even after the introduction of the scythe hook the heuk was still extensively used. Many farmers found the former produced rougher work, and it was argued that it was not suited to thin crops of grain.[46]

From the beginning of the nineteenth century, the scythe began to be used as an implement for cutting grain. Like the sickle, it is an implement of antiquity and originally it was used to cut grass. From the fourteenth century it began to be used as a grain-cutting tool on the European mainland. Initially the scythe was a short-handled implement, but gradually the blade and the handle were lengthened to improve its cutting potential, and it became heavier. Unlike the sickle, it was held by the user in both hands. Its basic design and principle have remained with us to this day.[47]

The motion used in cutting with the scythe was quite different from that used with the sickle. When using the latter the reaper employed a sawing motion, but with the scythe the sawing motion became a chopping and more violent action. The long-handled scythe was gripped palm downwards in the right hand and palm upwards in the left. The attachment of handles to the scythe handle (sned) allowed for easier holding and better handling. Basically, two long-handled scythe types were used in Scotland from the beginning of the nineteenth century. In the north and north-east, where grain cutting with the scythe took root, a sned with a Y-shape was used and, by contrast in the south, where English imports and influence were stronger, the sned with an S-shape was more commonly employed.[48]

The emergence of the scythe as a grain-cutting tool — it was extensively used for cutting grass and hay[49] — radically altered the harvest work pattern in areas where it was adopted. Its most fundamental impact on the work force lay in the total exclusion of the female from her role as a cutter of grain, although it did not substantially change the number of ancillary workers required at harvest. The long-handled scythe was much heavier than the sickle, and consequently required much greater strength to work.

From mediaeval times, therefore, scythe cutting had been associated with male strength. Mowing was a job which only the more experienced and better-paid male servants would be expected to do.[50] The move from reaping with the sickle to mowing with the scythe required harvesters to acquire and master a totally new skill.

In contrast to the small swathe cut by the sickle, a skilled mower using a blade four feet long would be required to cut between seven and eight feet of standing corn in a good sweep with a forward cut of between 12 and 15 inches.[51] Higher productivity, therefore, gave the scythe a clear advantage over other forms of hand reaping. It was estimated that a team of scythesmen could cut over four acres of oats or barley in a ten-hour day compared with just over two acres with the scythe hook and just under two with the heuk.[52] George Robertson estimated that five scythers were equal to nine sickles or nine scythers to twelve sickles.[53] In extensive experiments to determine the comparative merit of scythe and sickle carried out on farms on the Dunglass estate in East Lothian in 1793, detailed costings showed the substantial saving in time and labour achieved by using the scythe.[54]

The physical strength required to use the scythe was considerable, and it took time to acquire.[55] According to one source, scythesmen had to be 'strong men capable of undergoing great fatigue'.[56] The size of the work team varied according to farm size but might consist of three scythers, invariably men, followed by three gatherers, usually women, and three binders or bandsters, normally men and reflecting the skill required in binding the cut corn. In addition a raker was employed as part of the work force.[57]

John Taylor, a farm overseer at Corriestone near Huntly, summed up the early difficulties experienced by workpeople using the scythe for the first time. He noted that beginners were fast cutters but not neat in laying the cut crop into swathes, and he opined that instruction was needed to get the mower to lay the grain evenly in the swathe.[58] As with the scythe hook, the mower used the scythe across the ridge. Ancillary operations required skill. Gathering the swathes of cut grain was regarded as an 'art' by one contemporary who found that the areas where the scythe was first introduced — Aberdeen and Banff — were models of good scything. He travelled through Berwickshire and the Lothians in the 1840s, and although he saw 'tolerable scythesmen', he found no good gatherers.[59] He complained that southern women had no idea how to gather the cut corn, and he found that they had petticoats tied to their knees 'whereas a good gatherer invariably stands at the stubble end of the sheaf with her petticoat down at her knees'.[60]

There was clearly a distinct economic advantage in using the scythe as it cut lower, so providing more straw for fodder, and it permitted quicker harvesting. This included quicker drying of the sheaf because sheaves were not bound so tightly from the scythe as those that were compressed in the shearer's hand before being passed on to the bandster.[61] But the scythe was not universally adopted despite its advantages. Farmers at first were reluctant to use it on wheat. They feared that it was liable to shake this most valuable of grains and initially, even in areas where it did catch on, was used primarily on oats. The scythe was not easily employed when the crop was lodged through wind or rain. In addition, land surface had to be relatively smooth to allow it free passage, and land had often to be rolled before the scythe could be employed.[62] In the south of Scotland, where large numbers of seasonal migrants provided the bulk of the harvest labour force, farmers did not see any immediate advantage in changing from the sickle, which their workers were completely familiar with, to the more productive scythe. But in the north-east, where seasonal harvest labour was negligible on the small family farms, the quicker-cutting scythe gained ground from the beginning of the nineteenth century.[63] It was noted for Aberdeenshire in 1811 that 'The scythe ... was introduced a few years ago and both from the high wages and the difficulty of procuring reapers in a precarious season, was employed last harvest [1809] on many farms to a great extent'.[64] In Banffshire, where the scythe was used for cutting grain crops from 1806, there was 'a difficulty in obtaining what may be called good shearers'.[65]

III

The coming of the mechanical reaping machine marked another great phase in the relationship between the harvester and his work. Reaping machines had been in limited use in Scotland from 1828, but early difficulties with complicated cutting mechanisms, the draught of the machine and the lack of supporting technical services (for example, for the machine invented by the Auchterhouse minister's son, Patrick Bell) restricted its use. It was only from the middle of the nineteenth century when the lighter, more manoeuvrable American types, principally the McCormick and the Hussey, came on to the British market that the mechanical reaper began to make an impact.

One of Patrick Bell's prime motives in creating the mechanical reaper was to reduce the burden of harvest work on the labourer, but at first mechanical reapers did not greatly reduce labour input or physical exertion in the harvest field.[66] The early manual delivery type had no form of mechanical delivery for the cut corn after it had been sheared by the reaper blade. One man had to drive the horses, another had to deliver the cut sheaves of grain, and large numbers of harvesters were still required to bind and stook the crop. Its only saving in the early days was in the wages of shearers or scythesmen.[67] For the mechanical reaper to make any impact on the labour of harvest, one was required which would be light, would not represent a high capital outlay, would possess a simplified cutting gear and would be useful to small farmers.[68] In the early days, therefore, labour requirements of the mechanical reaper were still considerable. It was estimated in Kilberry in Argyllshire in the later 1860s that eighteen hands were required to keep the machine going: in east and central Scotland ten people were regarded as a fair number in attendance, and George Hope of Fenton Barns in East Lothian, one of the earliest and most enthusiastic proponents of the mechanical reaping machine, calculated that to work and keep up with the machine cutting an acre an hour, sixteen people would be needed.[69]

Eventually, from the 1850s and 1860s, light self-delivery types began to make an impact on labour requirements. One man could work the draught horses and attend to the reaper, and the principles embodied in McCormick's machine, where the cut grain fell on to a screw platform and was passed on to the ground at the side of the machine (side delivery), marked a major breakthrough in harvesting technology. The other major elements associated with McCormick's model were the knife that cut the grain by working to and fro; the fingers that gripped the corn stalks before cutting; the platform where the cut grain was gathered; the straw divider on the outside of the platform separating the cut from the standing grain; and the drawing wheel placed directly behind the horse and carrying most of the machine's weight.[70]

The other form of self-delivery was the back-delivery machine. In this instance the cut sheaves dropped behind the reaper and they had to be cleared from the machine's path before it made its next round. This type represented a smaller reduction in labour inputs. In contrast to the side-delivery model, with which an entire field could be cut without having to bind and stock before the reaper could carry on, a path had to be cleared for the back-delivery machine at once.[71]

The spread of the machine even after the 1850s was sporadic. A major limiting factor was the unevenness of field surfaces. The old high-crooked ridges were rapidly disappearing, and thorough drainage had gone a long way to smoothing out fields in some regions. The Lothians in particular, in the vanguard of improved Scottish farming practice, were ideally suited to mechanisation and, by 1860, East Lothian could boast 160 reaping machines.[72] But rougher, hilly, upland terrain blocked its passage, and consequently older methods of hand reaping and their attendant methods of work organisation lingered on in other areas. It was noted of Fyvie parish in Aberdeenshire in the early 1870s: 'No doubt the hilly nature of many of the larger farms has prevented the reaping machine from being more extensively used'. And even by the early 1870s John Milne noted: '...but even yet, however, incredible as it may appear to a south country farmer, some of our farmers have never seen a reaping machine at work'.[74]

In general terms, however, farmers saw the obvious advantage of the reaping machine as a means of reducing the labour required at harvest from the high numbers associated with hand-tool cutting. They were particularly keen to reduce the number of seasonal labourers — 'strangers' as they were often termed in agricultural accounts and treatises. As early as the 1830s it was noted: 'The reaping machine has been tried ... and although it will not prevent the necessity of hand labour, by the inhabitants of cultivated districts it may render the assistance of strangers less necessary'.[75] The prospect of drawing labour from the immediate locality, as opposed to the Highlands and Ireland, which could come and go on a daily basis and needed only victualling was more attractive to the farmer and his wife than having to feed and house an itinerant work force and have them loitering about the farm buildings on wet and idle days. The statement by the Reverend J. A. Honey of Inchture parish in Perthshire to the Royal Commission on the Employment of Women and Children in Agriculture in 1867 implied more than a slight sense of relief: 'The introduction of reaping machines, as far as harvest work is concerned, is lessening the necessity for a large influx of reapers and have so far done away with the harvest arrangements which have been far from proper'.[76]

While it was the moral aspect of housing itinerant workers in barns and stables that concerned the clergy, the farmer was more interested in making better use of his own specialist staff at harvest as machinery became more widely available. A Perthshire farmer observed in 1867: 'I use mowers and reapers and all the machinery I can find that is useful, hence the usual staff of the farm can get through our work in haytime and harvest'.[77]

Thus, on the large arable farms of the Lothians where the reliance on seasonal harvesters had been most pronounced, increased use of reaping machinery allowed the regular farm staff and their families to cope more readily with harvest work. In 1867 George Hope of Fenton Barns in Dirleton parish in East Lothian, for example, needed to recruit only fifteen extra harvesters to supplement the efforts of his fifty-eight regular hands.[78] In other areas where the resident farm staffs were smaller, a high input of seasonal harvest labour was still required. On a large unit in Errol parish in Perthshire, extra harvest labour in 1867 was supplied entirely by a hundred recruited females.[79]

But even after reaping machines became more general, harvesters had often to fall back on the older forms of hand-tool technology. Scythes, for example, were often used to cut a path in a field to allow the reaping machine to make a start on the crop, and in the early days of mechanical reaping the machine could not cope adequately with long soft grain stalks that became twisted and tangled in wet, windy weather.[80] The year 1857 was a case in point. There had been little sunshine in August, and September had been bedevilled by damp weather. On the 20th of that month a severe thunderstorm flattened much of the East Lothian crops which were still uncut at that late date. The situation was exacerbated by a heavier than usual crop, and as a consequence 'a greater proportion has been cut with the sickle and less by the reaping machine than in past seasons'.[81] The east coast suffered badly that year, and reports from Leven in Fife and Stow in the Borders tell the same story of weather defeating the machine.[82] 1882 was another wet summer: in Aberdeenshire a good crop of oats and an over-abundance of straw after lea was devastated by rain and had to be cut by sickle and scythe and not by the reaping machine.[83] Seven years later in 1889, and thirty years after the widespread introduction of the reaping machine, a large field in the Lothians had to be cut with the sickle because the weather had laid and twisted the crop.[84] It is significant that in 1860, when 160 machines were in use in East Lothian, Aberdeenshire scythesmen, contracted for the harvest, were still travelling south to work at the Lothian hairst.[85]

IV

Monetary payments to harvesters recognised two basic principles: the task for which the harvester was engaged and the sex of the harvester. Traditionally the most physically able male workers who could shear, stack and bind the crop were paid a higher wage than either less effective workers or women.[86] This principle, embodied in seventeenth-century wage regulations, was carried through into subsequent centuries.

Wage levels fluctuated in relation to labour supply and demand, but whatever the prevailing level, cutters of corn, shearers with the sickle or scythesmen were paid more than any other worker. These were regarded as the most skilled workers and their efforts were duly recognised. With the old heuk both men and women could share in top earnings to some extent, but with the coming of the scythe hook and the scythe, tools which the female did not use, her chances of earning on the top scale ended and she was relegated to the less well-paid ancillary tasks. Men, for example, were engaged for between 23/- and 25/- for cutting in Perthshire in the 1790s compared with 15/- to 20/- for women for three weeks' harvest work.[87] By the mid-1830s the difference was maintained. Men shearers in Kincardine were paid £2.5/- for the harvest and women were paid £1.5/-.[88] By the mid-1870s experienced scythesmen were paid at Crieff £6 a month for the harvest and bandsters were rewarded at the lower rate of between £4.5/- and £4.15/-. Women engaged to lift the cut grain behind the scythe obtained £4 and rakers, the least skilled of the harvest force, made only £2 per month.[89] At a hiring market in Perth in 1862, scythesmen were paid 27/- a week without victuals and lifters of grain were engaged at 12/- and 15/- a week with food and lodgings.[90] Workers employed casually at harvest were invariably paid a higher rate than workers similarly engaged at other times of seasonal demand such as potato lifting or turnip hoeing. On a daily rate it might be double the wage.[91] Extra payments were also often made to stackers of corn in the Lothians in recognition of their skill.[92]

K

The provision of food to harvest workers was an important element in their payment and it represented both a sizeable portion of the farmer's expenditure on harvest labour and the worker's income. Costings made in the middle of the nineteenth century were compiled by Henry Stephens. He calculated that it would cost the farmers on a daily basis 5d a day for bread to each harvester, with the provision of one loaf at breakfast each and two loaves each at dinner at midday. Each harvester received two and a half quarts of beer a day at a cost of one penny a quart, bringing the total daily expenditure per harvester to 7½d. At that time harvesters were receiving either two shillings a day or two shillings and sixpence, depending on their task.[93] By the late 1860s the provision of harvest food was costing farmers between seven and nine pence a day in the Lothians exclusive of the daily wage.

To the full-time farm servant harvest food was a valued addition to his yearly wage. By the middle of the 1860s, full-time married farm workers in Roxburgh were paid between £35 and £40 a year. The value of harvest food was calculated to be worth between £1.10/- and £2 of that sum. Taking as an example a full-time hind in Bedrule parish in 1867, the value of harvest food can be related to his other perquisites. He received oatmeal to the value of 1/9d a stone; barley at four shillings a bushel; peas at five shillings and four pence a bushel; potatoes at six shillings and two and a half pence per 100 yards; £9 for the keep of a cow; £3 for his cottage and garden; £2.17/- for coal and £1.4/- for harvest food.[94] The provision of food by the farmer for workers in harvest — both regular and casual labourers — underscores the special nature of the task and its importance in the agricultural calendar. With the possible exception of hay work, food was not normally provided to workers in respect of a specific task.

Harvesters were generally provided with three meals. Breakfast consisted of porridge and milk, dinner of beer and bread, and supper of porridge and milk, but there were variations according to regions and the whims of the farmer.[95] During the eighteenth century much of the food was prepared in the farm kitchen. Farmhouse staff were delegated to prepare food and, on some occasions, assist with the shearing.[96] The preparation and distribution of large quantities of food for large squads of harvesters placed a great strain on the resources of the farmer's wife and kitchen staff. George Robertson graphically described the fare and its method of distribution in the Lothians in the early part of the nineteenth century: 'The great pots of porridge for breakfast that were to be made and the large pails of buttermilk to be carried to the fields daily to them, was a work of no little toil and the great pots of kail [broth] composed of pot barley, beans peas shred cabbage and onion, in a mess as thick that a spoon could stand on end in it, together with a thick bannock of peasemeal for the main course, and for the second oatcakes, with milk for dinner was still a laborious undertaking'.[97]

During the nineteenth century, the accent on such a heavy diet changed

with a move away from the domestic preparation of harvesters' food.
There was a growing tendency to procure fare, notably wheaten bread,
from nearby towns. The food was 'of the best sort' for shearers, according
to one commentator.[98] Wheaten bread played an important role in the
harvesters' diet' at least in some areas. In Berwickshire at the beginning of
the nineteenth century shearers were given one pound of fine wheaten
bread at dinner in addition to a quart of good table beer.[99] In the Lothians
improvement came with the substitution of bread and beer for dinner
instead of kail.[100] A description of harvest diet for the middle of the
century on a farm in Edrom parish in Berwickshire showed that harvesters
were given, for four weeks, a daily diet of porridge and milk for breakfast,
a bottle of beer and seventeen and a half ounces of best wheaten bread for
dinner, and porridge and milk for supper.[101] Farmers would occasionally
dispense whisky to workers at harvest time, but as one Lanarkshire farmer
noted with relief: 'They don't drink much'. Butter — in some areas so-
called 'heuk butter' — cheese and ham or bacon were also given as part of
the harvest diet.[102]

Towards the end of the nineteenth century, according to the Royal
Commission on Labour of 1893, 'the question of [harvest] food became
ripe for alteration'.[103] The Commissioners noted a move away from the
provision of morning and evening meals by farmers (coupled with a greater
reliance on regular farm staffs and less need to recruit itinerant harvesters)
and a growing distaste for oatmeal in porridge form. In some instances
they noted that harvesters in the Lothians preferred to find their own fare
at these times, although the tradition of supplying food during the day
remained. Farmers felt that if they provided harvesters with a midday
meal, they would be kept near at hand and there would be no waste of
time before the afternoon start.[104] Bread still remained the basic element in
the harvesters' midday meal and it was brought 'fresh from the town or
village bakery every day'.[105] These developments were paralleled by a
tendency to commute the food to a simple extra cash payment in lieu of
food, or to pay harvesters in barley. As early as 1867 it was noted in
Roxburghshire, where one farmer offered one and a half bushels of barley
in lieu of a supper of porridge and milk in the field, that 'Nearly all prefer
the barley to the supper of porridge and milk and take their supper at
home'.[106] By the turn of the century it was common in some areas for
harvest food to be dropped completely from the harvesters' bargain and
replaced by a higher cash wage.[107]

Harvesters were a colourful social grouping, for the harvest was the time
of year when urban workers, spinners, weavers, colliers and even
schoolteachers 'took a hairst'.[108] They assembled at harvest hiring markets
throughout the country to be engaged, frequently in large numbers. The
West Port in Edinburgh was a recognised hiring centre, as were Glasgow
Cross, Perth, Crieff and Campbeltown, as well as many other centres.[109]

No clearer expression of the vivid nature of the harvest labour force can be found in the eighteenth and nineteenth centuries than the bothy ballads and songs of the north-east of Scotland. Some ballads give a valuable insight into the composition of the harvest work force and, indeed, of all the ballads dealing with life and work on the land, harvest ballads form the single largest category.[110] 'The Harvest Song', for example, singles out the individuals involved in the pre-mechanical cutting of the grain crops. The harvesters gathered at the farm and were organised into a working unit by the farmer:

> Frae baith toon and country to him they convene,
> And a' to the fields they gaither O;
> The maister he orders them a' as he thinks fit,
> And pits whom he pleases thegither O.[111]

Many ballads, such as 'Johnnie Sangster', emphasise the sheer physical fatigue in harvest work:

> Oh some complain on hacks and thraws
> And some on brods and bruises,
> And some complain on grippet hips
> And stiffness in their troosers;
> But as soon as they lay doon the scythe
> And a' the pipers yoke their blawvin,
> They ane a' forget their tools
> Wi' dafflin an' wi' tyawvin.[112]

One of the best known of this genre is 'The Lothian Hairst', which describes the seasonal movement of Aberdeen harvesters to the Lothian harvest fields. According to tradition, it was written c. 1860 by a female harvester from Deeside who travelled from there to the Lothians as part of a contracted harvest band which agreed to cut, gather and stook the grain crops at an agreed price per acre. The contractor then engaged a foreman who was responsible to the farmer for carrying out the work. The ballad in part tells the story of the foreman, Logan, who was employed by the contractor William Matheson.[113] According to the ballad, one of Logan's main tasks was to supervise the sleeping arrangements in the Lothian bothies and ensure that the mixed group of contract harvesters were kept strictly apart. In the opinion of the female authoress, Logan did his job only too well:

> My mate and I could get nae chance,
> For Logan's watchful eye,
> And wi' the lads we got nae sport,
> For Logan was so sly.
> He cleaned oor bothy every nicht
> Before he went to sleep,
> And he never left behind him ane,
> But strict his rules did keep.

V

Harvest operations in the eighteenth and nineteenth centuries underwent major changes. The coming of the scythe hook and the scythe, predominantly tools used by male harvesters, served to reduce female opportunities as cutters of grain and relegated women to the ancillary tasks of harvesting. Developing harvest technology can thus be taken as an important barometer of the sexual division of labour. The mechanical reaper finally removed the burden of grain cutting by hand and brought and end to the bandwin and threaving systems of labour organisation. These systems in themselves were highly organised and suited to hand-tool technology, and they represent the relationship between man and his work tools and between male and female workers on the harvest field. In addition they reflect the availability and expertise of harvest labourers and the farmer's ability to harness that labour to his regional and local requirements.

I have also tried to outline the special nature of harvest work: workers were paid special rates which reflected their skill in cutting or binding the corn, and the harvest diet was a further reflection of the exceptional nature of harvest work. Regional variation within Scotland was important in determining the harvester's working regime and the rate at which technological change affected him, not only in terms of the final adoption of the mechanical reaper, but within the world of hand-tool technology.

NOTES

1. I. H. Adams, *Agrarian Landscape Terms* (Edinburgh, 1976), p. 147.

2. W. Grant and D. Murison, eds., *Scottish National Dictionary* (Edinburgh, 1960–1976), see entry under 'heuk'.

3. J. Slight and R. Scott Burn, *The Book of Farm Implements and Machines* (Edinburgh, 1858), p. 481.

4. A. Fenton, 'Sickle, Scythe and Reaping Machine', *Ethnologica Europaea*, vii (1973/74), p. 361.

5. J. Taylor, 'On the Comparative Merits of Different Modes of Reaping Grain', *Transactions of the Highland and Agricultural Society of Scotland (T.H.A.S.)* (1843–5), p. 270.

6. A. Fenton, *The Northern Isles: Orkney and Shetland* (Edinburgh, 1978), p. 337.

7. *New Statistical Account of Scotland* (N.S.A.) (Edinburgh, 1845), xv, p. 138.

8. National Library of Scotland, Castletown Farming Papers, Ms. 2790.

9. 'Memoirs of Ayrshire, c. 1780 by the Reverend John Mitchell DD', in *Miscellany of the Scottish History Society*, vi (Edinburgh, 1939), p. 277.

10. J. Thomson, *A General View of the Agriculture of the County of Fife* (Edinburgh, 1800), p. 296.

11. F. H. Groome, *Ordnance Gazetteer of Scotland* (Edinburgh, 1885), i, p. 85.

12. *Old Statistical Account of Scotland* (Edinburgh, 1791–1799) (O.S.A.), xviii, p. 311.

13. *N.S.A.*, viii, p. 160.

14. *O.S.A.*, xviii, p. 311.

15. M. M. Postan, ed., *Cambridge Economic History of Europe: Agrarian Life in the Middle Ages* (Cambridge, 1966), p. 156.

16. J. Webster, *A General View of the Agriculture of Galloway* (Edinburgh, 1794), p. 15.

17. J. Singer, *A General View of the Agriculture of the County of Dumfries* (Edinburgh, 1812), p. 139.

18. R. Somerville, *A General View of the Agriculture of East Lothian* (Edinburgh, 1805), pp. 71–2.

19. *Farmer's Magazine* (Edinburgh, 1800–1825), xxii, p. 504.

20. P. Graham, *A General View of the Agriculture of the County of Stirling* (Edinburgh, 1812), p. 150.

21. *Farmer's Magazine*, xxiii, p. 55.

22. G. Robertson, *A General View of the Agriculture of Midlothian* (Edinburgh, 1794), pp. 62–3.

23. G. Buist, 'A Sketch of the Agriculture of Fifeshire', *Quarterly Journal of Agriculture*, xi (1840–41), p. 302.

24. R. Kerr, *A General View of the Agriculture of the County of Berwick* (London, 1809), p. 226.

25. J. Smith, *Remarks on Thorough Drainage and Deep Ploughing* (Stirling, 1843), p. 146; H. Stephens, *The Book of the Farm*, I (Edinburgh, 1844), p. 172.

26. Kerr, *Agriculture of Berwick*, p. 226.

27. Stephens, *Book of the Farm*, p. 302.

28. G. Robertson, *A General View of the Agriculture of Kincardineshire or the Mearns* (London, 1813), p. 261.

29. H. M. Neville, *A Corner in the North* (Newcastle, 1909), p. 47.

30. 'Letters from a Young Farmer to his Father', *Farmer's Magazine*, viii (1807), pp. 369–70.

31. Scottish Record Office (S.R.O.), Dalhousie Muniments, GD 45/18/704 (1658), Notebook of Reapers required for Panmure and Carmyllie.

32. *Scottish National Dictionary*, entry under 'threave'; H. Stephens, *Book of the Farm* (1871 edn.), II, p. 301.

33. *N.S.A.*, x, p. 438.

34. *Farmer's Magazine*, xxii (1821), p. 497; 'On Threaving or a New Mode of Paying for Reaping Corn, according to the extent of work executed', *Farmer's Magazine*, vi (1805), pp. 466–67.

35. *N.S.A.*, xiii, p. 370.

36. *Farmer's Magazine*, vi (1805), p. 467.

37. A. Fenton, *Scottish Country Life* (Edinburgh, 1976), p. 58.

38. J. Macdonald, 'On the Agriculture of the County of Fife', *T.H.A.S.*, viii, (1876), p. 38.

39. J. E. Handley, *The Irish in Scotland, 1798–1845* (Cork, 1943), p. 164.

40. Stephens, *Book of the Farm* (1855 edn.), II, p. 342.

41. *Ibid.*, p. 332.

42. Fenton, 'Sickle, Scythe and Reaping Machine', p. 38.

43. *Farmer's Magazine*, xxii (1821), p. 505.

44. Fenton, *Scottish Country Life*, p. 58.

45. G. Fortune, 'On Reaping Hooks', *Quarterly Journal of Agriculture* (1832), p. 1082.

46. *Ibid.*, p. 1081.

47. Axel Steensberg, *Ancient Harvesting Implements* (Copenhagen, 1943), p. 230; Michael Roberts, 'Sickles and Scythes: Women's work and Men's work at harvest time', *History Workshop* (1979), p. 15.

48. Fenton, 'Sickle, Scythe and Reaping Machine', p. 41.

49. R. Douglas, *A General View of the Agriculture of Roxburgh and Berwick* (Edinburgh, 1813), p. 111.

50. Roberts, 'Sickles and Scythes', p. 9.

51. J. Farquharson, 'On cutting grain crops with the common scythe as practised in Aberdeenshire', *T.H.A.S.*, x (1835), p. 188.

52. Stephens, *Book of the Farm* (1855 edn.), II, p. 342.

53. G. Robertson, *Rural Recollections* (Irvine, 1829), pp. 236–237.

54. S.R.O., Dunglass Papers; GD 267/25/7, Estate Diary, Barnyard Park, Black Castle. Long Reed, 1793–1797.

55. G. Buist, 'A Sketch of the Agriculture of Fifeshire', *Quarterly Journal of Agriculture*, xi (1840–41), p. 302.

56. Stephens, *Book of the Farm* (1844 edn.), III, p. 1058.

57. Farquharson, 'On Cutting Grain Crops', p. 192.

58. Taylor, 'Comparative Merits', p. 264.

59. *Ibid., p. 265.*

60. *Ibid.*, p. 266.

61. *N.S.A.*, xii, p. 336.

62. J. Home, *A General View of the Agriculture of the County of Berwick* (London, 1797), p. 46; Steensberg, *Harvesting Implements*, p. 244.

63. G. S. Keith, *A General View of the Agriculture of the County of Aberdeenshire* (Edinburgh, 1811), p. 258.

64. *Ibid.*, p. 258.

65. D. Souter, *A General View of the Agriculture of the County of Banff* (Edinburgh, 1812), p. 271.

66. Fenton, 'Sickle, Scythe and Reaping Machine', p. 44.

67. 'Competition of Reaping Machines at Stirling', *Quarterly Journal of Agriculture* (1853–55), p. 176.

68. *Ibid.*, p. 546.

69. *Royal Commission on the Employment of Children, Young Persons and Women in Agriculture. Fourth Report. Appendix Part II. Parliamentary Papers*, 1870, xiii (hereafter *Fourth Report on Women in Agriculture, 1870*), p. 258.

70. S. Nielson, 'The First Reaping Machines in Denmark', *Tools and Tillage* 1:3 (1970), p. 170.

71. Stephens, *Book of the Farm* (1908 edn.), II, p. 176.

72. R. S. Skirving, 'On the Agriculture of East Lothian', *T.H.A.S.*, iv (1873), p. 25.

73. A. Smith, *A New History of Aberdeenshire* (Aberdeen, 1875), I, p. 241.

74. J. Milne, 'On the Agriculture of Aberdeenshire and Banffshire', *T.H.A.S.*, vi (1871), p. 396.

75. A. Gorrie, 'An Account of the Carse of Gowrie', *T.H.A.S.*, ix (1832), p. 247.

76. *Fourth Report on Women in Agriculture, 1870*, Appendix, part ii, p. 74.

77. *Ibid.*, p. 92.

78. *Ibid.*, p. 183.

79. *Ibid.*, p. 73.

80. Stephens, *Book of the Farm* (1844 edn.), III, p. 1075.

81. *Scotsman*, 4 September 1867.

82. *Ibid.*, 3 September 1867.

83. 'The Cereal and other Crops of Scotland for 1882', *T.H.A.S.*, xv (1883), p. 289.

84. Stephens, *Book of the Farm* (1908 edn.), II, p. 170.

85. *Scotsman*, 29 Aug. 1860.

86. C. H. Firth, ed., *Scotland and the Protectorate 1654–1659* (Edinburgh, 1899), pp. 405–406.

87. *O.S.A.*, iv, p. 486.

88. *N.S.A.*, ix, p. 94.

89. *Scotsman*, 9 Aug. 1875.

90. *Ibid.*, 23 Aug. 1867.

91. *Fourth Report on Women in Agriculture, 1870*, Appendix, part ii, p. 177.

92. *Royal Commission on Labour: The Agricultural Labourer, vol. III, Scotland, Part II. Parliamentary Papers*, 1893–5, xxxvi. (hereafter *R.C. on Labour, 1893*), p. 107.

93. Stephens, *Book of the Farm* (1855 edn.), II, p. 346.

94. *Fourth Report on Women in Agriculture, 1870*, Appendix, part ii, p. 177.

95. *R.C. on Labour, 1893*, part ii, p. 106.

96. H. Hamilton, ed., *Life and Labour on an Aberdeenshire Estate*, Third Spalding Club (Aberdeen, 1946), p. 103.

97. Robertson, *Rural Recollections*, p. 240.

98. *Ibid.*

99. Kerr, *Agriculture of Berwick*, p. 229.

100. Robertson, *Rural Recollections*, p. 240.

101. *Fourth Report on Women in Agriculture*, 1870, Appendix, part II, p. 133.

102. *Ibid.*, pp. 225–226.

103. *R.C. on Labour, 1893*, part II, p. 106.

104. *Ibid.*

105. *Ibid.*

106. *Fourth Report on Women in Agriculture, 1870*, Appendix, part II, p. 133.

107. *R.C. on Labour, 1893*, part ii, p. 107.

108. *O.S.A.*, viii, p. 484; *Glasgow Herald*, 27 September, 1841.

109. 'List of Markets and Fairs now and formerly held in Scotland by Sir David Marwick', *Market Rights and Tolls, Parliamentary Papers*, 1890/1, p. xxxvii.

110. D. Buchan, *The Ballad and The Folk* (London, 1972), p. 265.

111. G. Greig, *Folk Song in Buchan and Folk Song of the North East* (Pennsylvania, 1963), article 98.

112. *Ibid.*, article 3.

113. J. Ord, *The Bothy Songs and Ballads of Aberdeen, Banff and Moray, Angus and the Mearns* (Paisley, 1930), pp. 16, 264.

8

The Country Tradesman

Gavin Sprott

The period of farming improvement was a distinctive era in the Lowland countryside. The processes of industrialisation started early, and have only been substantially completed in our own day. By the 1790s substantial parts of the countryside were worked by wage labour, when cities and towns were still centres of trading and old-style craft industry. The spinning mills, the precursors of modern industrial production, were at first located in rural areas, yet powered mechanisation was only adopted on a wide scale in the 1950s. Before that the direct application of steam power to farming was of very limited use.[1] The result was a period of drawn-out change of very distinct character, the flavour of which lingers strongly in the memory of those who knew it. Although this period is identified in popular memory with that of the horse-worked farms and the labour-intensive methods that these entailed, and therefore of the horseman himself, as much of that character belonged to the country tradesman, his family and his adherents.

The tradesman stood in contrast to the farm servant in a number of ways. The whole ethos was one of male monopoly. Although the work of the farm servant was male-dominated, the man frequently had the companionship of women outworkers. As a previous essay in this volume has shown, it was difficult for an East Lothian farm servant to get a *single fee*. His wife and family were a valuable part of the bargain.[2] Although subjected to the control of the *wumman gaffer* (a man), the fields of the Lothians could not have been worked without the woman workers, later loosely termed bondagers. The bothies and chaumers of East-Central and North-East Scotland were male institutions, but the neeps were clatted, the tatties lifted, the harvest cut, stooked, led, stacked and threshed only with a substantial amount of female (and child) labour.

The tradesmen for most of the nineteenth century relied little on female assistance. There are instances that are recalled merely on account of their rarity.[3] The only notable exception was that of the weaver, when the trade had so declined in the 1840s that the man had to seek subsistence elsewhere.

This male status of the tradesman's situation was tied to another

143

characteristic which set him apart from the farm servant. Despite the recent clearance of Lowland farming folk brought about by mechanisation, the population that remains is now geographically more stable than it has been for two centuries. If farm servants get on well with the farmer, have a reasonable house and their children settled at the local school, they will tend to *bide*. But even into the last days of horseworking some families would flit at every term. The result was severe discontinuity at the institutional level. For example, as recently as 1956–67, the son of a Galloway farm servant attended eight different schools. He also recalls the impatience of the teachers with this shifting population, resulting in scant interest or attention on their part.[4] By contrast, the relative stability of the tradesman allowed him to participate fully in the local masonic lodge, the kirk session, and his children to get the benefit of a continuous education. The archetypal *lad o' pairts*, such as Carlyle and Telford, was often the son of a tradesman.

All this was underlain by the fact that the master tradesman, whether a tenant or owner of his premises, was in himself his own master. His skills and the goodwill of his business could go down the generations, and the journeymen and other employees could also prosper in its shadow. The present incumbents of East Saltoun Smiddy in East Lothian, father and son, are respectively the seventh and eighth generations to follow that trade, a span that goes back to the early days of farming improvement.[5]

That example alone is a significant pointer to a more general pattern. There have always been tradesmen in the countryside, as attested by the baron court books and records of monastic administration. Their situation as small farm tenants underlies their part as members of the rural community. Their rent was often payable in produce as well as trade work. Although the miller was ubiquitous, he was not always indispensable, as the constant breach of thirlage shows. Although still not numerous, the most prominent tradesman was probably the smith. Pre-improvement ploughs had their *irons* — the sock, coulter, and also the slee-band, yetling and soam chain — to which a considerable draught of oxen was yoked. A basic level of metal technology was indispensable, and there is ample record of pre-industrial techniques of smiddy-work almost to within living memory.[6]

The old trades of smith, miller and weaver all required some fixed plant. Yet overall, the old-style farming was the great age of do-it-yourself, a tradition which survives in the crofting counties. The old-style farmer built and thatched his own house, found his own fuel, and devised his own harness, tools and transport. His wife span wool from his sheep and made most of the family's clothes.[7] What tradesmen there were often subsisted on a part-time basis.[8] Before the mid-eighteenth century the furnishing of rural houses was so sparse, often making use of the fabric of the building for seats and beds, that there was little or no trade of that kind for a skilled joiner. Kists and simple shelves were supplemented by a wide range of straw, willow and bent grass basketwork, which provided the storage capacity now expected of dressers, presses and other fitments. Although the iron age has been with us for over two thousand years, the scarcity of iron use and the range of ingenious alternatives up to and beyond the eighteenth century is remarkable.[9]

With the eighteenth century came two vital changes — the availability of raw materials and the development of new farming technology. The foundation of the Carron Ironworks (1759) and the availability of cheaper malleable iron through Henry Cort's puddling process (1784) were of major importance. The result was that iron had the same impact then as the synthetic derivatives of coal and oil have today. Iron started to replace timber in countless small details — hinges, nails, latches, locks and household utensils, as well as important developments in mills (Carron started casting cogwheels in the 1780s) and farm implements. Timber itself became available in what were previously unheard-of quantities. This derived from various sources. The growth of trade during the eighteenth century provided the cash with which to import increased amounts from the Baltic through the East-Coast ports, a trade which still continues in such small harbours as Kirkcaldy and Perth to this day. Although during the seventeenth century timber had been floated down the Tay, and down the Dee to the *Timmer market* at Aberdeen, during the following century this was put on an industrial level with the coming of the York Buildings Company to the Spey Valley.[10] This involved a new emphasis on sawn timber, and was vital, because the enormous building of new housing and steadings that came with farming improvement depended on getting the timber in a straight, semi-finished state.[11] If there were no straight lines in the buildings of the pre-improvement countryside, there was scarcely a natural bend in those that followed. It was impossible to build a timber floor or frame up roofing couples or purlins to take slates, tiles or indeed improved thatches out of split and eeched timber, except with enormous trouble and expense.[12] Coupled with these new sources was the growth of metalled roads in the later eighteenth century along which the supplies could travel, and the production of home-grown plantings of Scotch pine and the introduction of larch. The new plantings of hardwood, particularly ash, oak and elm for millwrighting and cartmaking work, and beech and plane for turning, loom parts and furniture, were also important.

The evidence of this extraordinary new availability of timber is reflected in the transformation of domestic interiors of even the older tradition of housing in the Lowlands during the second half of the eighteenth century. The communal sleeping arrangements round the central hearth could be abandoned for the box-bed and the subsequent division of the living areas of the house. This is when the *but* and *ben* rooms became commonplace. This upgrading of the fitments of the house was also part of the widespread movement in which the fabric of the house ceased to be part of the organic cycle of farming in the reduction of raw materials to a usable form.[13] As long as the former situation obtained, there was no room for the tradesman's skills in housebuilding. The construction of a *hallan* or *trance* near the entrance to deflect the draught, the box-beds with shelves, the framing up of the *hingin lum*, the *benches*, *skelfs* and various shelving, the appearance of dressers and tables, and the multiplication of *ambries*, *lang seats* or *settles*, and the appearance even of the wooden armchair for the man of the house, are all amply documented in the literature of the time.[14] This is summed up by Sir John Sinclair, writing in 1795, that 'the cottager or mailer's house has been improved in the last 30 years because timber is more easily got'.[15] Luxuries many of these various things would have been — some home-made with acquired timber, some made by a joiner — but by the early nineteenth century they were generally attainable by Lowland country folk.[16]

The demands of the new farming were many, but they have often been misunderstood. It is tempting to focus on the technical aspects — the trials of new plough-types and techniques, and to dwell on curiosities of old-style farming such as the apportionment of rigs, which although they were important were not basic issues. The heart of improvement was the reorganisation of land use. The old-style farming kept the arable and grazing in generally separate zones, with the outfield as general resource area giving some flexibility in between. The arable ground was worked as most gardens still are — intensive cultivation and manuring — although the standards of tidiness would have been somewhat different. The grazing relied on the natural regeneration of the pasture. Improved farming scrapped the distinction, and integrated the functions of arable and grazing into new combined rotations. Knowledge later credited to the improvers was often current well before their time.[17] The change required the capital generated by trade, a growing market for the products, and not least the degeneration of the old-style farming under population pressure and the exhaustion of the resources of natural meadow grass and of fuel on which it depended, to enforce change. The changes of the first generation of improvement were carried out almost entirely with the old-style tools and techniques to the point where distinct advances in kind became feasible, drawing in their wake a new technology.

A constant theme which runs through Andrew Wight's surveys of improving farming during the 1770s and 1780s is the importance of cleaning the ground and getting a good crop of sown grass.[18] Underlying this was the drive to get ground on which sown fodder crops — turnips as well as grass — would thrive. The result of assiduous drainage, stone, whin and broom clearance, realignment and scaling down of rigs, was ground suited to lighter ploughs and a greatly reduced draught. The road was now open for Small's improved swing plough and its derivatives. One result was a vast shedding of labour. The old Scotch plough was labour-intensive, requiring a minimum of two to three people. The remarkable change is illuminated in one case in Monikie parish in Angus: 'About 30 or

40 years ago [i.e. 1750s] a farm which is now worked by 3 ploughs, having each 4, sometimes only 2 horses, employed 5 cattle ploughs, having each 10 oxen'.[19]

However, this economy of labour — in this case a reduction of at least two thirds — could only be achieved with the back-up of skilled trades. Small's earlier wooden frames of the 1760s were developed into iron-framed ploughs, and although an attempt was made at industrial manufacture, the vast majority of the new swing ploughs were produced in country smiddies bred out of the needs of improved farming. Indeed, there was a whole complex of developments that meshed to make demands on what was virtually a new class in the countryside. Horses replaced oxen generally during the late eighteenth and early nineteenth centuries throughout most of the Lowlands. This followed from the extension and the improvement of roads and the transport needs of improved farming. Horses were not only faster, but their hooves would hold a shoe and their backs bear the weight of cart shafts much better. However, they all had to be shod.[20] The old-style ox-harness was home-made, but by the late eighteenth century substantial horse tackle made by saddlers was becoming common in the Lowlands.

Not least, making of the improved two-wheeled carts provided a large amount of work for both joiner and smith. The wheels in particular, with their *dish* and toed-in alignment at the iron axle-ends, complete iron tyres, nave-rings and cast-iron boxes, were an innovation of the late eighteenth century, and the corresponding skills were new ones that must have been acquired initially by trial and error.

The rebuilding of much of the country housing has already been referred to. This was the consequence of the re-location of the population resulting from the spread of improved farming, and also the greatly increased size of the new farming units themselves. To work efficiently, they required steadings on a scale that was totally new — adequate byres and milkhouses, barns and grain lofts, cart sheds and stabling for horses — and this generated perhaps the biggest single demand for new skills. The scale of this first round of building is not always evident to the eye, for there were repeated cycles of rebuilding, during the 'high farming' times of the 1840s and the movement for rebuilding or roofing in cattle courts in the 1870s. Beyond this came the supplying trades of quarrying and stone-breaking, brick and tilemaking, and sawmilling, which all became distinct rural industries.

The other block of trades that impinged directly on the new farming was that to do with grain processing. The combination of improved yields and increased arable acreage forced both the improvement of corn mills and the development of threshing technology. Until Andrew Meikle produced the first successful threshing mill in 1788, the process of hand threshing was a bottleneck in the line of grain production. The rapid spread of Meikle's mill throughout the 1790s, despite the scarcity of skilled millwrights to install them, testifies to this urgent need. A complementary development was the Thirlage Act of 1799, which opened the road to the removal of threshing from estate-owned corn mills. The real consequence was to put the miller on the same basis as other tradesmen, with his prosperity dependent upon his reputation and skill.

The stable character of these 'main' trades is demonstrated by their continuity through the generations, and the structures of apprenticeships which were the *sine qua non* of entry to these trades. One point which is not clear is to what degree apprentices would be the sons of farm servants. There was little cultural difference between country tradesman and farm servant. They both spoke the same language — *Scotch* as native speakers still refer to it. Many cottar bairns would have had a distinct raggedness compared with those of the tradesman of the more 'respectable' sort. That 'the soutar's bairns is aye the worst shod' had more than merely proverbial truth in it. There was an element of hierarchical status within the range of country trades, and some of these will be referred to. This blurred the distinction between tradesman and farm servant. Much more lay in the matter of degree than of kind. Traditionally the bothy man cared little for church attendance, and when he married and cottared, his wife was the more likely to carry the standard of religion, particularly in the upbringing of the children. On the other hand the institutional side of organised religion was a male affair, and as has been stated, the tradesman was in a position to fill kirk rôles at local level. Also, the theological bent of many weavers was well known. Another difference of emphasis would have been that of literacy and reading tastes. But on the whole there were enough literate and canny farm servants and enough harum-scarum tradesmen to make any wide distinction in character meaningless. The main difference lay in their expectations in life. Unlike David Brown, a joiner in Rosehearty who died in 1898, the farm servant would not expect to leave a mahogany table and eight hair-stuffed chairs, carpets and all the gear that went with a settled existence of modest but not overweening prosperity.[21]

There are various manifestations of these expectations once a young man had enjoyed his *prentice lowsin*.[22] A perusal of surviving account books of the various main trades reveals that the greater part of the work was done on account, generally settled every six months or so. In most cases, casual jobbing work accounted for less than a third of the work, so work continued in the expectation of continuity. For instance, the accounts of Ninewells Smiddy, Chirnside, Berwickshire which cover the latter half of the last century show the price of a new horseshoe creeping up from eight pence to a shilling, a gradual increase over the years with no intervening drop.[23] The system of working to accounts reveals longstanding relationships between the tradesman, not just with local farmers, but other local businesses and small industries, and the occupants of the surrounding *big hooses*. In the 1790s in Midlothian farmers could contract for the maintenance of their horses' shoes, cart-wheel rings and plough irons for the year.[24] In fact, it has long been the practice in country smiddies to keep patterns of the feet of individual horses from surrounding farms, and make up shoes ready during slack periods.

It is evident, however, that far from all the country tradesmen were self-employed. This is not so clear from smiddy accounts, where most of the work was brought into the smiddy, and a man's time was not set off against particular jobs. Yet much joiner work was done on the customer's premises, and as the materials were either supplied, or in the case of repairs were a minor part of the cost, men's time figures more in joiner's accounts, revealing the frequent employment of journeymen by the master tradesman. Unlike the smith or miller, the joiner or mason was much less dependent on fixed plant to ply his skill, and these trades are likely to have supported a much bigger floating population of employed men.

In other directions came openings for more specific skills which fed on the prosperity of improved farming. More people could afford shoes and boots, to have their clothes made by a tailor, to have their agreements and wills drawn up by a writer. The growing fashion for wheaten loaves in the countryside in the late eighteenth century meant employment for bakers, and likewise the fairly novel consumption of fresh meat meant employment for butchers. Up to the later nineteenth century there was an element of luxury in these things, and often the only fresh meat a farm servant's family saw was culled from the local rabbit population, or for a few days after their or a neighbour's pig was killed. Yet there were enough takers, partly no doubt amongst neighbouring tradesmen and their families, for these 'service' tradesmen to be numerous in small country villages as early as the late eighteenth century.[25] However, the domestic trades did not always have the same stability as the 'main' trades just mentioned, and sometimes the lesser of them took on casual work. This was particularly the case with weavers, but it also applied to other occupations.[26]

There have always been followings that required skills, for which there is no strict apprenticeship, but which are just 'picked up'. Weaving and shoemaking shaded into that category, but there were others which were to be encouraged in generous measure by farming improvements. The enclosure of the fields — to separate stock from the crops — required a lot of effort. It was in fact a long drawn-out process, as children could be used to herd stock instead of relying on dykes. A lot of ground lay unenclosed even into the 1860s, right to the eve of compulsory schooling. The demands of repairing dykes, replacing the first makeshift enclosures of fail dykes, meant that dyking, hedging and, from the 1860s, fencing was not a one-off but a continuous process. Some of those involved were the *groat men* of Berwickshire, working as day labourers.[27] Their wages could vary quite widely from summer to winter, and even within these seasons, reflecting both the variety but perhaps also the instability of the work.[28] Yet the ditcher or drainer — often also the dyker — came into his own with the drainage revolution which followed the introduction of subsoil ploughing and tile drains in the 1830s. The ditcher who *redd* blocked drains was often a water diviner as well and, if skilled, ensured himself constant employment. Other typical non-apprenticed skills were those of the rabbit-catcher and mole-catcher. Again, these were often linked to other field skills such as dyking.

On the edge of the settled population were the travelling people, the tinkers, who also had their trades, principally in tin-smithing and basketwork. These may have been skills which they took over from the settled population as both the disruption and the surplus produced by improvement pushed these do-it-yourself activities into the background. Also pursuing an itinerant but solitary minor trade were the chapmen, cadgers and so on.

An important consequence of the whole range of trades that fed on farming improvement was paradoxically to open up new opportunities for the unskilled and semi-skilled. A perennial problem of the countryside before improvement was that of the sturdy beggar. The old-style farming, with its emphasis on joint and kindly tenancy and the communal apportionment of natural resources, left little leeway for the unattached, those forced out by broken tenancies or other misfortunes. The combination of public road works, the labourers required to support the building trades in particular, and the growth of the new rural industries provided opportunities for this group for the first time on a significant scale.

The things we take for granted as time-hallowed fixtures are often surprisingly transitory. There has been cultivation in Lowland Scotland for upwards of five thousand years, but for only a little over two centuries by the horse. Although there were tradesmen before improvement, and tradesmen remained after it, the same general perspective applies. During this period the country tradesman had a degree of interchangeability with his counterpart in the towns, a situation that obtained neither before and not so much since for a large part of the country population. However, from the 1830s, there were various factors which were working to change this, although for many years they actually created more work for the country tradesman. They might be summarised as the developments by which the obstacles to making the Industrial Revolution effective in the countryside were overcome.

The first major step was the introduction of subsoil ploughing, by which means much previous drainage effort became really effective, and new and more ambitious schemes could be undertaken. In 1831 James Smith published his *Remarks on Through Drainage and Deep Ploughing*. The result, in conjunction with the recently introduced tile drains, was to dispense with the *rigs* and create the even field surface which opened the road for industrially produced field machinery. By the time the light American reaping machinery had been popularised in the 1850s, enough progress had been made in levelling field surfaces for them to have a market in Lowland Scotland.[29]

During the same decade, railways were becoming an established fact in rural Scotland. For instance, by 1860 the Strathmore line had thirteen branches into primarily agricultural areas. It is no coincidence that there now followed the growth of a number of implement manufacturers based with few exceptions on small country towns with railway connections.[30] The maintenance of these implements, together with the reapers which were spreading in the 1860s and the binders in the 1880s, kept the tradesmen busy. Although Jack and Allan carts were an alternative but never a serious rival for locally made carts, and the mass-produced Yankee digger ploughs were incapable of drawing a good seed-fur, the working tradesmen were becoming the agents of other people's work.

Moreover, by the 1850s industrial production was demolishing the country weaver's trade. The technology of power looms was available in the 1840s. Power loom factories were set up in many small country towns in the 1860s. They did not simply do some of the weavers out of business, but forced them on to more specialised lines and so reduced their returns as to stop recruitment to the trade. Country weavers worked on into the end of the century, but as a dwindling and ageing population. Themselves working as the agents of other people's trade, they were the first victims of industrial rationalisation.

Millers were also exposed to new competition from steam mills in the coastal towns which were processing cheap prairie grain from the 1870s, but the general adherence of the rural population to a large proportion of oatmeal in their diet kept many of the country millers going. The continuing payment of a proportion, though a diminishing one, farm servants' wages in meal, almost to the end of horse-working, was also partly responsible.

Some trades vanished into oblivion, such as those of the country tailor or shoemaker, or the tinker's tinsmithing skills, driven out by cheap factory goods. Others adapted and changed. Many firms of agricultural engineers, country garages, and even some steel fabricators had their genesis not in small-town factories but roadside smiddies. The firm of Alexander Wait in Chirnside is an example. In the 1890s they were hiring out bicycles, and early this century acting as agents for car tyres and parts. For 1904 the expenses for hiring out cycles were £13..18..9, the income £40..9..10, a surplus (but one which did not include depreciation costs) of £26..11..1, amounting to 30 per cent of their total profit. Cycle hire, and eventually motor engineering, was a more profitable venture than smiddy work. The firm is still trading under the same name.[31]

Although outwith the time-span of this study, a postscript is not inappropriate. As long as horses continued on the land, they had to be shod. Socks had to be relaid, carts made and repaired, horse field machinery maintained, horse harness renewed, and steadings maintained in their traditional form. Legislation of the 1930s enforced the upgrading of farm-servant housing, bringing another of those periodic surges of building

L

activity to the countryside. But in 1945 came the Standard Ferguson tractor — the *Wee Fergie*. It was the first adequate mass-produced tractor with hydraulically operated three-point linkage, capable of working system-machinery, to be widely adopted. In conjunction with the combine, it was the first real alternative to the horse. With the passing of the horse went the horseman and numerous small tradesmen in a large exodus from the countryside. For those who can remember the smiddy as a place where the men gathered to discuss the news, youngsters listened to their elders, and people crowded to wonder at the occasional travelling showman, it was the end of an era.

NOTES

1. Gavin Sprott, *The Tractor in Scotland* (Scottish Country Life Museums Trust, 1978).

2. Information from Allan Hamilton, 1983, Edinburgh, formerly Gifford. He referred to the period prior to 1914. See above, pp. 104–6.

3. For instance, the smith at Tealing, Angus, 1920s, whose wife often worked with him when he needed someone to strike or hold the work. Her hands were reputedly as strong as her husband's. Information from Isobel Smith, 1983, Monikie, Angus.

4. Information from William Findlay, 1981, Castle Douglas. The schools were Borgue, $\frac{1}{2}$ year; Castle Dykes, $\frac{1}{2}$ year; Applegirth, $1\frac{1}{2}$ years; Glenlochar, $1\frac{1}{4}$ years; Crockettford, 2 years; Dalbeattie, 2 years; Haugh of Urr, $\frac{1}{2}$ year; Castle Douglas High School, 3 years.

5. Information from Alexander Duff, 1982, East Saltoun. 'Dynasties' of tradesmen were common — for instance, the Meikle family of millwrights, most notably James, Andrew and George; the Hally family of smith and ploughmaking fame in Perthshire and Angus throughout 19th and first half of this century; the Umpherston family of millwrights at Loanhead throughout the 18th century. The list could be multiplied indefinitely.

6. For instance see *Scottish Studies*, Vol. 8, 1964, pp. 108–13. Donald Maclean of Carinish, S. Uist describes the making of peat charcoal as late as 1909–10. Known as *gual gaidhealach* — gaelic coal — it was little inferior to smiddy coal.

7. For instance, P. Graham, *The Agriculture of Stirlingshire* (Edinburgh, 1812), p. 77. Until the time of writing (early 19th century) the tenants were 'left every one to provide a house and offices for himself according to his ability'.

8. For instance, *Old Statistical Account* (hereafter *O.S.A.*), V, p. 361, Lochlee, Angus. The two smiths and four wrights were 'only occassionally employed', otherwise rearing black cattle and sheep. This was still a predominantly 'unimproved' district. The partial exception might be the South-East of Scotland. It is notable that the specifically farming occupational surnames such as Hynd, Shepherd, Harrower, Tasker (thresher) come from this area. Although thatching, using 'improved' materials and techniques, became a full-time occupation on the East Coast in the 19th century, in the early 1800s there were five families of *thackers* in Pencaitland alone. See J. Martine, *Reminiscences* (1894), p. 16.

9. Tradesmen often had crofts — but as a supplement to their trade, not an alternative. For instance, pre-industrial mills with a vertical waterwheel employed timber shafting and gearing, with wooden cogs engaging in cages of parallel rungs. Although these needed frequent replacement, the only indispensable metal part was the iron *rynd* which rested on the spindle and supported the upper or *runner* wheel. On a simple level, very sufficient locks could be made completely of timber.

10. See 'The Currach in Scotland, with notes on the Floating of Timber', *Scottish Studies,* Vol. 16, 1972, pp. 61–85.

11. There are numerous references in the literature of the late 18th century and early 19th centuries to the drastic nature of this process throughout the Lowlands. See, for instance, *O.S.A.* IV, p. 194 (1792) for Inchture, Perthshire: 'almost the whole houses in this parish have been built anew within these 16 years past'.

12. For instance, W. Aiton, *The Agriculture of Ayrshire* (London, 1811), p. 123. When roofs are thatched, native timber is used, and when slated, 'foreign' timber is used.

13. For instance, P. Marshall, *The Agriculture of the Central Highlands* (Edinburgh, 1784), pp. 19–21. He describes the sod huts once common in the Central and still in use in the Northern Highlands, where the walls were spread after a few years as manure, and with the roof sometimes used as fuel. The integration of the house fabric with the organic cycle in early 20th-century housing in Lewis is described in Alexander Fenton, *The Island Blackhouse* (H.M.S.O., 1978).

14. Two good descriptions are to be found in, Rev. J. Headrick, *The Agriculture of Angus* (London, 1813), pp. 127–129 and Rev. C. Findlater, *General View of the Agriculture of the County of Peebles* (London, 1802), pp. 45–6.

15. Sir John Sinclair, *The Agriculture of the Northern Counties* (Edinburgh, 1785), p. 50.

16. For instance, (1) Ms. Account Book of *McKellar,* High Fenwick, Ayrshire

17/12/1830	kitchen chair 5/9d.
10/6/1834	box bed £2.10s.
7/7/1839	salt box, wall press, including grounds, facings & linings 9/6d.

(2) Ms. Account Book, *Wm. & Rbt. Ford,* Borders area.

30/1/1808	dresser with 2 drawers, 2 doors, handles £3.4s.
24/9/1808	bed, framed and panelled at front & ends £4.15s.

17. T. C. Smout & A. Fenton, 'Scottish Agriculture before the Improvers — an Exploration', *Agricultural History Review,* XIII/II (1965), pp. 73–93.

18. Andrew Wight, *The Present State of Husbandry in Scotland* (Edinburgh, 1778–1784).

19. *O.S.A.* IV, pp. 347–8 (1792), Monikie, Angus.

20. A working horse had to be shod on average every 6–8 weeks.

21. Country Life Archive, National Museum, Edinburgh. MS 1972/3.

22. The ceremony which attended the end of an apprenticeship, which speaks of the status of a time-served man. For instance, *66th Report of the British Association* (Kirkcudbright, 1897), p. 466. There was a feast, usually high tea with a little whisky. Sometimes friends organised a dance, the *lowsin ball.*

23. Ms. Account Book, *James & Alexander Wait,* Ninewells Smiddy, 1854–1904. Prices in the western borders lagged by 1d–2d a shoe. The 8d. for 1854 compares with 2d. in the late 18th century in Midlothian.

24. G. Robertson, *The Agriculture of Midlothian* (Edinburgh, 1783), pp. 30–31.

25. For example, *O.S.A.,* IV, p. 194 (1792), Longforgan, Perthshire. This includes an interesting list of tradesmen and occupations residing within the village, although some practised their occupations outside it.

26. For instance, *Turriff Advertiser,* 8.3.1967. It is remembered in the Turriff district that in the late 19th century, when work was slack, the soutars of Turriff often found work building *rumble dykes* in the district.

27. *O.S.A.,* XIV, p. 22, Chirnside, Berwickshire.

28. J. Hume, *The Agriculture of Berwickshire* (Edinburgh, 1797), p. 149. Labourer rates per day quoted:

Winter	10d.–1s.
Summer	1s.–1/6d.

This compares with a year's fee for a single man of £6.9s. and bed and board, or that of a married hind of £18.14.6d. which did not include bed and board. The labourer would have been lucky to make £15 a year assuming constant work.

29. For an interesting summary of this process, see A. Fenton, *Scottish Country Life* (Edinburgh, 1976), pp. 18–23.

30. Exceptions are Wallace of Glasgow, Reid of Aberdeen, and Garvie of Aberdeen. Other firms included, for instance, Jack of Maybole, Bisset of Blairgowrie, Pollock of Mauchline, Begg of Dalry, Allan of Murthly, Kemp and Nicholson of Stirling, Cruickshank of Denny, Sellar of Huntly, Macdonald of Portsoy, Sherriff of West Barns, Elder of Berwick, Wallace of Castle Douglas, Newlands of Linlithgow, and Shearer of Turriff.

31. Ms. Account Book, *James & Alexander Wait,* cited above.

Part III. The World of Farm Labour

9

Farm Workers' Incomes in 1843

Ian Levitt and Christopher Smout

1. The wages of male farm servants hired by the year

The data on which this essay relies were gathered for the Scottish Poor Law Commission Report of 1844, and the methods used to process them in order to compile the maps and tables are described in the introduction to our book, *The State of the Scottish Working-Class in 1843* (Edinburgh, 1979). The commission interested itself in a wide range of social and economic questions regarding the labouring classes, sending out a questionnaire to every parish in Scotland to elucidate problems of diet, wages, prices, employment patterns, migration, education and poor relief (among others).

In rural areas in particular the response was excellent, and the information on various aspects of farm workers' incomes was of good quality. The calculation of the value of their wages is not easy, partly because wages were still paid to a considerable, but variable, extent in kind, and partly because several different types of worker were involved. In the first part of this essay we shall concentrate on the male farm servant hired by the year (or by the half-year in some cases). We are not for the moment concerned with day-labourers, or with women and children on the land. Characteristically such a farm servant was a ploughman, called a hind in the south-east of Scotland. He was the subject of Question 9 in the questionnaire:

> Q.9. What are the average allowances, and average wages of hinds or servants, hired for farming work by the year, in your parish?

There were, however, three distinct categories of worker subsumed even in this question. One was a cottager, who lived in a rented cottage. The second was a bothy-man, who lived in a purpose-built bothy, or barrack for farm-workers. The third was a living-in servant, who lived within the farmer's own household, eating in the kitchens and sleeping in an attic or outhouse of the farm itself. The cottager was married: the other two generally were not. The balance between the numbers of married and

156

unmarried farm servants varied enormously from district to district; another question in the inquiry sought to throw light on this:

Q.24. Is any preference shown to unmarried labourers over married labourers, as farm servants in your parish, or the reverse?

Before we consider the level of wages we should first consider the replies to this inquiry. There were 814 responses (89 per cent of all Scottish parishes) divided into 263 (32 per cent) that declared married servants were preferred, 315 (39 per cent) that declared unmarried servants were preferred and 236 (29 per cent) that could find no preference. Table 1 and Maps 1 and 2 show how this varied by district.

There was a strong preference for married servants or cottagers in the grain-producing districts of the south-east of Scotland, especially in East Lothian and the eastern Borders. This was the traditional area of the hind who served with his wife and children as a family work unit, the wife being called the 'bondager' — she had to perform a set number of days' free labour at harvest time (often 20 days) in order to pay the rent of the cottage, and she was expected to be available on other days (often 4 a week) to do paid labour as required.[1] The same socio-economic pattern was found in Northumberland, which suggests a very ancient origin, perhaps even from the seventh century when a single Anglian kingdom of Northumbria stretched from the Humber to the Forth. Some preference for married servants was also evident in parts of the south-west, though it was less strong: here they were known as 'cottars' or 'benefit men', and there was no formal obligation on their wives to work though no doubt they often did so.

The replies to Question 24 show that there was also a strong preference for married men in Fife and that this also stretched north (though in a weaker form) into Angus and lowland Perthshire. At first sight this is extremely surprising, as this area (especially beyond the Tay) was the heartland of the bothy system for unmarried farm servants. Perhaps married cottagers would indeed have been 'preferred' on economic grounds (as well as on social and moral ones) if they could have been obtained. One Angus farmer said that he did not approve of the bothy system 'where it can be avoided', as married men were steadier 'and he, besides, gets the labour of their families ... and they are absolutely necessary to him'.[2] This was a region of labour-intensive arable and root husbandry competing for labour with a widespread linen industry which was particularly suited to female and to family employment. So sharp was the competition that there were even reports of married women and their children remaining as weavers in Forfar and living apart from their husbands, who became ploughmen in bothies outside the town.[3] Plainly this was exceptional, but it is reasonable to suppose that the bothy system for single men was effectively forced on the farmer when he could no longer obtain family labour. It was new in the nineteenth century but certainly lingered on until after the First World War.[4]

Outside these areas married men were not widely preferred, except in certain northern arable pockets like Easter Ross. The unmarried were strongly preferred throughout most of the Highlands, but this has little significance in the crofting areas where there was seldom wage employment for farm-hands of any kind. In the north-eastern counties there was also a strong and important (but not a total) preference for the unmarried. A system of boarding single men in a 'chaumer' in the farmhouse prevailed in this region, though here, too, married ploughmen sometimes lived in 'chaumers' and visited their wives and families in villages several miles from the farm.[5] Less well known is the tendency also to avoid married farm servants throughout west-central Scotland — cottagers were scarce in Lanarkshire, parts of Stirling, Dumbarton and Renfrew. This may again be connected both with the small size of farms in this area and the structure of the labour market in heavily industrialised districts: families could earn more in industry than in farming. As these counties (like the others that clearly preferred unmarried labour) depended more on pastoral than on arable farming, they were also less thirsty for labour than Perthshire and Angus and had less need to try to marshal a force in a bothy. The ratio of family labour to employed labour in East Lothian in 1861 was 1:8.3. In Aberdeenshire it was 1:0.7.[6]

It is striking that so many areas should, for whatever reason, employ few married farm servants: it implies that in a majority of parishes the ploughman's job was likely to be a phase in a life cycle rather than a whole-time career. What did farm servants do when they got married? Many, particularly in pastoral counties where the farms tended to be smaller, may have been the children of other farmers and returned to inherit their fathers' farms. In the north-eastern counties at least, as Malcolm Gray has conclusively demonstrated,[7] they might become crofters occupying poor-quality smallholdings on the fringe of the main farming areas, supplying occasional help as day-labourers when required. Alternatively they might become whole-time agricultural day-labourers, living in a rented house; they might become involved in mining or textile industry within the parish; or they might migrate into the towns. Carters were often former farm servants putting their expertise with horses to a new use.

The pattern in pastoral areas was nowhere simple or uniform, but it was undoubtedly often determined by the wish of farm servants ultimately to own a little land, or at least to have some independence. That in the dairy county of Ayrshire was described by an experienced factor for several large estates. Most farm servants, he explained, were unmarried and lived as boarders in the farmhouse, but a number married and lived in rented cottages. It was common for the unmarried to 'look forward to having farms of about twenty acres. I could point out a dozen instances of farmers who were originally merely ploughmen. And these, after having been for a time in the small farms generally feel inclined to have larger farms'. They achieved their ambition by carefully saving enough wages to begin stocking a farm, and then marrying a female farm servant who had been equally thrifty. On their marriage both left paid employment and set up as farmers with their joint capital. If they could not attain this the couple might marry, the man remain a farm servant and his wife rent a certain number of cows from the farmer: 'the farmer supplies [the] food ... the produce becomes her own ... instead of farming his land, she farms the cows'.[8]

Information on the wage of married farm servants is summarised in Table 2. From 201 replies where it is either explicitly stated or is implicit in the context that a married worker is involved, it appears that the mean total value of the wage was around £24 a year.[9] From 139 replies that state the money component, however, it appears that the average for this in Scotland was only around £10 a year. About 60 per cent of the wage was paid in kind.

Such an overall mean, however, conceals remarkable variations from district to district in the nature and value of the payments in kind. The following account depends on a scrutiny of over 200 statements in the questionnaire, and all entries under farm servants' wages in the *New Statistical Account of Scotland* (15 volumes, Edinburgh, 1845) — a formidable body of data that can, nevertheless, only give a sketch of the complexity of regional practices.[10]

In the heart of the eastern Borders there were three districts, the Dunbar area, South Berwick and the Kelso area, roughly coterminous with the counties of East Lothian, Berwickshire and Roxburghshire, where the most valuable item in the hinds' wages was an allowance of unground grain — generally 10 or 12 bolls of oats, 3 of barley and 1 or 2 of peas or beans, their total value at current 1843 prices being about £12. In addition they were often allowed free carriage of up to four tons of coal, free manured potato ground (between 600 and 1200 yards in linear extent), the keep of a cow (worth £5) and a cottage paid for by 18 to 20 days' labour by the wife, the 'bondager'. The most valuable things a hind could possess, according to an East Lothian farmer, was 'a good wife, a good cow and a good razor'.[11] The hind's traditional right to enough ground to sow a capful of lint (flax seed) was generally commuted to £1 in cash; in Berwickshire and Roxburghshire a traditional right to keep sheep was commuted to £3 'sheep siller'; in Roxburghshire there was a right to keep chickens or 10 shillings in lieu. In fact in the Dunbar district cash wages were often as little as £1, in South Berwick were under £5 and in the Kelso district under £4 — in other words the only money items in the wage were generally fixed and identifiable commutations of traditional allowances in kind. Between 80 and 95 per cent of the hinds' wages were thus in kind.[12] Yet unquestionably these areas were among the most advanced in Scotland in terms of their agricultural practice: it was the region of the largest farms and the most sophisticated capitalist farmers. Why was the cash component of their most skilled workers' wage so extremely small?

Part of the answer must be that it was fixed by tradition, evidently one of extraordinary antiquity since, again, it spanned each side of the Anglo-Scottish border.[13] But such a tradition probably would not have continued unless it had been satisfactory to both employer and employee. For the farmer payment in kind was payment out of his own barns — it was simple, fixed and easily calculable. For the worker it represented a comfortable subsistence in good harvests and in bad; so much food was as much as a large family might want, and the south-east corner of Scotland was consequently well fed. If there was a surplus the ploughmen sold or exchanged the grain with others in the community — you could buy your shoes with oats from the village cobbler.

Such an economy might seem to presuppose that there was no great shortage of labour that would begin to bid up the wage dramatically. It was true that allowances in kind could in theory be increased from time to time, but it would have been foolish to increase them if they had lost all relation to a family's subsistence needs — paying a cash bonus would then become a simpler and more acceptable solution.

It is astounding to discover that the earliest extant detailed description of the hinding system in Scotland, the Midlothian justices' assessment of wages in 1656, described allowances in kind very close indeed to those in mid-nineteenth century East Lothian. A Midlothian hind in the Cromwellian period was to have 15 bolls of oats; $1\frac{1}{2}$ bolls peas, ground for sowing $1\frac{1}{4}$ bolls of oats and a firlot of beer, and pasture for two, or three, cows. When an East Lothian hind in 1843 is described above — it is basically the same, with potato ground instead of grain ground. The significant difference, however, between the Cromwellian period and the Victorian is that the woman bondager in the seventeenth century had worked for nothing, but in the nineteenth received a money wage, and the associated junior hind, or 'half-hind', who was presumably his son, also got a higher wage. In other words, the increased bargaining power of labour that came about over 200 years of change was manifested not in the wages of the adult male but in those of the dependent members of his family. He earned the food and they earned the cash, though surplus foods were often marketed.

For payment in kind to persist on this scale, however, also presupposes no great local demand for urban consumer goods that would have to be paid for in cash. For all their advanced nature these eastern Border districts were deeply rural, far from the main manufacturing and retailing centres. The fact that payment in kind persisted here more strongly than elsewhere in Scotland, while at the same time the wage was more valuable than anywhere else, suggests the Border hind ate better but spent less on clothes, small luxuries and general town wares than other ploughmen. Certainly the *Poor Law Report* data on diet confirm that more meat, wheatbread and peasemeal was consumed here than was normally the case in rural Scotland, and that meals were more varied and more frequent.[14]

Outside this area there was a crescent of east-coast districts where married cottagers were common, reaching from Fife, through West Lothian, the Edinburgh area, Peeblesshire and the Hawick area. The basis of the hinds' allowances here was payment in ground oatmeal, usually $6\frac{1}{2}$ bolls (worth nearly £6), together with enough potato ground to raise between 3 and 6 bolls (a privilege worth about £2), free house rent and often coals driven. In the southern districts here it was customary to allow the keep of a cow, and the value of the wage in kind would be at least 55–60 per cent of the total wage. In Fife, an allowance of a Scotch pint of sweet milk a day generally replaced the cow — as that was worth only about £2 or £3 in place of £5, the cottager's money wage was proportionately higher, and often 50 per cent of the total wage. In the Edinburgh area and West Lothian there were no allowances of milk or cow's keep at all: here, oatmeal, potato ground, house rent and driven coals were together worth £10 or £11, but the money wage rose to £14 or £15 — so the value of the allowance was only 40 to 45 per cent of the total wage. Evidently over this whole area the nearer the hind was to the urban centres and to industry, the smaller the proportion of his wage that was paid in kind.

Married farm servants in the south-west, the 'benefit men' as they were called locally, were again paid allowances of $6\frac{1}{2}$ bolls of oatmeal, ground for at least 6 bolls of potatoes, house rent and carriage of coals, but generally nothing for milk or cows. Because the carriage of coals was rather expensive and the potatoes plentiful, allowances in Wigtown were worth around £13, or 60 per cent of the total wage. Further north in Ayrshire such cottagers as there were had rather fewer potatoes but a little extra in cash — the money element again slightly exceeded the kind element as the industrial heartland was approached.

Elsewhere, there were only pockets in which cottagers were found. Such as there were in Angus, Kincardine and Perth were paid like those in Fife, with $6\frac{1}{2}$ bolls of oatmeal, 1 to $1\frac{1}{2}$ Scotch pints of milk, potato ground, house rent and sometimes coals driven. In Argyll the system was the same, with a cow's keep replacing the milk allowance. In Aberdeenshire married farm servants were less common, but where they occurred they had peats driven instead of coals driven, and sometimes no potato ground — an indication of the singular aversion of the north-east to potatoes.[15] Cottagers in the strip between Orkney and Inverness were given the traditional $6\frac{1}{2}$ bolls of meal, a quantity of potatoes, house rent, generally pasture for a cow, or a certain quantity of milk. The privilege of keeping a cow was less valuable in the north than in the south. South of Caithness they also often had 6–10 barrels of coal. The total value of allowances came to about £11 to which £6–£8 was added in cash — again approximately 60 or 65 per cent of the wage was in kind. In such deeply rural and relatively undeveloped areas one would expect kind to be a high proportion, but it is remarkable that even here it never came near to approaching the figure for south-eastern Scotland.

From 553 replies in the questionnaire it is possible to calculate the money wages of unmarried farm servants (see Table 3). To arrive at a total wage that would be comparable with that of the cottagers, however, we must add their payments in kind. For some reason evidence on this for living-in servants and bothy-men is unusual in the 1843 report, but there is a certain amount in the *New Statistical Account*. To derive the second column in Table 3 we have added £8 to the money wage in the far north and the northern and western Highlands, £9 in the central Highlands and the north-east, £10 in the bothy districts of the Tay area and £11 elsewhere.

Except in the bothy areas, unmarried servants living in were simply given board and lodging. In the south of Scotland the value of 'victuals' was often quoted at 6d. a day, but in the well-fed districts some were given slightly more — £10 a year for food plus £1 for lodging (half the rent of a cottage) seems a fair average. In the north-east, victuals were certainly worth less: £8 a year was the estimate for Drumblade in Aberdeenshire,[16] to which something must be added for lodging. Further north and west it is likely that living would be slightly inferior again. The bothy-workers enjoyed in their districts an allowance system not unlike that of the cottagers: each got 6½ bolls of oatmeal, a Scotch pint of milk and often some potatoes. They could not possibly consume so much (the allowances were the same as a married couple would get to stay alive on) and often sold half.[17] It was estimated, for example at Panbride in Angus,[18] that the meal was worth £6 and the milk £3: a little extra must be added for the potatoes and their very poor lodging in the bothy. These figures are necessarily rough guesses and the gradations are no doubt more subtle between districts than we can indicate on the evidence available. Overall, unmarried servants were paid roughly 15 per cent less than married ones, no doubt because the married brought with them wives and children who could be employed at cheap rates, or be made to labour for the rent of the cottage at harvest time in the case of the Border bondager. They were also likely to have been younger and therefore less skilled.

An overall picture of how the farm servant was remunerated is presented by Table 4, which puts the data on both married and unmarried servants together to arrive at a mean wage for each district irrespective of marital status. Its most interesting feature is the degree of regional variation, from the extremely poor pay in the north where most districts had less than 80 per cent of the Scottish mean, to the relatively high pay of the industrial areas and the rural south-east, which hovered some 20 per cent above the mean. It needs to be stressed again, however, that there would be few farm servants employed in the far north and on the west Highland coast where most people were crofters; the overwhelming majority elsewhere would receive a wage within the range of £20–£26 per annum.

2. *Agricultural day-labourers*

In addition to the farm servants, hired on annual contracts and provided with free accommodation, there were also varying numbers and types of agricultural labourers, generally less skilled, hired on a short-term basis and finding their own places to live. Question 10 asked about them in the following terms:

> Q. 10. What are the average wages of able-bodied agricultural day labourers in your parish?

There were 807 replies covering 89 per cent of parishes, divided in an interesting way between three-quarters that quoted rates per day and one quarter that quoted rates per week. The latter type suggests more regular and stable employment. Map 6 shows that such parishes were commonest in two areas, the central industrial belt where there was most competition for general labour, and the south-east where the high wages of hinds already noted suggests a strong market for specifically agricultural labour. In North Lanarkshire 75 per cent of the parishes quoted agricultural labourers' wages by the week, although there were scarcely any quotations here of farm servants' wages: it looks like a district where small farmers and their families did most of their own work but hired outsiders on a regular basis, perhaps for the less skilled tasks. In most of the districts of the eastern Borders four-fifths of the quotations were also for weekly wages, though here many of the labourers were probably the unmarried sons of hinds, work being regular partly because whole families were employed to cultivate large farms where the farmer was essentially a manager.

In Fife also there were many agricultural labourers who depended entirely on day wages. Such men were described at Leuchars (as also at Inveresk in Midlothian) to be past the age when they could hold down a job on yearly contract as farm servants, and as single or without families; but at Kingsbarns some, at least, were family men.[19] In Wigtownshire the labourers were often Irish immigrants working for Scottish farmers: their influx was said to have brought the rate of wages down heavily for the native Scots, but they certainly had large families: 'a labourer in this country gaining 8s. a week in summer, and 7s. in winter, will support a family of at least six or seven children, and keep them all decently dressed and make a very respectable appearance at church'.[20] Probably in most arable districts south of the Tay there were a good many who were agricultural labourers by profession.

In the Highlands and the north, however, where there were scarcely any wage quotations by the week, few were labourers by profession except in Easter Ross. Most day-labour was needed for a specific task — like digging a drainage ditch — or was seasonal — like harvesting and hay-making:

small tenants and crofters worked for farmers in this way to supplement their income, but did not try to live off such employment alone. Thus in Orkney 'there are scarcely any persons who come within the class of what would be called day labourers in Scotland or England, [but] those who have very small bits of land sometimes come and work as day labourers'.[21] There was a similar situation in the Hebrides, except that there a crofter would often have been fortunate even to get casual employment. In Aberdeenshire and the surrounding counties most work of this kind was also supplied by crofters, perhaps with three or four acres and a cow or two, as at Tough: 'the circumstances of this class of persons, when they are provident and careful, are on the whole comfortable. In the few instances in which our labourers have not bits of land, they have not the same abundance of supply'.[22] In the Black Isle of Easter Ross, however, there were a good many without cows or holdings, just as in Fife:[23] this northern patch of good arable land reproduced in many respects the social relationships of the south.

Agricultural labourers everywhere, like farm servants, were often paid partly in kind, though in this case it was simply an allowance of victuals worth (at least in 27 out of the 38 cases in which their value was quoted) 6d. a day — scarcely more than one-third of their average weekly wage. Wages also varied to a marked extent between the lows of winter and the highs of summer. Over Scotland as a whole it appears the labourer's wage rates tended to be about 12 per cent below the mean in winter and 10 per cent above it in summer, though, interestingly in the Highlands and the north the range was greater — from about 20 per cent below to about 20 per cent above. This reflects the more severe climate: in winter little could be done and labour was in gross oversupply; in the brief summer it was needed quickly to perform the essential tasks of gathering the crop before the weather failed again.

Naturally, the mere quotation of a daily or weekly wage rate can tell us nothing in detail of the real annual earnings of agricultural labourers. Jobs were not only less well paid in the winter, they were harder to come by; day-labourers in Easter Ross worked only nine or ten months in the year,[24] and in Fife winter destitution through unemployment was often severe.[25]

Table 5 and Map 7 show the regional variation in agricultural day-labourers' wage rates, including the value of victual allowances. In order to standardise the data the median was taken wherever a range was given for summer and winter work in the same parish, and a six-day week was assumed where day rates alone were given: but such a table cannot so closely reflect earnings throughout the year as those on the farm servants do, for the reasons just stated.

If the wage rates of the farm servants are compared with those of the day-labourers, by dividing the yearly wage of the former by 52 to arrive at a weekly rate, it appears that, despite the greater skill assumed to be needed by the farm servant, the day-labourer has a better rate. The last column in Table 4, shows the pattern: generally the differential is greater in the north and least in the south, especially where married farm servants are preferred. But as pay was not earnings, the yearly contract was everywhere preferred by the worker because of the certainty of income which it implied. Agricultural day-labour should perhaps be considered as a topping-up process as far as the employer was concerned, a way of supplementing the work of his own family and his yearly hired servants: as such it was an extra for a special task, paid over the odds. In many parts of the country a day-labourer was called the 'orra-man' or 'owrie' — the extra man.[26] This incremental nature of day-labour was particularly true in Shetland or the western Highlands where a crofter had to be tempted into special employment for a short period. It was less true in Berwickshire, where a day-labourer (or, more strictly, a weekly paid labourer) could expect a job for more of the year and would be paid less on a *pro rata* basis, not absolutely, but relatively; in the south-east the wage rates of farm servants and labourers were virtually identical in real terms, though of course the former was paid mainly in kind and the latter mainly in cash.

3. *Women and children in agriculture*

In the middle decades of the nineteenth century women worked on the land almost everywhere, and children over the age of 8 or 9 also worked in farming in many places: these features of rural life only began to disappear after 1870 when males began to earn sufficient to be able to withdraw their dependants from backbreaking toil in the fields. The commissioners asked about this type of employment in these terms:

> Q. 13. Are women and children usually employed in field labour, and at what rate of wages?

There were 825 replies (from 91 per cent of all parishes) of which 793 (96 per cent of responding parishes) were positive; of these, 57 per cent implied that women were employed but not children; 40 per cent that children as well as women were involved; 3 per cent gave an ambiguous reply. A fifth of the responses were, however, qualified by the remark that female and juvenile labour was used only seasonally or irregularly, although the question had not been framed to elicit this information. This suggests that their employment was often more spasmodic even than that of the male day-labourers.

In arable districts women and children probably only had jobs for about half the year at best. In Easter Ross they were used for cleaning the land of couch-grass and rubbish when it was to be prepared for a turnip crop, for manure spreading, for putting bone-meal in the turnip drills, for hoeing and cleaning the crop subsequently, for hay-making and for harvest work.[27] Certainly more parishes reported the employment of children in the south-east and other arable districts than elsewhere. The later phases of the agricultural revolution with the spread of turnip and potato husbandry must have created many more family jobs in agriculture (even if only seasonal ones) than had been available in the eighteenth century, and augmented total family earnings accordingly.

In pastoral districts, however, the pattern of employment had changed less: there were jobs for women as dairy hands throughout the year, and also some jobs for children as herds tending the animals especially where there was rough grazing. Of course, everyone also worked at harvest who could wield a sickle or tie a sheaf. Some women were hired by the year, mostly in the pastoral districts of the west, the south-west and the north-east, as living-in farm servants. Eighty-two parishes reported these in their replies to Question 9: presumably they were mainly dairy maids.

How well were the women paid? The quotations for day-labour were generally given in pence and inclusive of the value of victual payments which are less common than with men: 8d.–9d. was the mean day wage; to facilitate comparison with male labourers, however, we have reduced the figure to a national weekly wage on the basis of a six-day week (see Table 6). Generally a woman was paid about half the man's wage for labour over the same period, though it fell to as little as 35 per cent in parts of the western Highlands and rose to 57 per cent in Dumbarton and Renfrew district where there was a great deal of alternative employment for women (see also Map 8).

Industrial work for women was usually better paid than agricultural: even in these years when handloom weaving was falling on hard times, a woman at Girvan in Ayrshire was said to be able to earn 1s. or 1s.4d. a day at the loom compared to 8d. for outdoor work.[28] Overall the differential was not so great, however. Quotations from 127 parishes that were urban-industrial or rural parishes with a mixed economy suggest that women in industry obtained only 10 per cent more than women on the farm, measured as a day wage rate; in 16 parishes of farming or crofting character they were actually paid a quarter or a third less than those working on the land — but 'industrial' employment in such deeply rural locations was often only knitting stockings or plaiting straw on a very casual basis. Such calculations perhaps aggregate too much. It can hardly be doubted that a girl in a cotton factory working six days a week winter and summer would bring home much more than an outdoor farm girl in the same district who could only find a job for a few months of the year.

Those women farm servants hired by the year who lived in had (from 82 reports) a mean cash wage of £5, taking the country overall. Again, this is about half the male equivalent.

For children, the position is shown in Table 7 and Map 9. A wage of a little under 6d. put them at 30 per cent of the rate earned by adult males for a day's field labour; and, again, the overall differential in areas where there was much industry put children in industrial employment 10 per cent above the wage rate for those in farm work. The most highly paid children in farmwork were, however, those in the western industrial districts where there was most juvenile employment in manufacturers. Weeding was better paid than herding: in the Black Isle (where squads of 8 or 9 children would work a field) they were paid 6d. a day for the former but only 4d. for the latter.[29]

The narrowness of the overall differentials between industrial and agricultural rates for women and children's labour, combined with the clear way in which the agricultural rates rise in the vicinity of towns, suggests an active labour market in the Lowlands, with ready mobility from one type of occupation to another. Indeed, it was a great advantage to live within reach of the magic pull of industry, even if you did not choose to work in industry yourself. Conversely, the farm-worker and his family in the north were deprived of high wages, of such constant employment and of the possibility of shifting to other jobs. It would have been better for everyone if the jam of the industrial revolution could have been spread over a wider area than it actually was.

4. *Long-term wage changes and regional inequality*

How does our picture of agricultural wages compare with that of other scholars investigating different periods of Scottish history? Valerie Morgan[30] considered the wage data in the first *Statistical Account* of the 1790s, concentrating mainly on male farm servants paid by the year: she studied only the cash element of the wage and disregarded the extraordinary variations in the proportion paid in kind, a weakness that detracted from the value of her findings and misled her into thinking that Fife, the Lothians and the south-east generally were a low wage area. Otherwise, however, there is an interesting general resemblance between her maps of the distribution of wages and ours. On both, the Clyde appears as a 'high-wage region'; wages north of a line from south Argyll to the Angus–Kincardine border are lower than those south of that line, and very much lower in the islands and in the northern and western Highlands. It is interesting that these features should have appeared so early in the history of Scottish industrialisation.

Comparing the overall national picture from the 1790s with that from 1843 in detail, it seems that yearly cash wages for male farm servants increased from £6.8 to about £11.0 and for female farm servants from £2.9 to about £5.0 an increase of 62 per cent and 72 per cent respectively. For day-labourers the weekly wage rate rose from 6.0s. to 9.1s., an increase of 52 per cent. It is hard to say much about the cost of living, but the biggest single item in it — the cost of oatmeal — was almost identical at the two dates. Such a comparison of benchmark dates scarcely throws light on trends in the standard of living between the two, but agricultural

M

workers were clearly better off by a substantial margin at the second date than at the first.

Perhaps even more significant than the overall national picture for Scotland is the question as to whether the prosperity of the different regions grew at the same rate — whether there was divergence or convergence. Many regional economists believe that the first effects of sustained economic growth in a capitalist society will be to increase the gap between incomes in different regions of the developing nation, since wages and salaries in those areas that first experience growth will rise most rapidly.[31] Some, however, hold that it is likely that regional differentials will narrow again as labour moves to where it is best rewarded and capital to where labour costs are lower: if there is perfect competition, factor mobility will restore equilibrium. Others object that the advantages which initially favoured the growth points may prove cumulative, and institutional factors arise to impede a free factor market: in that case the 'backwash' effects of development at the centre will perpetuate if not exacerbate the regional imbalance.

Valerie Morgan's work appears, indeed, to confirm the first part of the thesis: variation in agricultural wages increased very substantially between the earlier eighteenth century and the 1790s, 'an indication perhaps that there was rather less contrast in the type and level of economic development in different parts of Scotland' before 1745 than at the end of the century.[32]

It is not easy to use a comparison between Valerie Morgan's work and ours to measure the degree to which convergence or divergence took place between the 1790s and the time of the Poor Law Inquiry in 1843 because of the different geographical bases on which the data were collected. There is, however, another way into the problem. A. J. Bowley gathered agricultural wage rates on a simple county basis for a series of years between 1790 and 1890–2.[33] Table 8 shows the results of applying a measure of inequality based on the coefficient of variation (adapted from J. G. Williamson's work in another context).[34] Wages are not income, of course: yet the trend of the day-labourer's wage may indicate at least the general direction of working-class living standards, especially as unskilled labour in farming was relatively free to switch to industry if higher incomes were available there. The drop in the coefficient by a quarter between 1810 and c. 1840, and by a further half between c. 1840 and 1892 (though apparently not evident between 1790 and 1810 or between 1860 and 1880) is fairly impressive, and supports to a certain extent the views of the 'convergence' school. Ultimately economic growth did bring wages closer together, but it took a long time to do it. Progress was twice as rapid in the second part of the century as in the first.

If there is a single reason for the prevalence of regional inequalities in the 1840s, it must be sought in the immobilities of the north. Highlanders did not leave the Highlands, nor Shetlanders the Shetlands, and so on, in sufficient numbers to bring the labour into closer line with what it was in the south. Nor did capital determinedly pursue labour into the wilder fastnesses — transport costs and the absence of a commercial superstructure in many parts made it unlikely that it would.

Scotland in the 1840s was a dual economy, not unlike similar economies in Latin America today.[35] The south was economically sophisticated, capitalist, oriented around growth in textiles and heavy industry; the north was a world of traditional values, oriented round the peasant desire to cling to a holding of land despite intolerable demographic pressures. It would take the shock of famine and clearance after 1846 combined with the slower erosion of local values by greater familiarity with the south (in which railways, boats, migrant labour and schools played a part) to alter this situation in any basic way: and that was a story belonging more to the second half of the nineteenth century than to the first.

NOTES

1. *Report of the Royal Commission on the Poor Law (Scotland)*, *Parliamentary Papers*, 1844, xxii, p. 790 (hereafter *Poor Law Report*).

2. *Ibid.*, Vol. 22, p. 94.

3. *Ibid.*, Vol. 22, p. 69.

4. Gavin Sprott, 'A Weel Plou'd Rig', in Billy Kay, ed., *Odyssey: Voices from Scotland's Recent Past* (Edinburgh, 1980), pp. 99–109.

5. Ian Carter, *Farmlife in Northeast Scotland, 1840–1914* (Edinburgh, 1979), esp. chapter 4.

6. Ian Carter, 'Oral History and Agrarian History — the North East', *Oral History*, Vol. 2 (1974), pp. 35–6.

7. Malcolm Gray, 'North-East Agriculture and the Labour Force, 1790–1875', in A. A. MacLaren, ed., *Social Class in Scotland: Past and Present* (Edinburgh, 1976), pp. 86–104.

8. *Poor Law Report*, Vol. 22, p. 498.

9. Throughout the tables on wages, we have chosen the mean rather than the median for representational purposes. This was largely the result of the SPSS packages which produces means and associated statistics, rather than medians in its tabulations. In order to satisfy ourselves that the representation of data would not be distorted (i.e. its distribution), we also computed medians for a certain number of wages and found very little difference in scores. These results, plus the fact that we were dealing with parish scores of distinct sets of wages and not the wages of individuals, gave us a reasonable confidence in the use of the mean as an average of wages.

10. We are also grateful to Professor George Houston for allowing us to consult his unpublished Oxford University D.Phil thesis, 'A History of the Scottish Farm Workers, 1800–1850'. See also above, chs. 2–5.

11. *Poor Law Report*, Vol. 22, p. 803.

12. For a detailed example, see *ibid.*, Vol. 22, pp. 732–3.

13. For the practice in Northumberland, see W. S. Gilly, *The Peasantry of the Border* (1842, reprinted with an introduction by R. H. Campbell, Edinburgh, 1973), Appendix, pp. 2–4. For Midlothian in 1656, see C. H. Firth, ed., *Scotland and the Protectorate* (Scottish History Society, 1899), pp. 405–7.

14. Ian Levitt and Christopher Smout, *The State of the Scottish Working Class in 1843* (Edinburgh, 1979), Chapter 2.

15. *Ibid.*, pp. 24–5, 38, 46.

16. *New Statistical Account*, (*N.S.A.*), Vol. 12, p. 306.

17. *Poor Law Report*, Vol. 21, p. 35.

18. *N.S.A.*, Vol. 11, p. 70.

19. *Poor Law Report*, Vol. 22, pp. 282, 295, 300, 304, 768.

20. *Ibid.*, Vol. 22, p. 535.

21. *Ibid.*, Vol. 21, p. 229.

22. *Ibid.*, Vol. 21, p. 676.

23. *Ibid.*, Vol. 21, p. 31.

24. *Ibid.*, Vol. 21, pp. 31, 480.

25. *Ibid.*, Vol. 22, pp. 295, 300.

26. *Ibid.*, Vol. 22, p. 295.

27. *Ibid.*, Vol. 21, p. 56.

28. *Ibid.*, Vol. 22, p. 442.

29. *Ibid.*, Vol. 21, pp. 56, 60.

30. Valerie Morgan, 'Agricultural Wage Rates in Late Eighteenth-Century Scotland', *Economic History Review*, 2nd series, Vol. 24 (1971), pp. 181–201.

31. The problem is discussed in H. W. Richardson, *Regional Economics: Location Theory, Urban Structure and Regional Change* (Penguin, Harmondsworth, 1969), and in J. G. Williamson, 'Regional Inequality and the Process of National Development: A Description of the Patterns', *Economic Development and Cultural Change*, Vol. 13 (1965), pp. 3–45.

32. Morgan, 'Agricultural Wages', p. 190.

33. A. J. Bowley, 'The Statistics of Wages in the United Kingdom during the Last Hundred Years, Part II, Agricultural Wages, Scotland', *Journal of the Royal Statistical Society*, Vol. 62 (1899).

34. Williamson, 'Regional Inequality', pp. 3–45.

35. Alan Gilbert, *Latin American Development: a Geographical Perspective* (Penguin, Harmondsworth, 1794), Chapter 7.

Table 1 *Percentages of Parishes clearly Preferring (a) Married or (b) Unmarried Farm Servants by District*

	(a)	(b)	N
1. Shetland	44	56	9
2. Orkney	17	72	18
3. Caithness	0	92	12
4. East Sutherland	36	36	11
5. East Ross	58	8	12
6. N.-E. Inverness	0	62	16
7. North-west coast	18	82	11
8. Skye and Outer Hebrides	18	92	12
9. West Argyll	33	47	15
10. North Argyll	0	80	10
11. South Argyll	11	67	18
12. Highland Inverness, Banff, Moray	17	67	12
13. Highland Perth, Aberdeenshire	30	60	10
14. N.-W. Perth	21	64	14
15. Nairn, Lowland Moray	0	67	21
16. Lowland Banff	19	39	26
17. Buchan	8	56	25
18. S.-E. Aberdeenshire	4	73	26
19. Inner Aberdeenshire	15	50	20
20. Kincardine	17	50	18
21. Inner Angus	31	40	35
22. Coastal Angus	42	27	26
23. East Perthshire	35	50	20
24. South Perthshire	18	59	22
25. East Fife	62	15	34
26. West Fife	59	4	27
27. North Stirling-Clackmannan	29	53	17
28. West Lothian, East Stirling	38	10	21
29. Edinburgh area	80	0	19
30. Dumbarton, Renfrewshire	5	85	20
31. North Ayrshire	25	42	24
32. South Ayrshire	50	31	16
33. North Lanarkshire	15	50	20
34. South Lanarkshire	11	42	19
35. Peeblesshire	47	23	17
36. Dunbar area	83	0	18
37. South Berwick	63	0	30
38. Kelso area	100	0	22
39. Hawick area	30	0	10
40. Inner Dumfries, Kircudbright	43	5	21
41. South Dumfries	30	13	23
42. South Kirkcudbright	29	24	21
43. Wigtown and south tip of Ayr	38	6	16
SCOTLAND	32	39	814

Table 2   *Married Farm Servants' Wage Rates, by District*

	Mean value of money wage (£p.a.)	N	Mean value of total wage (£p.a.)	N	Total wage as % of Scottish mean
1. Shetland	—	0	—	0	*
2. Orkney	6.0	1	14.0	1	*
3. Caithness	7.5	2	16.0	3	*
4. East Sutherland	8.3	3	18.0	1	*
5. East Ross	6.9	7	18.3	4	76
6. N.-E. Inverness	8.2	8	19.0	1	*
7. North-west coast	7.7	3	—	0	*
8. Skye and Outer Hebrides	—	0	—	0	*
9. West Argyll	7.7	3	20.0	1	*
10. North Argyll	9.5	2	—	0	*
11. South Argyll	11.3	3	—	0	*
12. Highland Inverness, Banff, Moray	—	0	—	0	*
13. Highland Perth, Aberdeenshire	—	0	—	0	*
14. N.-W. Perth	12.0	2	—	0	*
15. Nairn, Lowland Moray	—	0	—	0	*
16. Lowland Banff	—	0	—	0	*
17. Buchan	9.0	2	22.0	2	*
18. S.-E. Aberdeen	5.0	2	—	0	*
19. Inner Aberdeen	13.0	1	—	0	*
20. Kincardine	9.9	7	25.0	1	*
21. Inner Angus	9.8	5	24.0	2	*
22. Coastal Angus	11.3	6	23.0	3	*
23. East Perthshire	11.3	3	—	0	*
24. South Perthshire	12.0	1	—	0	*
25. East Fife	10.2	16	22.2	13	93
26. West Fife	11.9	10	23.6	9	98
27. North Stirling-Clackmannan	13.7	3	23.0	2	*
28. West Lothian, East Stirling	15.3	6	25.0	9	104
29. Edinburgh area	14.8	8	25.5	21	106
30. Dumbarton, Renfrewshire	—	0	24.0	2	*
31. North Ayrshire	14.0	1	24.2	6	101
32. South Ayrshire	12.0	3	23.0	5	95
33. North Lanarkshire	—	0	—	0	*
34. South Lanarkshire	11.0	3	24.0	2	*
35. Peeblesshire	11.1	8	23.5	11	98
36. Dunbar area	9.0	1	25.5	17	107
37. South Berwick	4.7	6	26.5	24	111
38. Kelso area	3.7	3	26.2	19	109
39. Hawick area	10.0	3	25.5	6	106
40. Inner Dumfries, Kircudbright	12.5	2	22.3	3	*
41. South Dumfries	10.0	3	22.6	9	94
42. South Kirkcudbright	—	0	22.3	11	93
43. Wigtown and south tip of Ayr	9.0	2	21.7	13	90
SCOTLAND	10.2	139	24.0	201	

Table 3 *Unmarried Farm Servants' Wage Rates, by District*

	Mean value of money wage (£p.a.)	S.D.	N	Mean value of total wage (£p.a.)	Total wage as % of Scottish mean
1. Shetland	3.33	0.82	6	11.33	55
2. Orkney	6.24	0.83	17	14.24	69
3. Caithness	8.44	2.24	9	16.44	80
4. East Sutherland	6.60	2.30	5	14.60	71
5. East Ross	7.00	—	1	15.00	*
6. N.-E. Inverness	7.89	1.17	9	15.89	77
7. North-west coast	6.43	1.90	7	14.43	70
8. Skye and Outer Hebrides	6.00	1.28	12	14.00	68
9. West Argyll	8.00	1.29	7	16.00	78
10. North Argyll	9.70	1.16	10	17.70	86
11. South Argyll	12.21	2.04	19	20.21	98
12. Highland Inverness, Banff, Moray	9.50	1.09	12	18.50	90
13. Highland Perth, Aberdeenshire	11.70	1.42	10	20.70	100
14. N.-W. Perth	11.42	1.08	12	20.42	99
15. Nairn, Lowland Moray	10.58	1.64	19	19.58	95
16. Lowland Banff	11.27	0.96	26	20.27	98
17. Buchan	11.85	1.09	20	20.85	101
18. S.-E. Aberdeenshire	10.71	1.49	24	19.71	96
19. Inner Aberdeenshire	11.75	1.29	20	20.75	101
20. Kincardine	11.13	1.85	15	20.13	98
21. Inner Angus	11.10	1.60	31	21.10	102
22. Coastal Angus	10.84	1.12	19	20.84	101
23. East Perthshire	11.90	1.10	19	21.90	106
24. South Perthshire	12.18	1.71	22	22.18	108
25. East Fife	10.69	0.75	13	20.69	100
26. West Fife	12.54	2.47	13	22.54	109
27. North Stirling-Clackmannan	13.55	1.44	11	24.55	119
28. West Lothian, East Stirling	14.00	2.79	10	25.00	121
29. Edinburgh area	14.00	2.83	2	25.00	*
30. Dumbarton, Renfrewshire	14.36	1.69	11	25.36	123
31. North Ayrshire	13.75	2.18	16	24.75	120
32. South Ayrshire	12.64	1.29	11	23.64	114
33. North Lanarkshire	14.64	2.37	14	25.64	124
34. South Lanarkshire	12.13	1.78	16	23.13	112
35. Peeblesshire	11.00	0.74	12	22.00	107
36. Dunbar area	10.00	—	1	21.00	*
37. South Berwick	10.00	—	3	21.00	*
38. Kelso area	11.00	1.41	2	22.00	*
39. Hawick area	11.40	0.55	5	22.40	109
40. Inner Dumfries, Kirkcudbright	11.67	0.97	18	22.67	110
41. South Dumfries	10.94	1.71	17	21.94	106
42. South Kirkcudbright	10.47	1.33	17	21.47	104
43. Wigtown and south tip of Ayr	10.00	1.05	10	21.00	102
SCOTLAND	10.99	2.55	553	20.65	

Table 4   *Married plus Unmarried Farm Servants' Wage Rates, by District*

	Mean value of total wage (£p.a.)	N	Total wage as % of Scottish mean	Farm servants wage rate as % of agricultural day-labourers wage rate
1. Shetland	11.3	6	53	76
2. Orkney	14.2	18	66	81
3. Caithness	16.3	12	76	75
4. East Sutherland	15.2	6	71	76
5. East Ross	17.6	5	82	95
6. N.-E. Inverness	16.2	10	74	77
7. North-west coast	14.4	7	67	67
8. Skye and Outer Hebrides	14.0	12	65	83
9. West Argyll	16.5	8	77	86
10. North Argyll	17.7	10	82	77
11. South Argyll	20.2	19	94	86
12. Highland Inverness, Banff, Moray	18.5	12	86	84
13. Highland Perth, Aberdeenshire	20.7	10	96	89
14. N.-W. Perth	20.4	12	95	89
15. Nairn, Lowland Moray	19.6	19	91	84
16. Lowland Banff	20.3	26	95	90
17. Buchan	21.0	22	98	88
18. S.-E. Aberdeenshire	19.7	24	92	80
19. Inner Aberdeenshire	20.8	20	97	85
20. Kincardine	20.4	16	95	86
21. Inner Angus	21.3	33	99	91
22. Coastal Angus	21.1	22	98	86
23. East Perthshire	21.9	19	102	91
24. South Perthshire	22.2	22	103	92
25. East Fife	21.4	26	100	92
26. West Fife	24.0	22	112	98
27. North Stirling-Clackmannan	24.4	13	113	96
28. West Lothian, East Stirling	25.0	19	116	96
29. Edinburgh area	25.5	23	119	100
30. Dumbarton, Renfrewshire	25.2	13	117	93
31. North Ayrshire	24.6	22	114	92
32. South Ayrshire	23.4	16	109	98
33. North Lanarkshire	25.6	14	119	90
34. South Lanarkshire	23.2	18	108	93
35. Peeblesshire	22.7	23	106	89
36. Dunbar area	25.3	18	117	100
37. South Berwick	25.9	27	120	102
38. Kelso area	25.8	21	120	95
39. Hawick area	24.1	11	112	89
40. Inner Dumfries, Kirkcudbright	22.6	21	105	97
41. South Dumfries	22.2	26	103	98
42. South Kirkcudbright	21.8	28	101	101
43. Wigtown and south tip of Ayr	21.4	23	100	104
SCOTLAND	21.5	754		91

Table 5 *Agricultural Day-Labourers' Wage Rates, by District*

	Shillings per week	S.D.	N	% of Scottish mean
1. Shetland	5.70	0.26	10	62.4
2. Orkney	6.78	1.32	15	74.5
3. Caithness	8.33	0.97	12	91.4
4. East Sutherland	7.68	1.08	10	84.2
5. East Ross	7.11	0.82	11	77.9
6. N.-E. Inverness	8.11	0.75	14	88.9
7. North-west coast	8.22	1.37	9	90.3
8. Skye and Outer Hebrides	6.52	1.42	11	71.6
9. West Argyll	7.35	1.04	12	80.7
10. North Argyll	8.81	1.33	11	96.8
11. South Argyll	9.04	1.21	20	99.3
12. Highland Inverness, Banff, Moray	8.50	1.24	12	93.5
13. Highland Perth, Aberdeenshire	8.98	1.82	10	98.4
14. N.-W. Perth	8.80	0.86	13	96.7
15. Nairn, Lowland Moray	9.01	1.09	21	98.9
16. Lowland Banff	8.73	1.59	26	95.8
17. Buchan	9.17	1.18	22	100.7
18. S.-E. Aberdeenshire	9.51	1.36	26	104.3
19. Inner Aberdeenshire	9.41	1.21	20	103.3
20. Kincardine	9.12	1.17	18	100.2
21. Inner Angus	8.98	0.93	34	98.6
22. Coastal Angus	9.48	0.89	26	104.1
23. East Perthshire	9.21	0.48	19	101.2
24. South Perthshire	9.27	0.83	22	101.8
25. East Fife	8.92	0.70	33	97.9
26. West Fife	9.43	0.84	27	103.5
27. North Stirling-Clackmannan	9.81	0.94	18	107.6
28. West Lothian, East Stirling	10.02	0.82	22	110.1
29. Edinburgh area	9.81	0.61	22	107.8
30. Dumbarton, Renfrewshire	10.45	1.26	19	114.9
31. North Ayrshire	10.35	1.02	26	113.7
32. South Ayrshire	9.18	0.73	17	100.8
33. North Lanarkshire	10.95	1.65	20	120.3
34. South Lanarkshire	9.62	0.78	20	105.7
35. Peeblesshire	9.84	0.87	16	108.1
36. Dunbar area	9.71	0.35	19	106.6
37. South Berwick	9.79	0.66	29	107.5
38. Kelso area	10.51	0.95	22	115.5
39. Hawick area	10.48	0.93	10	115.1
40. Inner Dumfries, Kirkcudbright	8.95	0.75	21	98.3
41. South Dumfries	8.73	1.21	23	95.8
42. South Kirkcudbright	8.27	1.06	21	90.9
43. Wigtown and south tip of Ayr	7.94	0.95	18	87.1
SCOTLAND	9.12	1.39	807	100.1

Table 6 *Women Field Workers' Wage Rates, by District*

	Shillings per week	S.D.	N	% of Scottish mean
1. Shetland	3.27	0.66	11	78.1
2. Orkney	3.31	0.47	11	79.1
3. Caithness	3.27	0.39	12	77.9
4. East Sutherland	3.21	0.56	7	77.0
5. East Ross	2.89	0.20	12	69.5
6. N.-E. Inverness	3.06	0.21	13	73.3
7. North-west coast	2.25	0.42	6	66.0
8. Skye and Outer Hebrides	2.94	0.13	4	70.5
9. West Argyll	4.00	0.70	10	95.2
10. North Argyll	4.62	0.64	8	110.0
11. South Argyll	4.85	0.76	15	115.4
12. Highland Inverness, Banff, Moray	3.60	0.90	10	85.8
13. Highland Perth, Aberdeenshire	4.06	0.53	9	96.4
14. N.-W. Perth	3.92	1.28	12	103.1
15. Nairn, Lowland Moray	3.60	0.49	21	85.6
16. Lowland Banff	4.00	0.71	21	95.2
17. Buchan	4.39	0.97	19	104.7
18. S.-E. Aberdeenshire	4.33	1.15	24	107.8
19. Inner Aberdeenshire	3.95	1.04	20	99.3
20. Kincardine	3.61	0.42	16	85.8
21. Inner Angus	3.94	0.47	35	93.7
22. Coastal Angus	4.11	0.46	26	97.8
23. East Perthshire	4.26	0.59	19	101.3
24. South Perthshire	4.25	0.60	22	101.0
25. East Fife	4.00	0.25	33	94.7
26. West Fife	4.17	0.71	26	102.2
27. North Stirling-Clackmannan	5.21	0.74	18	124.0
28. West Lothian, East Stirling	4.91	0.53	22	116.9
29. Edinburgh area	4.42	0.38	22	105.1
30. Dumbarton, Renfrewshire	5.81	0.71	17	138.4
31. North Ayrshire	5.47	0.81	19	130.4
32. South Ayrshire	4.60	0.76	15	109.4
33. North Lanarkshire	5.59	0.69	19	133.2
34. South Lanarkshire	4.83	0.81	20	114.9
35. Peeblesshire	4.72	0.81	16	112.4
36. Dunbar area	4.76	0.29	19	113.3
37. South Berwick	5.09	0.43	29	121.1
38. Kelso area	4.98	0.42	22	118.5
39. Hawick area	5.13	0.43	10	122.0
40. Inner Dumfries, Kirkcudbright	4.64	0.61	20	110.3
41. South Dumfries	4.31	0.43	21	102.5
42. South Kirkcudbright	4.35	0.46	20	103.5
43. Wigtown and south tip of Ayr	3.84	0.57	17	91.2
SCOTLAND	4.32	0.91	749	

Table 7 *Child Field Workers' Wage Rates, by District*

	Shillings per week	S.D.	N	% of Scottish mean
1. Shetland	3.00	0	1	*
2. Orkney	1.97	0.24	7	70.8
3. Caithness	2.00	0	1	*
4. East Sutherland	2.13	0.25	4	76.3
5. East Ross	2.00	0.55	6	71.8
6. N.-E. Inverness	3.00	0	1	*
7. North-west coast	*	*	0	*
8. Skye and Outer Hebrides	3.00	0	1	*
9. West Argyll	2.75	0.50	4	98.7
10. North Argyll	2.70	0.67	5	96.9
11. South Argyll	3.10	0.65	5	111.3
12. Highland Inverness, Banff, Moray	2.40	0.90	5	86.2
13. Highland Perth, Aberdeenshire	1.75	0	1	*
14. N.-W. Perth	2.81	0.38	4	100.9
15. Nairn, Lowland Moray	2.75	0.50	4	98.7
16. Lowland Banff	2.50	0.71	2	*
17. Buchan	2.00	0	1	*
18. S.-E. Aberdeenshire	2.50	0.50	3	*
19. Inner Aberdeenshire	3.00	0	2	*
20. Kincardine	2.40	0.55	5	86.2
21. Inner Angus	2.64	0.55	11	94.7
22. Coastal Angus	2.67	0.54	12	95.8
23. East Perthshire	2.25	0	1	*
24. South Perthshire	2.89	0.68	6	101.7
25. East Fife	2.82	0.34	11	101.2
26. West Fife	2.72	0.61	9	97.7
27. North Stirling-Clackmannan	3.25	0.38	8	116.7
28. West Lothian, East Stirling	2.95	0.39	9	105.7
29. Edinburgh area	2.92	0.49	13	104.9
30. Dumbarton, Renfrewshire	3.25	0.74	6	116.7
31. North Ayrshire	3.50	0.89	6	125.7
32. South Ayrshire	2.78	0.39	7	100.0
33. North Lanarkshire	3.46	0.89	7	124.4
34. South Lanarkshire	4.00	0	1	*
35. Peeblesshire	3.17	0.76	3	*
36. Dunbar area	2.73	0.43	14	98.1
37. South Berwick	2.83	0.46	21	101.7
38. Kelso area	2.79	0.52	13	100.1
39. Hawick area	3.25	1.06	2	*
40. Inner Dumfries, Kirkcudbright	2.79	0.35	9	100.3
41. South Dumfries	2.61	0.60	9	93.8
42. South Kirkcudbright	2.87	0.33	11	102.8
43. Wigtown and south tip of Ayr	2.80	0.59	10	100.5
SCOTLAND	2.78	0.59	261	

Table 8   *Co-efficients of Inequality in Agricultural Wage Rates in Scottish Counties, 1790–1892*

	Married farm servants	Day-labourers
1790	—	0.17
1794	0.16	0.17
1810	—	0.16
1834–45	0.13	0.12
1860	—	0.09
1867–70	—	0.10[1]
1880–1	—	0.09
1892	0.10	0.06

[1]This is arrived at by excluding one eccentric report, Argyll; if it is included it becomes 0.12.

The co-efficient of variation is Williamson's measure Vuw.

$$\text{Vuw} = \frac{\sqrt{\sum_i (yi - \bar{y})^2 / N}}{\bar{y}}$$

Where N = number of counties
yi = wage rate of the ith county
$\bar{y}$ = mean wage rate for Scotland.

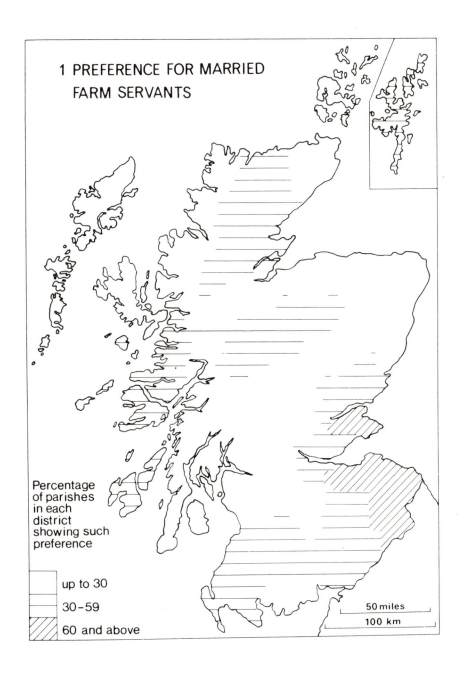

1 PREFERENCE FOR MARRIED
FARM SERVANTS

Percentage
of parishes
in each
district
showing such
preference

up to 30

30–59

60 and above

50 miles

100 km

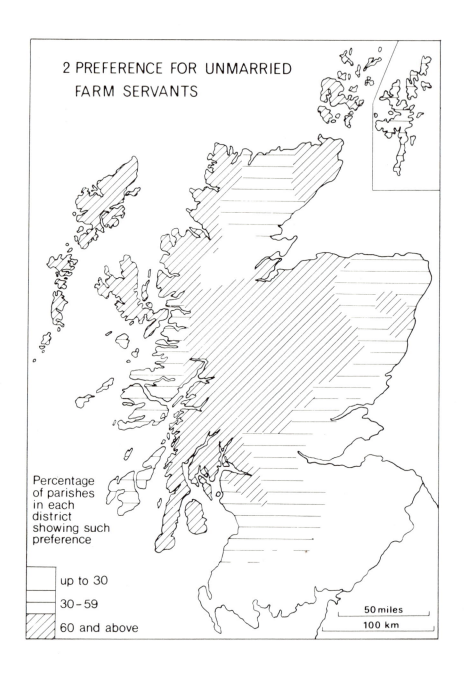

2 PREFERENCE FOR UNMARRIED
FARM SERVANTS

Percentage
of parishes
in each
district
showing such
preference

up to 30

30 – 59

60 and above

50 miles
100 km

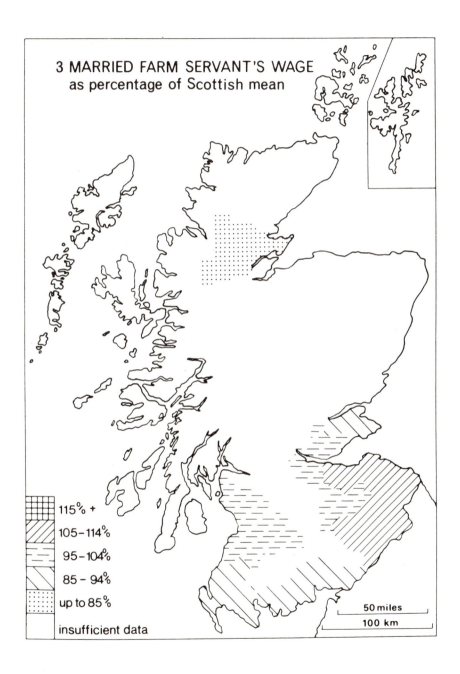

3 MARRIED FARM SERVANT'S WAGE
as percentage of Scottish mean

115% +
105–114%
95–104%
85–94%
up to 85%
insufficient data

50 miles
100 km

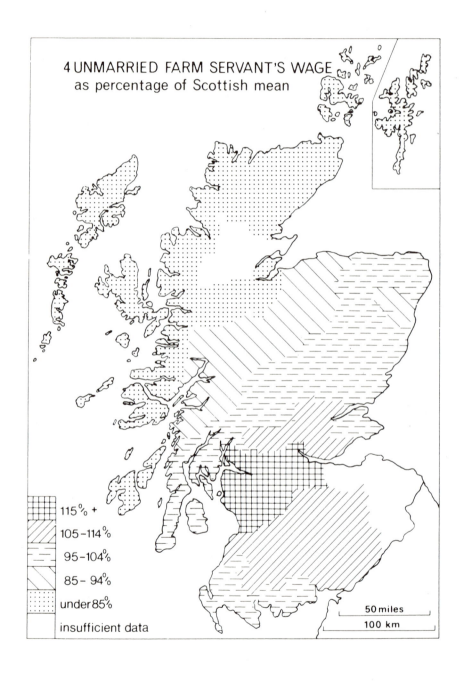

4 UNMARRIED FARM SERVANT'S WAGE
as percentage of Scottish mean

115% +
105–114%
95–104%
85–94%
under 85%
insufficient data

50 miles
100 km

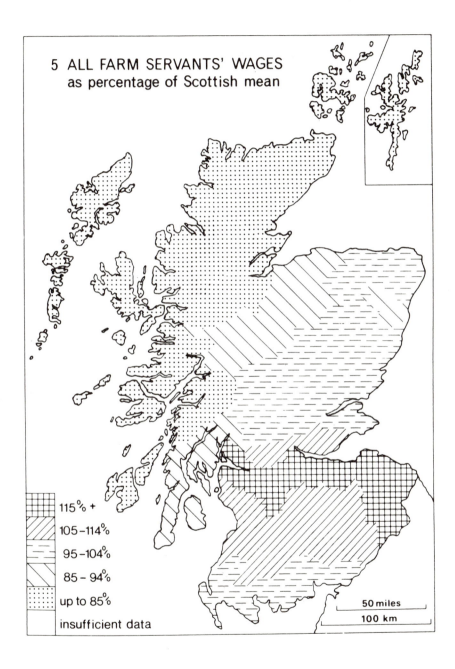

5 ALL FARM SERVANTS' WAGES
as percentage of Scottish mean

115% +
105–114%
95–104%
85–94%
up to 85%
insufficient data

50 miles
100 km

N

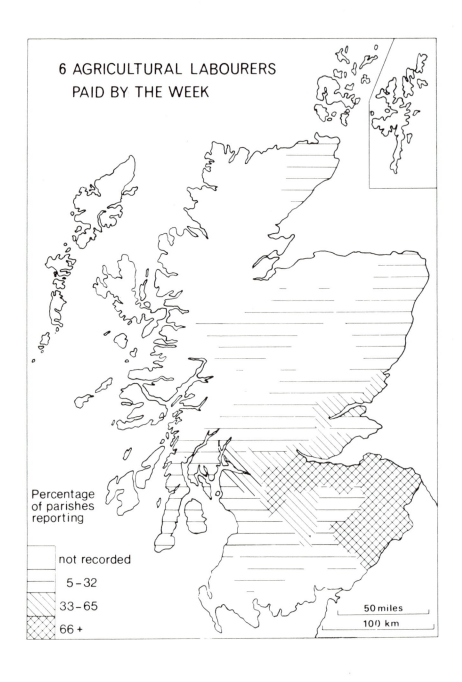

6 AGRICULTURAL LABOURERS
PAID BY THE WEEK

Percentage
of parishes
reporting

not recorded

5–32

33–65

66 +

50 miles

100 km

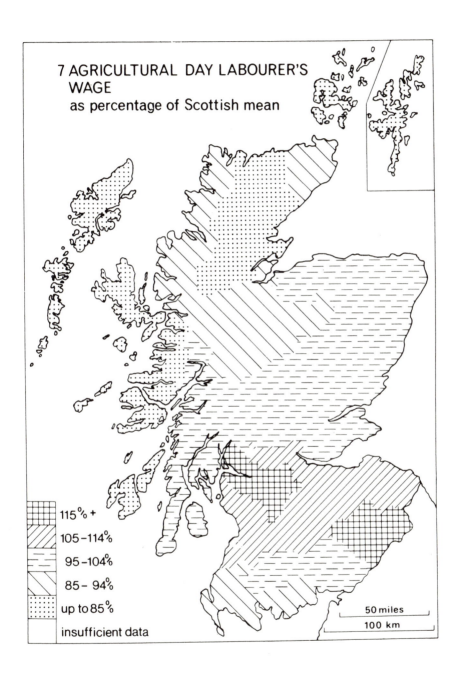

7 AGRICULTURAL DAY LABOURER'S
WAGE
as percentage of Scottish mean

115% +
105 –114%
95 –104%
85 – 94%
up to 85%
insufficient data

50 miles
100 km

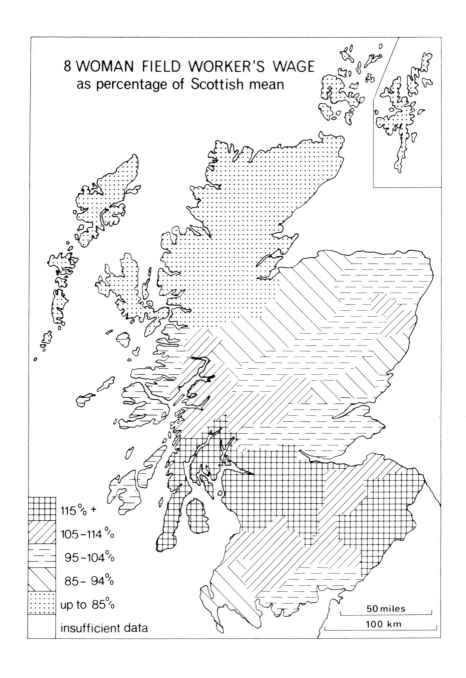

8 WOMAN FIELD WORKER'S WAGE
as percentage of Scottish mean

115% +
105–114%
95–104%
85–94%
up to 85%
insufficient data

50 miles
100 km

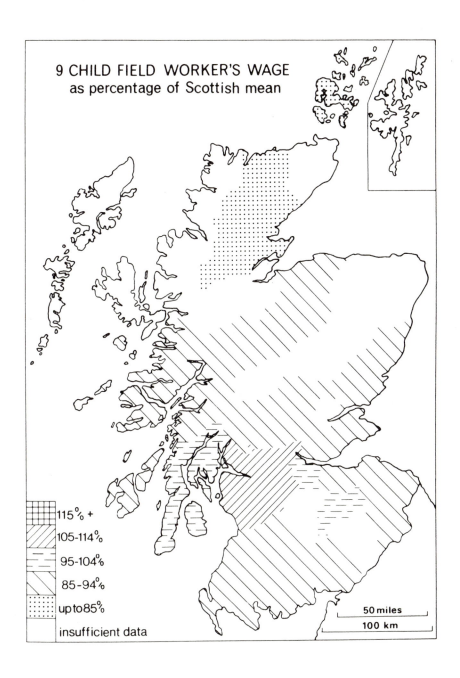

9 CHILD FIELD WORKER'S WAGE
as percentage of Scottish mean

115% +
105-114%
95-104%
85-94%
up to 85%
insufficient data

50 miles
100 km

10

The Housing of Agricultural Workers in the Nineteenth Century

Alexander Fenton

The concept of agricultural workers excludes farmers and crofters, who also make a living from the land. Though, as recently shown in a book on servants in husbandry in early modern England, the concept has changed substantially over the centuries,[1] by the nineteenth century the modern senses of farm-servant, farm-labourer, farm-worker and hind had been established. A well-defined social and economic gap between employers and employed had also appeared, obscuring the less clear situation of an earlier date.

To some extent, developments were being foreshadowed before the century began. In Roxburgh, it was noted in 1794 that the system for keeping servants differed from that in most parts of Scotland. Whether hinds, shepherds or barnmen, they lived with their families in houses on the farm, and were paid in kind.[2] The system of having houses for the married servants was by no means, however, unique to Roxburgh. It was also to be found, for example, in Angus. In the parishes of Fern and Menmuir, cottagers were almost universally employed, being regarded by farmers as cheaper and more steady than hired servants.[3] In Edzell it was said that though this useful class of cottars formed 'the best nurseries of male and female servants', nevertheless it was 'going fast out of fashion', which indicates that a preference for unmarried servants was developing.[4] This was also the case in the Carse of Gowrie where servants seldom or never ate in the farmer's family, but had 'a house adjoining to the offices, allotted for them, in which they lodge and eat'.[5] As a modest concession, it could happen in Angus that boiling water would be got ready in the farm-kitchen, for the men to make their brose with on their return from work.[6]

In Fife, cot-houses were being improved along with the farm-houses, and were said to have become in general better than the farm-houses of 30 to 40 years before.[7] Those built just before 1800 were 15′ –16′ wide, with stone-and-lime side-walls 6′ –7′ high, thatched, well-lit and 'sufficiently large to accommodate any ordinary family'. They were in units of from 3 or 4 to 8 or 10 dwelling houses, and were seen as of great benefit to the farm to which they were attached, 'as indeed they generally are and ought to be', since they could be let not only to married servants, but also to tradesmen or labourers to ensure a labour supply at the hay and grain harvests and other busy seasons. Such cottages were not, however, general in Fife. In the North division they were rare, since there the tenant farmers were unwilling to provide cottages with patches of ground to graze a cow. This inhibited the settling of mechanics, tradesmen and labourers.[8]

In Clackmannan, two forms of farm-service were noted. Those employed by the year, not residing in the farm-house, got an allowance of 'livery-meal' in lieu of board. This term was recorded in 1750 in the Atholl MSS, in relation to a servant who had a free house and kailyard, and was also used in Midlothian and Peebles (see *Scottish National Dictionary* s.v. *Livery*), so indicating other areas where some, at least, of the farm-servants lived separately. It marks a kind of hangover from the custom, formerly common, of boarding ploughmen in their employer's house, but by 1795 most of the principal Clackmannan farmers had already moved away from it. They had come to prefer married servants, 'as being more orderly and tractable', providing for them a house and a small kailyard as near the farm as possible. Some tenants were so eager that they had been known to erect a double cottage at their own expense. The cottar house principle was much praised.[9]

By 1795 in Midlothian, much renewal of cottages had taken place. The older style had walls of stone with mud mortar, ponderous roofs of thatch and sods, and low walls propped up with buttresses of unhewn stone. A wide chimney set against a gable wall let in the weather as well as light, which was supplemented by a slit or bole in the wall. Such light-boles were as often as not unglazed, and could be closed by a wooden shutter or simply a wisp of straw (the term *bole* is recorded in this sense in Angus, Midlothian and Selkirk). Newer cottages, however, were of good mason work, with walls 7' to 8' high, and neatly thatched with straw. Some were ceiled, and some had timber floors. In size they measured around 16'–18' square, 'which is found sufficient to hold the furniture commodiously'.[10]

In Ayr, though little information specifically about cottar houses is available for the late eighteenth century, nevertheless labourers who were employed on hedging, ditching, mowing, threshing, reaping and the like usually endeavoured to have a small house and garden, with a cow's grass and a patch of potato ground, for which they paid a rent.[11] In Renfrew, married ploughmen predominated. They were said to have lived in their masters' houses, a comment which is a little ambiguous, since it would be possible to interpret it as relating to cottar houses belonging to the farm.[12] Nevertheless, it could well mean that the married ploughmen did live in the farm-house, for a Midlothian source of 1725 speaks of 'hyndroumes in the farme howse at Fulfoord', where the farm servant or *hind* lived with his wife and child.[13] It was usual enough for single servants to lodge in the farm-house, especially in areas where such were or came to be preferred, for example in Nairn and Moray,[14] but this practice should not be allowed to obscure further the admittedly faint indications that similar conditions existed at an earlier date for married servants.

Marital status began to play an increasingly important role in the nature of accommodation as the eighteenth century ended. Some areas came to prefer single workers, others preferred married couples, and sometimes where the size of the farm justified it, both forms could co-exist.[15] In 1656, the Justices of the Peace for Midlothian drew up an Assessment of Wages. It referred to hinds and shepherds living in their own houses, and men like the *tasker* (flail-thresher), who might also have a house if employed on a big farm. The unmarried ploughmen, farm lads, female servants and maids lived in.[16] The servants with houses at this period, and in the following century (for example in Lanarkshire in 1708),[17] were required to provide a female servant, known as a bondager and usually in practice the wife, to carry out a range of duties which, in effect, paid the rent of the cottage.[18] Later, as this requirement lost its force, the term 'hind' came to mean, specifically in the south of Scotland and north of England, a skilled, married worker, occupying a cottage on the farm and receiving certain perquisites in addition to money wages. This was the stage that had been reached in Roxburgh, Angus and other places by the end of the eighteenth century.

It is possible to establish a broad view of areas of preference for married or single servants, as a pointer to forms of accommodation, thanks to an analysis made by Robert Hope, farmer at Fenton Barns in East Lothian. By 1814, servants hired by the year, and married, were general through much of Scotland, but more numerous in some districts than in others. They lived in cottages attached to the farm. Unmarried servants, whether male or female, were hired by the half-year and boarded in the farm-house.

In geographical terms, the breakdown in the first part of the nineteenth century — which was not, however, fixed for all time — was as follows: *East Lothian, Berwick, Roxburgh, Selkirk* and *Peebles* had mainly married hinds who got a house and garden (for which a reaper had to be provided), a cow's keep for the year, potato and flax ground, permission to keep a pig and half a dozen hens (or 4–6 stones of pork, or money in lieu). Unmarried servants on a half-year fee were paid in cash. Where a farm-worker lived in the farmhouse, he was named in Roxburghshire the *ha-man*.[19]

In the south-west, *Dumfries, Lanark, Renfrew, Galloway, Ayr* and *Dumbarton,* the farms were in general smaller, and family-sized. In such an area the difficulty of defining the concept of 'farm servant' becomes apparent, for sons not needed on the small farms of their parents normally hired themselves out to less fortunate neighbours, and saved till they could acquire a small farm for themselves. Thus married servants were less common, and the regular work was done by single men, hired by the year or half-year. They boarded with the farmer for whom they worked, and since they tended to be of the same social class, this situation was facilitated, with no special sense of social differentiation. Galloway was specified as an area where such farm-servants as were married lived in cottages on the farm, being engaged for a year and often longer.

In *Stirling*, especially among the farmers in the Carses, there were few married servants. Here, as in most of the western counties, the demand was for single men only.

In *Midlothian, West Lothian, Clackmannan, Kinross* and *Fife* a good proportion of the servants were married, and living in houses attached to the farms.

In *Perth, Angus (Forfar)* and *Kincardine* many of the servants were also married. On some farms, however, 'where a number of unmarried servants are employed, they live in what is provincially called a *bothy*, that is to say, they have a room or cottage for themselves, where they prepare their victuals, eat and sleep'. This practice, in the first decade of the nineteenth century, was described as 'peculiar to the north-east Lowlands, and some parts of Perthshire'. Robert Hope saw nothing in it to deserve imitation, however.

In the north-east — *Aberdeen, Banff, Moray* and *Nairn* — a great proportion of servants were single, hired by the year or half-year, and boarded by the farmer. But 'fortunately for the interest of agriculture', the use of married servants was spreading, and the bigger farms were already employing one or two. On small farms there was a kind of intermediate arrangement, whereby a married servant was taken on for nine months, and the three summer months were left to him to cast his peat fuel and to hire as a day labourer. In such a case a house was not provided, but the married worker had a small croft and a little grass for his cow at night, when she was brought home from amongst the farmer's cattle. Whilst employed, breakfast and midday dinner were provided, and an allowance was given in meal for supper. Wages were, in money, 1/- to 2/- a day, which was better than for regular day-labourers who at this period normally earned around 1/- a day, without necessarily getting any extras.

In the Highland districts, farm-service as such was almost unknown. Farmers depended on the labour of themselves and their families. Landlords got much of their work done for them by the crofters and their families, especially during the hay and corn harvests, under the conditions of lease for the crofts, but this system was dying out. In the agricultural parts of *Inverness, Ross* and *Cromarty*, married farm-servants were to be found in their own houses, as well as single servants living in. *Argyll*, in particular, had hardly any other than single men, getting their victuals in the house of the farmer. In the *Hebrides*, servants who were hired made it a condition that they should have summer leave of absence to work at kelping or fishing.

Caithness had married servants; in *Orkney*, men and women were given board as part of their wages; and in *Shetland*, full-time farm-servants were unknown, since they engaged in farm-work only outside the fishing season.[20]

Already by the end of the eighteenth century indications are to be found of the variations in farm-servants' housing, often directly related to marital status, that came to characterise the nineteenth. Such improvements in accommodation had begun (at least in the southern districts), and though writers might still remember housing like that described by John Ray in 1661 as 'pitiful Cots, built of Stone, and covered with Turves, having in them but one Room, many of them no Chimneys, the Windows very small Holes, and not glazed' this image was beginning to fade.[21] Nevertheless, farm-servant housing remained fairly basic, and though walls and roof might be better built, the single room of about 15-16 feet wide by 18 feet long remained for long the standard unit for a married family. The percipient Robert Hope summed up the state of affairs in 1814:

> Though some of them are on a proper construction, yet in too many instances they are far from being comfortable, having neither a floor except of earth, nor ceiling. The windows, also, are very small, which may admit a little light, but are rarely calculated for the admission of fresh air ... At the same time, from the great expense of keeping up cottages, farmers are never anxious to have more than what are barely sufficient to accommodate the labourers, necessary for all the different operations of the farm.

Hope went on to note that the number of cottages attached to farms was very different in the various districts of the country. Where married men were usual, cottages were plentiful, and farmers were willing enough to build to attract the kind of labour they preferred. As a result, 'more attention is paid to the comfort of the occupiers, when new ones are erected, than can be found in those built thirty or forty years ago, particularly by making the windows larger, and to open when necessary, and also by setting apart a by-corner, into which the ashes and other filth from the house may be thrown, instead of allowing the dunghill to be placed within a step of the threshold, as is still too commonly to be seen in some districts, to the great injury of the inhabitants, and the disgust of every stranger who witnesses such scenes'.

Elsewhere, cottages were scarcer, and farmers had the choice between drawing extra labour from the towns and villages, or not getting the work done. The situation was even worse in areas where work in loom-shops or cotton-mills was available, taking workers off the land. Hope did not think there would be any great change till arable farms became larger than they generally were in the early 1800s.[22] It is out of such conditions that the bothy system, already foreshadowed for east-central Scotland, eventually grew.

Broadly speaking, farm-servant housing in the areas dealt with here can be divided into three categories: *cottar houses* for married servants, *chaumers* for single men in areas of smaller farms, especially in the north-east of Scotland, and *bothies* on large farms in districts where unmarried workers were preferred.

In earlier days, a *cottar* was a tenant on a farm, occupying a cottage to which a small amount of land was often attached. In this respect what has come to be known as the 'tied cottage', about which controversy still appears with annual regularity, was a natural follow-on. This earlier sense of cottar equates to some degree with the class of tenants known as *mailers*. The two names are often seen as being synonymous, as in the Invercauld Records in Aberdeenshire in 1760.[23] A *mailer* was one who rented a piece of arable ground with a house attached, and hired out his services to a farmer (or sometimes to the surrounding farmers). According to a Morayshire description of 1795, they had houses but no farm. They generally kept a few sheep, with their master's stock, and some received grass for a cow or a horse.[24] Later, they came to play a part in the reclamation of moors and peat bogs by building their huts on the edges of such areas, and reclaiming an acre or two for a cow and a horse, paying little or no rent at first, and eking out a living by acting as tradesmen of various kinds. This term characterises the class from Aberdeenshire up to Inverness-shire; elsewhere in Highland areas such as Skye, the term *lotter* was an equivalent,[25] and as far north as Caithness almost every farmer had a 'cottage' or two on the outskirts of his farm, on the edge of the common, with a house and kailyard, and often a cow and a few sheep on the common, for which he paid some days' labour in spring and harvest plus a little money rent. A day's work a week on the farm was known as 'cottar-work'. By the early 1800s the division of commons, which made the keeping of a cow difficult, had eroded the old system, and some farmers had begun to build cottages themselves to house married servants.[26] To some degree *mailers* and *lotters* preserved in their forms of tenure, in the north-east, north and west of Scotland, something of the character of what cottars had once been in the east and south of Scotland, but as the nineteenth century advanced and as forms of labour organisation hardened to match the needs of improved farming, the cottar came to be simply a married servant on a farm living in a tied cottage as part of his contract. It may be argued, indeed, that this was a decline in status, and it is worth drawing attention, in this context, to the Aberdeenshire subtlety (recorded in 1825) whereby the ploughman, who had formerly had a separate house and a piece of land, was known as the *cottar,* and other lesser sub-tenants as the *cottar-men* or *cottar fouk.*[27]

As has been noted, one-roomed cottar-houses prevailed in the earlier period, or, if double, each room was occupied by a separate family.[28] Improvements in the scale and internal arrangements of such housing came slowly, though theorising and practical admonishment were not lacking. Sir John Sinclair was having his say already by 1814. He noted that in the more northerly parts of Scotland, walling materials for cottages and outhouses were of the simplest kinds. If stones were difficult to get, sods alone, or alternating layers of sods and stones, in each case with a bottom course of stones, 'when properly constructed', were used.[29] Though long abandoned in the more improving districts, this form of construction remained in the remoter parts. In some places mud- or clay-walled cottages were built. Sinclair specified Dumfries and Perth, but they were much more widespread, being found as far north as Sutherland, but in the main less for farm-servant accommodation than for other types of buildings.[30] Bricks were possible also, but Sinclair recommended walls of stone, two feet thick, packed and bedded in clay or mud, the outer 5–6 inches built with lime, and closely pointed. If lime was allowed for the whole wall, it need be no more than 18–20 inches thick.[31]

As far as roofs were concerned, sods were bad in a moist climate; reeds were good, but available only in places; heather was desirable; straw was so valuable for animal feed that it was scarce for thatching, and had ceased by the early 1800s to be much used on farm offices, though still occasionally on detached farm cottages; pantiles, widely used, were poor for insulation; slates were preferred as the best and most desirable roofing, though their expense for cottages and 'inferior buildings' was acknowledged.[32]

The least expensive form of flooring was clay, but also available were composition floors made with lime, floors of flagstones or brick, and of fir deals.[33]

Sinclair concluded by giving his advice on the best construction of cottages, praising East Lothian examples, and noting that 'the cottager should be taught the value as well as the comfort, of a necessary house; though in some parts of the country, it will take some time before they learn this truth'.[34]

But even East Lothian was not progressing with any degree of scorching speed. The minister of Aberlady thought, in 1845, that there was 'ground to hope, that the cottages on every farm will, at no very distant period, have two apartments instead of one'.[35] In Morham, most hinds' and cottar houses were still one-roomed, except at Morham Mains where two-roomed houses were being built.[36] In advance of her time, however, and exceptional for long after, was Lady Ruthven on her Pencaitland estate, where she was building three-roomed houses with a kitchen-cum-sleeping room, a bedroom, and a room for dairy produce and household necessaries, all with internally plastered walls.[37]

This patchy situation may be compared with what was happening just across the Border, in Northumberland. Dr. W. S. Gilly, vicar of Norham from 1831 to 1855, and President of the Berwickshire Naturalists' Club in 1851, published a small booklet on the agricultural workers of his area in 1841, in order to exert pressure for better housing with two rooms, as a matter of preserving morality and decency. 'Let us take care.' he said, 'to lodge our peasants as well as we lodge our beasts',[38] and it is, indeed, true that accommodation for animals was often improved well in advance of that for workers.

Gilly noted that mobility of hinds who, through regular moving from one engagement to another, could scarcely be said to have a home — a

Fig. 1. A hind's cottage at Norham, Northumberland. From Gilly, *Peasantry of the Border* (1841) C12485.

point equally true of Scotland — and since they did not bargain especially for good homes, the proprietors took little care to provide such: 'there are many old tenants of *farms*, but few of *hinds' cottages*'.[39] In Norham, there were 174 hinds' houses; of these, 83 had changed inmates within the two years before he was writing, 145 within seven years before, and 156 within ten years before. Only 13 had had no change since 1831. There were two rooms in 27 of them, and in many, 'human beings and cows are littered under the same roof'.

Internal conditions could vary greatly. Some houses were tidy, with comfortable furniture, colourful crockery and little bookshelves, but others were wretched. Essentially, what was provided was the building framework. The servants had to bring their own oven, copper, grate, shelves, and fixtures including partitions and window frames, and some form of substitute for a ceiling. There was no byre, pigsty, pump or well as a rule. The windows, many no larger than 20 × 16 inches, did not open, and the houses themselves averaged 24 × 16 feet (which is longer than sizes specified for Scotland).

In these up to a dozen people might live, perhaps including a young woman, not a member of the family, hired as a 'bondager' to do the field work. A house of 24 × 15 or 16 feet would contain three beds; in an example noted, one bed accommodated the parents with a daughter of 6 and a boy of 4, a second a daughter of 18, a son of 12 and a daughter of 8, and a third three sons of 20, 16 and 14. In some one-roomed houses, the entrance area lodged a cow in winter, and farther in there were two beds along a whole side of the room, separated by a door opening on a storage space behind the beds for pails, tubs, etc. There could be a third bed in the corner. All these were enclosed box-beds, closed with sliding panels.

By 1840, improvements were just beginning in Norham parish. There

Fig. 2. A group of hinds' cottages, at Norham, Northumberland. From Gilly, *Peasantry of the Border* (1841). C12486.

was a new row of cottages with one room each, but now bigger in size, and each with a separate byre and pigsty; other cottages had two rooms with the same separate outbuildings, and toilets, which were, however, rare. Ceilings were beginning to be inserted, and opening windows.[40]

Much of this also applied in Scotland, where, it appears, servants might carry their own locks with them when they flitted, for an East Lothian writer noted, in 1861, how a cottager's door was 'covered with key-holes, made to suit the size of the lock of each successive occupant'.[41] Change was coming by the 1840s not only in the south-eastern districts, but also in areas farther north, such as Easter Ross which was, however, admittedly much influenced by the south-east. There, it was said in 1842, dunghills and cesspools were now rare at the front of cottages, and cattle were no longer under the same roof. The main defects were said to be lack of ventilation, since the small wooden windows were rarely left open, and the lack of a neat, well-ordered garden. In the parish of Kincardine, where farms had 4–5 servants, there was a mixed situation; half were married and lived in detached or connected cottages each with two rooms and a closet; the rest were single men in bothies, where they fed themselves and lived 'comfortably and cheerfully'. The cottar houses were built near the steading, in line so as to make a short street. Some had a causeway or pavement in front. Bigger farms had cottar houses with tiled or blue-slated roofs; elsewhere straw and clay thatch was used. Pigsties were normal, but rarely attached. The house walls were of stone or mud-work, the floors of earth and clay (rarely of timber), and there was a good fireplace and chimney. The walls were whitewashed with lime. Furnishings consisted of a few chairs, a cupboard, a table and a bed. Significantly, these were attached to the improving farms. The homes of crofters and day-labourers were in general not so good, often having the cattle under their roofs, and being built of turf, without a chimney.[42]

Fig. 3. a–b. Front and back views of an improved hind's cottage on the Thornton Estate in Norham, Northumberland, showing the facilities at the rear and the rainwater spout and barrel. From Gilly, *Peasantry of the Border* (1841). C12487–8.

The description of the houses as resembling a small street is also a reflection of what was happening in the south-east in the first part of the nineteenth century. In the Lothians, Roxburgh and Berwick, the *hind's row* was a row of cottages occupied by farm workers (*Scottish National Dictionary*, s.v. *Hind*). They were single-storey buildings (it appears that though English farm-workers liked an upstairs bedroom since they generally did not sleep in the kitchen-cum-living room,[43] it took some time for their Scottish equivalents to wish to sleep so high above the ground) in long rows, built in such a way that they had alternately a thick and a thin partition wall. The thick wall contained the fireplace. Examples in

Fig. 4. A range of six improved cottages on the Thornton Estate in Norham, Northumberland, each with its own garden. From Gilly, *Peasantry of the Border* (1841). C12489.

Berwickshire, in existence by 1809, had roofs of pantiles, slates or thatch, and floors of clay, hard rammed earth, or bricks. Internally they measured 21 × 16 feet, and were divided by the placing of box-beds into a chamber, a closet for storing milk, meal and potatoes, and a lobby with a coal-hole.[44] It was, of course, cheaper to build in rows, since walls and roofs were shared.

By the 1840s, church and social conscience stirred up activity to such an extent that there was a minor flood of writings on the subject of farm-workers' housing. Architects produced designs for cottages, often submitting them to the ever active Highland and Agricultural Society of Scotland, in the hope of winning a premium.[45] This plethora of publication marked the end of an era. The author of *Designs for Farm Cottages and Steadings* contrasted the old hinds' houses with what he was providing as the new. No longer should there be the old 19 × 15 feet one-room house, with no closets, plaster, ceiling or floors; where the door opened on a 3 foot wide space partitioned off by a 'hallan wa' from the front to the back of the house, with a pig sometimes parked at the far end; where the inner chamber was divided into two unequal parts by two 6 foot long box-beds with a 3 foot passage between leading to a space at the back for storage, or for holding an extra bed for the female employed on the farm; where the fireplace was set against the 'hallan wa' under a conical vent, and the furniture consisted of a chair or two, a deal table, a large open cupboard known as a *bink*, a large wooden press and, where possible, a clock.[46] Instead there should be all sorts of improvements in structure, living space, heating, sleeping accommodation, ventilation and sanitation. Practical architects and theorists (not always distinguishable), and farming economists, expounded their views in plenty. According to D. Low (1844), 'small, warm, and not expensive apartments, are required in the cottage ... an undue extension of the size and number of rooms, is useless and inconvenient to persons whose means of furnishing and heating them are so limited', but at any rate, 'the subject of the dwellings of the rural population, whether they exist as detached cottages, or as groups of houses, in the form of hamlets or villages, merits more regard than has hitherto been paid to it'.[47]

Stone and lime walls and a slated roof were the best materials. Tile roofs were cheaper, but less durable and not good for keeping an even temperature. Thatch was a good non-conductor of heat, especially if of heather, though wheat and rye were the main materials used, with reeds, where obtainable, for preference. Clay was the cheapest form of wall, but it had to be well-built and well-plastered with mortar, above a ground course of stone or brick to keep moisture off it. Flagstones formed the best and most durable floors on the ground, but upper rooms should have floors of wood. Sash windows, opening top and bottom, were preferred, but hinged windows, which never fitted so well, were in frequent use. The fireplace should have a register grate or a stove, with constructed flue orifices, to conserve heat, and should serve for all purposes, including heating water

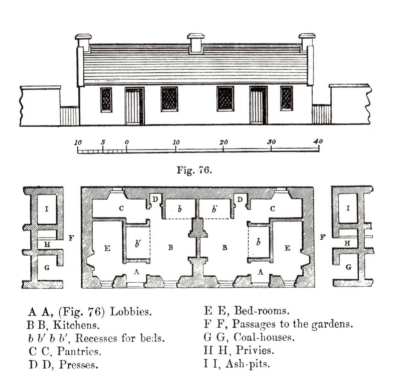

Fig. 76.

A A, (Fig. 76) Lobbies.
B B, Kitchens.
b b' b b', Recesses for beds.
C C, Pantries.
D D, Presses.

E E, Bed-rooms.
F F, Passages to the gardens.
G G, Coal-houses.
H H, Privies.
I I, Ash-pits.

Fig. 5. A double cottage design by Mr. Newlands, a model of which had been put into the Agricultural Museum of the University of Edinburgh, as a great improvement on former cottages. From Low, *Landed Property* (1844), p. 194. C12591.

P

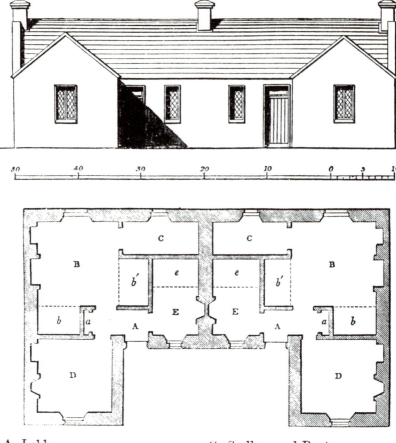

A, Lobby.

    a, Press.

B, Kitchen.

    b b′, Recesses or beds.

C, Scullery and Pantry.

D, Room which may be a shop.

E, Small bed-room.

    e, Bed.

Fig. 6a–b. A double cottage design incorporating an extra room in each half. From Low, *Landed Property* (1844). C12589–90.

and cooking. Cottages should be in rows to save walling and roofing materials, and to increase the warmth, but a two by two arrangement (which became extremely common everywhere) left easy access to the rear.[48]

The course was set by this period. Implementation continued throughout the nineteenth century, sometimes well, sometimes ill, so that still in the twentieth century not everyone was satisfied. The pages of *The Scottish Farm Servant* are full of more, or less, strident comment:

> The house accommodation provided for farm servants in most parts of Scotland is a disgrace to the country.[49]

'Let us admit that some attention is now being given to the housing of farm servants, and that here and there improvements are being made. In some counties the authorities have been active, and the worst of the hovels in their area have been condemned. In some districts, too, you will find landlords who are doing something to provide habitable dwellings. All this but throws into blacker relief the conditions in other areas. There are still many houses where the kitchen floors are of earth, or what is often as bad, dilapidated brick, or broken and uneven flags, which increase the labour of the housewife, and rob the family of health and comfort. It is still the rule to find no proper water supply convenient, and to find sanitary conveniences non-existent. I have heard of an old but-and-ben which was "improved" by heightening the roof and slating it, and into the gable of which the coat of arms of the Duke who owned the property was placed, but for which no water supply was provided, and no privy erected.' Even for new houses, the walls could be of the cheapest masonry possible, with 'flimsy wood fittings, and jerry windows ...; two small rooms, with a poky closet, and sometimes not even the latter. Sculleries or outhouses are the exception'.[50]

Even in the formerly pioneering Lothians, some one-roomed houses were still to be found in 1913, mostly tiled, and without sanitation. There was no regulation to enforce the erection of privies, though the 1897 Act laid down that the local authority may require the owner of a house to provide a proper supply of wholesome water 'at or reasonably near the house'.[51].

Some of the voices raised were women's, pointing to a new degree of post-First World War emancipation. The 'average woman in the farm cottage' was beginning to be heard: 'she has very definite ideas as to what exactly she does want. She wants ample bedroom accommodation, she wants more cupboards, she wants water in the house, and a bath, and a scullery with sink and boiler so that the washing-up and all the other odds and ends of housework need not be done in the kitchen ... She wants fireplaces in the bedrooms ...'[52] And the Tory Government of 1923 was blamed for believing 'that working people have no right to parlours in their houses', since their housing improvement scheme of the period was for 'non-parlour' houses only.[53]

Such comments give the more extreme views, but it is true enough — even in the experience of the present writer, in the Aberdeenshire of the 1930s–40s — that cottar houses long remained without water or indoor sanitation. Perhaps the farm-servants themselves did not start complaining loudly soon enough. Stephens noted in 1855 that they made no formal complaints about accommodation if they got work under a good master on a good farm,[54] and even though *The Scottish Farm Servant* was seeking to co-ordinate complaints in the 1920s, the editorial and branch secretarial effort in the three months up to January 1923, for example, produced only three responses.[55] Nevertheless, much improvement had been taking place

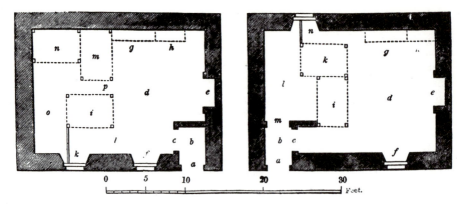

Fig. 7. Two ground plans of houses for small families.
Right, 22 × 15 feet internally: *a,* door; *b,* porch; *c,* inner door; *d,* main apartment
with *e,* fireplace, *f,* window, *g,* plate-rack; *h,* dresser; *i k,* two box-beds placed to
form a living room *d* and a store-room *l*; the bed *i* is entered from the store-room,
which has a door *m* and part of a window *n* (the female field worker could sleep
here, along with, if need be, a grown-up daughter or other girl). Basically suitable
for hind, wife and field-worker.
Left: details as above, but with 3 beds; *i* entered from the space lit by window *k*
via a door *l*; *m* entered from the living room *d*; *n* from the store-room *o,* entered by
a passage with a door *p.* Suitable for a hind, wife, 3 children and 1 field-worker.
From Stephens, *Book of the Farm* (1844), III, p. 1369. C12933.

since the 1840s, and in some places earlier. One of the last sources for
establishing the theory and practice of farm-servant housing between that
period and the early 1800s is Stephens' *Book of the Farm,* the six editions
of which were each thoroughly revised and updated between 1844 and
1908 (which also gives Scotland the best and most detailed survey of
agricultural development in the second half of the nineteenth century for
any country of Europe). In the first edition of 1844, Stephens noted that it
was usual to build cottages on a standard plan, but pointed out that it was
just as easy to build on different plans, to suit family needs. The plans he
gave exemplified this theory. His small family houses remained essentially
as single rooms divided by box-beds, for 'nothing is more uncomfortable to
work people than to be obliged to occupy a house much larger than the
small quantity of furniture they usually possess can occupy'.[56] He allowed
also for double cottages, in many ways the pattern for the rest of the
century, each 'capable of affording ample accommodation for an ordinary
family'.[57] The living space was again 22 × 15 feet, with the addition of a
rear projection to give an extra room. An extension in length of 2 feet
allowed for a fourth box-bed, making sleeping space for 8 individuals. For
larger families, Stephens recommended the addition of a second storey. In
terms of price, the simplest cottage cost £53, the next £62, the double
cottage £122.18.1.[58] Though Stephens preferred the double cottage to

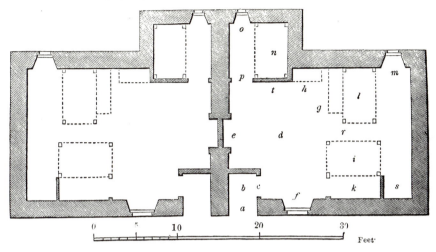

Fig. 8. A one-storey double cottage, each half measuring 22 × 25 feet internally, with an additional rear projection to give an extra room. The key is as for Fig. 7. The bed *i* is entered from space *k*; *l* through a door *p*, and is lit by a window *o*. If extended by 2 feet, an extra bed could go at *s*. For 8 persons on one floor. From Stephens, *Book of the Farm* (1844), III, p. 1371. C12934.

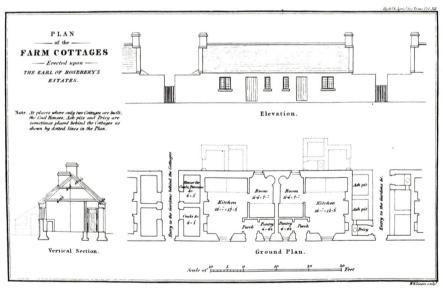

Fig. 9. Part of a row of double, single-storey cottages built on the Earl of Rosebery's estates, *ante* 1839, showing a well-thought out use of available space. Outside privies are provided. From 'Remarks on Cottage Premiums' (1839). C12932.

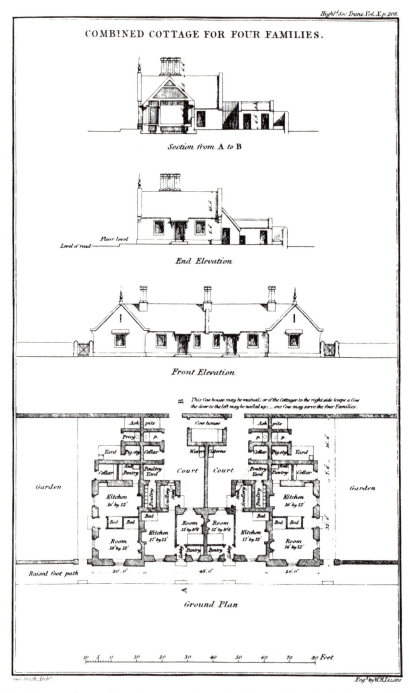

Fig. 10. a–c. A combined cottage for 4 families, with all 'mod. cons.', and tightly packed space for poultry, pigs and cows as well. From 'Construction of Cottages', facing p. 205. C12931.

rows, hinds' houses were, nevertheless, most commonly built in long rows. On large farms, they could occupy three sides of a square.[59]

Stephens stuck to the simpler, less expensive plans. Others were more evolved, as for example the single-storey cottages built on the Earl of Roseberry's estates which, for their time, were compact and conveniently planned.[60]

For a time improvements appear to have lain in the domain of architectural ingenuity in fitting in as many spaces as possible in a kind of amoebic growth at the back, without adding appreciably to the living space.[61] It is probably true to say, however, that in the later nineteenth century, there was an increase in internal space due to the general adoption of two-storey cottar houses, mostly designed by local architects such as James Duncan of Turriff, Aberdeenshire,[62] even though Scottish farm-servants, unlike their English counterparts, did not at first appreciate them greatly and were slow to learn to sleep upstairs.[63] A late nineteenth-century plan of Lendrum, amongst the Hatton Estate papers in Aberdeenshire, shows proposals for the alteration of an old house to such a new-style two-storey building. In north-east Scotland, this was part of an improving movement that became common to most estates. On the Haddo estate, 56 new cottages were built within 3 years, 1861–64; the Duke of Richmond and Gordon is said to have always agreed to requests from his tenant farmers to erect cottar houses; Findlay of Aberdour put up 35 new ones and renovated 12 in a 9-year period in the 1880s.[64]

Two-storey cottages became general in all areas where cottar houses were required, some being particularly good. One Dumfriesshire estate is said to have put up houses with a boxroom and three bedrooms upstairs.[65] In general, however, space remained relatively limited, and it is not a matter of wonder that at the present day many of the old double cottages are being knocked into single houses for their occupants, often commuters rather than farm-servants any more.

Alongside the cottage for married servants, there came to exist in west-central, but especially in north-east, Scotland, a form of accommodation known as *chaumers*. These were for single men.[66] They were furnished as for bothies, with wooden built-in beds and the men's kists where they kept their few belongings, but table equipment was unnecessary, since they had their meals in the kitchen of the farm. For this reason, the term *kitchie* (kitchen) system has been used, though in fact it is no real system in itself, but only part of a bigger complex. Chaumers were above or at least close to the stable, and descriptions indicate that they could be very rough places indeed. Carter has quoted some of the less savoury descriptions,[67] but these should not obscure the fact that some were perfectly comfortable, with a good fireplace to keep out winter cold. This was the present writer's experience of chaumers visited on farms in the Turriff area of Aberdeenshire, though it may well be possible to regard such examples as improved survivals of a type of accommodation that has now, effectively, vanished.

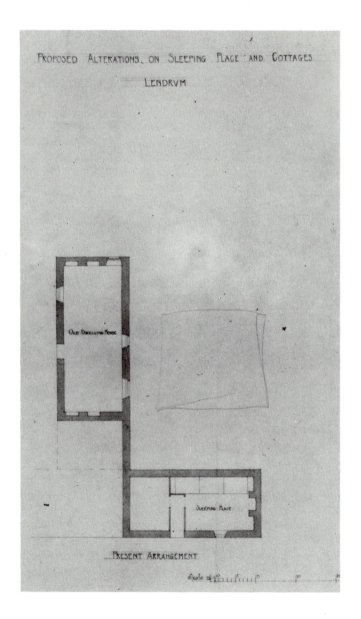

Fig. 11. a–b. A late nineteenth-century plan from the Hatton Estate papers, showing an old cottage and proposed improvements into a two-storey unit for two families, at Lendrum, Aberdeenshire. C12936.

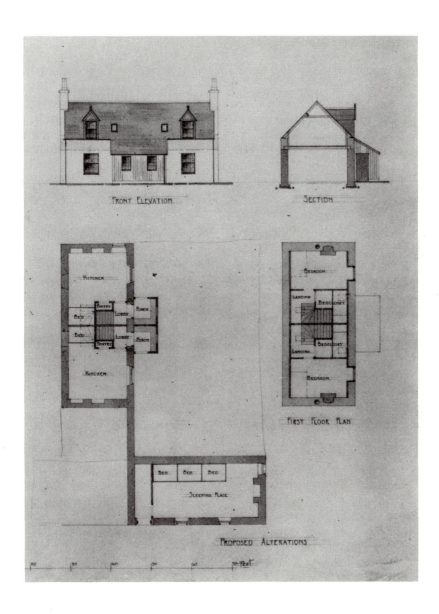

FRONT ELEVATION

SECTION

KITCHEN

PANTRY LOBBY PORCH
BED
BED
PANTRY LOBBY PORCH

KITCHEN

BEDROOM

LANDING
BEDCLOSET

BEDCLOSET

LANDING

BEDROOM

FIRST FLOOR PLAN

BED BED BED

SLEEPING PLACE

PROPOSED ALTERATIONS

Finally, there is the question of bothies. As noted earlier, these originated in areas where single men were preferred, with a place in the steading where they both slept and ate.[68] Since the late eighteenth century their pros-and-cons have been discussed, and recent writers have dwelt on the poor quality of the accommodation.[69]

Angus and the Mearns seem to have been the primary bothy areas, with a later spread in parts of Fife, the Lothians, Berwickshire, the eastern parts of Ross and Cromarty, and Caithness.[70] As a rule, bothies housed single men, but some were specifically for women workers. In the arable districts there were often more female than male labourers. They were usually immigrants from Ireland, or from the Highlands and Western Islands, who were provided with bothy accommodation and given a money wage, with an allowance of milk. In the 1830s, 9d a day was the rate; by the 1870s, scarcity of labour was allowing them to demand terms which included the use of a bothy with furniture as well as bedding, coals supplied free, money wages of 1/4 a day, increasing to 2/- a day during potato lifting, and with food added during harvest. Some potatoes might also be provided.[71]

In considering the spatial relationships between bothies, cottar houses and chaumers, it is necessary to remember that we are dealing with a changing situation. Speaking of Angus, Mr. Cowie of Halkerton Mains noted in 1852 that most proprietors and farmers were removing old cottar houses, or letting them fall down, without replacing them. This made the employment of married men difficult, and cut out the possibility of using the cottar house and its associated piece of ground as a base for bringing up and training good servants, and providing reservoirs of extra labour at peak periods. The bothy, therefore, became 'a stereotyped establishment throughout those districts'. Interestingly, the meeting of the Fettercairn Farmers' Club, at which Mr. Cowie was speaking, endorsed his call for a return to the cottar house and married men.[72]

Further evidence of the spread and decline of bothies has been documented by Carter for Aberdeenshire. By the 1860s one was to be found on almost every lowland district farm in Angus and Kincardineshire, but in Aberdeenshire there is little evidence of them till the 1830s, on large farms only. Their numbers slowly grew, predictably with the greatest numbers towards the two bothy counties to the south. Northern Buchan had none. By 1849 there were said to have been about 520 men in bothies in Aberdeenshire, i.e., around 5% of the total farm servant population, the bulk of whom were 'chaumered'. From then on the numbers began to shrink. The last three closed in Insch in 1895, and by the First World War little evidence of any remained. The pattern was similar for Banffshire, though with an even lower degree of bothy penetration. To the north, in Moray and Nairn, the chaumer reigned supreme till after 1860, when a movement of servants from Ross-shire brought the bothies to which the men were accustomed with it to such an extent that it was the leading form of accommodation by the 1880s on the

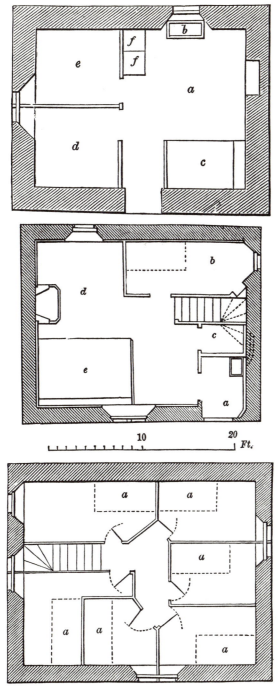

Fig. 12. a. A single-storeyed bothy. From H. Stephens and R. S. Burn, *The Book of Farm Buildings* (Edinburgh, 1861). C7705.

Fig. 12. b–c. A two-storeyed bothy. From Stephen and Burns, *Book of Farm Buildings*. C7703, 7704.

majority of farms. From the 1890s, however, it waned in Nairn, and the chaumer remained the norm there for single men.[73]

The subject of farm worker housing is far more complex than might appear from a casual glance. The present notes do little more than scratch the surface. In terms of building, there is a great deal of local variation arising out of a local circumstances which may include the kinds of workers that farmers preferred as well as the degree to which estates took an interest, sometimes also with an eye to decorative appearance as well as simple functionalism. However, the importance of the subject lies not in terms of architecture, but in the considerable extent to which it is a reflection of the social history of the countryside.

NOTES

1. A. Kussmaul, *Servants in Husbandry in Early Modern England* (Cambridge, 1981), pp. 3–10.

2. D. Ure, *General View of the Agriculture of the County of Roxburgh* (London, 1794), p. 54.

3. *Old Statistical Account (O.S.A.)*, iii (1792), p. 441; iii (1793), p. 155.

4. *O.S.A.* x (1974), p. 109.

5. J. Donaldson, *General View of the Agriculture of the Carse of Gowrie, in the County of Perth* (London, 1794), p. 24.

6. Mr. Rogers, *General View of the Agriculture of the County of Angus or Forfar* (Edinburgh, 1794), pp. 17–18.

7. R. Beatson, *General View of the Agriculture of the County of Fife* (Edinburgh, 1794), p. 19.

8. J. Thomson, *General View of the Agriculture of the County of Fife* (Edinburgh, 1800), pp. 80–81.

9. J. F. Erskine, *General View of the Agriculture of the County of Clackmannan* (Edinburgh, 1795), pp. 72–74.

10. G. Robertson, *General View of the Agriculture of the County of Mid-Lothian* (Edinburgh, 1795), p. 42.

11. Col. Fullarton, *General View of the Agriculture of the County of Ayr* (Edinburgh, 1793), p. 73.

12. A. Martin, *General View of the Agriculture of the County of Renfrew* (London, 1794), p. 20.

13. A. F. Steuart, *The Woodhouselee MS. A Narrative of Events in Edinburgh and District during the Jacobite Occupation, September to November 1745* (Edinburgh, 1907), p. 76.

14. J. Donaldson, *General View of the Agriculture of the County of Nairn* (London, 1794), p. 16.

15. A.Z., 'On the Comparative Advantages of keeping Married and Unmarried Servants upon Farms: and the Policy of Encouraging the Increase of Cottages and Villages', *Farmer's Magazine*, ix (1 Feb., 1802), pp. 1–8.

16. C. H. Firth, ed., *Scotland and the Protectorate* (Scottish History Society, Edinburgh, 1899), pp. 605–8.

17. C. A. Malcolm, ed., *The Minutes of the Justices of the Peace for Lanarkshire, 1707–1723* (Scottish History Society, Edinburgh, 1931), p. 19.

18. A. Fenton, *Scottish Country Life* (Edinburgh, 1976, reprint 1977), pp. 159–71.

19. G. Watson, *The Roxburghshire Word-Book* (Cambridge, 1923), s.v.

20. R. Hope, 'On Rural Economy, and the Relative Prices of Provisions and Labour', in Sir John Sinclair, *General Report of the Agricultural State, and Political Circumstances of Scotland* (Edinburgh, 1814), III, pp. 225–41.

21. W. Derham, ed., *Select Remains of the Learned John Ray* (London, 1960), pp. 187–8.

22. Hope, 'Rural Economy', pp. 249–52.

23. J. G. Michie, ed., *The Records of Invercauld, 1547–1828* (New Spalding Club, Aberdeen, 1901), p. 143.

24. *O.S.A.*, xiv (1795), p. 75.

25. *Report of Her Majesty's Commissioners of Inquiry into the Condition of the Crofters and Cottars in the Highlands and Islands of Scotland. Parliamentary Papers,* 1884, xxxii. Appendix A, p. 30.

26. J. Henderson, *General View of the Agriculture of Caithness* (London, 1812), pp. 231–32.

27. J. Jamieson, *An Etymological Dictionary of the Scottish Language* (Edinburgh, 1825), s.v.

28. *O.S.A.*, i (1792), pp. 344–5: Yester.

29. A. Fenton, 'Alternating Turf and Stone — An Obsolete Building Practice', in *Folk Life* 6 (1968), pp. 94–103.

30. A. Fenton, 'Clay Building and Clay Thatch in Scotland', *Ulster Folk Life* 1970, pp. 28–51; A. Fenton and B. Walker, *The Rural Architecture of Scotland* (Edinburgh, 1981), pp. 76–84.

31. J. Sinclair, *Appendix to The General Report of the Agricultural State, and Political Circumstances of Scotland* (Edinburgh, 1814), I, pp. 257–8.

32. *Ibid.*, pp. 262–8.

33. *Ibid.*, pp. 268–71.

34. *Ibid.*, pp. 271–75.

35. *New Statistical Account (N.S.A.)*, ii (1845), p. 255.

36. *N.S.A.*, ii (1845), pp. 268–9.

37. *N.S.A.*, ii (1845), pp. 351–2.

38. W. S. Gilly, *The Peasantry of the Border* (Berwick-upon-Tweed, 1844; 2nd edition London, 1842) (reprinted Edinburgh, 1973), p. 6.

39. *Ibid.*, p. 6.

40. *Ibid.*

41. *George Hope of Fenton Barns: A Sketch of his Life,* compiled by his daughter (Edinburgh, 1881), p. 231.

42. J. Cameron, *Report on the Sanitary Condition and General Economy of the Town of Tain and the District of Easter Ross, made to the Poor Law Commissioners* (1842), pp. 3–6, 13, 16–17.

43. D. Low, *On Landed Property, and the Economy of Estates* (London, 1844), pp. 186, 193–4.

44. R. Kerr. *General View of the Agriculture of Berwick* (London, 1809), p. 102.

45. G. Smith, 'Essay on the Construction of Cottages, Suited for the Dwellings of the Labouring Classes, and Adapted to the Climate of Scotland', *Prize-Essays and Transactions of the Highland and Agricultural Society of Scotland* (1835),

pp. 205–16; 'Remarks on Cottage Premiums, and Description and Specification of Cottages Built on the Estate of the Earl of Roseberry', *Prize-Essays and Transactions of the Highland and Agricultural Society of Scotland* (1839), pp. 527–34; 'Plans and Specifications of Cottages', *Transactions of the Highland and Agricultural Society of Scotland* (1851), pp. 275–80.

46. J. Cunningham, *Designs for Farm Cottages and Steadings* (Edinburgh, 1849), I, p. 12.

47. Low, *Landed Property*, pp. 175–6, 202–3.

48. *Ibid.*, pp. 175–98.

49. C. A. Paterson, 'The Housing of Farm Servants', *The Scottish Farm Servant* (May 1913), p. 16.

50. '"Good enough for Farm Servants". The Housing Scandal', *The Scottish Farm Servant* (October 1913), p. 17.

51. 'Some Notes on Housing', *The Scottish Farm Servant* (November 1913), p. 2.

52. 'Another Word on Housing', *The Scottish Farm Servant* (May 1922), p. 514.

53. 'Should Workers have Parlours?', *The Scottish Farm Servant* (June 1923), p. 42.

54. H. Stephens, *The Book of the Farm* (Edinburgh and London, 2nd ed., 1855), II, p. 542.

55. 'Housing Complaints', *The Scottish Farm Servant* (January 1923), pp. 678–9; (July 1923), p. 62; (October 1923), p. 111.

56. H. Stephens, *The Book of the Farm* (Edinburgh and London, 1844), III, p. 1370.

57. *Ibid.*

58. *Ibid.*, III, pp. 1368–80.

59. Stephens, *Book of the Farm* (1855), II, p. 545.

60. 'Remarks on Cottage Premiums', following p. 528.

61. Smith, 'Construction of Cottages', facing p. 205, Figs. 10a, b, c.

62. Fenton, *Scottish Country Life*, p. 187; Fenton and Walker, *Rural Architecture*, p. 151.

63. I. Carter, *Farm Life in Northeast Scotland, 1840–1914* (Edinburgh, 1979), p. 131.

64. *Ibid.*, p. 130.

65. E. B. Mitchell, *Today and Tomorrow in Rural Scotland* (Edinburgh, n.d. (1921)).

66. R. S. Skirving, 'Farm Labour and Labourers', *Report on the Present State of the Agriculture of Scotland, arranged under the auspices of the Highland and Agricultural Society* (Edinburgh, 1878), pp. 104–41.

67. Carter, *Farm Life*, pp. 120–22.

68. Donaldson, *Carse of Gowrie*, p. 24; Rogers, *County of Angus*, pp. 17–18.

69. T. C. Smout, *A History of the Scottish People, 1560–1830* (London, 1969), pp. 321–23; Carter, *Farm Life*, pp. 123–7.

70. Fenton, *Scottish Country Life*, p. 188; Fenton and Walker, *Rural Architecture*, pp. 146–7.

71. Skirving, 'Farm Labour', pp. 139–40.

72. 'Fettercairn Farmers' Club, Forfarshire', *The North British Agriculturist* (May 1852), pp. 275–76.

73. Carter, *Farm Life*, pp. 125–27.

11

Unions and Myths: Farm Servants'
Unions in Aberdeenshire, 1870–1900

Ian Carter

The experience of collective action is fugitive. Something of what it meant to join with others for compelling personal or social reasons might cheat the grave in the form of written reminiscences, or as oral accounts awaiting the ubiquitous tape-recorder. But what remains is no more than a scrap of what existed: random threads from the tissue of hopes, fears, plans, setbacks, intentions and consequences that impelled men and women in days beyond recall to attempt to gain more control over the conditions of their lives. Yet we, in our turn, are impelled to try to understand why those others, long dead, did what they did. In the absence of first-hand accounts we construct our own accounts, fixing our current concerns on the photographic plate of the past. This means that social historical work is ineluctably political. It also means that an attempt to reconstruct the experience of collective action is not concerned to discover the truth. There is no truth to be discovered. Instead there is a limitless field of possible ways of expressing what collective action might have meant to those involved. The choice rests partly on one's personal political position; but it should also rest on the threads of what we can know about the experience of those under study.

British labour history provides a good example of a genre in which this second condition is not met. Constructed within a rather limited political matrix, it trammels our view of trades unionism and inhibits attempts to understand the meaning of unionism for rank and file members:

> Despite strictures against the Webbs for punctuating Trade Union history with institutional rather than economic turning points (the 'new model' Trade Unions rather than the trade cycle), little better has been offered in its place. Nor is this surprising so long as the history of particular groups of workers is equated with a history of their trade union organisation, and the trade union history itself is derived from the activities of head office rather than from the social relations of the work-place.[1]

To attempt to understand the experience of agricultural unionisation in Scotland by focusing on the social relations of the work-place means that

213

we must move from the national level to consider a much smaller unit: the demonstration of earlier chapters in this volume of the dramatically wide variation in farming systems in the lowlands dooms attempts to discuss unionisation at a higher level of generality. As luck will have it, we do have one detailed examination of agricultural[2] unionisation at the county level: Gwenllian Evans' thirty-year old study of Aberdeenshire.[3] This will provide the basis for the argument in this chapter.

Evans examines attempts at unionising hired farm workers in Aberdeenshire between 1870 and 1900. By ending her survey in the last year of the nineteenth century, Evans avoids discussion of Joe Duncan's successful attempt to organise farm workers that began in Turriff in 1912. Her period is the pre-history of Aberdeenshire unionism, the time of fitful attempts and little success. She identifies three attempts in these years. In February 1872 Longside farm workers formed a union. Their initiative was taken up in other places, and unionisation spread rapidly through the county, culminating in a meeting in the Sailors' Mission Hall in Aberdeen on 25 July 1872 at which the Aberdeenshire Agricultural Labourers' Union was formed. It had a brief life: the November term delivered the quietus. Eight years later 'well-wishers' in Aberdeen organised a meeting for farm workers on Muckle Friday, the great feeing market for the May term. More than four hundred farm servants turned up to the meeting in the Song School.[4] A committee was formed, which distributed questionnaires but then expired. Six years later came the most determined attempt at organisation. On 17 January 1886 a group of Kintore farm workers met to form a union. Their efforts were supported by the Aberdeen Trades Council, and the movement flourished. In 1887 it was formalised as the Scottish Farm Servants' Union, an organisation with its membership base in Aberdeenshire. By the following year the SFSU had thirty branches in the county. In 1894 it merged with the Perth-based Ploughman's Federal Union, to form the Scottish Ploughmen's and General Labourers' Union. This body had strong support in Aberdeen city, but was weak in the countryside. With its dissolution in 1900 Evans brings to an end her chronology of attempts to form farm workers' unions in Aberdeenshire.

That chronology is unexceptionable. The only possible objection is that by limiting attention to the years between 1870 and 1900 Evans might miss a fourth fleeting attempt at organisation, in 1866. By February of that year efforts at organisation in Midlothian were spreading to other counties. Within a month these efforts had reached the Howe of the Mearns: sufficiently close to Aberdeen city for the Tory *Aberdeen Journal* to warn its more exquisitely masochistic readers of Fenian influence among the ploughmen. By late April meetings were being held to form union branches throughout lowland Angus and Kincardine. These meetings were well attended; on several occasions newspaper reports assert audiences in excess of two hundred farm workers. Curiously, however, this movement does not seem to have crossed the Dee with any force. In April the *Journal* carried a gnomic report from the Garioch to the effect that,

> Sometimes we find a little interest is elicited among farmers in regard to those meetings or gatherings here and there of the farm servants for certain objects, and the ultimate object, it may be, apparently, to prepare the way for ability to coerce their employers into submission to any terms they might deem meet to dictate.[5]

Four months later, in August 1866, the radical Liberal *Aberdeen Free Press* reported a public dinner in the Vale of Alford. The principal speaker was Robert Anderson, Wellhouse, a prominent local farmer. He disparaged recent attempts to establish farm workers' unions urging the improvement of relations between farmer and hired workers as a better alternative.[6] These scattered cases suggest that the 1866 agitation did reach Aberdeenshire, but the lack of any more systematic treatment in newspapers (particularly in the *Journal* which, like any conservative organ, could turn a muck-cart into a tumbril on the slightest pretext) must mean that not much happened in the county. Thus we may forgive Gwenllian Evans for having given the 1866 episode no attention.

But if her chronology is unexceptionable, the same cannot be said for the explanations offered for the trajectory of farm worker unionisation in Aberdeenshire. Dr. Evans insists that we must admire farm workers' attempts at organisation, and none will disagree. Yet she takes those attempts to have been doomed:

> Despite their fine aspirations, the farm workers were, in fact, too unorganised, too isolated from each other and altogether too weak to put up a united front to the farmers. Unlike urban workers they had few opportunities of coming together and realising their identity of interests. Even though the fairs provided a meeting place, the excess supply of labour encouraged individual bargains, usually on the masters' terms. Moreover, the multiplicity of fairs (for every market town had its fair) made concerted action quite impossible, while the six-monthly flittings which resulted from the system of hiring made it almost impossible to build up strong branches of the union. The attempt to form a union failed also because of the lack of organising ability among the farm servants, and the absence of any strong leader or group of leaders.

We will return to particular assertions in this explanation a little later. Before doing that, we must follow the general line of argument further, and see to what view of the farm worker and his (or her) potential for collective organisation it gives rise.

While Gwenllian Evans was writing her article, one academic neighbour was Ken Buckley, at that time engaged on his history of Aberdeen Trades Council. It is not surprising, then, that Buckley should echo Evans' conclusions. Farm servants were relatively isolated one from another, he argues, and were hired on annual or six-monthly engagements. It was not possible to erect a strong union on this shifting basis.[8]

This conclusion is repeated by Dyer, writing on Kincardineshire in a rather more recent period, but allowing us to make an important move in unpacking the implications of Evans' argument:

> Most of them [hired farm workers] have not received the kind of education likely to give them the skills and imagination to act politically, while the most resourceful, the potential leaders amongst them, are more than likely to leave the land. These are not to mention the influence which the landowners and farmers have historically held over them by their tenancy of tied cottages. Furthermore, as in Scotland as a whole, these disadvantages have not been compensated for by the prevalence of Nonconformist chapels, as was the case in certain parts of rural England and Wales.[9]

The Free Church of Scotland is swept out of existence with a stroke of the pen, and with it the long and bitter struggle after the Disruption to connect the interest of crofter and landless farm labourer and farm servant to that of the Free Church.[10] More importantly for our purposes, however, Dyer shows us how easy it is to move from a recognition of structural constraints inhibiting farm worker unionisation to a perception of the hired farm labour force as a passive *lumpenproletariat,* the dupe of superior classes. Thus we arrive at the opinion of James Leatham, radical printer and union activist in Aberdeen,[11] about the reasons why it was so difficult to unionise local farm workers:

> To remain on the land and try to make the life feasible to a man of some self-respect would seem to be beyond Aberdeenshire Sandy. Other counties make some show of organisation; and the result in improved conditions warrant, as might be expected, the efforts made. But the Aberdeenshire labourer, pluming himself on his self-imputed shrewdness, and absorbing the interested flattery of those who seek to keep him as he is, steadily resists all the efforts of those who would organise him into unions, with the improvement of his lot in view.[12]

This assertion of ubiquitous false consciousness among Aberdeenshire hired farm workers seem to have brought us a great distance from our starting point in Evans' argument. Her concern, it will be remembered, lay with structural conditions which inhibited hired workers from forming unions. When she summarised her argument she did so by emphasising two principal difficulties facing intending unionists. One, the fact that 'the method of employment and the bi-annual flittings deprived the unions of that nucleus of permanently placed young men which was necessary to build up strong local branches', is consonant with her more elaborate account of structural constraints considered above. But the second summative factor shifts the focus: in Evans' view hired farm workers also suffered from 'the lack of powerful leaders, either from amongst the farm labourers themselves or from the socialists of the city'.[13] Her structural constraints explain why leadership could not rise within the ranks of the Aberdeenshire hired farm labour force: the problem of that class becomes the fact that no member of a more advanced class stepped forward to represent farm workers' interest until Joe Duncan answered the call from Turriff in 1912, and finally established continuing agricultural unionisation in the county.[14] Thus while Leatham's language is more pungent, we see that Evans' argument is set within the same universe of discourse. False consciousness is a necessary element in that discourse.

This will not do. The false consciousness hypothesis requires us to assume that hired Aberdeenshire farm workers were fully proletarianised. That proletariat had only one weapon in its resistance to rural bourgeois class fractions; trades union organisation. That organisation was an unproblematic index of the development of class consiousness among hired farm workers, either at their own hand or through the interjection of comradely assistance from members of more advanced classes. None of this can be accepted for Aberdeenshire farm workers between 1870 and 1900.

Let us revisit Evans' three episodes of unionist activity. Her first case, the 1872 movement that began in Longside, supports her general argument. Newspaper accounts of the Longside meeting suggest that this was called by farm servants for farm servants. The *Aberdeen Journal* drew an instructive parallel with Joseph Arch's contemporaneous agitation in the English midlands:

> The Warwickshire movement has extended to the North more speedily than is usual with any movement of the kind. In Warwickshire, and where the farm labourers are moving, in the South, for higher wages and shorter hours. they began under the direct guidance of certain enthusiastic members of Parliament. In Aberdeenshire, they are acting for themselves, and at least deserve that consideration which is due to self-reliance.[15]

Things get much more complicated in the 1880 episode. In this case, it will be recalled, a group of 'well-wishers' convened a meeting in the Song School on Muckle Friday. Who was it that wished hired farm workers well? Newspaper reports of the meeting, taken in conjunction with the relevant Post Office directory, produce some interesting evidence. Thirteen men are listed: Alexander Walker, Dean of Guild and tobacconist in a large way of business; Baillie Peter Esslemont, of the still celebrated Aberdeen emporium called Esslemont and Macintosh (the Jenners of the North); Shoremaster James Paterson, wholesale druggist; William Alexander, editor of the *Free Press* and major local literateur; Archibald Gillies, manager of the *Journal*; William Lindsay, bookseller; John Miller, owner of a large business involved in distilling tar, refining paraffin wax and general agricultural dealing; A. Cook, tailor and outfitter; Rev. J. Smith, minister of St. George's in the West Church; J. B. Taylor; George

Taylor, former President of Aberdeen Trades' Council; Alexander Taylor; and Robert Stornach, farm servant.[16]

The imbalance between one farm servant and a cluster of local worthies is striking. Equally striking is the preponderance of merchants among those worthies, though the Post Office directory also reveals that in 1880 five of our thirteen were directors of the Bon Accord Property Investment Company, four were directors of the Aberdeen Café Company, two were directors of the Aberdeen Building Company, and one was a director of the Aberdeen and Northern Heritable Property Company. Two sat on the Aberdeen School Board, and two were councillors of the Aberdeen Philosophical Society.

Wholly unsurprising, one might think; a platform full of stuffed shirts, with a token farm servant and a former Trades Council President to dispel any whiff of paternalism. But things get more interesting if we ask questions about the political complexion of these 'wellwishers'. Most were Liberals; Alexander and Esslemont were notoriously radical. The Tories were represented only by Walker, Gillies and, one assumes, the hapless Auld Kirk minister. Thus while Dean of Guild Walker urged the meeting that improvements in farm workers' life conditions could come about only through public pressure — and hence that direct action by farm workers would be futile — some fellow Tories thought the meeting less apolitical than it might have appeared. A dialect letter to the *Journal* from 'Andra Tamson' asserted that the Song School meeting was a Liberal plot that had gulled innocent Tories. Alexander Taylor, who had organised the meeting and acted as chairman, was a farm servant who had written a book about his experiences on the farms and had seen it published by the *Free Press*. His aim was to get elected to Parliament on the Liberal ticket. Beyond that,

> "Radical Esslemont" ... and the like o' him, wi' the *Free Press* at their back, wi' this flatterin' and cozenin' o' the servant class ... are only mischief makers.[17]

'Andra Tamson' was wrong on one point. Alexander Taylor did not write the book to which he referred.[18] It was written by John Taylor, who almost certainly was the J. B. Taylor in the list of Song School wellwishers. John was a former farm servant who turned to science and to Liberal journalism through contact with a well-known north-east autodidact, John Duncan.[19] But it is noticeable that while Alexander Taylor denied authorship of the book, he did not deny 'Andra Tamson's' description of the Song School meeting as a Liberal plot.[20] With the scheme blown and the token Tories scuttling for cover, it is not surprising that we hear no more of this attempt to unionise farm workers. Who needs a broken conspiracy?

But the most illuminating of Evans' three episodes is that of 1886. On 17

January a meeting was called in the Free Church schoolroom at Kintore to form a local 'association for the improvement of the condition of the agricultural labouring classes'.[21] This spark ignited a considerable conflagration; the Trades Council-sponsored gathering of local branches in Aberdeen city on 10 April was attended by delegations from local associations at Alford, Tarves, Monymusk, Ellon, Forgue, Fyvie, Banchory Durris and Strachan, Udny, Newmachar, Drumblade, Newhills, Enzie and Fochabers, Gartly, Monquitter, Strathdon, Rhynie, Insch, Echt Skene and Midmar, Pitcaple, Grange, Drumoak, Glenlivet, and Rayne.[22] The report of the initial Kintore meeting gives no indication of who was there, except that a farmer — Hay, Wardhouse — was elected President of the nascent local association. In later meetings of this association a prominent part was played by a very well-known local farmer, H. D. McCombie, Milton of Kemnay;[23] other farmers were also active in this branch. The inaugural meeting of the Tarves local association was attended by a galaxy of local big farmers: Hay, Little Ythsie; Marr, Cairnbrogie; Garden, North Ythsie; Argo, Braeside; Bean, Braikley; Hay, East Shethin; and Duthie, Tarves.[24] This pattern was repeated wherever one looked. The city unionists saw dangers in the presence of farmers at farm servants' meetings:

> Your farmers, ministers, and other may, at the outset, attend your meetings and express sympathy with the movement, but depend on it your experience will be different from that of every other trades union if, when you become a power and are in a position to resist the oppression of capital or to enforce your demands, you do not find yourselves bitterly opposed and your position and purposes misrepresented by all classes in the country.[25]

These dangers notwithstanding, farmers were allowed to continue to play a major role in local associations. What was their interest in so doing? Altruism, perhaps; a disinterested concern for the condition of hired farm workers? This was the farmers' line, but others claimed to see other motives. McCombie, Milton of Kemnay urged a shift from six-monthly or annual engagements with perquisites as part of the farm servant's fee to weekly engagements with a single cash wage.[26] Hay, Little Ythsie urged the adoption of piece-work systems in farming.[27] To these suggestions 'An Old Farm-Worker' responded that however rational these suggestions might appear to capitalist farmers, they held dangers for farm workers, including the threat of wageless weeks and months in winter, as in southern England, when bad weather stopped farm work.[28]

Farmers could attempt to guide the policies of local branches in directions which made sense to big farmers, then. But some also had a second, deeper purpose in associating themselves with farm workers' attempts at unionisation. At meeting after meeting one finds incongruous matters raised. At Banchory, Joseph Milne 'read a lengthy paper criticising the land laws, condemning the House of Lords, and the present landowners'. At Bucksburn W. Thomson, Broomend, Kintore urged that 'they were living in a priest-ridden and a laird-ridden country'. An Echt meeting heard a demand for the 1886 Crofters' Holdings Bill to be extended throughout Scotland. At Forgue Fyvie, Templeland provided the integument that binds these elements together:

> Now ... that the G.O.M. has given you a vote, are you to be the dumb driven class you have been in the past? Are you to let the needy landlord and croft-grabbing farmers legislate for you, as they have hitherto done? So long as landlords have an unchecked monopoly of the soil of the country, you can never have a just or fair reward for your labour.[29]

Fyvie's speech shows us that we must pay attention to the political context in which the 1886 attempt at unionisation was set. Gladstone's ministry had a precarious life, maintained in office only by the Irish members and the crofters' representatives: the members elected in the name of the Highland Land Law Reform Association. The HLLRA members extracted the 1886 Crofters' Holdings Bill as the price of their support. Land agitation in the north-east had produced not a single-issue peasant party like the HLLRA, but a pressure group inside the Liberal Party, the Scottish Farmers' Alliance. Many of the demands associated with this group had been won by 1886 — the right to protect crops against ground game, better machinery for adjudicating the value of tenants' improvements at the end of a lease — and the SFA had lost much of its more conservative support. What remained was the Radical core, which sought the extension of the Crofters' Bill throughout Scotland and, more distantly, the wholesale transformation of social relations on the land in Britain on Georgite principles. This Radical core (rump might be a better word) nailed its colours to the mast by changing the SFA's name to the Scottish Land Reform Alliance, in direct emulation of the Highland party. But this remained a pressure group within Liberalism. In seeking the extension of the area covered by the Crofters' Bill the SLRA was constrained to exercise influence within the party, rather than bargain from outside. With much influence lost as farmers who had gained what they wanted from earlier reforms left the movement, the SLRA had to find ways to extend its constituency. The Kintore farm workers' meeting was a godsend. The brief newspaper account of the first meeting, on 17 January 1886, gives no hint about who was present. But we do know that the second meeting on 30 January received a letter from John Bruce, Fornet, Skene: a notorious, though eccentric, rural Aberdeenshire radical. More importantly, this meeting was attended (and addressed) by H. D. McCombie, Milton of Kemnay, the leading member in his generation of the rural north-east's most celebrated Radical family, and currently President of the West Aberdeenshire Radical Association. Similarly with other local branches: most of the farmers listed as attending these branches' meetings can definitely be associated with the SLRA. There seems little doubt that further research would link the rest to that body too, either directly or through other vessels of north-east Radicalism like the network of Mutual Improvement Associations.[30]

This fact was not lost on farm workers in 1886. At Drumblade a former farm servant quoted a case of victimisation:

> One farmer in the district ... had not asked his servants to remain in his service because they had been connected with the agitation, and yet that farmer was a member of the Farmers' Alliance. He strongly condemned such treatment as inconsistent and tyrannical.[31]

The tyranny needs no gloss. But the charge of inconsistency could only be made if both speaker and audience took it for granted that the SFA, and the SLRA in its time, was intimately connected with the farm workers' agitation. This fact was laid bare at the Trades' Council-sponsored congress of local branches in April 1886. A delegate noted that

> At Echt they were led astray at first, and he has been sorry to see so many associations led astray by giving their political aid at meetings to further the Farmers' Alliance and Radical movements, while, on the other hand, those people who proposed to be so willing to aid them were making political capital out of the movement, while at the same time they were making no advance towards meeting their demands. The farm-servants sought a half-holiday, and they shouted in their ear, "Crofters' Bill to the whole of Scotland".[32]

In 1893 G. R. Gillespie reported to the Royal Commission on Labour about the fate of attempts to unionise farm workers in Moray, Banff and Nairn. Those attempts had not met with much success:

> It is perhaps a sign of the prevalence of good feeling that no benefit societies or unions have ever flourished in the district. A few of the younger members are Oddfellows. The Gowan Guild was started as a benefit society, and a mutual improvement society some years ago. For a time it had a considerable membership, and then fell off, and now exists only as a benefit society. The Ploughman's Union has made various attempts to get a footing in the district, especially at election times. It has never succeeded, the men distrusting its political complexion, and doubting its financial soundness.[33]

If we assume that this passage could be taken to summarise the position in Aberdeenshire — not an unreasonable supposition, given the similarity of circumstance between farming in Aberdeenshire and Banffshire — then it provides us with a bridge back to Gwenllian Evans' argument. Taken in isolation, Gillespie's assessment might be seen to lend weight to Evans' argument: the difficulty of forming continuing organisation on a shifting membership base and the lack of leadership among hired farm workers inhibiting the formation and institutionalisation of agricultural unions. Suspicion of financial soundness could then be put down to north-eastern thrift; suspicion of political complexion would then be a rationalisation masking an underlying false consciousness.

We have seen that this will not do. The 1872 episode does appear to have been an attempt by hired farm workers to organise in defence of their own interests; but the same cannot be said of the 1880 and 1886 episodes. In the first case, radical Liberals in the city hatched a plot to establish a captive union that would deliver political support to the Liberal party. In the second case, rural Radicals battened on nascent discontent among hired farm workers and guided agitation in directions that benefited them (and, through them, the Liberal party) rather than farm workers. We can see that those workers were wise to take a leery attitude to the political complexion of organisations purporting to represent their interests. Their unwillingness to join represents not false consciousness, but a rational appraisal of the real nature of the organisation.

This could lead to deplorably conservative conclusions to Gillespie's assumption that 'the prevalance of good feeling' between farmer and hired farm worker rendered redundant the need for organisation in defence of underclass interests. That is not the conclusion to which I am drawn. Rather, we must understand the productive relations of Aberdeenshire agriculture in the later nineteenth century, and the way in which these relations influenced the possibility of defensive or offensive collective action by hired farm workers. Since I have written at inordinate length on this subject elsewhere, I will be brief here. Once again I will organise my argument around the invaluable framework provided by Gwenllian Evans' essay.

Evans assumes that the hired labour force on Aberdeenshire farms was a proletariat: landless workers who had to sell their labour power in order to purchase the necessities of life and, in the long run, raise a replacement labour force. Labour power was sold, it is assumed, to capitalist farmers whose mode of production is essentially similar to that of industrial capitalists. Evans' doctoral work, of which her work on agricultural unionism forms a part, was on the wage level in Aberdeen rather than on the social relations of agricultural production. Unfortunately, however, rural Aberdeenshire did not display the sharply polarised class structure that this argument requires. Taking one hundred tilled acres as the lower limit of capitalist production under prevailing productive conditions, only seventeen per cent of Aberdeenshire farmers were capitalists in 1885. The rest were middle and poor peasants; small farmers and crofters. Yet that seventeen per cent worked fifty-seven per cent of the tilled land, using hired labour. The 1881 census revealed that fifty-nine per cent of all male farm labour in Aberdeenshire was hired, rather than drawn from family members.[34]

Interpreted, these figures show that Aberdeenshire agriculture had not been fully penetrated by the social relations 'typical' of capitalist production. It remained a peasant county, both in the numerical dominance of small farmers and crofters over capitalist farmers and in the cultural expectations which set the frame within which agricultural production was undertaken. Hired farm servants, the basis of capitalist production, were recruited not from the children of hired workers, but from peasant farms which were in a labour-abundant phase of the family farm life cycle. They carried with them into farm service sets of expectations about how they would be treated which were an idealised version of the family-based ('kindly') relations of production on family farms. They also carried into farm service a determination not to stay there. By the age of thirty-five most men had left hired farm work. Some went to the towns; hence the strength of the Ploughman's Federal Union branch in Aberdeen city, filled with former horsemen now driving horse trams and carriers' carts. Very many returned to the land as peasant farmers, using for capital the wages accumulated through years of relentless thrift in farm service. Thus in Aberdeenshire farm service was not proletarianised: it was not a career in itself, but a stage in a career that began in peasant farming then moved through wage work and back to peasant farming.

Social relations of agricultural production thus undermine Evans' argument. She assumed that the Aberdeenshire hired farm labour force was proletarianised. The members of this rural proletariat naturally would seek to band together in pursuit of common class interests. A failure so to combine must be explained through structural constraints and false consciousness. But if the hired labour force was a peasant fraction, then much of this argument is redundant. Unionisation no longer serves as a simple index of class consciousness. One now starts to look for resistance in other places; resistance that is rooted in rural Aberdeenshire's peasant culture. And one finds it: the witchcraft Society of the Horseman's Word, a pre-capitalist trade union; the clean toon, which protected the most senior hired farm worker in his dealings with the farmer; gossip, including its unique institutionalised form of the north-east's bothy ballads; the critical importance of establishing and maintaining a good reputation. In the specific conditions of late nineteenth-century Aberdeenshire all these were alternative forms of struggle and resistance to farmers' abrogations of customary expectations. The one independent episode of union activity — that of 1872 — was killed by the term. At the heart of the term shift was the feeing market, which Evans takes to be an arena of weakness for farm workers, one of the most important constraints inhibiting unionisation. This is fatally mistaken. Not only did servants have a strong market position throughout Evans' period,[35] but the feeing markets served a critically important function for local farm workers that English farm workers had to establish unions to see performed: they established the prevailing wage level.[36] It was on the feeing markets that many defensive strategies focused, notably the famous (and splendid) bothy ballads.

Thus one arrives at the conclusion that it was so difficult to establish trade unions among Aberdeenshire hired farm workers between 1870 and 1900 because unions were irrelevant. The justification for this heresy is not a conservative assertion of community of interest between farmer and workers, but a more subtle appreciation of the nature of rural Aberdeenshire's social formation. That formation supported a culture which allowed a wider — and, one must say, though it is impossible to quantify the assertion, a more effective — defence of hired farm workers' interests. It is significant that Joe Duncan's successful attempt to establish continuing union organisation in the county came in 1912, by which date the older defensive strategies were losing their effectiveness very rapidly as the culture in which they were set atrophied. But we must recognise the value and effectiveness of those older strategies. Nineteenth-century Aberdeenshire farm workers, no less than the poor stockinger, the Luddite cropper, the 'obsolete' hand-loom weaver, the 'utopian' artisan, and even the deluded follower of Joanna Southcott, need to be rescued from the massive condescension of posterity.[37]

NOTES

1. Editorial Collective, 'British economic history and the question of work', *History Workshop Journal*, iii (1977), p. 3.

2. See above, Chapters 2–5.

3. G. Evans, 'Farm servants' unions in Aberdeenshire between 1870 and 1900,' *Scottish Historical Review*, xxxi, (1952), pp. 29–40.

4. Evans makes this the Long School, incorrectly.

5. *Aberdeen Journal*, 7 February, 11 and 25 April 1866.

6. *Aberdeen Free Press*, 10 August 1866.

7. Evans, 'Farm Servants' Unions', p. 31.

8. K. D. Buckley, *Trade Unionism in Aberdeen, 1878–1900* (Aberdeen, 1955), pp. 30–1.

9. M. C. Dyer, 'The politics of Kincardineshire', (unpublished PhD Thesis, University of Aberdeen, 1974), p. 1150.

10. I. Carter, 'To roose the countra fae the caul' morality o' a deid Moderatism: William Alexander and *Johny Gibb of Gushetneuk*', *Northern Scotland*, ii (1976), pp. 148–62.

11. R. Duncan, *James Leatham, 1865–1945: Portrait of a Socialist Pioneer* (Aberdeen, 1978).

12. J. Leatham, 'An Aberdeenshire classic — centenary of Dr. William Alexander', *Trans. Buchan Field Club*, xiii, (1926), p. 129.

13. Evans, 'Farm Servants' Unions', p. 40.

14. J. Smith, *Joe Duncan: the Scottish Farm Servants and British Agriculture* (Edinburgh, 1973).

15. *Aberdeen Journal*, 17 April 1872.

16. *Aberdeen Journal*, 21 May 1880; *Post Office Aberdeen Directory, 1880–1* (Aberdeen, 1880).

17. *Aberdeen Journal*, 27 May 1880.

18. Anon (J. M. B. Taylor), *Eleven Years at Farm Work, Being a True Tale of Farm Servant Life from 1863 Onwards* (Aberdeen, 1879).

19. W. Jolly, *The Life of John Duncan, Scotch Weaver and Botanist* (London, 1883), p. 343.

20. *Aberdeen Journal*, 28 May 1880.

21. *Aberdeen Free Press*, 18 January 1886.

22. *Ibid.*, 12 April 1886.

23. *Ibid.*, 1 and 22 February 1886.

24. *Ibid.*, 18 March 1886.

25. *Ibid.*, 12 April 1886.

26. *Ibid.*, 22 February 1886.

27. *Ibid.*, 18 March 1886.

28. *Ibid.*, 19 March 1886.

29. *Ibid.*, 22, 23, 25, 29 March 1886.

30. I. Carter, 'The mutual improvement movement in north-east Scotland in the nineteenth century', *Aberdeenshire University Review*, xlvi (1976), pp. 383–92.

31. *Aberdeen Free Press*, 2 April 1886.

32. *Ibid.*, 12 April 1886.

33. *Royal Commission on Labour. The Agricultural Labourer; Vol. III. Scotland. Part I. Parliamentary Papers*, 1893–4 (C 6894–XV), XXXVI, p. 113.

34. I. Carter, *Farm Life in Northeast Scotland, 1840–1914* (Edinburgh, 1979), pp. 29, 104.

35. *Ibid.*, p. 118. See above, pp. 116–119 and below, pp. 244–6.

36. J. P. D. Dunbabin, *Rural Discontent in Nineteenth Century Britain* (London, 1974).

37. E. P. Thompson, *The Making of the English Working Class* (London, 1968), p. 13.

12

The Expressive Culture of Nineteenth-Century Scottish Farm Servants

David Buchan

Culture may be conveniently, if not very precisely, portrayed on a continuum with markers for traditional (or folk) culture, popular (or mass) culture, and high (or elite) culture. The frequent overlappings and interactions of the three sectors mean that any attempt to demarcate between them with rigidity is doomed to failure, but the central distinctions, if viewed flexibly, lead to useful and at times essential discriminations in perspective. At the very least the distinctions counter the common misconception that equates culture with high culture and assumes the high culture forms to be the only cultural forms. It is of more than passing interest for Scottish cultural history that the two dominating figures of pre-twentieth century literature, Burns and Scott, both had a fair acquaintance with the expressive forms of all three cultures.

The expressive culture of nineteenth-century Scottish farm servants contained elements, varying in proportion as the century progressed, from the three sectors but, overall, was predominantly a traditional culture, that is, one transmitted primarily by word of mouth and customary practice. The main part of this essay consists of a survey of the expressive forms of the traditional culture, while the last section deals with the impact of the new forms. Since folk culture constituted the disciplinary concern of Folkloristics (or Volkskunde, Folklore, Folklife, Ethnology — the discipline has many aliases), the generic taxonomy of that discipline provides the apposite framework of discussion for the traditional expressive forms, the relevant genres in this case being folksong, folk narrative, folksay, folk custom, and material culture. In accordance with standard folkloristic method, the evidence derives from a range of written or documentary sources and from field-recordings.

The farm servants' culture makes a large subject, and its size dictates that in the short compass of this essay only an outline of its major features can be offered. Similarly, on its relationship to the rest of Scottish traditional culture a brief comment must suffice. Much, obviously, belonged to both, but the culture of the occupational group contained elements directly related to the life of the group and these elements are highlighted on the generic exemplification; one should bear in mind, however, that beyond the group-specific material is that shared with Scottish traditional culture in general.[1] The subject includes the two variables of region and time: on the first one can simply note that considerable differences existed in the social and cultural conditions of the various regions, between, say, the Lothians and Highland Perthshire; the second requires rather more extended comment.

For the decades before and after 1800 the traditional culture was in the process of adapting itself to the manifold effects of the agrarian and industrial revolutions and the consequent social upheaval. Patterns of labour altered, and so did patterns of leisure. In 1831 James Hogg, the Ettrick Shepherd, complained trenchantly of one alteration among 'the Border peasantry':

> On looking back, the first great falling off is in SONG. This, to me, is not only astonishing, it is unaccountable. They have ten times more opportunities of learning songs, yet song-singing is at an end, or only kept up by a few migratory tailors. In my young days, we had singing matches almost every night, and, if no other chance or opportunity offered, the young men attended at the ewe-bught or the cows milking, and listened and joined the girls in their melting lays. We had again our kirns at the end of harvest, and our ling-swinglings in almost every farm-house and cottage, which proved as a weekly bout for the greater part of the winter. And then, with the exception of *Wads*, and a little kissing and toying in consequence, song, song alone, was the sole amusement. ... I have given great annual kirns, and begun singing the first myself, in order to elicit some remnants, some semblance at least, of the strains of former days. But no; those strains could be heard from no one, with the exception of one shepherd, Wat Arnos, who alone, for these twenty years, has been always ready to back me. I say, with the exception of him and of Tam the tailor, there seems to be no songster remaining. By dint of hard pressing, a blooming nymph will sometimes venture on a song of Moore's or Dibdin's (curse them!), and gaping, and half-choking, with a voice like a cracked kirk-bell, finish her song in notes resembling the agonies of a dying sow.[2]

Although Hogg's is a high-coloured and decidedly personal plaint (and like many others premature in its declaration of the demise of song-singing), it does convey how one man (himself a performer) apprehended change in the patterns of traditional leisure between the late eighteenth and the early nineteenth centuries, and it also indicates, in the scornful reference to the nymph warbling Moore and Dibdin's songs, the changes in repertoire and performing style that had occurred within tradition.

Following his mother, Hogg blames the publication of Scott's *Minstrelsy*, by which 'a deadening blow was inflicted on our rural literature and principal enjoyment by the very means adopted for their preservation'.[3] The *Minstrelsy*, however, designed to capture the old disappearing Scots culture, was a symptom rather than a cause of the general social and cultural changes. These changes, particularly through the effects of widespread education and literacy and the new media dependent on them, altered cumulatively through the century the content and style of the expressive forms within tradition. Old forms of song and story and custom went out; new kinds came in. The participants in the old practices also changed, with some groups distancing themselves from traditional activities and others gradually forsaking certain of the expressive forms. Hogg laments that 'the *aristocracy* of farming ... has placed such a distance between servants and masters, that in fact they have no communication whatever, and very little interest in common', which destroyed the former unity where 'in all the sports the farmer or his family joined'.[4] By the end of the century the separation was physically symbolised in some areas by the piano for the farmer's daughter in the best room (though the separation may not have been entire for such daughters as Rose in 'John Bruce o the Forenit' who 'plays the piano, and whyles wi' the men'). A number of forms devolved from adults to children: the classic wonder tale, once the major fictional genre of the adult community, dwindled into the fairy tale for youngsters; guising and the guisers' play became in many regions an activity of the youths where formerly it had belonged to the community's male adults. Throughout the nineteenth century, then, there were, at different rates in different regions, changes within the genres and in the participants and practices of tradition.

The traditional genres were performed in a number of contexts. Frequently described is the farm kitchen on the long winter evenings, with a heaped fire crackling and men and women plying their different tasks — like spinning or shoe-mending — and telling stories, singing, making music, playing games, and 'speeran guesses' (posing riddles). Neighbours would drop in and various itinerants — chapmen, beggars, peripatetic tailors — would also enliven proceedings. Other milieux for performance during leisure hours were the bothy and the chaumer, while during working hours song or story could be heard in the field, to while away the dreary hours of hoeing for instance, or, in very bad weather, the stable when the men caught up on the indoor tasks. Away from the farm, performances also occurred at the smithy, the shoemaker's shop, or a local howff.[5]

In the genre of folksong most attention has fallen, understandably, on the bothy ballads.[6] Examples of the texts appear in John Ord's *Bothy Songs and Ballads of Aberdeen, Banff & Moray, Angus and the Mearns* and in Gavin Greig's *Folk-Song of the North-East*, which will be superseded in the coming years by the successive volumes of the Greig-Duncan MSS; examples of the sung ballads are to be heard on a record, *Bothy Ballads. Music from the North-East*, compiled from the archives of the School of Scottish Studies.[7] The bothy ballads are narrative songs composed largely by the farm servants about the lives of the farm servants and, as Gavin

Greig puts it, 'as illustrating bucolic life, manners, and ideals — often in a vivid and convincing way — they are interesting and instructive'.[8] Although largely recorded in the region, they are not, as a recent writer asserts, 'a unique cultural production of northeast Scotland', for they occur elsewhere.[9] From Angus come the bothy ballads 'Morphie' and 'The Mill o Lour', from Renfrewshire the quite early 'Faughill Shearing', and from Kintyre 'Killeonan'.[10] As far as can be ascertained, their dates of composition range from the 1820s, in the case of 'The Faughill Shearing', to the period just before the First World War.

The bothy ballads provide both a celebration and a criticism: they celebrate the accomplishments, cameraderie, and vagaries of the labouring life and they criticise the harsh and mean conditions of the employment. The largest group of songs deals with a feeing at a particular farm, normally in one of two patterns, by description of either a six-month term, as in 'The Barnyards o Delgaty', or a single day's work, as in 'Drumdelgie'. Two other broadly distinguishable groups treat specific aspects of life and work, such as harvest, feeing, harrowing, term day, the ploughing match, and humorous incidents from life about the ferm-toon. Recent sociological writing has emphasised their critical function, pointing up their purpose as protest songs, where the protest relates to the conditions of the farm servants' existence and lacks 'overt political overtones', for 'they represent a peasant reponse rather than a class response to the introduction of capitalist farming'. A number of the ballads attack specific farmers ('Swaggers' is the standard example) in a way that would both spread a bad reputation and ensure difficulty in his attracting a decent workforce, which would make it 'seem likely that they were conscious attempts to black certain farmers'.[11]

The bothy ballads constitute a distinctive subgenre, but it was just one subgenre among the many that made up bothy song since 'bothy-song', as Ord points out forcibly, 'is just another name for folk-song'.[12] Naturally, numbers of the other bothy songs bear directly on the farm servants' life. A not infrequent theme is the celebration of the ploughman's life, its superiority to other trades extolled comparatively or simply declared, as in the various songs entitled 'In Praise of Ploughmen'. Balancing this, though, is the sardonic critique of this 'slavery job of low degree' in such a song as 'Twa Recruitin Sergeants' (ascribed by one performer of a two-stanza version to the Duchess of Gordon on her famous recruiting drive for the Gordon Highlanders).[13] A few worksongs from the early decades have survived, such as one sung at the driving of the peats and a pair sung while manoeuvring the old 'aucht-owsen plough'.[14] But to appreciate fully the huge range of bothy song and its multiple subgenres (such kinds of song as the songs of custom, the women's worksongs, the lyric songs, the comic songs, the narrative songs, the multifarious broadside songs, the occupational songs, the classical ballads) one must turn to the collection of Gavin Greig, recorded largely from the farming community of one region.

Instrumental music too occupied an important place in the leisuretime activities. Among the farm servants were players of the fiddle, the bagpipes, the melodeon, and the trump (the Jew's harp); in at least one district the cornet attained a popularity in both bothies and balls, but it may have been a twentieth-century phenomenon.[15] Pipers in certain regions, especially those abutting the Highlands, accompanied and encouraged the shearers in the harvest field, a task undertaken in one area by a blinded ex-drummer-boy playing a fife.[16] Farming districts often produced a fiddler of some reputation who was sometimes also a composer. In Perthshire John Cuthbert, a miller's widow's son who started playing on a horse's skull laced with four strings, was able to advance from poultryman to earning his living as a violin and piano player and teacher.[17] In the early decades of the century in the southern counties, itinerant fiddlers made a living in the country districts. James Stuart, based on Tweedmouth, traversed the south-east, it was said, until he was 114 years old.[18] Blind John Jameson travelled with his wife through Peeblesshire, 'playing at kirns, penny-weddings, and fairs' and being lodged in farm-steadings.[19] James Hogg gives this account of them:

The itinerant fiddlers were a great source of amusement, and a blithesome sight to many a young eye; but every farmer acknowledged one only as his family musician, and the reception of interlopers was rather equivocal. The family musician, however, knew well when to make his appearances. These were at the sheep-shearing, when he got his choice fleece; at the end of harvest, to the kirn supper; at the end of the year, for his cakes and cheese; and at the end of seed time, for his lippie of oats. On all these occasions the neighbours were summoned, and the night spent in dancing and singing; and then, besides the farmer's bounty, it was customary for every man to give the musician sixpence ... .[20]

Dancing occurred not only on the occasions listed by Hogg but also at the larger 'balls' of a district. In the Cromar bothies one of the ploys of the lang nichts was step-dancing, 'each man bi himsel', and from near Huntly comes a memory of 'the towel dance' performed in a farm-kitchen and involving two people and two towels.[21] The institution of the dancing class established itself in many areas throughout the century, but what proportion of the pupils were farm servants would be difficult to determine. The dancing instructor exercised an influence outside the class: 'during the winter months the dancing-master, besides being the recognised master of the revels, was generally the country model of elegant and polite bearing, and his port and sentiments were more attended to than the instruction and example of the parson and church clerk'.[22]

Folk narrative was the other main performative genre. Hugh Miller provides an illuminating account of a tale-teller in a Ross-shire 'barrack' or bothy:

At times a song or story secured the attention of the barrack; and there was in especial one story-teller whose powers of commanding attention were very great. He was a middle-aged Highlander, not very skilful as a workman, and but indifferently provided with English; and as there usually attaches a nickname to persons in the humbler walks that are marked by any eccentricity of character, he was better known among his brother workmen as Jock Mo-ghoal, i.e. John my Darling, than by his proper name. Of all Jock Mo-ghoal's stories Jock Mo-ghol was himself the hero; and certainly most wonderful was the invention of the man. As redorded in his narratives, his life was one long epic poem, filled with strange and startling adventure, and furnished with an extraordinary machinery of the wild and spernatural; .... The workman used, on the mornings after his greater narratives, to look one another full in the face, and ask, with a smile rather incipient than fully manifest, whether 'Jock wasna perfectly wonderfu' last night?'[23]

The importance of these 'wonderful personal narratives that had not a word of truth in them' for people in oppressed circumstances should not be underestimated, for Miller declares that 'in getting into conversation with individuals of the more thoroughly lapsed classes of our large towns, I have found that a faculty of extemporary fabrication was almost the only one which I could calculate on finding among them in a state of vigorous activity'.[24] Storytelling of this kind can afford a creative fulfilment and a sense of worth to an individual otherwise denied these by the conditions of his existence.

For Jock Mo-ghoal all story forms became grist to his personal narrative mill, but the various genres require some distinguishing since their purposes and effects differ. The major genre of the older tradition, the equivalent in narrative of the muckle songs, is the Märchen or wonder tale, an imaginative excursion into a fictional world filled with unreal marvels and realistic mundanities by an ordinary hero or heroine who undergoes trials and tests to emerge rewarded by gear and partner. Although a considerable harvest of these stories has been recorded from the Travellers in the last thirty years, texts from the nineteenth century are relatively scanty in number, but evidence exists that certainly in one region farm servants performed Märchen. In 1859 Donald Macraw, a drover of North Uist, told John Francis Campbell, following a Märchen he had just recounted (as they walked along the road for several miles), that 'in Kinross and Perthshire it is the custom for the hinds and farm-labourers to assemble and repeat stories in broad Scotch, which closely resemble those told in the islands, but which are not garnished with measured prose'.[25] It is, of course, distinctly possible that some at least of the recorded texts lacking contextual information about the informant derive from farm servants. This possibility would apply not only to Märchen but also to such genres as fable and Novella (or realistic tale).

Various kinds of international jocular tales enlivened an evening's entertainment. The Schwank (or comic story), for instance, of the beast-owner who trains his horse or donkey to do with less and less food and then is bewildered when the beast dies after existing on one straw a day appears in Galloway.[26] In a number of regions evidences occur of a strong tall tale tradition, with local reputations for such masters of the art as Lang Lamb: 'Lang Lamb's a lear, but he aye gies his lees feet to stan' on'.[27] Jokes, of course, abounded and this unregarded genre actually offers some revealing insights into the concerns and attitudes of those who told them. The targets of the jokes include such topics as the working conditions or the failings and foibles of stereotypical figures like the farmer, the grieve, the haflin and so on. On the former is this gem from the south-west:

> There was a farm in Dumfriesshire which had the reputation of working its men pretty hard, and one man went there to work and after a while met a friend who asked what it was like on the farm, to which he replied 'Oh, it's just like heaven,' 'Just like heaven?' replied the friend, taken aback. 'Aye' he said, 'there's nae night there either.[28]

Of the latter kind is a joke told with different subjects (grieve, wife, for example) in different tellings. A, who has a tendency to sleep late, is wakened one morning by B shouting 'Fire, fire!' 'Where?' says A getting up in a hurry. 'In aabody's hoose bit this een. Get up, ye lazy vratch'.[29] Close kin to the joke, the anecdote often serves similar purposes, such as the wry encapsulation of social relationships. An anecdote still encountered concerns the farm servant who reluctantly asks the farmer for a day off the following Tuesday; 'Why?' says the farmer, to which he replies 'gettin mairriet'. As is customary with many traditional items, different emphases of meaning can be brought into play with different presentations of the anecdote's core.[30] Quite unequivocal in its meaning is the Galloway anecdote:

> Another day twa cairts wus sent wi a pleughman across the water tae Kirkcubrie. Whun they wur comin back yin o' the horses reestit at the soun' o' the ladles, and backit aff the ferry-boat inta the water. The man try't a' he could tae save the horse, but it pu't him into the water, and he wus droon't too.
>
> Whun the ither horse was brung hame, an the farmer was tell't aboot the accident, he exclaim't wi an oath — 'If it had only been the man a wudnae 'a mindit; but the guidd hoerse'.[31]

While the jokes and anecdotes tend to typify aspects of the ordinary everyday life, the legends deal with the more extraordinary events and characters of the past or of the supernatural world. An example of the historical legend is this one, in its printed form, from Aberdeenshire:

> Here [the farm of Tombeg] the last of the Highland 'caterans' that ever troubled the parish made a descent, but were caught and made an example of. They had ordered the 'cow-baillie' to drive all the cattle out of the byres, but the faithful servant, while he obeyed the reivers' orders, took care to knock out

a few 'sods' in the back wall as he unbounded the cattle. Just as he drove out the last he fled through the hole to the laird's, and the result was that the cattle-lifters were overtaken and several of them duly 'justiced'.[32]

In the bothies and chaumers were also to be heard formula tales, where, for example, each person in a group repeats what has come before, a sentence being added every round, and recitations.[33]

The two major genres of folksay figure as prominently as one would expect in a largely traditional culture. The posing of riddles — the speeran o guesses — occupied a standard place in the evening's entertainment in the farm kitchens.[34] Proverbs and the proverb-related subgenres permeated the everyday speech of rural folk, in ways that are best perceived within those regional ethnographies which re-create specific scenes and include typical dialogue.[35] Each occupational group develops its own lexicon, not only of those terms directly connected with the pursuit of the occupation itself, but also of words which carry a particular connotative freight, such as 'plodderan':

PLODDERAN — Toiling night and day almost; the first that disgusted me with a farmer's life, and what disgusts thousands at it, is the not having a moment of time that can be said to be our own.[36]

An area of folksy often unregarded but quite instructive for the insights it provides is that of rhymes.[37] For present purposes, they can be seen in three groups, the first group comprising those used in certain social situations. At festivities there were toasts:

> Peace and plenty, and nae killing;
> Beef at a groat, and meat at a shilling;
> Whisky for naething, yill at the same;
> A canty bit wifie, and a cosy wee hame,

and, before meals, graces of both solemn and unsolemn cast like the West Lothian one said 'when there appeared to be little for dinner':

> Lang kail an' few o' them,
> Louse, lads, an' let's to them,

or that 'referring to the treatment of farm-servants in the matter of their food':

> Guid an gracious noo is deid an' gone,
> Deil an' sorrow's noo come on:
> Thin brose an' nae breid,
> Oh! God, gin she were deid![38]

At work, there was a rhyme for the last shearer of the band in the Fife fields:

> Oh dear!
> My back's sair, shearin' bear, And up I canna win,
> And my bonnie love has left me i' the lang tail-win.[39]

The second group of rhymes are concerned with knowledge: they record and fix in memorable form features of the landscape, the social environment, and the group's history. From Berwickshire comes a rhyme on a noteworthy past event:

> Far up on Lammermoor amang the heather green
> The earliest ha'rst that e'er was seen
> Was seen at Bentydod.
> Because, they were shearing the remainder of their crop
> there, on a New-years morning.[40]

Most districts had rhymes listing farms found in the locality, like these from Ayrshire and Speyside respectively:

> Doughtie, Auchengairn, Dawine, and Dahairn,
> Clasgalloch, the Balloch, the Challoch,
> The Chang, and the Cairn,
> and   Dipple, Dundurcas, Dundaleith and Dalvey,
> The four bonniest haughs on the rin o' the Spey.[41]

Sometimes these lists turn into a *blason populaire,* as in this account of the places in the Berwickshire parish of Hutton:

> Hutton for auld wives,
> Broadmeadows for swine;
> Paxton for drunken wives,
> And saumon sae fine:
> Crossrig for lint and woo',
> Spittal for kail,
> Sunwick for cakes and cheese,
> And lasses for sale.[42]

On occasion these rhymes could become descriptions of certain farms that would serve as warnings:

> The ploughmen at the hiring fairs had rhymes to denote their likes and dislikes for particular farms or farmers, and the fare they got from their masters, as in the jingle, which had many alterations to suit the case, of which the best known form describes the fares of the Kinross district:

> Witches in the Watergate,
>   Fairies in the Mill,
> Brosy lads o' Neviston,
>   Can never get their fill.
> Sma' drink in the Punful,
>   Crowdie in the Kirk,
> Grey meal in Boreland
>   Waur than ony dirt.
> Bread and cheese in the Easter Mains,
> Cauld sowens in the Wester Mains,
> Hard heads in Hardeston
>   Quakers in the Pow;
> The brae lasses o' Abdie (Aldie)
>   Cannaspin their ain tow.[43]

The third group of rhymes provide a commentary on the nature of the life. A West Lothian version of a rhyme found elsewhere, suitably adjusted, captures tersely the pressure of a hard-driven toun:

> The Lang Toon, the Lang Toon, has neither watch nor clock,
> But parritch-time an sowens-time an' aye 'Yoke, Yoke.'

Angus supplies 'The Ploughman's Week':

> Soor Monday
> Cauld Tuesday
> Cruel Wednesday
> Everlasting Thursday
> Oh Friday will ye ne'er gae dun,
> Sweet Setterday and the efternin
> Glorious Sunday rest forever,
> Amen.

And Fife furnishes 'the only commandment' of the ploughman:

> Six days shalt thou labour and do all
>   That you are able;
> On the Sabbath-day wash the horses' legs
>   And tiddy up the stable.[44]

The rhymes, then, can be seen to serve at least three major functions: they celebrate, they record, and they criticise.

The events of folk custom provide both contexts for the performance of some of the genres already mentioned and occasion for expressive behaviour appropriate to the event. For brevity's sake, the kinds of events may be highlighted as the festivals of periodic custom, the rituals of rites of passage, and the recreations of episodic custom. The periodic customs

include those of the farming year and of the calendar year:[45] in the first
category come, for example, the end of harvest festivals — the kirns and
meal-an-ales; and in the second the festivals of the quite lengthy Yuletide
season. At Hogmanay, just one element of the Yule season, the young men
might go round the district performing a version of the folk play often
known in Scotland as 'Galations',[46] or make a round of house-visits as
guisers, or indulge in pranks which sometimes carried social meaning. In
Banffshire, they armed themselves with turnips from a farmer's field and,
if he were stingy, battered his door:

> When the farmer or his men came out, they had the pleasure of looking at a
> smashed door, a heap of the farm turnips, and also had the advantage of
> knowing what some of their neighbours thought of them. But if a cottager
> were poor and well thought of, our *modus operandi* was different. The door was
> unmercifully battered just the same (ou, he'll jest hae tae mend it, ye ken), but
> a big heap of turnips presented from fields other than his own by unknown
> hands, testified to the respect in which he was held.[47]

The rites of passage mark the special stages of an individual's life, such as
birth, marriage, and death.[48] The ceremony of initiation into the
Horseman's Word, in effect initiation into adulthood, constituted a rite of
passage particular to the ploughman community.[49] Recreational customs
included such indoor activities as song and rhyme games, cards, and the
dambrods, and such outdoor ones as curling, football, feats of strength,
tilting at the ring, and quoits; sufficiently different from the ordinary to be
classed as at least partly recreational were otterhunts and foxhunts.

In the generic area of material culture expressive activity went into the
making of things, in arts and crafts both occupational and non-
occupational. A farmwork craft such as harness-making demanded skill and
allowed for an individual's creativity, as did the non-occupational ones that
involved the fashioning of whistles or 'peeterie dicks' or the making of
clickit rugs. Some farm servants turned their creative attention to the
visual arts and produced drawings and paintings.[50]

Throughout the period there developed the new print culture, which
entered into a sometimes quite complex co-existence with the old oral and
customary culture. The spread of education and mass literacy resulted in
the creation of new ambiences for the rural population — libraries, reading
rooms, Mutual Improvement Societies, and evening classes in such
subjects as land surveying — which all provided opportunities for the
engagement of intellectual and emotional energies. The educational
changes also led to the country folk being exposed to various productions
of the print medium. For the most part the libraries contained educational,
'improving' material whose usefulness was matched by its heaviness.
Literature, doubtless because of its dubious enjoyment quotient, did not
constitute a staple element of these institutions, which meant that
individuals had to find their own means of satisfying literary tastes. A

rarity was the farm servant who could accumulate his own library:

> ...such a farm servant ... I had never met before and have not met since.
> On going to our sleeping apartment [an outhouse connected with the stable]
> the second night, he opened a trunk filled with books which he had bought out
> of his savings.... . In Jamie's trunk were the works of Shakespeare, Milton,
> Burns, Byron, Bacon, Macaulay's *Essays,* Addison, Hume, De Quincey, Hugh
> Miller, Boswell's *Life of Johnson, Noctes Ambrosianae,* a number of Sir Walter
> Scott's novels and many other excellent works — in fact, he had not a trashy
> book in his possession.[51]

Buying, however, became easier as the century progressed. One writer
comments in 1880, 'The aged can remember when *the Waverley Novel*
costs 31s. 6d., and was hired out to read at 1s. per volume for 12 hours. It
is now retailed, with all the Notes, at 3d'.[52] Certain kinds of poetry
achieved popularity, most especially when they could be adapted to the old
social patterns and sung in the company of small groups, but poetry could
also be viewed as an improving force, as by Janet Hamilton (of the village
of Langloan in Lanarkshire) in her essay on 'The Uses and Pleasures of
Poetry for the Working-Classes': '[the workman] while holding communion
with the spirits of the mighty masters of song in their immortal pages, may
feel every noble principle of his mind strengthened, every emotion of his
heart warmed and purified, and every feeling refined and elevated'.[53] It is
distinctly possible that the purveyors of this view of poetry hoped that
'proper' poetry would counteract the improper effects of the 'roch' strain
in the old culture with its vigorous bawdy tradition.[54]

For some decades into the nineteenth century, however, the only
affordable literature for the farm servants population was that dispensed by
the chapmen — the chapbooks and broadsheets. These, wrote William
Chambers, 'disappeared slowly through the united effects of education, and
a demand for something equally exhilarating and much more conformable
to improved manners and feelings'.[55] A demand he and his brother Robert
met with *Chambers' Journal* and a series of cheap instructional
publications. The *Journal,* according to Allan Cunningham, was widely
read by Galloway shepherds who would pass it on to the next in a chain by
leaving it under a mountain-top stone at an appointed time.[56] Newspapers
eventually achieved a wide audience, but when still costly they would be
bought by groups of rural people who would read the paper in turn, or
who would hold a special evening session when one person would read
aloud the entire paper from first to last page for the assembled group in an
interesting adaptation of the usual performance patterns.[57] On the other
hand, it was Hugh Miller's experience in the barrack or bothy that 'during
the whole season a newspaper never once entered the barrack door'.[58]

People engaged actively as well as passively in the new culture. They
acted, for example, in the plays and operettas produced by Gavin Greig in

Aberdeenshire or by The Burrelton and Woodside Young Men's Mutual Improvement Society in Perthshire. Poem-making, however, is the activity most likely to be associated with farm servants, for was not the National Bard a ploughman, one who inspired a legion of followers? Certainly nineteenth-century Scotland boasted a number of poets who came from a working-class background, James Hogg the Ettrick Shepherd, Allan Cunningham the stonemason, William Nicholson the pedlar, and Robert Tannahill and William Thom the weavers, but remarkably few poems clearly attributed to farm servants appear in such publications as Robert Ford's *Harp of Perthshire* or Malcolm Harper's *Bards of Galloway* or the D. H. Edwards *Modern Scottish Poets* series.[59] Since a number of contributors worked on farms in their early life, one is led to the conclusion that those involved in prestige publication of their poetry were also interested in moving out of farm work. Rural themes, of course, figure prominently in nineteenth-century poetry, and that the National Bard followed the plough seems to have cast a symbolic glamour over the poetic role of the ploughman. William Lillie, 'Buchan's Ploughman Poet', became both clerk and miller but, 'after the fashion of Burns, still regarded himself as essentially a ploughman'.[60] Lillie in fact furnishes a case study instructive not only in his adoption of the ploughman role but also in the fact that he wrote many of his poems within the song tradition, and although only two poems were published during his lifetime, Gavin Greig recorded nine pieces sixty to seventy years after his death. The farm servants did not appear in numbers in the conventional nineteenth-century poetic volumes because, it would seem, they pursued a more limited fame, by performance of their works in their district, or perhaps by print in local newspapers. Few pieces, however, can have had as limited an original audience as the poem written in 1858 on the walls of the chaumer at Crichmalade, in the Aberdeenshire parish of Fyvie:

> On the 16th October in the year 58,
> I went to the ploo, nae doots to haud straucht,
> Mysel' in good humour, my horses the same,
> I ploo'd till eleiven, and then I cam' hame,
> Gaed Nell and Nansy some corn to eat,
> An' syne took a besom and swypet my feet.
> Then to the barn I quickly withdrew,
> To bundle some straw, but, oh, what a stew!
> When denner was over to the stable we went,
> To clean up oor horses it was oor intent.
> Oor orders fae Dawson for plooin, again,
> Nae sinsheen, but cloody and some draps o' rain.
> Noo my day's wark is finisht, and I'll hae a smoke,
> An' I'm boun for my bed, for it's past nine o'clock.[61]

By 1914 the expressive culture of the Scottish farm servants contained a variety of strands, drawn from high, popular, and traditional cultures.

Over the period 1780 to 1914 taken as a whole, however, it was predominantly traditional in cast. In consequence, most of this essay has been directed to providing an account, through a rapid survey of the genres, of the nature and range of the traditional cultural forms, with indications of some of the functions served. In general terms the functions fulfil the neoclassical aims of instruction and delight; in more specific terms the three major functions are those of imaginative entertainment, as in the Märchen, transmission of knowledge, as in the historical legends and the proverbs, and direct commentary on the life lived, as in the bothy ballads, the jokes and anecdotes, and the rhymes. The commentary genres will provoke the most immediate interest for the social historian, as well they might since they furnish valuable insights. But, on a cautionary note, a balanced understanding of the expressive culture, and of what precisely is being expressed, requires that they be considered not in isolation but along with the other genres in a cultural system that has a range of forms and interwoven functions. Taken in their totality, the forms and functions of the farm servants' expressive culture demonstrate a quite comprehensive response to the arduous business of living, encompassing record and fantasy, celebration and criticism.

NOTES

1. In David Buchan, *Scottish Tradition*, (London, 1984). An attempt is made to exemplify the range of the verbal genres in Scottish folk literature.

2. James Hogg, 'On the Changes in the Habbits, Amusements, and Condition of the Scottish Peasantry', *Quarterly Journal of Agriculture,* iii (1831–32), pp. 256–7.

3. *Ibid.,* p. 257.

4. *Ibid.,* pp. 263, 261.

5. The performance contexts of the nineteenth-century farm servants are the subject of a forthcoming paper.

6. David Buchan, *The Ballad and the Folk* (London, 1972) and *A Scottish Ballad Book* (London, 1973) furnish a brief introduction and a group of representative texts. David Kerr Cameron, *The Ballad and the Plough* (London, 1978) shows the interrelationships of the bothy ballads and their social context in splendidly evocative fashion. Edward K. Miller provides an illuminating contextualist account of the repertoires and lives of two Angus farm workers who bothied early this century in 'An Ethnography of Singing: The Use and Meaning of Song within a Scottish Family' (unpublished, PhD thesis, University of Texas at Austin, 1981). Bob Munro adopts a revealing sociological perspective in 'The Bothy Ballads: the social context and meaning of the farm servants' songs of North-Eastern Scotland', *History Workshop,* No. 3 (1977), pp. 184–93. Ian Carter, *Farm Life in Northeast Scotland 1840–1914* (Edinburgh, 1979), pp. 137–59, follows the same approach. See also T. J. Byres, 'Scottish Peasants and their Song', *Journal of Peasant Studies,* 3 (1975–76), pp. 236–51; Hamish Henderson, 'The Bothy Ballads', *Journal of Peasant*

Studies, 2 (1974–75), pp. 498–501 (an extract from the booklet accompanying the record noted below); Alan Howkins, 'The Voice of the People: the social meaning and context of country song', *Oral History,* 3 (1975), pp. 50–75.

7. Paisley, 1930 reprinted Edinburgh, 1973; 2 vols., Peterhead, 1909, 1914, reprinted with 'Folk-Song in Buchan' and foreword by Kenneth S. Goldstein and Arthur Argo, Hatboro, Penn., 1963. Volume I of *The Greig-Duncan Folk Song Collection,* edited by Patrick Shuldham-Shaw and Emily Lyle, was published in 1982 (Aberdeen); London: Tangent Records, 1971, TNGM 109.

8. 'Northern Rustic or Bothy Songs', *Miscellanea of the Rymour Club* (Edinburgh, 1906–28), i, p. 20.

9. Carter, *Farm Life,* p. 137.

10. *Misc. Rymour Club,* ii, pp. 122–6; Ord, *Bothy Songs,* p. 255; E. B. Lyle, ed., *Andrew Crawfurd's Collection of Ballads and Songs* (Edinburgh, 1975), i, pp. 131–2; *Tocher,* no. 3 (1971), pp. 80–81.

11. Munro, 'Bothy Ballads', pp. 192, 193, 190. See also Carter, *Farm Life,* pp. 137–159.

12. *Bothy Songs,* p. 1.

13. *Trans. Rymour Club,* iii, p. 186.

14. Included in Buchan, *Scottish Folk Tradition.*

15. Tape 82:09: rec. W.M., 83, retired farm servant in Cromar.

16. George Robertson, *Rural Recollections* (1829), excerpted in J. G. Fyfe, ed., *Scottish Diaries and Memoirs, 1746–1843* (Stirling, 1942), p. 284.

17. [Duncan Macara], *Crieff: Its Traditions and Characters* (Edinburgh, 1881), pp. 2–3. See also [Macara], *Crieff,* pp. 1–7; James Godsman, *Glass, Aberdeenshire: The Story of a Parish* (Aberdeen, 1970), p. 115; James Pirie, *The Parish of Cairnie* (Banff, 1906), pp. 143–4.

18. J. F. S. Gordon, *The Book of the Chronicles of Keith . . .* (Glasgow, 1880), pp. 198–9.

19. William Chambers, *Memoir of Robert Chambers with Autobiographic Reminiscences of William Chambers* (Edinburgh, 1872), pp. 62–63.

20. 'Changes', p. 261.

21. 82:09, W.M.; 82:08, N.H., 78, Huntly, a retired banker brought up for part of his childhood on a farm in that district.

22. [Macara], *Crieff,* p. 5.

23. *My Schools and Schoolmaster* (Edinburgh, 1893), p. 101.

24. *Ibid.,* p. 103

25. John Francis Campbell, *Popular Tales of the West Highlands* (4 vols., Edinburgh, 1860–62, reprinted Paisley, 1890), ii, p. 316.

26. Andrew McCormick, *Words from the Wild-Wood* (Glasgow, 1913), pp. 108–9. The story is tale-type 1682 in Antii Aarne and Stith Thompson, *The Types of the Folktale* (rev. ed., Helsinki, 1961).

27. William Watson, *Glimpses of Auld Lang Syne* (Aberdeen, 1905), p. 257.

28. Recorded 25/3/76 from R.C., a Dumfriesshire man, who can trace the joke's telling back to a farm worker in the shire c. 1900.

29. A printed version is in Maitland Mackie, 'Personal Recollections of Farming in the North-East', in Archie W. M. Whiteley, ed., *The Book of Bennachie* (n.p., 1976), p. 8. It is described as an actual prank in Cameron, *Ballad and Plough,* p. 115.

30. A printed version in J. F. Fraser, *Doctor Jimmy* (Aberdeen, 1980), pp. 25–26,

has a cattleman asking for Saturday afternoon off and replying to the offer of the evening and Sunday too that 'he had the feeders to look after' before unwillingly agreeing. A recorded version has the farmer saying, 'I had a week off when I was mairriet' and the farm servant responding, 'Na, na, bit we've the wark gey weel in hand' (82:08: N.H.).

31. R. De Bruce Trotter, *Galloway Gossip* (Dumfries, 1901), pp. 19–20.

32. Alex. Inkson McConnochie, *Bennachie* (Aberdeen, 1890), pp. 32–33.

33. 82:03, rec. J.R., 59, former farmworker, Aberdeen; 82:09: W.M.

34. Robertson, *Rural Recollections*, p. 281.

35. See, for example, Helen Beaton, *At the Back o' Bennachie* (2nd ed., Aberdeen, 1923) and Alexander Gordon, *The Folks o' Carglen* (London, 1891).

36. John Mactaggart, *The Scottish Gallovidian Encyclopedia* (1824, reprinted Old Ballechin, Perthshire, 1981), p. 384.

37. See D. Buchan, 'Social Function and Traditional Scottish Rhymes' in Venetia J. Newall, ed., *Folklore Studies in the Twentieth Century* (Woodbridge, Suffolk, 1980), pp. 153–7.

38. *Trans. Rymour Club*, iii, pp. 176–7, 181, 178.

39. *Misc. Rymour Club*, i, p. 55: 'In other days when kemping ... was common in the harvest field, the last of two shearers, shearing the same rig, was said to be last in "the tail win"' (i, 234); John E. Simpkins, *County Folklore VIII...Fife, Clackmannan, and Kinross* (London, 1914), p. 211.

40. George Henderson, *The Popular Rhymes, Sayings, and Proverbs of the County of Berwick* (Newcastle-upon-Tyne, 1856), p. 19.

41. *Trans. Rymour Club*, iii, p. 180; Mactaggart, *Encyclopedia*, p. 357.

42. Henderson, *Rhymes*, p. 13.

43. Simpkins, *Fife*, p. 380, citing F. E. J. G. Mackay, *A History of Fife and Kinross* (Edinburgh, 1896), p. 294.

44. *Trans. Rymour Club*, iii, p. 182; Edinburgh, National Museum of Antiquities, Country Life Archive: Ploughmen, Angus; Simpkins, *Fife*, p. 207, citing the *Fife Herald and Journal*, 9 December, 1903.

45. See M. M. Banks, *British Calendar Customs: Scotland* (3 vols., London, 1937–41).

46. See, for example, Alex. D. Cumming, *Old Times in Scotland: Life, Manners, and Customs* (Paisley, 1910), pp. 145–6. See also E. C. Cawte, Alex Helm, and N. Peacock, *English Ritual Drama* (London, 1967), pp. 66–67.

47. Gordon, *Carglen*, pp. 293–4.

48. See, for example, Beaton, *Bennachie*, pp. 34–47.

49. Hamish Henderson, 'The Horseman's Word', *The Scots Magazine* (May, 1967), pp. 2–8; Carter, *Farm Life*, pp. 154–6; George Ewart Evans, *The Pattern under the Plough* (1966; London, 1971), pp. 220–39.

50. Kenneth S. Goldstein, 'William Robbie: Folk Artist of the Buchan District, Aberdeenshire', *Chapbook*, 3:3 (n.d.: late '60s), pp. 3–12, 22; David Toulmin, 'William Robbie', *A Chiel Among Them* (Aberdeen, 1982), pp. 67–78.

51. Watson, *Glimpses*, pp. 302–3.

52. Gordon, *Keith*, vi.

53. *Poems, Sketches, and Essays* (new ed., Glasgow, 1885), p. 432.

54. See Hamish Henderson, 'The Ballad, the Folk and the Oral Tradition', in Edward J. Cowan, ed., *The People's Past* (Edinburgh, 1980), pp. 79–84.

55. Chambers, *Memoir*, p. 234.

56. *Ibid.*, p. 253.

57. Walter Gregor, *An Echo of the Olden Time from the North-East of Scotland* (Edinburgh, 1874), pp. 32–33.

58. *Schools,* p. 101.

59. Paisley, 1893; Dalbeattie, 1889; and, for example, second series, Brechin, 1881.

60. William Lillie, 'Buchan's Ploughman Poet', *Aberdeen University Review,* xlv (1973), pp. 169–76. See also David Toulmin on Peter Still in 'The Bard of Ugieside', *Straw into Gold* (Aberdeen, 1981), pp. 202–18.

61. Greig, *Folk-Song,* article cliii.

13

Scottish Farm Labour in the Era of Agricultural Depression, 1875–1900

T. M. Devine

From the early 1870s, the prosperity of the agrarian economy of lowland Scotland began to falter as throughout the United Kingdom there was a severe and prolonged fall in the price of both wool and cereals.[1] The selling price of wool in 1883 was only sixty per cent of the average price and less than half the level of the highest price paid during the years 1805–1874. The prices of barley and oats began to fall rapidly too. Barley prices were reduced to 30/- per quarter in 1883 and reached 25/- per quarter ten years later. Oats fetched 20/- a quarter by 1883 and 15/- in 1895. Wheat prices remained fairly stable during the 1870s but fell from a level of 45/- per quarter in 1882 to 30/- in 1889 and finally to 24/- in 1894. From the early 1880s there were parallel reductions in the prices of meat, livestock and dairy produce. Between the years 1883 and 1895 best quality fatstock prices declined by twenty per cent while middling quality prices fell by twenty-five to fifty per cent over the same period. Wholesale butter and cheese prices dropped by about twenty per cent from 1883 to 1895.

These were the main price indicators of the 'Agricultural Depression' which afflicted British farming in the last quarter of the nineteenth century. Modern revisionist writing on the subject has shown that the experience of all regions and all sectors of the agricultural industry was not uniformly bleak.[2] Worst hit were specialist wheat farmers; least affected were dairy farmers, producers of quality livestock and market gardeners. There was wide variation in the fortunes of individual farmers depending on such variables as soil, market, agrarian specialisation and landlord responses. Yet, even when all the qualifications have been made, it remains clear that the period 1875–1900 was one of great difficulty for British agriculture. The industry was being affected by a transformation in the nature of food supply in the developed world. Foreign imports, especially from Canada, the United States and North America, increased in volume throughout the period and British farmers were confronted in consequence with a structural change in market conditions. The proportion of imported wheat consumed in the U.K. rose from forty per cent in 1872 to sixty per cent in 1892. About fifteen per cent of all meat consumed in 1872 was imported from abroad. Twenty years later the figure had more than doubled to thirty-one per cent.[3] The more competitive environment often meant reduced income for farmers and declining rentals for landlords. The purpose of this essay is to survey the experience of the agricultural labour force in Scotland during these difficult years and to outline its general condition in the final period covered by this volume.

I

It is hard to speak about agricultural wages in the last quarter of the nineteenth century in precise terms. There is, for example, the obvious difficulty, which has been noted elsewhere in this volume, of putting a value on payments in kind. This is a particular hazard in a study of the Scottish labour force, for whom such payments remained an important component of the total wage reward in 1875. The difficulty is compounded by the fact that some allowances in kind were reduced in the 1880s and converted to money payments. Increases in money wages for married servants may therefore often reflect commutation rather than real additions. Moreover, to form any idea of the true position of the labourer one would need to take into account the value of 'in kind' earnings later sold in the market, the assumed worth of rent-free cottages and, perhaps above all, the income of other members of the family. It is only possible to gain impressions of these vital elements in overall standards.

Fortunately, however, though precise figures are debatable, the general trend is reasonably clear. A comparison of wage rates gathered by the two Royal Commissions of 1867 and 1893 shows that between these two dates weekly wages for married farm servants in Scotland rose by about thirty per cent, though a proportion of this rise derived from changes from 'in kind' to cash earnings.[4] More meaningful are rates for unmarried servants paid mainly in cash, the *structure* of whose earnings did not alter in the same way over the period. In their case average money wages at spring feeing markets in the north-east show a sharp increase for all single servants from the 1860s to the late 1870s, a slump in the 1880s, but from 1887 a slow climb to a higher level which was retained until the end of the century.[5] A. L. Bowley calculated that the annual average wage of unmarried servants in 'southern Scotland' stood at £12 in 1834–5, had risen to £22 in 1867–70 and by 1892 was standing at £27.[6] A. Wilson Fox collected data from a variety of farming districts for his wage survey of 1900.[7] In Stirlingshire, the wages paid to unmarried horsemen rose from £16 to £20 in 1850 and to £30 to £34 in 1899, increases occurring in 1861, 1871, 1880, 1890, 1893 and 1897. Rates for single male servants in Dumfriesshire showed variation between £11 and £14 from 1852 to 1857. From 1858 they rose to £18 and continued to increase in the following years without interruption, reaching their highest level of £27 per annum in 1897, or about double the prevailing rate of the early 1850s. Similar evidence was produced from farms in Linlithgow, East Lothian and Kirkcudbright.

Three points are worth making about these figures. Firstly, they obviously do not take into account changes in real purchasing power. The increase in the value of real wages as opposed to money income must have been even greater. R. Hunter Pringle carefully estimated in his report on agricultural labour in Fife, in 1893, that the grocery bill for a family of six persons in that area had fallen by about twenty per cent between 1873 and the early 1890s.[8] It is impossible to say how accurate or how typical his calculation was.[9] Undoubtedly, however, the prices of most necessities were showing reductions over this period.

Secondly, the commutation of wages in kind to wages in money meant that more married workers spent more in the market and thus were able to take advantage of the fall in the price of consumables. The 1880s seem to have been a key decade in the erosion of 'in kind' payments.[10] In the Lothians and the Borders the 'boll wage' was gradually falling into disfavour. Several items disappeared (including the right to keep a cow) and were replaced by money. By 1890, hinds in East Lothian, who in the 1850s were almost entirely rewarded in kind, still received potatoes, a house and garden, cartage of coal and food during harvest, but the remainder of the wage was paid in money.[11] Allowances in kind at that date were only valued at £9 per annum, whereas money payments totalled over £41.[12] The decline in payments in kind reflected changes in transport and the expansion of new marketing networks in the Scottish countryside. The cottage of the farm servant was now less isolated from town suppliers and it was no longer necessary for the farmer to provide all the main items of consumption as part of the wage contract. So in the Lothians in the 1890s: 'On account of the keen competition among merchants, grocers, bakers and butchers, the labourer's wife has now no need to trudge away to town, bringing her burden home in a basket. Those days are gone. Vans and carts go regularly on set days from farm to farm, supplying all the necessaries of life, and although the system is pernicious to some whose powers of self-denial are regrettably weak, still it has its advantages to such as are possessed of self-control and prudence'.[13] Farm servants were also able increasingly to purchase from 'the passing van' because, although married men were still hired by the year, payment of the cash element in their wages was normally now made weekly or monthly; single men, although paid less regularly, were also able to obtain cash more frequently on application to their employer.[14]

Thirdly, there is an important contrast between the wage history of agricultural labourers in Scotland and England in this period. Farm wages in England rose by an estimated forty-six per cent between 1850 and 1877. Thereafter, in most counties of England, and in particular those of the southern and eastern regions, there was a marked change in trend. From

1878 until about 1894 wages in several counties began to fall and by 1894–5 were lower than they had been since the 'sixties. Only from 1895 did the upward movement resume.[15] The pattern in lowland Scotland (and in parts of northern England) was different. In the north-east single male servants did experience a decline in wages from the later 1870s until about 1886. But the recovery came sooner than in southern England, with a rapid increase from 1887, and the fall between 1877 and 1886 still left wages above the level achieved in the early 1870s. Moreover, the slump in money wages after 1877 affected farm servants less severely than might have been supposed, since the cost of living also fell. From 1880, real wages in that area rose inexorably until 1902.[16]

Several regions elsewhere in the lowlands excaped the full impact of the slump of the late 'seventies and early 'eighties.[17] In Stirlingshire wage levels seem to have been maintained in the 1880s until 1885 when the rise resumed. In Dumfriesshire, the Lothians and Fife, there appears to have been a steady increase over the entire period 1870–1900. Moreover, throughout these years Scottish farm servants remained relatively well paid by British standards of the time. According to Wilson Fox's calculations for 1898, male farm servants in the counties of Renfrew, Stirling, Lanark and Dumbarton were the highest paid farm workers in Britain, with an average weekly income of between 21/9 and 21/2 per week.[18] Next came agricultural labourers in Durham and Northumberland with earnings of just over £1 per week. In other Scottish lowland counties, male servants averaged from 19/6 to 16/8 per week. But even the county with the lowest earnings, Wigtownshire, had higher wages than twenty-six counties in England and Wales.

Lowland Scotland belonged to the category of high-earning agricultural regions in Britain, with the west-central district at the top of the premier league with earnings over £1 per week. This was followed by the south-east and east-central regions, which had estimated average earnings of between 18/- and 20/-, and finally by the north-eastern-counties of Aberdeen and Banff together with the Border counties of Wigtown, Kirkcudbright, Dumfries and Roxburgh with averages of 16/- to 18/-. These figures should be viewed with great caution. They all contain debatable estimates on the value placed on allowances in kind. Also Anglo-Scottish comparisons are rendered difficult by differences in the structure of payment and the composition of the labour force in the two countries. Nonetheless, the data suggest that Scottish farm workers were not seriously affected by the decline in agricultural prices between 1870 and 1900. On the contrary, over the period as a whole, real incomes rose for many workers, and not least of the problems assailing the farming class was the need to bid higher to ensure a regular supply of labour.

Other evidence tends to confirm this impression of improved standards in the last quarter of the nineteenth century. Accommodation for farm labour in Scotland was notoriously poor and is described in detail elsewhere in this volume.[19] In the later nineteenth century the picture often remained black, with accommodation for unmarried workers in bothies still very deficient.[20] Moreover, as late as 1871 it was estimated that forty per cent of farm cottages in Berwick and Roxburgh had only one window or none at all.[21] Government reports of the 1870s and early 1890s were full of evidence of the pervasive problem of dampness in farm workers' dwellings.[22] Nevertheless there was some progress in these decades. The advent of county Medical Officers of Health in the 1890s gave a further encouragement to those farmers who were bent on improving labourers' accommodation out of sheer economic self-interest. Thus, improved bothies were built, with cooking areas separate from sleeping areas, and with individual cubicles.[23] In the north-east it became less common for bothymen to do their own cooking. Increasingly, both cooking and cleaning were done by a woman hired to take charge of the bothy full-time.[24]

The diet of Scottish farm workers also became more varied, if perhaps less healthy. Tea, coffee, sugar, tobacco and meat were consumed to a greater extent. As allowances in kind diminished and marketing of groceries by cart or van in rural areas improved, so the old dependency on a restricted diet of milk, meal and potatoes disappeared. The change was particularly conspicuous in the Lothians where payments in kind had predominated in the first half of the nineteenth century:

> Porridge is the chief breakfast food where milk can be got, but I heard of many houses where tea with bread, cheese, butter and jam has supplanted porridge. There are two courses for dinner, either broth and meat or meat and pudding. Herrings, either fresh or salt are in great esteem; they may be seen hanging in a row outside the door of many a cottage. Eggs, too, are purchased from farmers or "egglers". Tinned meat I do not hear much about. Coffee and tea, costing 2/6 to 3/- per pound are drunk. I met with no instance of beer or porter being kept for ordinary consumption, and if there be whiskey in the cupboard it is produced on high-days and holidays only. Some good housewives buy flour and bake scones. The barley and peasemeal scone seems to have altogether disappeared.
>
> Formerly the crockery and delf of a hind's house consisted of a porridge bowl for every member of the family, a few cups and saucers of unpretentious pattern and not overburdened with handles, a thick strong wine glass, and a brown earthenware teapot, possibly half a dozen soup plates. There were always sufficient horn spoons (called "hornies") to admit of a simultaneous family attack on the porridge ... Go into a labourer's cottage now and the "dresser" will be seen filled with plates for three courses. The cupboard below holds its pretty flowered breakfast and tea-set, its half-dozen tumblers and wine glasses, its jugs and mugs, but no horny spoons.[25]

The Lothian hind had a family income higher than that of most agricultural workers, but changes in diet were not restricted to the biggest earners. In the north-east, bothymen sold a proportion of the meal

s

obtained as part of their fee and used the money to buy jam, tea and wheaten bread.[26] Indeed, the diets of many Scottish farm labourers in the later nineteenth century began to show a definite preference for bought-in provisions, including white bread from the travelling van.

There were more subtle indicators of changing times. Conditions of employment hardly altered — married servants were still hired by the year, single servants by the half-year. Holidays were few and hours remained long. But expectations were rising generally among the farm work force. The Royal Commission on Labour of 1893 discovered that farmers with poor reputations as master were finding difficulty in recruiting experienced men in some areas.[27] It was becoming more common also for some servants, almost certainly a small minority, to break their engagements early or not to turn up for work after taking a fee at the hiring fair.[28] Women were reckoned to be particularly guilty of this offence. Moreover, a successful campaign against the 'bondage' system of recruiting female workers had been waged in the Lothians, and no trace of it remained in that area by the later nineteenth century.[29] The mechanisation of the grain harvest, with the arrival of the self-binding reaper, the adoption of the 'potato digger' and the employment of rick-lifters, worked by windlass or horse, took some of the hard labour out of farm work.[30] Since these devices meant a reduction in the number of seasonal hands for some tasks, their growing popularity ensured that more of the income to labour accrued to employees living permanently in the farm steading. Finally, the growing popularity of the bicycle increased the farm servant's mobility and enlarged the quality of his life.

There is no way of measuring these advances, and their effects varied significantly from area to area and between different groups of workers. For many, farm labour remained a dirty, monotonous and poorly paid job with excessive hours and few prospects.[31] Yet in no sense was the period 1870–1900 one of 'depression' for the Scottish agricultural labour force. In these years wages and conditions changed for the better. The second part of this essay will explore this apparent paradox of rising rewards for labour in a phase of agrarian difficulty.

II

The 'Agricultural Depression' in Scotland caused problems but did not result in a crisis. The economic context of the period 1870–1900 was much tougher than that of the preceding decades, but it was one to which the lowland farming community was able to adjust without massive savings in labour requirements. The Scottish agrarian economy had several advantages in the new era.[32] Wheat had fallen most in price, but wheat production in Scotland was mainly limited to parts of the south-east lowlands and its cultivation was in decline even before 1870. The Scottish regime of mixed farming was better placed to adjust to a collapse in cereal prices. Lower grain prices meant cheaper costs of feed and a rising market for meat and dairy products. Scottish livestock farming in the lowlands with its traditional emphasis on quality of production was insulated in several of its sectors from lower quality competition from imported refrigerated meats. Dairy farming and soft fruit cultivation, together with the supply of horses for transport, were likely to prosper as industrial and urban expansion continued.

These advantages should not be overstressed. Areas of marginal land in the valleys of the Forth and Tay were badly hit and most farmers were faced with reduced profit margins.[33] But lowland farming in general remained resilient. No structural change was necessary; adjustment only was required. The response is made clear in Table 1: a continued reduction in wheat acreage and an increase in permanent and rotation pastures.

Table 1   *Crops and Livestock in Scotland, 1875–1895*

	1875	1880	1885
Thousand Acres			
Wheat	102	74	55
Barley	265	264	237
Oats	1005	1037	1046
Pulse, etc.	39	28	32
TOTAL Corn	1411	1404	1371
Potatoes	158	187	149
Root and Green Crops	427	510	511
Rotation Grass	1385	1456	1572
Bare Fallow	17	22	23
TOTAL Arable	3398	3579	3626
Permanent Grass	1110	1159	1220
Orchards	—	—	8*
Thousand Head			
Horses: for agric.	136	141	142
unbroken and mares	47	53	47
Cattle	1143	1099	1176
Sheep	7101	7072	6957
Pigs	151	121	151

*Including market gardens and nursery grounds.
Source: C. S. Orwin and E. H. Whetham, *History of British Agriculture, 1846–1914* (Newton Abbot, 1971 ed.), pp. 252, 268.

Increased grain imports did not force Scottish farmers to cultivate less but rather, as grain prices fell, to cultivate as much as ever in order to produce corn to feed more livestock because in that sector they had a comparative advantage. On balance, the net result was probably to marginally reduce labour requirements. The change from the five-course shift to six-shift rotation (whereby one tenth more of the land was in grass) lessened demand for servants.[34] The reduction was especially marked in the Lothians.[35] Overall, however, there was no widespread decline in employment. For decades Scottish farmers had tailored their labour needs to the number of horses which could effectively work a given area of land. Since they had long practised effective economy of labour, there was little surplus to shed after 1870 in the manner characteristic of southern English arable farmers. This was also less necessary anyway given the continued integrity of mixed husbandry in the new market situation. Scottish workers gained, therefore, because farming in the lowlands was still viable and, in some areas, conspicuously successful. At the same time, while demand for their services remained buoyant in most years, they also reaped the benefit of falling food prices and improved marketing in the countryside as allowances in kind were steadily replaced by payments in cash.

Yet, the main reason why money wages rose in the late nineteenth century was that farmers were forced to bid higher to attract labour. The wage history of Scottish agriculture after 1870 was but a reflection of a deeper structural change in the pattern of employment in Scotland. Industrial and urban employments (as shown in Table 2) were expanding at a particularly fast pace.

Industry had competed for labour with agriculture in the lowlands since the later eighteenth century, and this had long distinguished the rural

Table 2 *Male Employment in Scottish Agriculture and Some Industrial Sectors, 1841–1911*

Year	Agriculture (inc. farmers)	Mining/ Quarrying	Metals	Transport/ Communications	Ship-building
1841	221,583	25,035	22,478	24,256	4,089
1851	255,614	53,146	36,107	48,396	4,395
1861	248,462	62,013	44,342	56,794	9,146
1871	273,960	76,461	58,461	70,476	16,250
1881	208,502	82,507	68,218	85,126	18,470
1891	214,255	100,793	72,847	117,394	23,433
1901	198,124	132,433	86,784	143,899	34,527
1911	195,174	164,513	93,345	158,498	50,856

Source: Clive Lee, *British Regional Employment Statistics, 1841–1971* (Cambridge, 1979).

labour market in Scotland and northern England from that of the far south. In the second half of the nineteenth century, however, the level of competition became particularly intense with the rise of heavy industry based on coal, iron and steel, mining and engineering. Moreover, migration from country to town was already well-established by 1870.[36] The geographical distribution of urban areas, the structure of labour recruitment in agriculture and the social attitudes of the people of rural Scotland all helped to promote mobility. In the later nineteenth century, however, migration from the land speeded up, and the number of male and female farm servants reached a peak from which there was a steady decline. A long-term process of accelerated demographic adjustment was underway.

Precise measurement of numbers engaged in farm work is complicated by changes in census categories over time. The problems are especially pronounced in the case of females and they are analysed separately in an earlier essay in this volume.[37] Difficulties exist too in the case of male servants and labourers, though to a lesser degree. The census indicates that their numbers fell from 137,440 to 127,960 in 1861, to 108,818 in 1871, 91,801 in 1881 and 81,309 in 1891. This represented a gross reduction of about thirty-three per cent over the period. The figures are merely a rough guide, an illustration of trends, but they vividly demonstrate the exodus from farm employment. Literary evidence and the views of experienced observers suggest that the movement of women from the land was even greater.[38] This migration of labour forced farmers to raise wages.

In one sense the movement was puzzling because it occurred when conditions in farm work were modestly improving. Nor could it be explained by mechanisation: contemporary opinion was unanimous that most mechanical innovations were a consequence rather than a cause of labour shortage.[39] Nor was it simply a matter of industry offering higher wages than agriculture, though this was a central factor in many cases. In Britain as a whole, the 'crude wage ratio' between agriculture and industry was about fifty per cent for most of the second half of the nineteenth century, though the differences may have been less in Scotland.[40] Higher wages were said to be a particularly powerful incentive for former farm servants to enter mining in Lanarkshire.[41] The police and the railways were especially attractive employments for farm servants in the north-east, and in many towns there and further south former ploughmen became carters and vanmen and put their skills in the management of horses to good use.[42] It is by no means obvious that these jobs always offered higher earnings than those on the land. As contemporaries pointed out, even single farm servants received bed and board as part of their engagement and obtained security of employment over a given period. Some contrasted this with the urban worker who was exposed to a fluctuating labour market conditioned by the trade cycle. Moreover, it was possible to cite individual cases where farm servants gained little in the way of increased income by seeking industrial employment:

> At the present rate of agricultural wages there are many men now employed
> in towns or on railways, for smaller wages than they could readily get as farm
> labourers. Mr. Younger of the Alloa Brewery, has many men in his employ
> who were once farm servants, and he kindly took from his books the wages
> paid to such. They run from 20/- to 22/- for the best and 18/- to 20/- for the
> less intelligent men, but out of these wages a house rent amounting to £7 or
> £8 per annum has to be paid. Mr. Younger thinks it is the easier work about
> the brewery that draws them, and the general attraction and society of a
> town.[43]

Conditions of employment in agriculture were seen by an increasing
number of farm workers as less attractive than life in industry and the
towns. Significantly the rural trade unions of the later nineteenth century
were not mainly concerned with raising wages (as was the case in England)
but with attempting to reduce working hours, to secure more holidays,
encourage the erection of better houses and bothies and protect members
from what was described as 'all oppression and tyranny'.[44] Life on the land
had improved but advances were still patchy and failed to keep pace with
the rising expectations of many workers in the later nineteenth century.
There was a new awareness of what constituted comfort. Agriculture was
condemned because it offered few openings for the ambitious to climb
above the level of grieve (or foreman).[45] Again, by the end of the
nineteenth century the Saturday half-holiday was hardly known in farming:
the need to maintain and feed the work animals made employers unwilling
to concede it.[46] Officially farm servants worked a ten-hour day but this did
not take into account the early morning feeding and preparation of the
horses and evening grooming. As late as the 1930s some farmers in the
north-east insisted on horses being 'suppered' as late as 8.00 p.m.[47]
Increasingly, too, the lack of community and social life in agriculture
attracted criticism. Scottish farm workers were dispersed in groups of
cottages, bothies and chaumers attached to individual farms. This, together
with long hours of labour and the habit of changing employers at the end
of a term, had the effect of restricting social life to the occasional fair or
agricultural show.[48] As earnings in industrial occupations rose and the new
urban society generated a new range of skilled jobs, some farm labourers
also became aware of a relative fall in status. Farm servants around Paisley
in the early 1890s complained: 'We consider our condition very poor
because we are not estimated as other trades. We object to being called
unskilled labourers. A man cannot be a ploughman in a day'.[49] A
ploughman from Dumfries put the point in even more extreme terms: 'To
my opinion, the life of the agricultural labourer is altogether colourless and
sordid; in fact, his life throughout is sleep, eat and work; no time for
enjoyment as other labourers have; no half-holiday on Saturday, although
it is earnestly asked for; no holidays as a right, only as a favour; we get
from three to four in a year'.[50]

Not all felt as bitterly about life on the farm as this man but there was nonetheless widespread recognition that rural life was backward and that the town provided not only higher earnings but also shorters hours, more leisure and freedom in the evening and at the weekend from employers. It therefore offered an irresistible attraction, particularly to young farm workers of both sexes. As the Royal Commission on Labour of 1893 concluded: 'There is much drudgery and very little excitement about the farm servant's daily duties, and I believe the young men dislike the former and long for the latter. By the labourers themselves, slight importance is attached to the healthy character of country life in comparison with various branches of town labour. That phase of the question sinks into insignificance in their estimation, and only the shorter hours, numerous holidays and ever present buzz, bustle and excitement of town life or the neat uniform and genteel work of the police constable or railway porter, are present to the mind of our young farm servant'.[51]

NOTES

1. C. S. Orwin and E. H. Whetham, *History of British Agriculture, 1846–1914* (Newton Abbot, 1971 ed.), pp. 241–2, 259. There is an interesting and original survey of the problem in Scotland in Retta McLachlan, 'The Impact of the "Agricultural Depression" of 1879–1896 on the Life and Work of the Agricultural Labourer in Scotland', B.A. dissertation, Department of History, University of Strathclyde, 1979.

2. Summarised in P. J. Perry, *British Farming in the Great Depression, 1870–1914* (Newton Abbot, 1974).

3. J. Scott, 'British Farming and Foreign Competition', *Trans. of the Highland and Agricultural Society of Scotland (T.H.A.S.)*, 4th ser., X (1878), p. 121.

4. John W. Paterson, 'Rural Depopulation in Scotland', *T.H.A.S.*, 5th ser., X (1897), p. 270.

5. R. Molland and G. Evans, 'Scottish Farm Wages from 1870 to 1900', *Journal Royal Statistical Society*, Series A (General), CXIII (1950), pp. 223–226. See also Ian Carter, *Farm Life in Northeast Scotland, 1840–1914* (Edinburgh, 1979), pp. 86, 117–119.

6. A. L. Bowley, 'The Statistics of Wages in the United Kingdom during the last Hundred Years. Part I. Agricultural Wages', *Journal Royal Statistical Society*, LXII (1899), p. 148.

7. *Report by Mr. Wilson Fox on the Wages and Earnings of Agricultural Labourers in the United Kingdom. Parliamentary Papers*, 1900 Cd. 346. (Hereafter *Wilson Fox's Report* (1900)), p. 85.

8. *Royal Commission on Labour. The Agricultural Labourer. Volume III. Scotland. Part II. Parliamentary Papers*, 1893–4, XXXVI (hereafter *R.C. on Labour, 1893*), p. 82.

9. Carter, in his study of the northeast lowlands, reckons that real wages of farm servants there rose by thirty per cent between 1870 and 1900. See Carter, *Farm Life*, p. 86.

10. *Wilson Fox's Report* (1900), pp. 79, 85–86.

11. *R.C. on Labour* (1893), Part II, p. 24; R. S. Skirving, 'On the Agriculture of East Lothian', *T.H.A.S.*, 4th ser., V (1873), p. 45.

12. *Ibid.*

13. *R.C. on Labour* (1893), Part II, p. 119.

14. *Report of an Enquiry by the Board of Trade into the Earnings and Hours of Labour of Workpeople of the United Kingdom. V. Agriculture in 1907. Parliamentary Papers*, 1910 cd. 5460, pp. xxi–xxiv.

15. *Wilson Fox's Report* (1900), p. 2.

16. Molland and Evans, 'Scottish Farm Wages', pp. 223–226.

17. *Wilson Fox's Report* (1900), p. 85.

18. *Ibid.*

19. See above, pp. 188–210.

20. Alexander Fenton and Bruce Walker, *The Rural Architecture of Scotland* (Edinburgh, 1981), pp. 143–159.

21. *Ibid.*, p. 145.

22. See, for example, *R.C. on Labour* (1893), Part II, pp. 21–22, 28–30.

23. J. McDonald, 'On the Agriculture of the Counties of Forfar and Kincardine', *T.H.A.S.*, 4th ser. XII (1881), p. 170.

24. Carter, *Farm Life*, p. 124.

25. *R.C. on Labour* (1893), Part II, p. 109.

26. W. Diak, 'The Scottish Farm Labourer', *Independent Review*, VII (1905), p. 322.

27. *R.C. on Labour* (1893), pp. 63–64.

28. *Ibid.*

29. See above, pp. 105–6.

30. John Speir, 'Changes in Farm Implements since 1890', *T.H.A.S.*, 5th ser. XVIII (1906), pp. 47–62.

31. See below, pp. 252–3.

32. What follows is based on *Royal Commission on Agricultural Interests. Minutes of Evidence. Parts I and II. Parliamentary Papers*, 1881, Cd. 2778–1, 3096, XV, XVII; *Royal Commission on Agricultural Depression, Reports of Assistant Commissioners. Parliamentary Papers*, 1894, Cd. 7342, XVI Part I and 1895, Cd. 7742, XVII.

33. J. A. Symon, *Scottish Farming Past and Present* (Edinburgh, 1953), p. 197.

34. Paterson, 'Rural Depopulation', pp. 270–1; *R.C. on Labour* (1893), Part II, pp. 9, 51, 97.

35. *R.C. on Labour* (1893), Part II, pp. 9, 51, 97.

36. M. Gray, 'Migration in the Rural Lowlands of Scotland, 1750–1850', in T. M. Devine and D. Dickson, eds., *Ireland and Scotland, 1600–1850* (Edinburgh, 1983), pp. 104–117.

37. See above, pp. 112–113.

38. For evidence on this point see above, pp. 113–114.

39. John Wilson, 'Half a Century as a Border Farmer', *T.H.A.S.*, 5th ser., XIV (1902), p. 39; Orwin and Whetham, *British Agriculture*, pp. 347–8; Carter, *Farm Life*, p. 119; Paterson, 'Rural Depopulation', pp. 265–6.

40. J. R. Bellerby, 'Distribution of Farm Incomes in the U.K., 1867–1938', *Journal of the Proceedings of the Agricultural Economics Society*, X, no. 2, February, 1953.

41. *Royal Commission on the Employment of Children, Young Persons and Women in Agriculture. Fourth Report. Appendix. Parts I and II. Parliamentary Papers,* 1870, Cd. 222. XIII, p. 275.

42. *R.C. on Labour* (1893), Part I, pp. 109, 130; Part II, p. 45.

43. *Ibid.,* Part II, p. 48.

44. *Ibid.,* pp. 70, 161–2.

45. *Ibid.,* pp. 10, 52.

46. *Wilson Fox's Report* (1900), p. 54.

47. *Report of the Committee on Farm Workers in Scotland,* 1936. Cd. 5217. 1936, pp. 20–22.

48. *Board of Agriculture for Scotland: Report of the Committee on Women in Agriculture in Scotland* (1920), pp. 38–40.

49. *R.C. on Labour* (1893), Part I, p. 57.

50. *Ibid.,* p. 74.

51. *Ibid.,* Part II, p. 10.

Index